Learn Microsoft SQL Server 7.0

José Ramalho

Wordware Publishing, Inc.

Library of Congress Cataloging-in-Publication Data

Ramalho, José Antonio
    Learn Microsoft SQL server 7.0 / by José A. Ramalho.
      p.   cm.
    Includes index.
    ISBN 1-55622-639-X (pbk.)
    1. Client/server computing.   2. SQL server.   I. Title.
    QA76.9.C55R36   1999
    005.75'85--dc21   99-12468
                                                    CIP

ISBN 1-55622-639-X
10 9 8 7 6 5 4 3 2 1
9904

All inquiries for volume purchases of this book should be addressed to Wordware Publishing, Inc., at the above address. Telephone inquiries may be made by calling:

(972) 423-0090

Contents

Contents

Contents

Contents

Contents

Introduction

SQL Server 7.0 represents one of Microsoft's major investments and strategic components, along with the Windows NT version called Windows 2000, as a definite attempt to enter the market of corporate applications. The new SQL Server is a completely new version that breaks the links with the original product's source code based on Sybase's SQL Server. Version 7's interface brought many innovations and ease of use, incorporating at the same time sophisticated tools for the power user. With this product Microsoft intends to approach and gain an important market share in the data warehousing, mobile computer, and e-commerce sectors. The new version has versions that run on Windows 95/98 and NT with 100 percent code compatibility. It integrates an OLAP server and a module for Data Transformation Services (DTS), as well as integrated management of multiple servers, besides other new features.

OLE DB substitutes the DB Library as an internal interface for all of SQL Server's internal operations, allowing the use of heterogeneous queries that use the SQL Server's processor to run the queries made to the server store engine. The product is now much easier to operate due to the changes in the interface and the extensive use of wizards to perform many administrative tasks. Scalability is one of its strengths, which makes it competitive with the main products of the corporate market. The product database was designed to run on systems ranging from a notebook running Windows 95 to multiprocessing machines running applications of terabytes in clusters.

The new version now has line level lock, intra-query parallelism, and better distributed queries to support VLDB (very large databases), one point that is vital for Microsoft's strategy of acting in the data warehousing segment.

The Objective of This Book

This book is a practical guide and introduction to Microsoft's SQL database Server 7 and a reference guide for the Transact-SQL language used by the product. There are 18 chapters about the program's main modules and resources and a reference guide for the functions and commands of the Transact-SQL language. SQL Server 7 is an extensive product with many resources and features. Although its graphical interface makes it easy to operate, it is a complex and detail-intensive product—just like any other corporate database—and only time and practice will allow the reader to gain comprehensive knowledge of it. Due to these characteristics, we chose to cover SQL Server 7's main resources and new items in this book.

The CD that accompanies this book contains the official trial version of SQL Server 7. It is the full product and is limited to a 120-day trial period. We recommend that you use Windows NT as the operating system to run it. With this copy the reader will be able to immediately practice the subjects covered in this book. This is a good option for those who want to evaluate the product.

Target Audience

Due to its practical approach, this book can be used by all who want a general overview and want to put immediately into practice the concepts presented here. We recommend that you use it in introductory courses to SQL Server 7 or in self-training. The book covers only the operation of SQL Server 7, making it a good option for the reader with a minimum knowledge of databases. Computer professionals, developers, and students will also benefit from use of this book.

Structure

The book has 18 chapters covering the product almost in its entirety. It starts with an overview of SQL Server 7 and its components, showing how to create a database, tables, and database diagrams, and using the main user interface, called Enterprise Manager. Then it shows how to use Query Analyzer, which is responsible for the execution and viewing of the Transact-SQL language commands. Creating indexes and views of a database, as well as stored procedures and triggers, which are responsible for the routine automation, are also covered. The next step is to show you SQL Server 7's replication resources and to enter the world of data warehousing, bringing you the resources of DSS (Decision Support Systems), such as OLAP Manager and DTS (Data Transformation Services). The administrative tools are covered next, as well as backing up and restoring resources. Following is a summary of each chapter:

1—Overview

This chapter explains some basic concepts of a database and the components of a SQL Server 7 database.

2—Creating a Database

Creating a database using the Database Wizard and the Transact-SQL language is covered in this chapter.

3—Tables

A table is the basic element of a database. Here we cover the operations of creating, changing, and excluding tables using different methods.

4—Database Diagrams

The database diagram is a module that visually creates in just one screen the tables and accessory files of a database using drag and drop.

5—Query Analyzer

Query Analyzer, the SQL tool used to run queries directly in the database through the Transact-SQL commands, is covered in this chapter. The tool is also responsible for the query analyses and makes suggestions on how to improve the command execution.

6—SQL Basics

Everything in a database ends up being SQL, regardless of whether a query was made through a client program or a graphical interface. The command responsible for the results is a SQL command. Knowing this language is fundamental for those who work with a database.

7—Indexes

This chapter shows the index types and how to create, change, and exclude them. This is very important for improving access to a database.

8—Views

This chapter introduces the concept of views, which are virtual tables that allow the user to view a subset of columns in one or more tables.

9—Stored Procedures

Stored procedures are routines written in the Transact-SQL language that automate tasks. This chapter shows the types of routines and how to create and maintain a stored procedure.

10—Triggers

Triggers are routines written in Transact-SQL language that are automatically triggered when an event, such as inserting, updating, or deleting, occurs. This chapter gives detailed information on creating and maintaining triggers.

11—Replication

This chapter explains the concept of database replication and transactional replication, two of three possible types that can be executed by the SQL Server 7.

12—Merge Replication

This chapter continues the discussion of replication, showing how to create a merge-type replication.

13—Data Warehousing and OLAP

This chapter is an introduction to the concept of data warehouses and OLAP, and shows the capacities that the OLAP Manager offers for the creation of data warehouses.

14—OLAP Manager Practical Example

After the theory, we give you a practice example using a sample database on the companion CD.

15—Data Transformation Services

The DTS is one of the SQL Server's modules, and that alone justifies its inclusion. It allows the transformation of data from one format to another in an extremely practical way.

16—DTS Practical Example

This chapter gives you a practical example of a database transformation.

17—Tools

This chapter provides an overview of several tools and utilities that come with SQL Server 7.

18—Backing Up and Restoring

This chapter shows how to create and restore database backups through the dialog boxes or the Backup Wizard.

Appendix A—Transact-SQL Reference Guide

This appendix contains an alphabetical list of functions and commands of the Transact-SQL language.

Appendix B—Installing the Software

Installing the software and working files from the companion CD is detailed here.

Summary

This book will provide the reader with a practical view of SQL Server 7's main resources. It is ideal as an introduction to the software. After you master the topics covered in this book, we suggest that you read specialized books on the software's modules or techniques to improve performance.

If you have any comments on this book, send them to **jose.antonio@ ramalho.com.br**. For information about the author's other books, visit **www.ramalho.com.br**.

Chapter 1

SQL Server 7.0 Overview

This chapter deals with basic database concepts as they apply to SQL Server 7 and its specific features.

Client/Server Architecture

SQL Server 7 is a relational database designed to support applications with client/server architecture, in which the database is resident in a central computer called a server, with information shared by several users that run applications in their local computers, or clients. Such architecture provides greater data integrity, since all the users are working with the same information. Through business rules, controls are enforced that apply to all the users concerning information added to the database. The client/server architecture considerably reduces the network traffic, since it returns to the user just the data requested. For example, if a search of a database containing 100,000 records returned just three records, only these three records will be sent through the network to the client machine. In a traditional system, all 100,000 records would be sent through the network. This helps make maintenance tasks, such as backing up and restoring, much easier to perform because data is located in only one place. Following is an example of the basic use of this architecture:

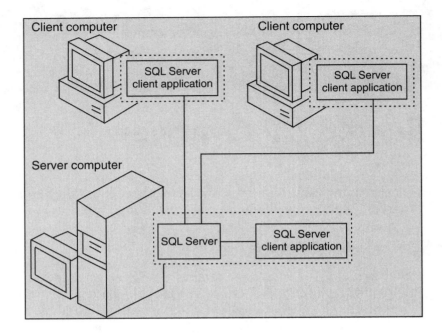

SQL Server Architecture

The SQL Server 7 database is divided into several logical components, such as tables, views, and other elements that are visible to the user. These elements are physically stored in two or more files in the disk. The file format or location where the logic elements are written to is seamless to the system's user.

A SQL Server 7 server can contain several databases pertaining to several users. A company can have one database that is used by many users throughout several departments, or it can have several databases that are exclusively used by specific users in each department. The next illustration shows the user's view in the form of three tables and the physical implementation of those tables through the use of a data file, an index file, and a log file.

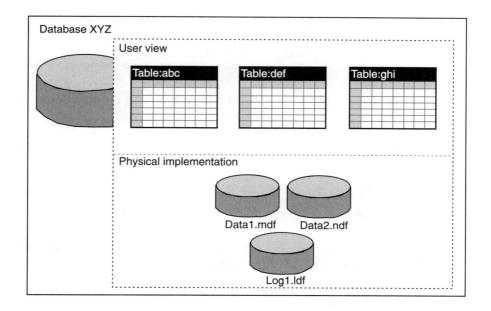

When a database is created, the users can have access permissions attributed to them. This enables the SQL Server to store several databases and limit the access to each one to specific users.

Components of the SQL Server

The table below shows the key components of SQL Server 7.

Component	Description
Database	Contains the objects used to represent, store, and access data.
Tables	Store lines or records of data and their relationship with other tables.
Database Diagrams	Graphically represent the database's objects, allowing them to be manipulated without the use of the Transact-SQL language.
Indexes	Auxiliary files that improve the access speed to the rows of the table.
Views	Provide an alternate way of looking at the data in one or more tables.
Stored Procedures	Transact-SQL programs stored in the server that execute predetermined tasks.

Component	Description
Triggers	A special type of stored procedure that is automatically executed when certain operations are performed in the table.
Full-Text Indexes	Special indexes that make the search easier in columns with Varchar and Text data types.

Below is a more detailed description of these elements.

Databases

A *database* is a collection of tables, views, indexes, triggers, stored procedures, and other objects. SQL Server 7 can maintain several databases. The next figure shows a server called ServidorNT2 that contains four databases called newpub, newpub2, Northwind, and pubs.

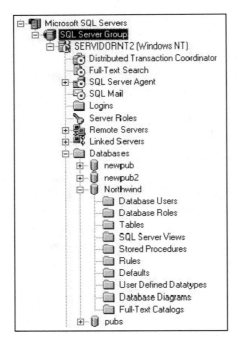

Note that the Northwind database shows the components it maintains such as tables, views, etc.

Tables

Tables are the core of a database. They store the data grouped in the form of rows and columns like a spreadsheet. Each row represents a record, and each column is an attribute or field. Each field maintains one type of information. For example, a field called Value has a Numeric data type, while a field called Name maintains Text type information. A table's fields can have restrictions as to the contents they are going to store. For example, a field called Quantity cannot store text, only numbers, and cannot accept values below 1 or above 100.

Database Diagrams

SQL Server 7 allows the creation of *database diagrams*. These diagrams are the graphic representation of tables, indexes, and views that are stored by the database and can be manipulated through the use of drag and drop and interaction with dialog boxes. This allows several tasks to be performed without needing to use the Transact-SQL language, such as changing the physical characteristics of a database or its tables.

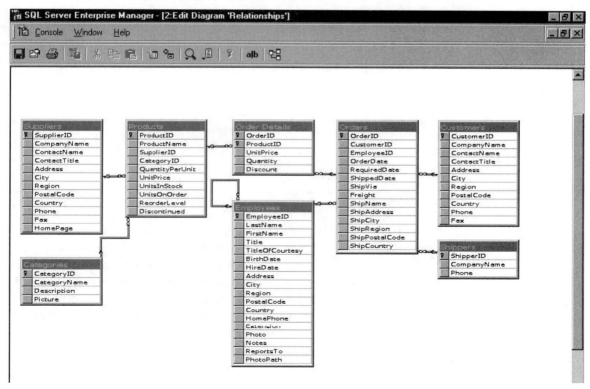

Indexes

Indexes are special types of files that work in association with tables. Their purpose is to speed up the process of accessing a certain record or group of records. They can be compared to indexes found in books, where instead of skimming through an entire book to find a specific page, you just use the index to locate the subject and its corresponding page number.

In the Pubs database the Employees table has an index based on the emp_id column, as shown below.

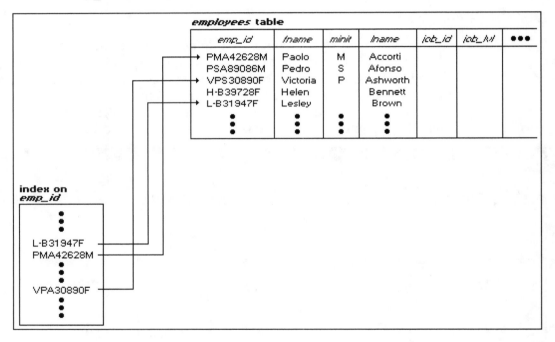

When conducting a search in the Employees table, the server detects the key column and searches in the index, which basically contains a copy of the emp_id column contents and the address of its row inside the table. Some indexes are automatically created, as is the case of primary key columns. The optimal situation would be that each column in the database had an index associated with it in order to improve performance. However, each index that is created takes up disk space and frequently will not even be used.

Views

A *view* is a virtual table with its contents defined by a query to the database. The view is not a physical table, but a set of instructions that returns a set of data. The next illustration shows two tables that serve as the basis for the creation of a query.

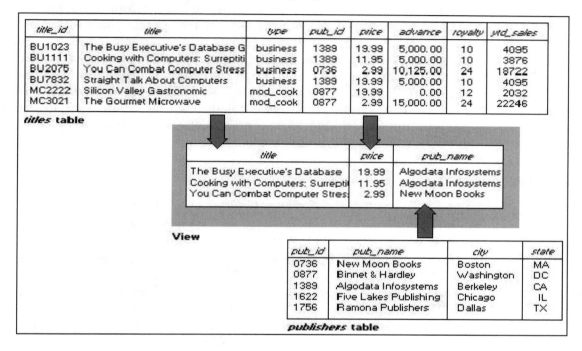

title_id	title	type	pub_id	price	advance	royalty	ytd_sales
BU1023	The Busy Executive's Database G	business	1389	19.99	5,000.00	10	4095
BU1111	Cooking with Computers: Surreptiti	business	1389	11.95	5,000.00	10	3876
BU2075	You Can Combat Computer Stress	business	0736	2.99	10,125.00	24	18722
BU7832	Straight Talk About Computers	business	1389	19.99	5,000.00	10	4095
MC2222	Silicon Valley Gastronomic	mod_cook	0877	19.99	0.00	12	2032
MC3021	The Gourmet Microwave	mod_cook	0877	2.99	15,000.00	24	22246

titles **table**

title	price	pub_name
The Busy Executive's Database	19.99	Algodata Infosystems
Cooking with Computers: Surrepti	11.95	Algodata Infosystems
You Can Combat Computer Stress	2.99	New Moon Books

View

pub_id	pub_name	city	state
0736	New Moon Books	Boston	MA
0877	Binnet & Hardley	Washington	DC
1389	Algodata Infosystems	Berkeley	CA
1622	Five Lakes Publishing	Chicago	IL
1756	Ramona Publishers	Dallas	TX

publishers **table**

Stored Procedures

The data in a database can be accessed only through the execution of Transact-SQL commands. When creating an application to serve as the interface with the database, the developer can choose to create a SQL program that is locally stored and sent to the server to be executed there, or to create and maintain the programs in the server itself, in stored procedures that can be triggered by a program in the client machine. A *stored procedure* can accept parameters (values that are passed to the procedure) for processing. However, unlike functions, they do not return any value. Once the stored procedure is created it can be used by any application that accesses the database. The stored procedures are created by the Transact-SQL CREATE PROCEDURE command and are changed by the ALTER PROCEDURE command.

Triggers

A *trigger* is a stored procedure that is automatically executed when data in the table changes due to the execution of a SQL INSERT, UPDATE, or DELETE command. One of its most common uses is to force limitations that are more complex than the ones allowed through the CHECK constraint, which limits the information inserted in a column. A trigger can be created in association with the INSERT command, which makes a query to other tables and returns a logic value that helps to limit the data attributed to a certain column. For example, a trigger can be created that executes an instant replication, i.e., when a row is inserted in database Z, a line with the same information is added to database Y. Or, when a row is deleted from a table, the trigger deletes the other rows associated to that one from other tables. A trigger is treated as a transaction and can be rolled back when a problem is detected.

Full-Text Indexes

This special type of index allows the execution of queries based on columns with contents of the Varchar and Text types. These are the main differences between a normal index and a full-text index:

Normal Index	Full-Text Index
Created and deleted through SQL commands.	Created and deleted through the use of stored procedures.
Can be several indexes in each table.	Can be only one full-text index in each table.
Automatically updated when the fields of the table change.	Updated only when requested.

Wizards

SQL Server 7 makes extensive use of wizards to perform several administrative tasks. Without the wizards, those tasks would have to be performed through Transact-SQL commands. Wizards show a series of dialog boxes that interact with the user, asking for information and using it to execute certain tasks. Below is a list of the main wizards:

Wizard	Purpose
Configure Publishing and Distribution	Configures a database for replication
Create Alert	Executes the creation of an alert
Create Backup	Creates a backup of the database
Create Database	Executes the creation of a database
Create Diagram	Executes the creation of a database diagram
Create Index	Executes the creation of an index
Create Job	Executes the creation of a job
Create New Data Service	Executes the installation and configuration of an ODBC datasource
Create Publication	Executes the creation of a publication for replication
Create SQL Server Login	Executes the creation of an access login to the users
Create Stored Procedures	Executes the creation of stored procedures for the addition, deletion, and updating of rows
Create Trace	Executes the creation of a trace
Create View	Executes the creation of a view
Database Maintenance Plan	Executes the creation of a maintenance file
Disable Publishing and Distribution	Executes the disabling of a publication and replication scheme
DTS Export	Executes the creation of a DTS package for data export
DTS Import	Executes the creation of a DTS package for data import
Full-Text Indexing	Executes the process of creating a full-text index
Index Tuning	Executes the process of fine-tuning an index
Make Master Server	Executes the process of creating a master server
Make Target Server	Executes the process of creating a target server
Pull Subscription	Executes the process of recovering data in a replication server
Push Subscription	Executes the process of sending data to a server for replication
Register Servers	Executes the process of registering SQL servers
Setup	Executes the process of installing and configuring the SQL Server
Web Assistant	Executes the creation of the steps needed to create a Web page based on the contents of a table or the importation of Web data

Summary

This chapter provided an overview of the SQL Server architecture and components. In the following chapters, we will show you how to create each one of these components, starting with a database.

Chapter 2

Creating a Database

Creating a database, particularly its basic structure, is extremely simple with the SQL Server 7 because of its graphical interface. The task takes no more than one or two minutes, whether you create it manually, with the help of a wizard, or with Transact-SQL commands. Creating a database involves providing the physical characteristics of the database, such as its size, increase rate, name, owner's identification, and group identification.

Three files form a database: the primary file, the secondary file, and the log file. Following is a description of each file's function:

Primary—This file contains information needed to load and initialize the database, as well as to store data. This is a default file in any database you create.

Secondary—The secondary file exists only when the primary file is not big enough to maintain all data files. Depending on the size of the database there may be a need for several secondary files.

Log—The log file is used to recover the database. There is at least one log file in each database, and a second can always be created. The minimum size is 512 KB.

When a database is created, all of its files are zeroed, i.e., they are filled with zeroes in order to overwrite any data left in the disk by deleted files.

A database can be created manually through the Enterprise Manager, by using the Create Database Wizard, or with the Transact-SQL language.

Creating a Database Manually

To create a database manually, follow these steps:

In the Enterprise Manager, click the Microsoft SQL Servers icon and then expand the server.

Click the right mouse button in the Databases folder and choose New Database, as shown in the following figure:

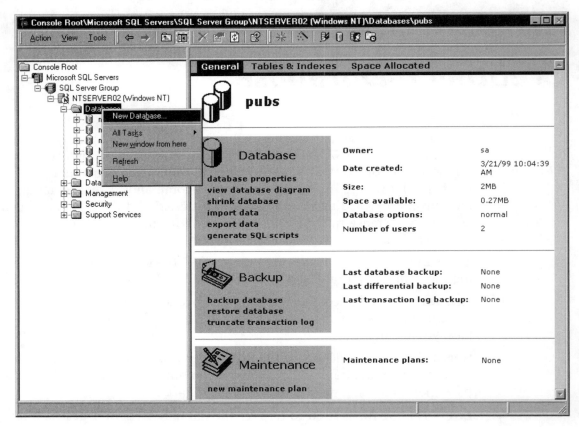

Enter a name for the database in the dialog box that appears. In this example, use **newpub**.

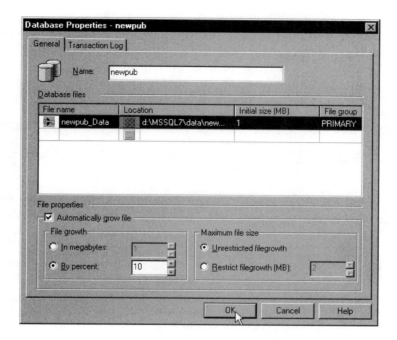

The primary database and the transaction log files are created using the name you specified as the prefix. In our example, these names are newpub_data.mdf and newpub.ldf. The initial size of the primary file and the log file are based on the model database. Before pressing the OK button, take a look at the Options tab.

The Options tab allows you to specify the type of access that the database will have. The DBO Use Only option allows only the creator of the database to access it. The Single User option allows only one user to access the database, thus preventing its shared use. Return to the General tab and click OK. The database will be created using the default values.

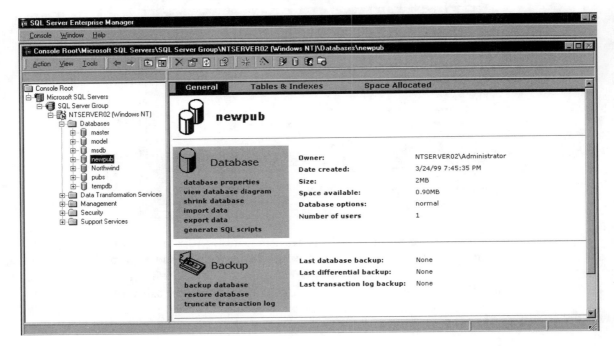

In the above figure, the newly created Newpub database is listed with the Northwind and Pubs databases.

Creating a Database with the Wizard

Using a database wizard is quite simple. A wizard can be activated through the menu command Tools|Wizards. This opens a window in which you click Database and double-click Create Database Wizard. You can also enable the wizard by right-clicking on the Databases folder in the left panel and choosing Tools|Wizard in the quick menu.

The first screen of the wizard contains only informational data. Press Next to continue. In the second screen you provide the name and confirm or specify another location for the database before pressing Next.

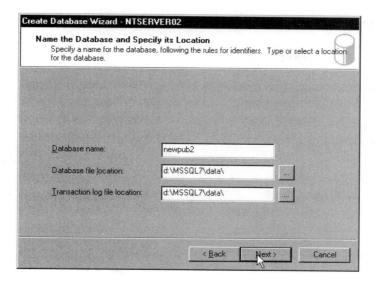

In the next step, you can accept the proposed value for the name of the database files and size or enter an initial size for the database files.

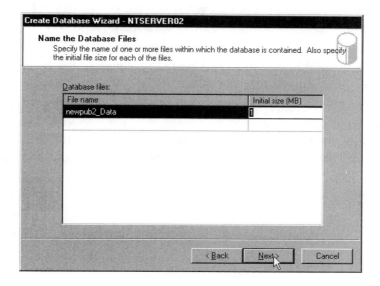

After pressing Next you must enter some data about database file growth.

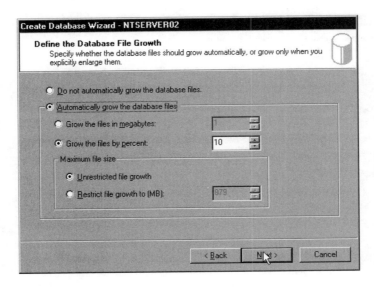

As the default the database will automatically grow at 10 percent increments from its current size. You can change this so the database grows in megabytes instead of percentage by selecting the option Grow the Files in Megabytes. The default is to grow one megabyte at a time.

The maximum size of the database will not be limited except for the physical available space. In order to set a maximum size you must select Restrict File Growth and indicate the final size that the database can achieve. Press Next.

In the next step, illustrated in the figure on the following page, you need to specify the size of the transaction log file. The wizard offers a default of 1 MB. Press Next and repeat this operation with the log file.

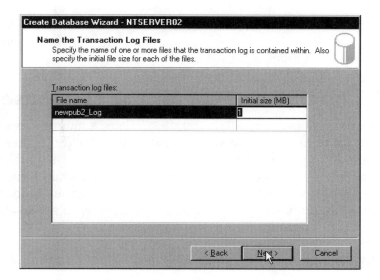

A screen asking you to confirm the growth type and maximum file size will appear. Enter the data according to your preferences. In this example we are keeping the indicated values. Press Next; a window appears with a summary of the characteristics of the database to be created, as shown below.

Press Finish to create the database. The wizard then asks if you want to create a maintenance plan for the database now. If you answer Yes, the Database Maintenance Plan Wizard will be invoked.

Defining a Maintenance Plan for the Database

Once the database is created, you must create a maintenance plan for it. Through a wizard you can specify several preventive maintenance tasks that aim to improve the performance or security of the database. Tasks such as integrity checking for files and indexes, backup frequency, and control report generation are some of the tasks the maintenance plan will execute automatically. This section describes how to set up the maintenance of the database we have just created.

The Database Maintenance Plan Wizard

The first screen of the wizard contains only informational data. After pressing Next, you will see a screen where you must enter the names of the databases that will be part of the maintenance plan. The Newpub2 database is selected as the default, since the wizard that created it invoked the maintenance wizard. Here you can choose the option All Databases in order to have all files, including the system databases, in the maintenance plan. You could also choose All System Databases or All User Databases.

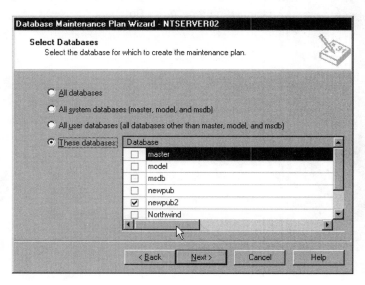

Pressing Next brings up an update optimization screen. These options help you reorganize data and indexes to improve performance. Make sure all the boxes are checked for this example. Then press Next.

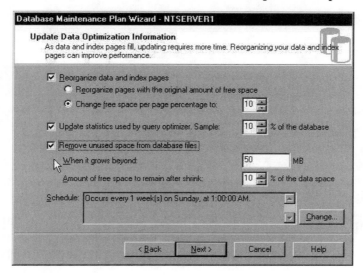

In the next step you select the data integrity tests to be performed. Check the appropriate tests and specify in the Schedule box when the tests must be performed, as shown below.

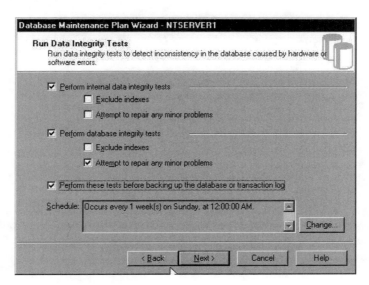

Press Next. In the next screen, the wizard wants to know if it can invoke the backup tool as part of the maintenance plan. You must confirm the backup configuration in this step.

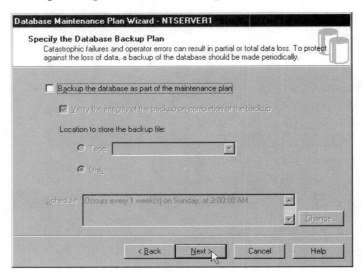

Press Next. A screen appears similar to the previous one concerning the execution of the log files backup. Press Next. The following screen, similar to the figure below, asks for authorization to issue reports.

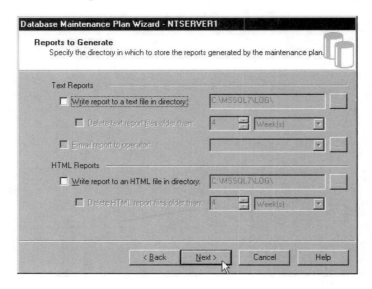

If you wish to issue reports, select the type and specify where they must be created, as well as how often they should be deleted.

Next, the wizard wants to know if the maintenance history must be kept in the server where the maintenance is done or in another server. If you choose another server, enter its location. In any of the options you can limit the number of rows for the maintenance table.

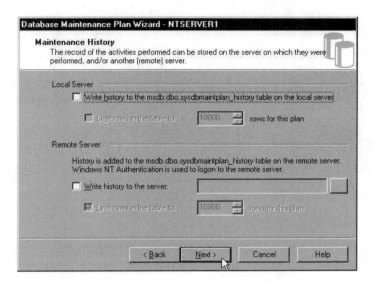

Press Next. The final screen appears, showing a summary of the operations that will be performed. Here you can change the name for the maintenance plan or accept the proposed name.

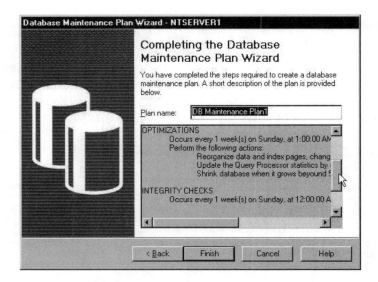

Pressing the Finish button creates the maintenance plan with the selected characteristics.

Creating Other Maintenance Plans

The Database Maintenance Plan Wizard can be invoked anytime through the Tools|Wizard menu. When the Wizards box is open, click in Management and choose the Database Maintenance Plan Wizard. You can create several maintenance plans according to the needs and characteristics of your database.

Creating a Database Using Transact-SQL

A database can also be created through the CREATE DATABASE command. Its complete syntax is described in the reference guide in Appendix A. Below is an example of a command that creates a database called Test1. The primary file is called Test1_dat. It has an initial size of 20 MB and a maximum of 50 MB, with growth in increments of 5 MB. The log file has an initial size of 6 MB and a maximum of 20 MB, and will grow at increments of 4 MB.

```
USE master
GO
CREATE DATABASE Test1
ON
( NAME = Test1_dat,
FILENAME = 'c:\mssql7\data\test1dat.mdf',
```

```
SIZE = 20,
MAXSIZE = 50,
FILEGROWTH = 5 )
LOG ON
( NAME = 'test1_log',
FILENAME = 'c:\mssql7\data\test1log.ldf',
SIZE = 6MB,
MAXSIZE = 20MB,
FILEGROWTH = 4MB )
```

Changing Database Characteristics

Once the database is created, you can change its characteristics through the Properties dialog. To activate this dialog box, right-click on the name of the database and select the Properties option in the quick menu.

The dialog box is the same as the one used to create the database but with the addition of a Permissions tab. This tab lets you grant or remove database access privileges for registered users.

Deleting a Database

In order to delete a database and all its contents, activate the quick menu with a right-click on the database name and choose the Delete option. This brings up a message box asking for confirmation. If you choose Yes, the database is deleted and cannot be recovered.

Viewing the Database Components

After a database is created, you can view its main physical characteristics, such as the file space and log space, or the number of tables and rows per table, through the viewing panel.

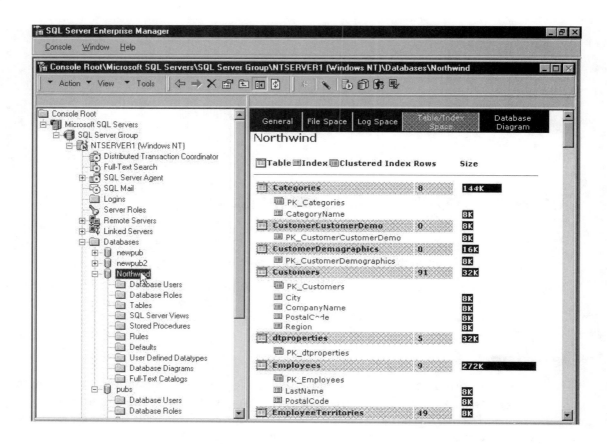

To get this information, double-click on the database name. As an example we will perform this operation with the Northwind file. In the right panel a bar appears at the top showing five topics: General, File Space, Log Space, Table/Index Space, and Database Diagram. When you click one of them, the appropriate information appears. In the above figure, the Northwind tables are shown with the fields, number of rows, and size.

In order to view a specific component of the database, click on the corresponding folder in the tree and then click on the item in the viewing panel. For example, to access the contents of a view, you must click on the SQL Server Views folder. If the database has previously created views, they will be shown in the right panel, as shown in the following figure.

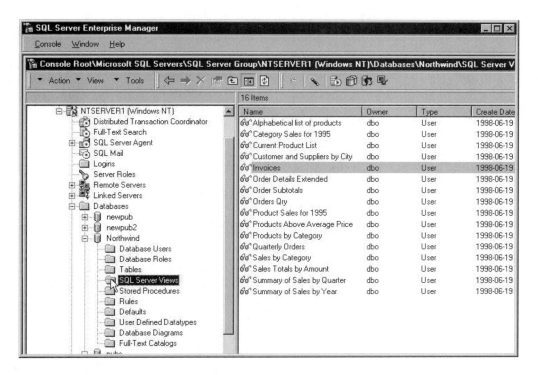

When you want to open, edit, or view one of the views, click with the right mouse button on the view name. The quick menu shows all available options for that object. This procedure is the same for any of the database objects.

Summary

This chapter demonstrated how to create a database manually, by using the Create Database Wizard, and with Transact-SQL commands. Setting up a maintenance plan was also discussed. The next chapter addresses tables.

Chapter 3

Tables

Tables are the heart of the database. Knowing how to create and maintain tables is among the most important pieces of knowledge for database users. In order to create a table, you must know the concepts and characteristics of the database used.

The process of creating a table must begin only after the database has been carefully defined. Many developers have the bad habit of defining the database "online," i.e., they open the module that creates the tables and then start thinking about the database. This can cause many problems.

Characteristics of Tables

The SQL Server 7 allows the creation of temporary and permanent tables. Temporary tables are those created in memory while permanent tables are those that are written to disk.

A SQL Server 7 table can contain up to 1,024 columns. Each column must be created through the specification of basic information such as its name, the data type it will store, and the optional specification of default values and constraints imposed on the contents.

The name of a column must be exclusive inside a database. There cannot be two columns called State inside the same table. However, different tables inside a database can contain columns with the same name. For example, two tables called Clients and Suppliers can each contain address information data in columns called Street Address, City, and State.

The name of a table must be exclusive among the tables created by an owner. However, inside a database there can be tables with the same name pertaining to different users.

Filegroups

When a table is created, it is automatically put in the default filegroup. However, if the table contains fields of type Text, Ntext, or Image, they can be put in a filegroup different from the rest of the table.

Data Types

Each column in a table must have a data type specified to it. In other words, one must indicate that the column will store a particular type of data such as text, number, data, or image. The SQL Server 7 can use several types of data and also allows the user to create his or her own data types.

Data stored in a SQL Server 7 table can be of these types:

Integer	
Bit	Integer with a 0 or 1 value
Int	Integer number with values between -2^{31} ($-2,147,483,648$) up to $2^{31}-1$ ($2,147,483,647$).
Smallint	2^{15} ($-32,768$) up to $2^{15}-1$ ($32,767$).
Tinyint	Integer between 0 and 255
Decimal or Numeric	Number with fixed accuracy between $-10^{38}-1$ up to $10^{38}-1$.
Money	Monetary data values from -2^{63} ($-922,337,203,685,477.5808$) through $2^{63}-1$ ($922,337,203,685,477.5807$), with accuracy to a ten-thousandth of a monetary unit.
Smallmoney	$-214,748.3648$ through $214,748.3647$, with accuracy to a ten-thousandth of a monetary unit.
Float	$-1.79E+308$ through $1.79E+308$.
Real	$-3.40E+38$ through $3.40E+38$.
Datetime	January 1, 1753, up to December 31, 9999, with accuracy up to the 3.33th millisecond.
Smalldatetime	January 1, 1900, up to June 6, 2079, with precision of up to 1 minute

Miscellaneous	
Cursor	A reference to a cursor
Timestamp	An exclusive number recognized by the database
Uniqueidentifier	An exclusive global identifier

Strings	
Char	A fixed field with maximum size of 8,000 bytes
Varchar	A fixed field with maximum size of 8,000 bytes
Text	Variable with size up to $2^{31}-1$ (2,147,483,647) bytes

Unicode Strings	
Nchar	Unicode character with fixed size of up to 4,000 bytes
Nvarchar	Unicode character with variable size of up to 4,000 bytes
Ntext	Variable with size up to $2^{30}-1$ (1,073,741,823) bytes

Binary Strings	
Binary	Fixed size of up to 8,000 bytes
Varbinary	Variable size of up to 8,000 bytes
Image	Variable size with up to $2^{31}-1$ (2,147,483,647) bytes.

Synonyms

Some synonyms were created for compatibility with the SQL-92 language.

Synonym	**Equivalent to**
binary varying	varbinary
char varying	varchar
character	char
character	char(1)
character(n)	char(n)
character varying(n)	varchar(n)
dec	decimal
double precision	float
float[(n)] for $n = 1$-7	real
float[(n)] for $n = 8$-15	float
integer	int
national character(n)	nchar(n)
national char(n)	nchar(n)
national character varying(n)	nvarchar(n)
national char varying(n)	nvarchar(n)
national text	ntext
numeric	decimal

Constraints

Constraints are a way to ensure the integrity of a database through the filtering of information inserted in a table's column. Constraints are the basic mechanism to ensure the integrity of a field. They have priority over triggers, rules, and default values. There are five types of constraints:

NOT NULL specifies that a column cannot accept the value Null.

CHECK limits the values that can be put in the column by testing for a condition. Boolean is based on the contents that are attributed to the column. If a tested condition returns TRUE, the entered value is attributed to the column.

UNIQUE forces the columns to have exclusive values; in other words, in a column that is designated UNIQUE, there cannot be two records with the same contents. For example, a product code or social security number must be exclusive. On the other hand, the contents of a state or city field can be duplicated.

PRIMARY KEY creates the primary key of the table, a column, or combination of columns with values that must be exclusive inside the table in order to identify a row. A column with a primary key constraint cannot have the Null value attributed to it. When the primary key is formed by more than one column, just one of them will be considered the primary key. The other columns that form the key are called candidate keys.

FOREIGN KEY identifies the relationship between the tables. This is a field in the current table that points to a key field in another table. The use of a foreign key prevents the deletion of rows in the current table when there are references to key fields of external tables. This kind of constraint prevents a value from being introduced in the current table that is not found in the key fields of the external table that was joined.

Sample Tables

In this chapter, we will create one table with author data, another with book data, and a third that will be used to join the author and book table. Those tables will be created in the Newpub database. The Authors table must have the structure shown on the next page, with the au_id column as the primary key with an exclusive value defined by ID.

Column	Name	Type	Size	null?	Default
1	au_id	Int	10	no	
2	au_name	varchar	30	no	
3	au_phone	varchar	18	yes	
4	au_email	varchar	25	yes	
5	au_addr	varchar	40	yes	
6	au_city	varchar	30	yes	
7	au_state	char	2	yes	
8	au_zip	char	8	yes	
9	au_country	char	15	yes	'Brazil'
10	active	bit	1		

The Active field indicates whether the author has had a book published.

The Books table must contain the following fields. The book_id column must be the primary key with an exclusive value defined by ID.

Column	Name	Type	Size	null?	Default value
1	book_id	ID	4	no	
2	title	varchar	50	no	
3	price	money	8	no	
4	category	char	10	no	
5	comments	varchar	100	yes	'not available'
6	publidate	datetime	8	yes	

The Autbook table must contain the following structure, and the book_id column must be the primary key:

Column	Name	Type	Size	null?
1	book_id	ID	4	no
2	au_id	ID	10	no

Creating a Table with the Enterprise Manager

Follow these steps to create a table:

Expand the Databases folder and the database where you want to create the table. Then click with the right mouse button in the Tables folder and select the option New Table.

A dialog box, shown below, asks for the name of the table. In this example we will enter **authors**. Press OK. This will bring up a window in which you define the characteristics of the columns.

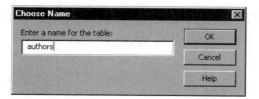

Characteristics of Columns

The following window must be used to enter the characteristics of the columns in the table we are creating:

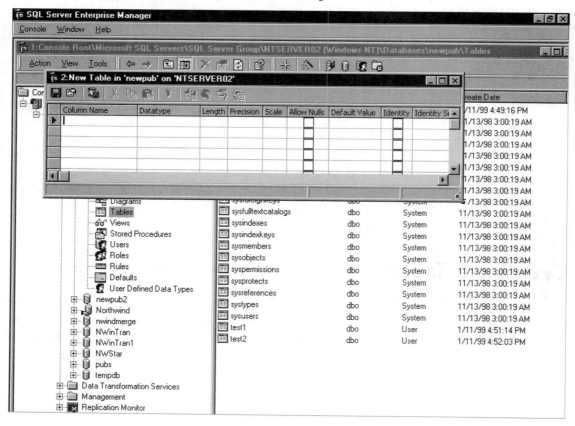

Below is a description of each column in this window:

Column Name	Indicates the name for the column or field
Datatype	Indicates the type of data stored by the column
Length	Indicates the size of the field
Precision	Indicates the number of digits in a number
Scale	Indicates the number of decimal places
Allow Nulls	When this column is checked, SQL Server will allow the inclusion of Null values in the field
Default Value	Used to specify a default value for the column
Identity	This column, when checked, indicates that the field will have an identity number automatically generated
Identity Seed	Indicates the initial value for the first record
Identity Increment	Indicates the incremental value for new records
Is RowGuid	Creates exclusive contents for the column at the global level. A table can have only one column of this type and it must be created with the data type Uniqueidentifier.

For a numeric field, Length holds the number of bytes used to store every number. For character or Unicode fields, this is the number of characters. For Binary, Varbinary, and Image fields, this indicates the number of bytes.

Identifier Columns

A table can contain one identifier column. This type of column contains only one value that identifies one row of the table. This type of column is ideal for the automatic creation of codes for records. For example, a table of sales orders can contain a field called ped_num that stores only one identifier in sequence for the order. Through the Identity property the SQL Server generates an incremental value for every row that is added to the table. You can specify an initial value (seed) and the value that will be used to increment this counter. When neither item is specified, 1 is used as the default. Only one column per table can have this property activated. The data type of the column must be Int or Smallint; it does not allow Null values.

Null Values

Some tables can contain columns that accept the Null value, indicating that the column has not received any contents as yet. The fields that must be filled out are created with the option Allow Nulls unchecked.

Primary Key

One or more columns of the table that identify that row exclusively inside the table form the primary key. The specification of a primary key assures the integrity of the table. The column or columns that form a primary key cannot contain the Null value. When specifying a primary key, SQL Server creates a specific index in order to guarantee that the key is exclusive.

In our table, au_id and book_id are primary keys of the Authors and Books tables. The Autbook table has its primary key composed of the au_id and book_id columns. The primary keys are also used in joins to relate one table to the other.

Foreign Key

The foreign key is a column or a combination of columns used to establish a link between two tables. The link is made through the creation of fields that are common to both tables. Its use is very common for maintaining the referential integrity between the two tables. For example, you have an Employee table with a field called Department. This field is associated to the dep_id field in another table called Dept that has data from the company's departments. If there is no foreign key, anybody can delete a row of a department in the Dept table when there are several employees in that department specified in your records. A foreign key allows only the insertion of those values found in the related fields of the foreign table.

Although it is common, a foreign key does not necessarily need to be associated to a primary key in another table. However, it must reference a column with exclusive contents.

UNIQUE Constraints

In addition to the primary key, we can create constraints of type UNIQUE in other columns. When this type of constraint is created, the SQL Server creates an exclusive index in order to assure the data is not duplicated.

CHECK Constraints

A constraint of type CHECK limits the values accepted by a column. The validity check of entered data is made against a list of values or the analysis of a logical expression, for example, price > 1 and < 100.

Using Tables

Let's look at other basic operations with tables.

Deleting a Table

You can delete a table from a database with the following steps:

Expand the Databases folder and the database that contains the table you want to delete. Then expand the Tables folder. Click with the right mouse button on the name of the table to be deleted and select the option Delete. The Drop Objects dialog will appear.

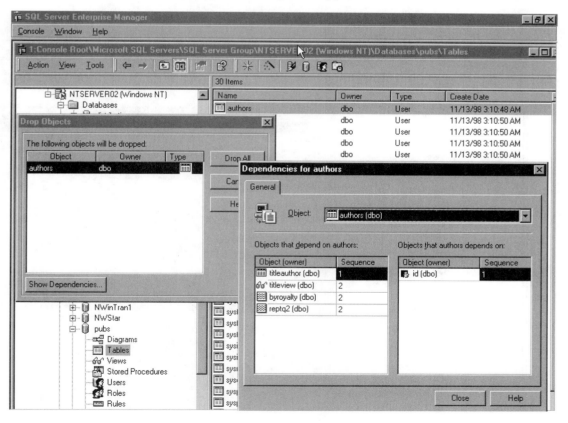

To delete the table, press the Drop All button. (Do not actually delete the table in this example.) To see all the dependencies involved with the table, press Show Dependencies. If dependencies exist, a new dialog box is shown. To return to the previous screen, press Close.

Renaming a Table

Expand the Databases folder and the database that contains the table you want to rename. Then expand the Tables folder. Click with the right mouse button on the table to be renamed.

Then enter the new name of the table and click outside the typing area.

Viewing a Table's Data

In the detail panel, click with the right mouse button on the name of the table you want to view. Select Open Table. Click on Return All Rows to see all the lines of the table or Return Top to enter how many lines you want to see.

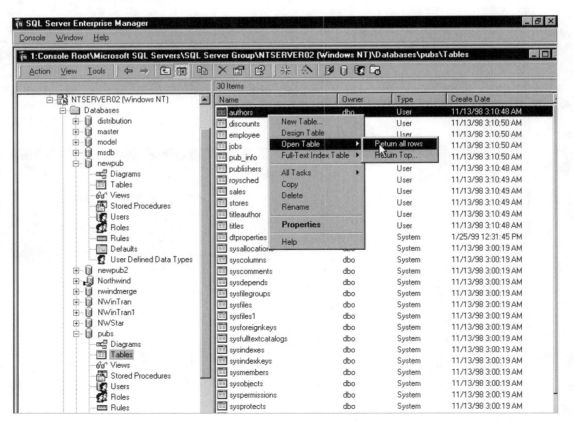

A new window opens, showing the table's records.

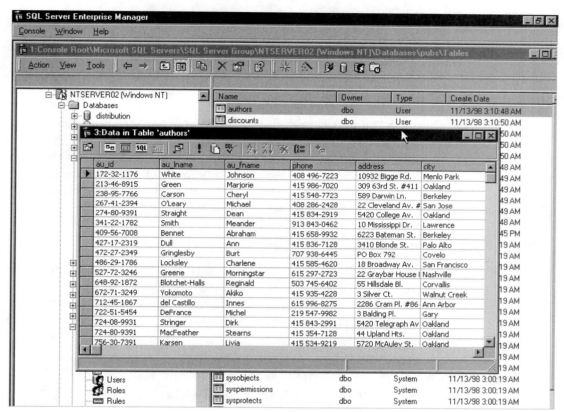

In this window you can use the scrolling bars to view more lines or columns.

Editing Data in a Table with the Enterprise Manager

To change data in a table's field, follow the same procedure used to view the table. Once the record to be edited is located, click on the field that you want to edit and enter the new contents.

Remember that the constraints created for the fields must be respected when editing the record. If we try to insert a new record in the Authors table of the Pubs database and we do not enter the proper contents to the Contract field, the following message will appear:

Adding a New Column to the Table

Expand the Databases folder and the database where the table is located. Then expand the Tables folder. Click with the right mouse button on the table to be changed. Click on the option Design Table. Select the column that will be to the right of the new column and right-click on the name of the column; select Insert Column. After entering the data, press Save. To cancel the deletion of the line while typing, press Esc.

Removing a Column from the Table

Expand the Databases folder and the database where you want to edit the table. Then expand the Tables folder. Click with the right mouse button on the name of the table to be changed. Click on the option Design Table. Select the column to be deleted and then click on Delete Column.

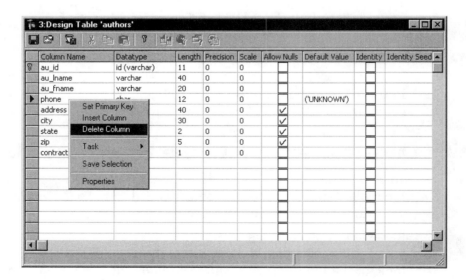

After the column is deleted, press Save. It is not possible to remove a column that is being used by an index, CHECK or UNIQUE constraints, or a primary or foreign key.

Viewing the Properties of a Table

To find out the structure of a table and details about its columns, you need to activate the properties box. Expand the Databases folder and the database that contains the table. Then expand the Tables folder. Click with the right mouse button on the name of the table and click on the Properties option. The screen below shows the properties of the Northwind database Products table.

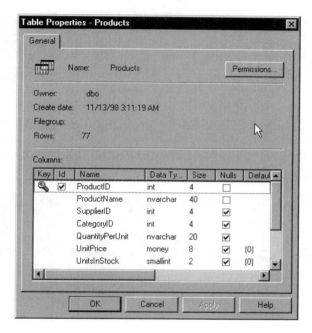

In addition to the properties of the columns, you can also find out the access permissions for the table by pressing Permissions. To close, press OK.

Creating the Authors Table

Let's create the Authors table in the Newpub database. To do this, expand the Databases folder, right-click Tables, and select New Table. Enter **Authors** in the first dialog box and complete the data on the Authors table as shown in the next figure. The word Brazil must be enclosed in single quotes; otherwise an error will occur when the table is written.

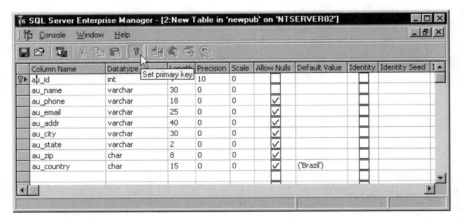

Creating the Primary Key

The primary key for this table is the au_id field. To define a primary key, click on the cell to the left of Column Name that corresponds to the desired field. Then click on the Set Primary Key button.

To finish creating the table, press Save. Create the Books and Autbook sample tables using the same technique and the information on page 31.

Summary

In this chapter you learned how to create, change, and insert data into a table. In the next chapter we will show how to create a relationship among tables and how to use a database diagram.

Chapter 4

Database Diagrams

Database diagrams are graphic representations of a database. With them you can manage database objects using a graphical interface and drag and drop in order to perform tasks that normally are done with SQL language commands. These include adding or deleting tables, triggers, stored procedures, table column constraints, and table relationships.

Here is an example of the Northwind database diagram:

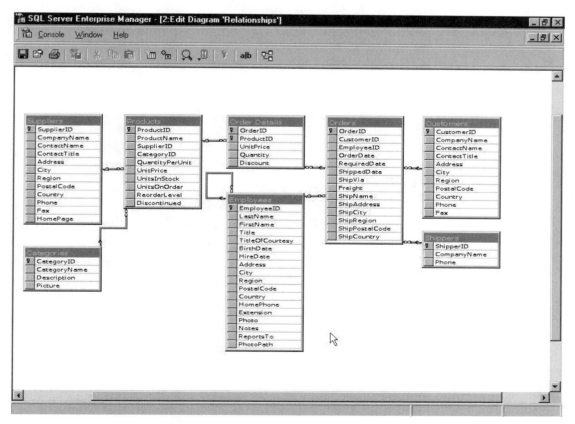

You can see the database tables and the relationships among them. Each table shown here is simply a reference to the table that is physically stored inside the database. Several diagrams can be created for the same database. These are some of the tasks you can perform through a diagram:

➤ View the table structure and its relationships

➤ Obtain several views of parts of a complex database

➤ Experiment with the database structure without executing the changes

➤ Change the database structure

You can also change the characteristics of a table by using a diagram. These changes are automatically reflected in other diagrams where the table appears. This also applies to deleted tables. The changes made in the tables of a diagram do not affect the physical table until the moment the diagram is written. The diagram allows you to make changes in several tables and to select just some tables in which the changes made will be written. The operations described below will cause the re-creation of the table when the diagram is saved:

➤ Adding a table that does not allow Nulls at the end of the current table

➤ Adding a column in the body of the table

➤ Reorganizing the existing columns

➤ Deleting an existing column

Creating a Diagram

To create a diagram, expand the desired database. Then click with the right mouse button on Database Diagrams and select New Database Diagram. This activates the Create Diagram Wizard.

Let's create a diagram for the Pubs database. After following the above steps, the first wizard screen appears. Just click on it and continue. Select all the tables in the next dialog box, as shown below. Press Add.

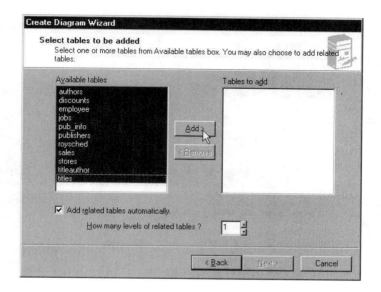

Press Next. In the next screen, the wizard lists the tables to be added. Press Finish.

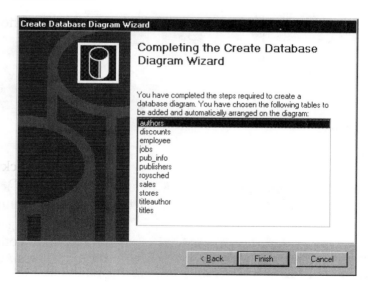

After you press Next, the program shows the names of the tables that were selected. Press Finish to create the diagram. The diagram is then shown in the working area, as illustrated below.

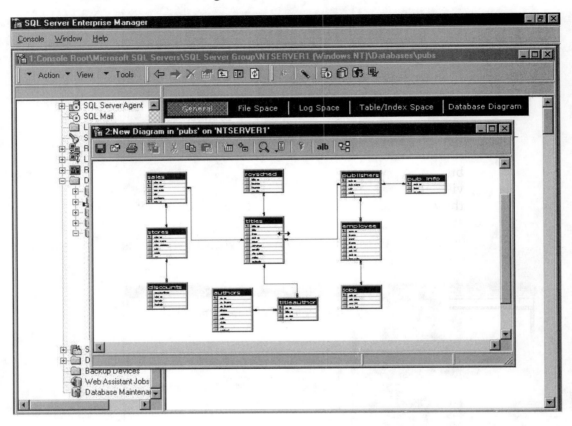

To save the diagram, click on the Save button (the diskette icon) and enter a name for the diagram. Let's call it **diagram02** in this example.

Using a Diagram

The following sections show how to perform some basic operations with the diagrams.

Opening a Diagram

To open an existing diagram, first expand the server and the Databases folder. Click on the Database Diagrams folder. The existing diagrams appear in the right panel. Double-click on the diagram you wish to open, or click with the right mouse button and select Design Diagram in the quick menu that appears.

This operation will open the Northwind database diagram shown at the beginning of this chapter.

Printing a Diagram

The database diagram is a good way of documenting a database. To print the diagram, click on the Print button or the Print option in the quick menu. Before printing, check where the page breaks will occur, as diagrams containing many tables often take up two or more pages. To view the page breaks, activate the quick menu by clicking with the right mouse button on a free space of the diagram, and select View Page Breaks. To view the entire diagram and have a better idea of the space it occupies in the page, click on the Zoom option in the quick menu and choose a smaller percentage. The figure below was displayed with a zoom of 50%.

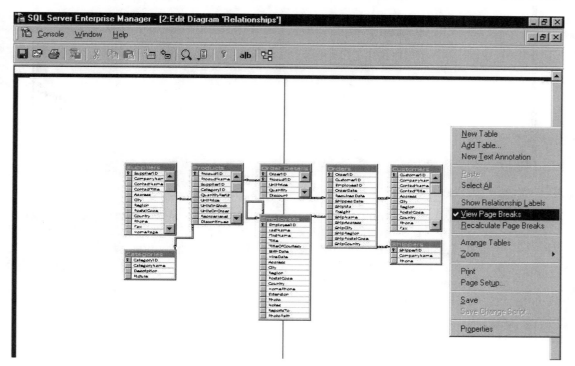

The thick lines around the diagram are the page borders. The vertical line in the middle of the screen is the page division. Note in this case that two tables would be cut in half. You can manually adjust the placement of the tables by clicking on the table's title bar and dragging it to the desired position, as shown below.

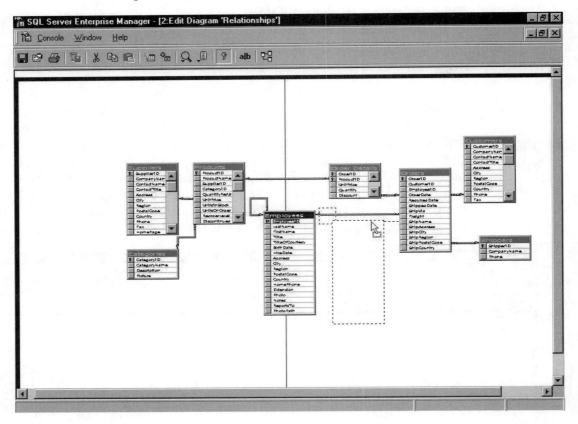

Instead of doing the adjustments manually, you can use the Arrange Tables option in the quick menu. It reorganizes the tables automatically and keeps the page breaks from dividing tables whenever possible. The next figure shows the diagram with a zoom of 25% after the tables have been adjusted.

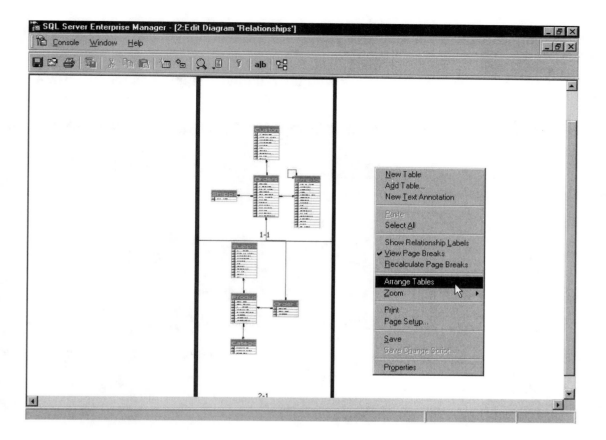

Quitting a Diagram

To finish viewing a diagram without saving changes you've made, click on the Close button (the x in the title bar) and choose No in the dialog box. If you answer Yes, all the changes made in the layout will be written and will affect the database.

Using Tables in Database Diagrams

The following sections explain how to use tables in database diagrams. These tasks include creating, adding, and removing tables, as well as creating relationships among tables.

Viewing a Table's Properties

To view the properties of a table and perform most operations related to tables, you must click with the right mouse button on the title bar. A quick menu opens with all the options that apply to that table.

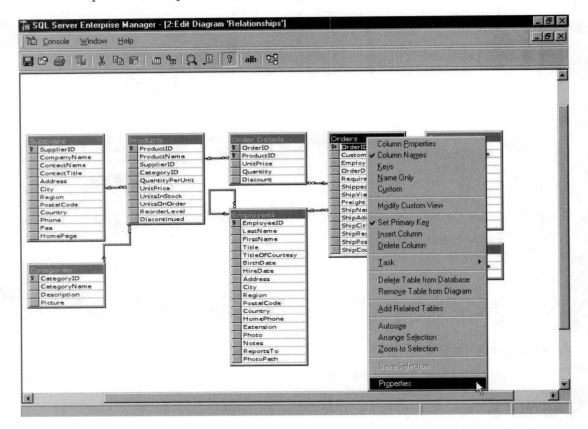

The last item is Properties. Since the Orders table is selected, when you click on this item a dialog box appears showing the properties of that table. In this dialog box there are three tabs. The Relationships tab shows the relationships between this table and the other tables. It shows the tables referred to in foreign keys and the tables that make reference to it.

For example, the Orders table is related through the CustomerID field to the Customers table that has the CustomerID field as its primary key, as shown in the next figure.

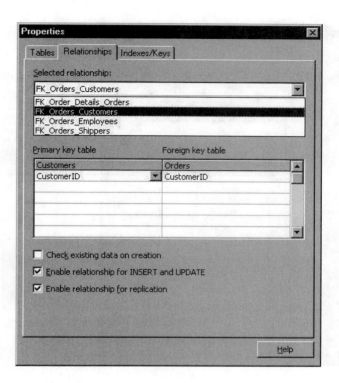

The Indexes/Keys tab allows you to view and create the index files of the table. In this example, the OrderID column is used as the table's primary key and the name of the index associated with it is PK_Orders.

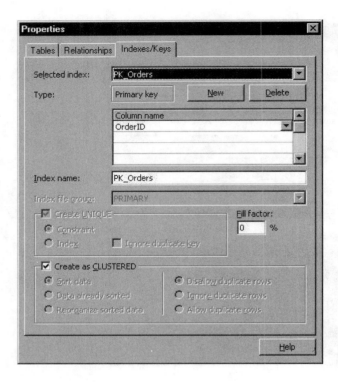

You can create new indexes by using the New button. To delete an index, select the index and then press the Delete button.

The Tables tab shows information such as the name of the table, the file where it is located, and its constraints. Through the Selected Table field you can select other tables in the diagram. The following figure shows the Products table which contains a constraint that limits the values of the UnitPrice column.

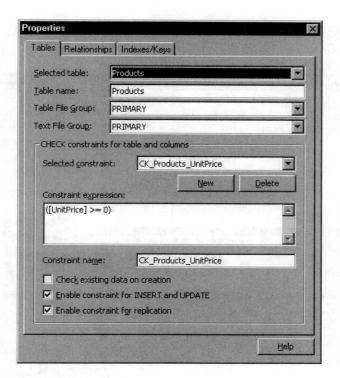

Changing the View of a Table

As its default, a database diagram shows the tables as a rectangle with the names of the table's columns. You can change this display through the quick menu. Each table can be viewed in the following formats:

➤ Column Properties—Shows a grid with all the columns of the table as its properties, such as size, if it accepts Nulls, data type, etc. When a new table is inserted in the diagram, this format is automatically enabled.

➤ Column Names—Lists the names of all columns. This is the default. When an existing table is added to the diagram, it appears in this format.

➤ Keys—Shows the names of all columns that are primary or foreign keys, or those that possess an exclusive characteristic.

➤ Name Only—There is only one title bar in the table.

➤ Custom—Shows only the columns that are user defined.

The next figure shows the Column Properties format selected for the Orders table.

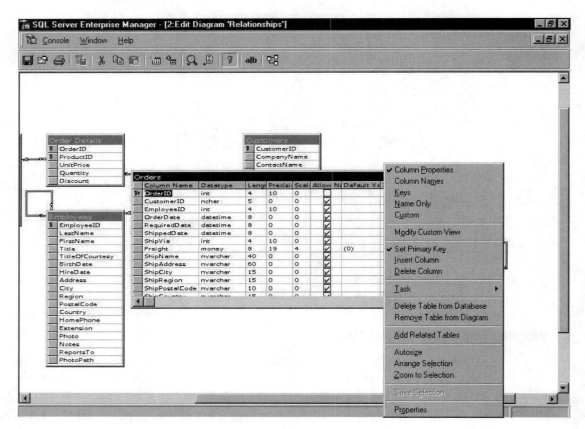

Adding Tables to a Diagram

In the Creating a Diagram section we used the wizard to create a diagram with all the data tables. Now we are going to create a small diagram and add the tables manually. Activate the Create Diagram Wizard and press Cancel in the first screen. Then click with the right mouse button on the working area and select Add Table. A dialog box appears, showing the database's tables. We are going to create a diagram containing the Authors, Titleauthor, and Titles tables. First choose the Authors table and press the Add button.

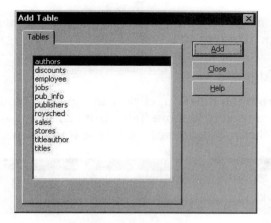

The selected table appears immediately in the working area. Then select Titleauthor and Titles simultaneously, keeping the Shift key pressed while clicking on the names of the tables. After they are selected, press Add. The tables are overlapped on the diagram's working area. You can adjust them quickly by activating the quick menu and clicking on Arrange Tables.

Examine how the diagram appears after these tasks are performed. Note how the relationships between the tables are automatically created.

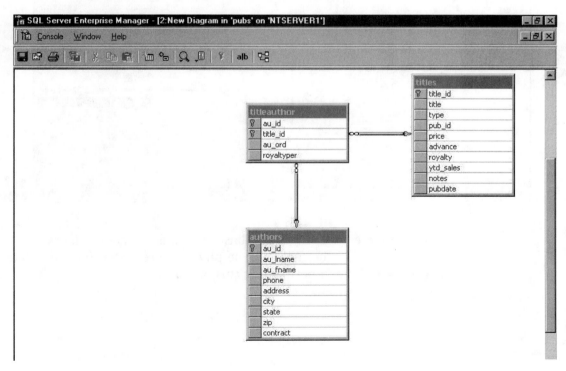

To complete this example, add the Publishers table to the diagram and save it with the name **diagram01**.

Removing a Table from a Diagram

To remove a table from the diagram, click with the right mouse button on the table's title bar and select Remove Table from Diagram. As shown in the next figure, we eliminated the last table that was inserted.

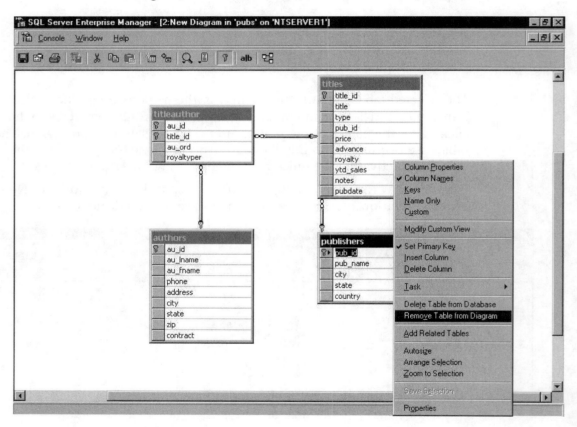

When the Delete Table from Database option is selected, a message appears saying that the table will be physically removed from the database. Be careful when performing this operation.

Adding Related Tables

The database diagram allows all the tables related to another table to be included at once. For example, the Titles table is related to the Publishers, Sales, and Roysched tables, in addition to the two tables that are already related (Titleauthor and Authors). To add all of the other related tables, click on the table from which all the relationships originate and choose Add Related Tables.

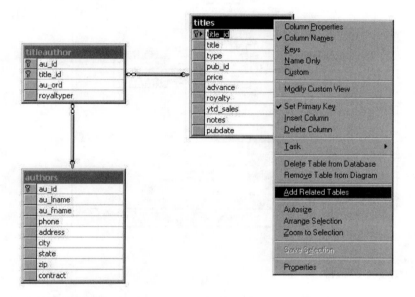

The related tables will appear in the diagram. Use the Arrange Tables option so the diagram appears like the one that follows.

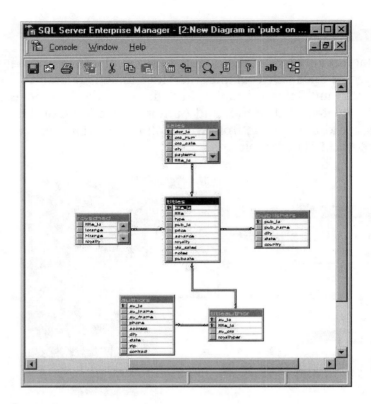

Including Annotations

The database diagram allows you to include annotations or comments in a text box in the working area. To do this, click with the right mouse button on the place where you want to insert the text and select New Text Annotation.

A rectangle will appear. Enter the text you want inside the rectangle. You can increase or decrease the rectangle's size and adjust the text by clicking and dragging its corners.

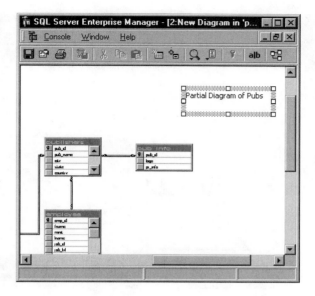

Creating a New Table

To create a new table, press the New Table button in the toolbar. Enter
TABLE1demo in the dialog box and press OK.

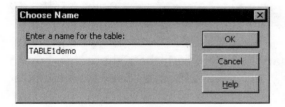

The grid to create the table appears in the working area. All you have to
do is to specify the characteristics of the new table. As an example, we
will create the two columns shown in the following illustration:

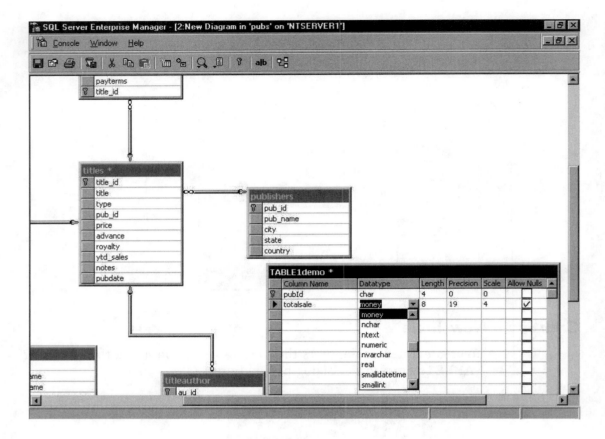

To create the primary key, click with the right mouse button on the first line of the grid and click on Set Primary Key in the toolbar.

Creating a Relationship Among Tables

Now that the new table is created, we will relate it to the Titles table. This operation is quite simple. Just select the line that defines the column with the primary key in the new table and drag it to the name of the corresponding column in the other table.

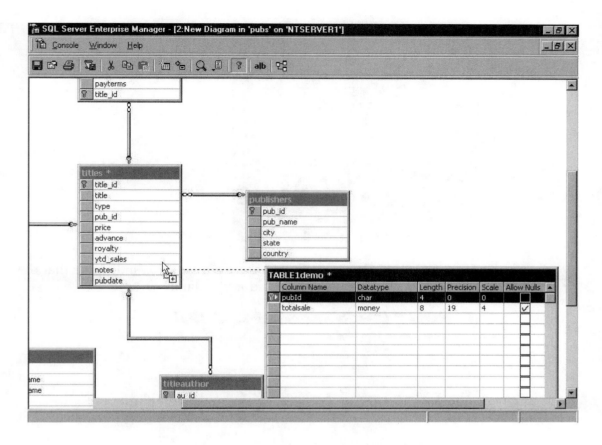

In this case we will select pubId from the TABLE1demo table and drag it to the pub_id column of the Titles table. This opens a new dialog box, in which you can press OK to confirm the creation of the relationship.

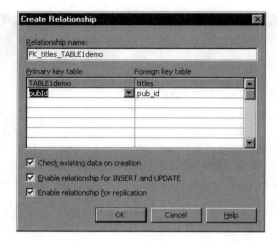

If you press OK, the program will show a dialog box indicating that the new table will be physically created in the database.

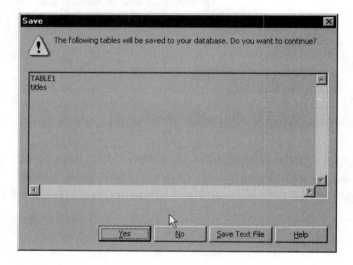

In our example we don't want to save the changes we made, so we press No.

Summary

In this chapter you saw that database diagrams can be very useful for the creation of models and prototypes of databases, in addition to helping with the work of creating and maintaining tables. In the next chapter we will talk about a fundamental tool for working with SQL Server, the Query Analyzer.

Chapter 5

Query Analyzer

In this chapter we will learn about one of the SQL Server 7 tools and how it works. The SQL Server Query Analyzer is a tool with a graphical interface that allows the user to perform a series of activities related to the recovery and optimization of the queries in a database. Among these activities are:

➤ Querying a SQL Server database using the SQL commands to view the text or grid

➤ Viewing a graphical representation of the steps to execute a query

➤ Running an index performance analysis

➤ Accessing the online help for the Transact-SQL language

➤ Executing Transact-SQL scripts of stored procedures

The Query Analyzer is the best option when you want to practice using the Transact-SQL language, since it allows the immediate execution of the commands and displays the results. In addition, it allows immediate access to Transact-SQL's help if you have problems with its syntax.

Connecting to the Server

After loading, the program displays a dialog box where you must specify the server to which you want to connect. This dialog box can also be accessed with File|Connect.

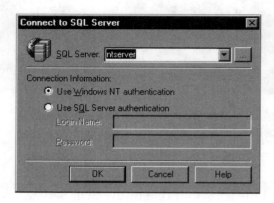

In the SQL Server box, enter the name of the desired server or click on Browse (the button with three dots) to access a list of the network servers. (Windows 95 does not have the Browse option.)

Choose a method of authentication in the Connection Information panel. Select Use Windows NT Authentication to connect with an identity and password in Windows NT or select Use SQL Server Authentication to enter a password and identity that is recognized by SQL Server.

In this case, the only available server is ntserver. The working screen of the Query Analyzer appears after you press OK.

The Working Screen

Two panels form the working screen. If you see only one panel, press the Hide Results button (to the left of the Database field) and open the second panel. In the top panel, the Query Panel, you enter the SQL commands or load the scripts to be run. The bottom panel shows the results of your query or error and warning messages.

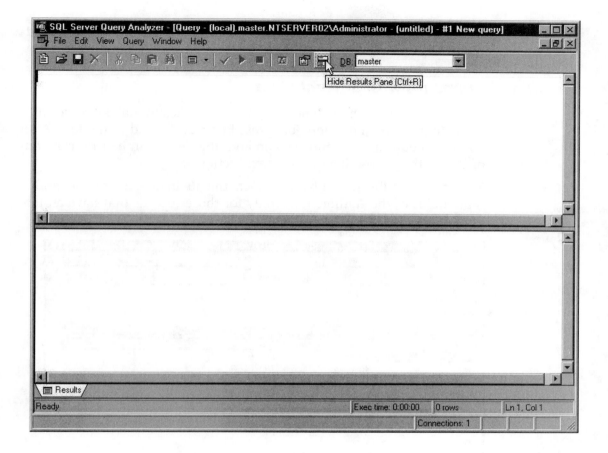

The toolbar has two buttons that are equivalent to some of the menu options. There is also a list of available databases in the server. You can select a database by clicking on the arrow of the Database box to open a list and then on the name of the desired database. In this example we will work with the Pubs database.

We will use some of the SQL commands to show how the Query Analyzer functions. These commands will be detailed in the next chapter and the entire syntax can be found in Appendix A. Before continuing, select the Pubs database in the Database field and make it the default database.

Changing the Panel Sizes

You can increase or decrease the size of the two panels by clicking and dragging the dividing line that separates them. When positioning the cursor in the dividing line, the format changes. Then you can drag and resize the window.

Executing Commands with Several Lines

A SQL command can be divided into several lines to make it easier to read. To go to the next line, just press Enter at the end of the line. After you finish entering the entire command, the query can be run using any of the methods described in the next section.

The command illustrated below selects the au_lname, au_fname, and State fields of the Authors table only for those records that have a State field other than "CA."

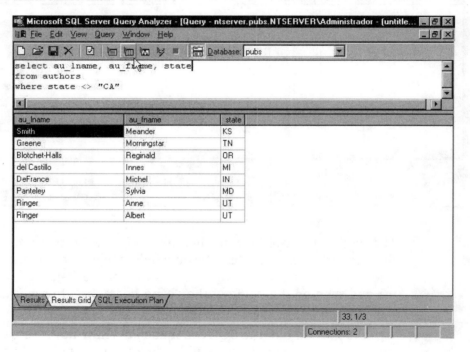

In this example it is not important whether the contents of the field are specified with capital letters; all the occurrences of "ca" or "CA" will be considered.

Executing a Query

Make sure you have specified the Pubs database as the default database. In the Query Panel enter the command **select * from authors**. Note that while you type, the words "select" and "from" become blue. This is because they are the fixed parts of the syntax of the SELECT command, which is the main command used to recover fields and rows in a database. Authors is one of the tables in the Pubs database. To execute and see the results of the query, you can use the Execute Query button as shown in the figure below, the Execute Query option in the Query menu, or the Ctrl+e key combination.

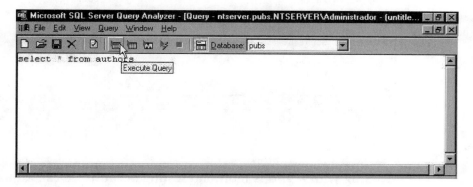

Viewing the Query with a Grid

Instead of using the Execute Query button, you can use the Execute Query Into Grid button or option. It works the same way, but it shows the data in a tabular format, including the name of the columns, and makes a better use of the screen space, as shown in the next figure.

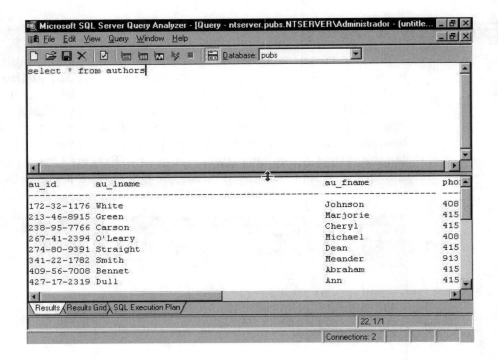

Working with a grid is more interesting because we can adjust the width of the columns and organize the order of the display. To do this, click with the right mouse button on one of the columns to activate the quick menu and choose the Sort Column option. Below is the previous example after it is organized by the au_lname column.

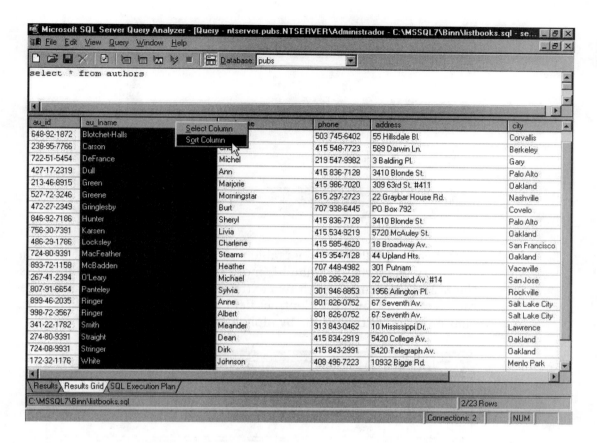

Viewing the Query Execution Plan

A very important task of the Query Analyzer is, as its name implies, to analyze a query. Through the Query Execution Plan option or button, we can see all the steps and procedures for executing a query. Some commands require several logical and physical operations that demand CPU time and hardware. To graphically see the steps for the execution of a query, you must press the Query Execution Plan button. The Results Panel shows the icons for the operations performed.

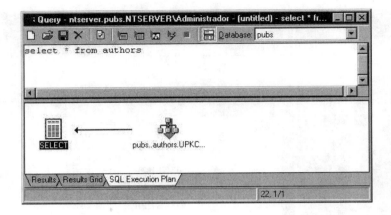

In this case, the Pubs.authors table was completely read. More steps are necessary when the command is more complex. The next figure shows the SELECT command with two extra clauses. The WHERE clause filters the records in which the Contract field is not zero and the ORDER BY clause organizes the results by alphabetical order of state and city.

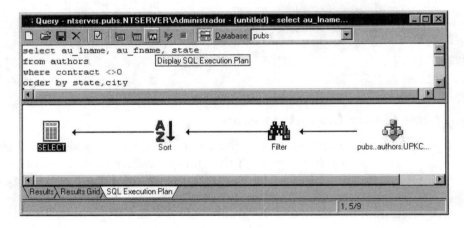

Note that in the bottom panel two new operations are displayed.

Adjusting the Execution Plan Display

More complex queries will require several operations that will not always be completely viewed in the bottom panel. To have a global view of the operations performed, you can zoom out and reduce the size of the icons. This operation can be done through the quick menu, which is activated by right-clicking in the bottom panel. In this menu, the first option, Zoom

To Fit, must be selected. The next screen shows that all the elements forming the query are displayed through the reduction and repositioning of its icons.

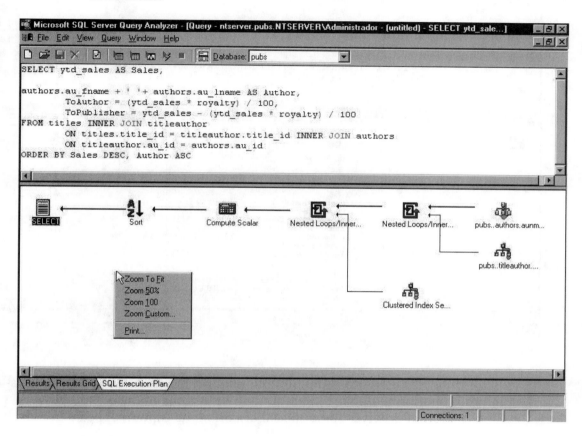

Analyzing a Query

After executing the query, the Results Panel can be used to obtain specific information about each operation displayed. Just pause the cursor on an icon for a description of the operation characteristics.

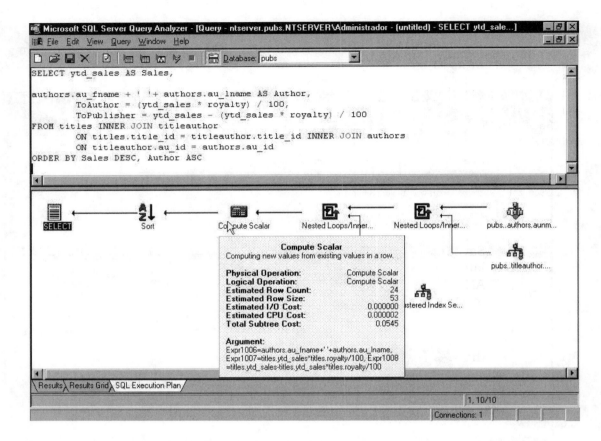

In the above figure, a description is shown related to the scalar calculation performed by the internal math operations of the query. When an operation deserves some special attention, its caption appears in red.

Saving and Recovering a Query

The text or script of a query can be written to disk for future recovery and execution. If you often execute the same queries, this will save you a lot of time.

To save a query, click on File|Save. Select where you want to save the query and enter the name of the query in the File Name field. In the File Format field, select the set of characters you want to use to save the query.

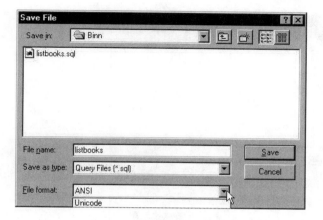

Save the query in the page code used by Windows if it will be executed later in a batch operation from the command line. Save the query in ANSI format if you want to use it again in the Query Analyzer. Save the query in Unicode format if it uses special international characters.

To load a query, click on File|Open. Select the place where this query is stored and enter the name of the query in the File Name field. Remember that the extension .sql is added to the query filename.

The last five queries saved are displayed at the end of the File menu.

Editing a Query

In the Edit menu you can perform basic operations such as editing the text of the query. With the Find option you can specify text to be located inside the command lines. With the Replace option you can replace text. The Go To option allows you to specify the line number of the query in which you want to position the cursor. Remember that some scripts can contain dozens of lines.

Saving the Results Panel

You can save the contents of the Results Panel when it is in the form of a grid and then export the data to other programs. To do that, select the Results Panel (press Shift+F6 to give it focus). Click on File|Save As. Then enter a name for the file in the File Name field. In the Column Delimiter field, select Comma Separated (CSV) to separate the fields with commas or Tab Delimited to use tab marks. Click on the Save button.

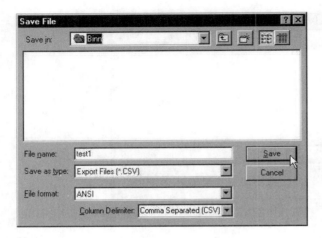

Printing Queries and Results

You can print the text of a query (script) or the contents of the Results Panel. To do that, give the focus to the panel you want to print and click on the Print option in the File menu.

Configuring the Display Options

Through the Set Options option in the Query menu you can change the format of the result or execution panels. Just click on the corresponding tab and check or change the desired items.

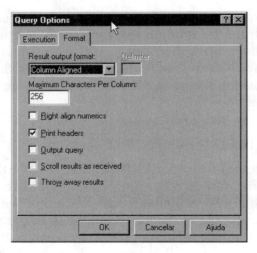

Obtaining Online Help

When you don't know the syntax of a SQL command, select the desired keyword and press Shift+F1. This operation will activate the online help and will show help items for the word specified, as shown in the next screen.

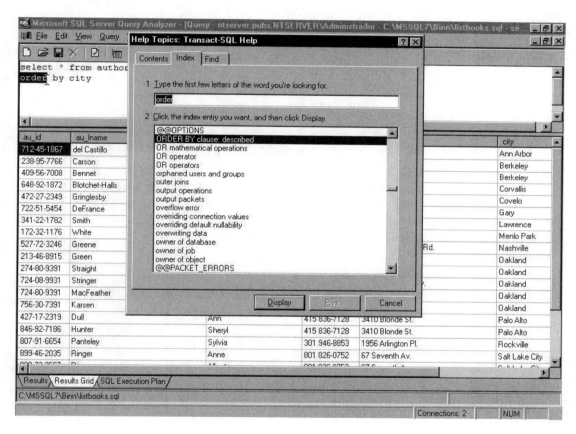

Summary

The Query Analyzer is one of the most important tools for the developer who wants to access and change the tables of a database through SQL commands. Its operation is quite simple because of its interface. The next chapter contains a brief introduction to the SQL language.

Chapter 6

SQL Basics

The SQL language is the basic tool for accessing data in a relational database. Mastering the SQL language is the first and most important step to understanding relational databases. In the last few years the SQL language has left the mainframe domain and gone down to the desktop. This move has been attributed to the fact that relational databases have also expanded their platforms and today have versions running on both PCs and mainframes. In addition, the Internet turned out to be an instrument that popularized this language. Because it has a structure that is suitable for the client-server architecture, more and more applications and pages that access relational databases are created using what is basically the SQL language.

This chapter does not intend to turn you into a SQL expert. Its purpose is to give you an overview of the language, so that you can make your first queries using SQL. We recommend that you read a book written specifically about SQL if you want to be a pro.

SQL Server 7 and SQL

Although there is an ever-growing standard for the SQL language, most database vendors have created their own extensions in order to explore the characteristics of a database, as is the case of SQL Server 7 and Transact-SQL. The commands shown in the following list are just some of the extensions of SQL Server 7 to the SQL standard. The complete syntax of these commands is found in the reference guide in Appendix A.

ALTER DATABASE	CREATE TRIGGER
ALTER PROCEDURE	CREATE VIEW
ALTER TABLE	DROP DATABASE
ALTER TRIGGER	DROP DEFAULT
ALTER VIEW	DROP INDEX
CREATE CLUSTER	DROP PROCEDURE
CREATE DATABASE	DROP RULE
CREATE DEFAULT	DROP STATISTICS
CREATE INDEX	DROP TABLE
CREATE PROCEDURE	DROP TRIGGER
CREATE RULE	SET
CREATE SCHEMA	TRUNCATE TABLE
CREATE TABLE	

Some of these commands are detailed here and in the next chapters; however, we will focus on the main commands of the SQL language.

SQL Essentials

With about a dozen commands and functions, the reader will be able to perform most activities related to the research and manipulation of a database. The table below shows the essential commands that will be discussed in this chapter. Most of the tasks performed by these commands can be executed through the SQL Server 7 graphical tools, and this is a great help for the user. However, mastering the bare minimum of the language also will help a lot when learning about SQL Server 7.

Commands	Functions
SELECT	SUM()
INSERT	AVG()
DELETE	MAX()
UPDATE	MIN()
CREATE TABLE	COUNT()
CREATE VIEW	SYSDATE()
CREATE PROCEDURE	

Types of SQL Declarations

SQL declarations, or commands, are divided into two main categories: DDL and DML, according to their functionality.

DDL (Data Definition Language)

DDL, or data definition language, is the part of SQL that is used to define a database's data and objects. When these commands are used, entries are made in the data dictionary of the SQL Server 7. In this category are the commands shown below.

Command	Description
CREATE TABLE	Creates a table
CREATE INDEX	Creates an index
ALTER TABLE	Changes or inserts a column in a table
DROP TABLE	Eliminates a table from a database
DROP INDEX	Eliminates an index
GRANT	Grants access privileges to a user

DML (Data Manipulation Language)

DML, or data manipulation language, is the part of SQL used to recover and manipulate data. These are the commands responsible for queries and changes made in tables. The following chart shows some of the most important commands in this category.

Command	Description
SELECT	This is the main command of the language; it is used to recover data from a table or view.
INSERT	Inserts a line in the table
DELETE	Deletes lines from the table
UPDATE	Changes the contents of columns (fields) in the table
COMMIT	Writes the changes made to disk
ROLLBACK	Undoes the changes made after the last commit

Data Types

Before learning more about SQL commands you must know what data types can be stored in a SQL Server 7 database. This is used, for example, when you create a table. You must supply certain information, such as the table's name and each field's name, the data type it will store, and so on.

In SQL Server 7 the data stored in a table can be of the types described in the following table:

Integer	
Bit	Integer with a value of 0 or 1
Int	Integer number with values from -2^{31} ($-2{,}147{,}483{,}648$) through $2^{31}-1$ ($2{,}147{,}483{,}647$)
Smallint	2^{15} ($-32{,}768$) through $2^{15}-1$ ($32{,}767$)
Tinyint	Integer from 0 to 255
Decimal or Numeric	Fixed accuracy from $-10^{38}-1$ through $10^{38}-1$
Money	Monetary data values from -2^{63} ($-922{,}337{,}203{,}685{,}477.5808$) through $2^{63}-1$ ($922{,}337{,}203{,}685{,}477.5807$), with accuracy to a ten-thousandth of a monetary unit
Smallmoney	$-214{,}748.3648$ through $214{,}748.3647$, with accuracy to a ten-thousandth of a monetary unit
Float	$-1.79E + 308$ through $1.79E + 308$
Real	$-3.40E + 38$ through $3.40E + 38$
Datetime	January 1, 1753, through December 31, 9999, with accuracy to 3.33 milliseconds
Smalldatetime	January 1, 1900, through June 6, 2079, with accuracy to 1 minute
Miscellaneous	
Cursor	A reference to a cursor
Timestamp	An exclusive number recognized by the database
Uniqueidentifier	An exclusive global identifier
Strings	
Char	Fixed field with maximum size of 8,000 bytes
Varchar	Fixed field with maximum size of 8,000 bytes
Text	Variable size up to $2^{31}-1$ ($2{,}147{,}483{,}647$ bytes)
Unicode Strings	
Nchar	Unicode character with fixed size of up to 4,000 bytes
Nvarchar	Unicode character with variable size of up to 4,000 bytes
Ntext	Variable size up to $2^{30}-1$ ($1{,}073{,}741{,}823$ bytes)
Binary Strings	
Binary	Fixed size of up to 8,000 bytes
Varbinary	Variable size of up to 8,000 bytes
Image	Variable size up to $2^{31}-1$ ($2{,}147{,}483{,}647$) bytes

Expressions and Operators

SQL Server 7 supports all of the most common operators found in most languages. The operators act on the operands, i.e., the elements that are analyzed by the operator. There are two classes of operators: unary operators that act on only one operand and binary operators that act on two or more operands.

Operator Precedence

There are several types of operators. When more than one type of operator is present in an expression, they are evaluated according to the following precedence order:

➤ + (positive), – (negative), ~ (bitwise NOT)
➤ * (multiplication), / (division), % (module)
➤ + (addition), + (concatenation), – (subtraction)
➤ =, >, <, >=, <=, <>, !=, !>, !< (comparison)
➤ ^ (bitwise Exclusive OR), & (bitwise AND), | (bitwise OR)
➤ NOT
➤ AND
➤ ALL, ANY, BETWEEN, IN, LIKE, OR, SOME
➤ = (assignment)

Operators

Following are the types of operators supported by SQL Server 7:

Arithmetic		
Multiplication	*	
Division	/	
Subtraction	–	
Addition	+	
Modulo	%	
Character		
Concatenation	||	

Comparison		
Equal	=	
Not equal	< >	
Greater than	>	
Less than	<	
Greater than or equal to	> =	
Less than or equal to	< =	
Not less than	!<	
Not more than	!>	
Not equal to	!=	

Logic	
NOT	Inverts the boolean value
AND	True when both expressions are true
OR	True when one expression is true
BETWEEN	True when the operand is inside the range
LIKE	True when the operand finds a standard
IN	True when some item is true
SOME	True when any item is true
ANY	True when some item is true
ALL	True when all the set is true

Bitwise	
	(realize operations of bit manipulation between two integer expressions)
& (Bitwise AND)	
| (Bitwise OR)	
^ (Bitwise Exclusive OR)	

Unary	
+ (Positive)	The numeric value is positive
– (Negative)	The numeric value is negative
~ (Bitwise NOT)	Returns the one's complement of the number

The SELECT Command

This command is likely familiar. Although you have not actually used it thus far in this book, it was the basis of almost all the examples we have seen so far. It is the essence of the SQL language.

```
SELECT [ ALL | DISTINCT ] [ TOP n [PERCENT] [ WITH TIES] ] <select_list>[ INTO
new_table ][ FROM <table_sources> ][ WHERE <search_conditions> ][ [ GROUP BY [ALL]
group_by_expression [,…n]] [HAVING <search_conditions> ] [ WITH { CUBE | ROLLUP } ]][
ORDER BY { column_name [ ASC | DESC ] } [,…n] ][ COMPUTE  { { AVG | COUNT | MAX | MIN
| SUM } (expression) } [,…n] [ BY expression [,…n] ][ FOR BROWSE ][ OPTION
(<query_hints>) ]


<select_list> :: = { [ { <table_or_view> | table_alias }.]* | {column_name |
expression | IDENTITYCOL | ROWGUIDCOL }[ [AS] column_alias ]| new_column_name =
IDENTITY(data_type, seed, increment) | GROUPING  (column_name)| { table_name |
table_alias}.RANK| column_alias = expression | expression column_name }[,…n]
```

Here are some of its main parameters:

DISTINCT returns only a copy of each set of duplicated lines, i.e., those lines that have the same contents.

The following example returns an occurrence of each state found in the Authors table. Although there may be several lines with "ca" as state, just one is returned.

Example:

```
SQL> select distinct state from authors

state
-----
CA
IN
KS
MD
MI
OR
TN
UT

(8 row(s) affected)
```

ALL is the default. It returns all selected tables.

* selects all the columns of tables or views specified in FROM.

<expression> selects one expression, normally the name of a column or an expression formed by one table or specified in a snapshot.

WHERE filters the lines that will be displayed by the query. Without this clause, all the lines will be displayed.

GROUP BY groups the selected lines based on the value of <expr> for each line, and returns only one line with information for each group. For example, in the Titles table we can use this clause to group or view information about editorial lines (type).

HAVING filters the lines returned, displaying just those that have an expression that evaluates to True. Normally it is used with GROUP BY to filter the group's lines.

ORDER BY *column_name* orders the lines returned by the SELECT command by the column specified.

COMPUTE generates a value resulting from the use of a function applied to the processing of a subgroup. The COMPUTE clause columns must appear in the list of selected fields. The resulting value is displayed as an additional line to the query result.

<column_alias> creates an alias for a column.

<table_alias> creates an alias for a table, view, or snapshot.

UNION returns all the exclusive lines selected by any of the queries.

UNION ALL returns all the lines selected by the queries, including the duplicates.

MINUS selects all the lines selected by the first query but not by the second query.

column_name is the expression, generally a field by which the lines will be ordered. ASC is the default and uses the ascending order. DESC uses the descending order. All the columns specified in ORDER BY or GROUP BY must be specified in the list of columns and expressions of the SELECT command.

Examples of SELECT

The next example shows the use of the LEFT() function in order to restrict the amount of text shown in the Title field. It also shows the use of the AS clause to create a title for the column formed by some expression, and the use of calculated columns from other columns.

```
select left(title,20) as title, ytd_sales, price, (ytd_sales*price) as total,
(ytd_sales*price*royalty)/100
  from titles
```

title	ytd_sales	price	total	royalty
The Busy Executive's	4095	19.99	81859.05	8185.90
Cooking with Compute	3876	11.95	46318.20	4631.82
You Can Combat Compu	18722	2.99	55978.78	13434.90
Straight Talk About	4095	19.99	81859.05	8185.90
Silicon Valley Gastr	2032	19.99	40619.68	4874.36
The Gourmet Microwav	22246	2.99	66515.54	15963.72
The Psychology of Co	NULL	NULL	NULL	NULL
But Is It User Frien	8780	22.95	201501.00	32240.16
Secrets of Silicon V	4095	20.00	81900.00	8190.00
Net Etiquette	NULL	NULL	NULL	NULL
Computer Phobic AND	375	21.59	8096.25	809.62
Is Anger the Enemy?	2045	10.95	22392.75	2687.13
Life Without Fear	111	7.00	777.00	77.70
Prolonged Data Depri	4072	19.99	81399.28	8139.92
Emotional Security:	3336	7.99	26654.64	2665.46
Onions, Leeks, and G	375	20.95	7856.25	785.62
Fifty Years in Bucki	15096	11.95	180397.20	25255.60
Sushi, Anyone?	4095	14.99	61384.05	6138.40

The next example shows the use of the WHERE clause to filter the records that belong to the computer line.

```
SELECT title,type FROM titles
where type = 'popular_comp'
```

title	type
But Is It User Friendly?	popular_comp
Secrets of Silicon Valley	popular_comp
Net Etiquette	popular_comp

```
(3 row(s) affected)
```

The next example shows the use of GROUP BY and ORDER BY to return the number of sales of each one of the editorial lines.

```
SELECT type, SUM(ytd_sales) AS total
FROM titles
GROUP BY type
ORDER BY type
```

```
type            total
-----------     -----------
business        30788
mod_cook        24278
popular_comp    12875
psychology      9939
trad_cook       19566
UNDECIDED       NULL

(6 row(s) affected)
```

The next example shows the use of the COMPUTE clause to create totals for each of the editorial lines that begin with "p." The LIKE clause uses the "%" character as a wild card, which in this example takes into consideration all characters after the letter "p." In this command, all the editorial lines are grouped by the Type column and put in ascending order by annual sales. The COMPUTE clause adds the ytd_sales field of all the records of the same type. It shows this value after displaying the group.

```
SELECT left(title,20) as title, type, ytd_sales
FROM titles
WHERE type LIKE 'p%'
ORDER BY type,ytd_sales
COMPUTE SUM(ytd_sales) BY type

title                 type            ytd_sales
--------------------  -----------     -----------
Net Etiquette         popular_comp    NULL
Secrets of Silicon V  popular_comp    4095
But Is It User Frien  popular_comp    8780

(3 row(s) affected)

SUM
-----------
12875

(1 row(s) affected)


title                 type            ytd_sales
--------------------  -----------     -----------
Life Without Fear     psychology      111
Computer Phobic AND   psychology      375
Is Anger the Enemy?   psychology      2045
Emotional Security:   psychology      3336
```

```
Prolonged Data Depri     psychology    4072

(5 row(s) affected)

SUM
-----------
9939

(1 row(s) affected)
```

Functions

A SQL function is a routine that performs a specific operation and returns a result. It is similar to a procedure, except that a procedure does not return any value. A function can receive arguments that will be used in processing.

The basic syntax of a function is:

```
Funcname(arg1,arg2,...ARGn)
```

Funcname is the name of the function, such as ABS, LOWER, etc. **arg1** and **arg2** are optional parameters to the function.

SQL functions are divided into single row functions, or scalars, and group functions, or aggregates. A single row function returns the result of each row in a table or view. A group function returns only one result to the group of rows. For example, the LOWER() function converts its argument into lowercase, and the UPPER() function converts its argument into uppercase. In the following example, when the function is executed it acts on all the lines of the table.

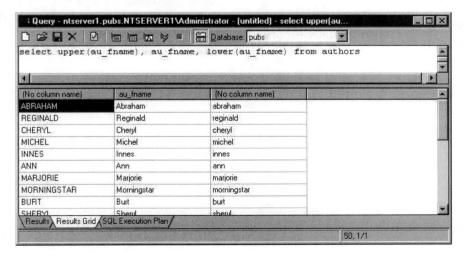

These functions can be used in SELECT commands that contain WHERE, START WITH, or CONNECT BY clauses. However, they cannot be used with GROUP BY.

The group functions process a group of rows from the table and return the result. As default, most of these functions act on all the rows of the table. They accept the following parameters:

DISTINCT Specifies that the function act only on the rows with different values.

ALL Makes the function consider all the rows, including those with duplicate data. This is the default.

With the exception of the COUNT() function, all other functions ignore Null values.

These group functions are:

AVG Returns the arithmetic average of *n*.

Syntax: `AVG([DISTINCT|ALL] n)`

COUNT Returns the number of lines of the query. *Expr* represents a non-Null field or expression.

Syntax: `COUNT({* | [DISTINCT|ALL] expr})`

MAX Returns the maximum value of *expr*.

Syntax: `MAX([DISTINCT|ALL] expr)`

MIN Returns the minimum value of *expr*.

Syntax: `MIN([DISTINCT|ALL] expr)`

Next are several examples of these functions. Follow along with these examples by opening the Query Analyzer and selecting the Pubs database. Note the complete contents of the Titles table used in the examples; it contains 18 records.

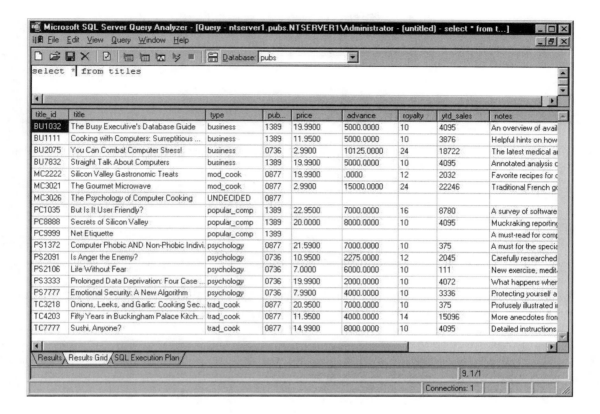

The following figure shows three columns corresponding to the average, minimum, and maximum of the ytd_sales field (number of books sold in the year) of the Pubs database's Titles table.

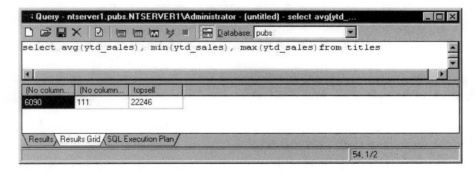

The next example shows the total of records in the Titles table.

```
SELECT COUNT(*)  FROM titles

-----------
18

(1 row(s) affected)
```

The next example returns only those lines with values other than Null in the Advance field.

```
SELECT COUNT(advance) FROM titles

-----------
16

(1 row(s) affected)
```

The next example returns how many books have royalty payments, that is, the lines that have a value other than Null in this column.

```
SELECT COUNT(royalty)
FROM titles

-----------
16

(1 row(s) affected)
```

The next example returns how many types of royalty exist and shows the number of distinct values in the Royalty column.

```
SELECT COUNT(distinct royalty)
FROM titles

-----------
5

(1 row(s) affected)
```

The CREATE TABLE Command

The CREATE TABLE command creates a new table in the database. SQL Server 7 allows up to 2 billion tables in each database, and up to 1,024 columns in each table. There is no limit to the number of rows in a table, except the physical space available. The maximum size of bytes per line is

8,092. The table is created in the current database, unless another name for the database is specified.

```
CREATE TABLE table_name({<column_definition>| column_name AS
computed_column_expression| <table_constraint> } [, ...n])[ON {filegroup | DEFAULT}
][TEXTIMAGE_ON {filegroup | DEFAULT} ]
```

table_name is the name of the table you are creating.

column_definition specifies the type of data in the column. Up to 1,024 columns are allowed.

Here is the syntax for column_definition:

```
<column_definition> ::= { column_name data_type }[ NULL | NOT NULL ][ IDENTITY
[(seed, increment )[NOT FOR REPLICATION] ] ][ ROWGUIDCOL ][ <column_constraint> ::=
[CONSTRAINT constraint_name] { { PRIMARY KEY | UNIQUE }[CLUSTERED | NONCLUSTERED]
[WITH [FILLFACTOR = fillfactor]][ON {filegroup | DEFAULT} ] | [FOREIGN KEY]REFERENCES
ref_table [ ( ref_column ) ] [NOT FOR REPLICATION]| DEFAULT constant_expression |
CHECK [NOT FOR REPLICATION] (logical_expression)}] [ ...n]
```

IDENTITY indicates that the field will have only one value that will be automatically generated by the system every time a new record is included. The Identity property can be assigned to Tinyint, Smallint, Int, Decimal (p,0), or Numeric (p,0) columns. Only one identity column can be created per table. Bound defaults and DEFAULT constraints cannot be used with an identity column. You must specify both the seed and increment, or neither. If neither is specified, the default is (1,1).

seed is the value that is used for the very first row loaded into the table.

increment is the incremental value that is added to the identity value of the previous row that was loaded.

column_constraint is optional and indicates some integrity control that is applied to the column, such as its contents not being empty.

DEFAULT is optional and indicates a default value for the column.

table_constraint is optional and indicates some control over the integrity applied to the table as a primary key.

Here is the syntax for table_constraint:

```
<table_constraint> ::= [CONSTRAINT constraint_name]{ [ { PRIMARY KEY | UNIQUE } [
CLUSTERED | NONCLUSTERED] { ( column[,...n] ) } ] [ WITH [FILLFACTOR = fillfactor] ]
[ON {filegroup | DEFAULT} ] ] | FOREIGN KEY [(column[,.n])] REFERENCES ref_table
[(ref_column[,.n])] [NOT FOR REPLICATION] | CHECK [NOT FOR REPLICATION]
(search_conditions)}
```

Example:

```
CREATE TABLE demo2
(       code int,
        name char(20),
        state char(2)CONSTRAINT default_name DEFAULT ('CA')
        )
```

The INSERT Command

The INSERT command inserts a new row in the table and fills those columns that have specific values. You don't have to enter contents in all the fields.

Basic syntax:

```
INSERT [INTO] {<table_sources>}{{ [(column_list)] VALUES ({DEFAULT |
constant_expression }[,...n] )| select_statement| execute_statement } | DEFAULT
VALUES }
```

INTO indicates the name of the table that will receive the data.

column_list is a list of the columns that will receive the data. They must be enclosed in parentheses and separated by commas. When the values specified by VALUES are not in the same order as the columns, the column_list option must be used to specify that the columns will receive such values.

VALUES specifies the list of values that will be inserted.

DEFAULT attributes the default value for the column. When a default value is not defined, it uses Null.

constant_expression is a literal value, expression, or variable.

The following example uses the DEFAULT clause in the State field. One of the records inserted uses the DEFAULT VALUES clause to generate the contents for all the fields. Note that because they do not have standard contents some fields contain a Null value.

```
CREATE TABLE demo2
(       code int,
        name char(20),
        state char(2) DEFAULT('CA')
        )

INSERT demo2 VALUES (1, 'first record',"FL")
INSERT demo2 VALUES (2, 'second record',"WA")
insert demo2 default values
```

```
insert demo2 (code, name) values (4, 'fourth record')
INSERT DEMO2 VALUES (5,"FIFTH RECORD","LA")
select * from demo2
```

The result is:

```
code         name                  state
----------   -------------------   -----
1            first record          FL
2            second record         WA
NULL         NULL                  CA
4            fourth record         CA
5            FIFTH RECORD          LA
```

The next example shows the use of the CHECK clause to restrict the information that can be distributed to the State field. Only those states contained in the list will be accepted in this field.

```
drop table demo2
CREATE TABLE demo2
(       code int,
        name char(20),
        state char(2) CHECK (STATE IN ("CA","FL","TX","CO")) DEFAULT('CA')
    )

INSERT demo2 VALUES (1, 'first record',"FL")
INSERT demo2 VALUES (2, 'second record',"WA")
insert demo2 default values
insert demo2 (code, name) values (4, 'fourth record')
INSERT DEMO2 VALUES (5,"FIFTH RECORD","LA")
select * from demo2
```

The result is:

```
Server: Msg 547, Level 16, State 1
INSERT statement conflicted with COLUMN CHECK constraint
'CK__demo2__state__5070F446'. The conflict occurred in database 'pubs', table
'demo2', column 'state'.
The statement has been aborted.

code         name                  state
----------   -------------------   -----
1            first record          FL
NULL         NULL                  CA
4            Fourth record         CA
```

Note that the second and fifth records were not included since the State field does not satisfy the specific requirements for this field.

```
CREATE TABLE demo1a
    (
    cust_id int NOT NULL IDENTITY (1, 1),
    name char(20) NULL default("----****----"),
    comments char(20) NULL,
    date datetime NULL CONSTRAINT date DEFAULT (getdate())
    ) ON [PRIMARY]
insert into demo1a default values
insert into demo1a (name,comments) values ('Jose Ramalho','no comments')
insert into demo1a (name) values ('Jim Hill')
insert into demo1a default values
select * from demo1a
```

Note that the contents of the cust_id and date fields are automatically generated by the system. The IDENTITY clause automatically increments the contents of the cust_id field and the GETDATE() function returns the system's date and hour.

```
cust_id       name            comments          date
-----------   -------------   ---------------   -----------
1             ----****----    NULL              1998-10-02 12:17:02.820
2             Jose Ramalho    no comments       1998-10-02 12:17:02.830
3             Jim Hill        NULL              1998-10-02 12:17:02.840
4             ----****----    NULL              1998-10-02 12:17:02.850

(4 row(s) affected)
```

The DELETE Command

This command removes rows from a table or view that satisfy a specified condition.

Basic syntax: DELETE FROM *scheme.table* WHERE *condition*

For example, to delete lines from the demo1a table that we have just created with the field name "----****----" we can use the following command:

```
delete from demo1a where name="----****----"
select * from demo1a

(2 row(s) affected)
```

```
cust_id     name               comments          date
-------     --------------     --------------    ---------------
2           Jose Ramalho       no comments       1998-10-02 14:46:17.170
3           Jim Hill           NULL              1998-10-02 14:46:17.180

(2 row(s) affected)
```

The UPDATE Command

The UPDATE command allows you to update one or more fields from a line or group of lines in a table or view. The contents of each field can be adjusted with the SET clause. When more than one column is updated, the column=value pairs must be comma separated. Identity columns cannot be updated.

Basic syntax:

```
UPDATE .table SET  column=value WHERE condition
```

```
UPDATE {<table_or_view>} SET {column_name = {expression | DEFAULT}| @variable =
expression} [,…n] [FROM {<table_or_view> | select_statement) [AS] table_alias [
(column_alias [,…m]) ] | <table_or_view> CROSS JOIN <table_or_view> | INNER
[<join_hints>] JOIN <table_or_view> ON <join_condition> | <rowset_function>}[, …n]]
[WHERE <search_conditions>| CURRENT OF { { [GLOBAL] cursor_name } |
cursor_variable_name} } ] [OPTION (<query_hints>, [,...n] )]
```

SET specifies the list of columns that will be updated.

column_name is the name of the column that will be updated. If it refers to a table other than the current one, it must be preceded by the name of the table/database.

expression is the new contents of the column; it can be the result of a subselect that returns only one value.

DEFAULT indicates the current contents that must be replaced with the default value that was previously defined when the table was created.

FROM specifies another table or view that will be used to provide the updating criteria for the operation.

WHERE specifies the conditions that must be satisfied to limit the number of lines that will be updated.

See the example below in which the contents of the Comments field is changed to "n/a" for all rows.

```
update demo1a
set comments ="n/a"
select * from demo1a

(2 row(s) affected)

cust_id      name                  comments      date
-----------  --------------------  ------------  --------------------
2            Jose Ramalho          n/a           1998-10-02 14:46:17.170
3            Jim Hill              n/a           1998-10-02 14:46:17.180

(2 row(s) affected)
```

In the next example we use the WHERE clause to filter the changes.

```
update demo1a
set comments ="xxxxxx"
where name="Jose Ramalho"
select * from demo1a

cust_id      name                  comments      date
-----------  --------------------  ------------  --------------------
2            Jose Ramalho          xxxxxx        1998-10-02 14:46:17.170
3            Jim Hill              n/a           1998-10-02 14:46:17.180

(2 row(s) affected)
```

The DROP TABLE Command

To remove a table from the database you use the DROP TABLE command. This command physically removes the table from the database, deleting its structure and data.

Syntax: DROP TABLE table_name

This example removes the demo2 table from the current database:

DROP TABLE demo2

To remove a table that is in another database, you must specify the name of the database followed by the extension .dbo and the name of the table.

For example: DROP TABLE pubs.dbo.demo1

The following figure shows that we have the master database active and we specify the demo1 table to be removed from the Pubs database.

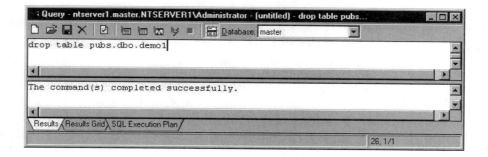

The IF EXISTS Command

There is a systems table called INFORMATION_SCHEMA.TABLES WHERE, and one of its columns (table_name) contains the name of the existing tables. Through the IF EXISTS command we can check to see if a particular table already exists so we can delete it before we try to create it. Here is an example of this command:

```
IF EXISTS (SELECT TABLE_NAME FROM INFORMATION_SCHEMA.TABLES WHERE TABLE_NAME = 'demo1')
   DROP TABLE demo1
```

Now we are going to create a table and insert some records in it through the Query Analyzer.

```
create table demo1
( cust_id int not null,
  name char(30),
  email char(40))
insert demo1  values (1,'xxxx','zzzz')
insert demo1  values (1,'xxxx','zzzz')
insert demo1  values (1,'xxxx','zzzz')
insert demo1  values (1,'xxxx','zzzz')
select * from demo1
```

The result of these commands would be:

```
cust_id     name          email
----------- ------------- ----------------------------------------
1           xxxx          zzzz
1           xxxx          zzzz
1           xxxx          zzzz
1           xxxx          zzzz

(4 row(s) affected)
```

However, if you try to run it again you will get the following error message:

```
Server: Msg 2714, Level 16, State 1
There is already an object named 'demo1' in the database.
```

By changing the script and including the IF command, we can run it without any problem. The existing table will always be deleted.

```
IF EXISTS (SELECT TABLE_NAME FROM INFORMATION_SCHEMA.TABLES WHERE TABLE_NAME = 'demo1')
    DROP TABLE demo1
create table demo1
( cust_id int not null,
  name char(30),
  email char(40))
insert demo1  values (1,'xxxx','zzzz')
insert demo1  values (1,'xxxx','zzzz')
insert demo1  values (1,'xxxx','zzzz')
insert demo1  values (1,'xxxx','zzzz')
select * from demo1
```

Summary

This chapter gave you a brief introduction to the SQL language. With the information contained here, you can query, navigate, and even create tables in many databases. In the next several chapters we will see how the Enterprise Manager replaces much of the manual work of creating and maintaining the tables you have seen here. The next chapter covers working with indexes.

Indexes

In Chapter 1 you learned that an index is an auxiliary file associated to a table, with the purpose of speeding up the access time to the table's rows. An index is formed by keys based on the contents of one or more columns of the table. The figure below shows the Employees table containing an index based on the emp_id column.

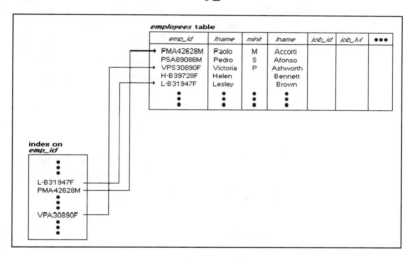

Types of Indexes

The SQL Server uses two types of indexes: clustered and non-clustered.

➤ Clustered—A clustered index organizes the rows of the tables in a particular order, such as alphabetical or numerical. For example, in an index that is ordered alphabetically, the record of author Bennet comes before author Yokomoto. This type of index is perfect when you don't have much table updating to do, since when the contents of a key field are changed, the table is reorganized. There can only be one clustered index per table. We can even say that the rows of the table themselves are the index, as is the case of a telephone directory where the line with the name serves as the data and the index. In other words, to find Jose Ramalho's phone number, you must locate the entry Ramalho, then Jose in the directory, and then obtain the phone number, which is next to the name.

➤ Non-clustered—A non-clustered index has a structure separate from the table. The physical order of the table's rows does not follow the order of the index file. A non-clustered index is similar to the index found at the end of a book. The data (the table's rows) are put in one place and the index is located in another place. The index file's data are stored in order of their values. The information of the table is stored in another order that does not follow the same sequence of the non-clustered index file. There can be several indexes of this type per table.

The indexes can also be configured as *unique*, indicating that there cannot be more than one row with the same contents. If it is not created with this option, the key field of the table may have more than one occurrence of the same contents. For example, if indexed, the lname column of the Authors table could have more than one record with the same author's last name.

Fill Factor

One characteristic of SQL Server is the ability to create files of indexes with room for the insertion of new keys, without having to physically reorganize all the index files.

When a clustered index is created, the SQL Server stores the table's data in a database according to the order of the key fields. When a new row is inserted inside the table or when the values of the key field change, you need to reorganize the storage of these rows in the database's pages. When a page is completely full, the server moves approximately half the rows from that page to a new one. This is called *page split*, and depending on the size of the table it can seriously affect performance, particularly when there is intensive updating in key fields. During the creation of an index, whether using the Enterprise Manager or a Transact-SQL command, you can use the Fill Factor option to leave free room inside the page. Thus, future additions or changes made in the rows of a table can fit in the page, without the need to reorganize them. The Fill Factor is a value between 1 and 100, and specifies how much free space there must be inside the page. The value 100 indicates that the page can be completely filled out. This value can only be applied when the table is used for queries. A value less than 100 will leave more space unused inside the page for future additions.

Creating Indexes

Indexes are created in the same file group of the table. Optionally, you can create non-clustered indexes in a group of different files to obtain performance gains, due to the use of different physical access media.

There are two ways to create indexes. One is using the Transact-SQL command called CREATE INDEX and the other is through the Enterprise Manager. Indexes can be created either during the creation of a table or in an existing table.

Creating an Index During Table Design

Expand the Databases folder and the folder of the database where the table/index will be created.

Click with the right mouse button on the Tables folder and select New Table.

Enter a name for the table in the Choose Name dialog box that appears. For this example, enter **test1**.

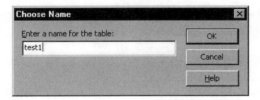

Fill out the fields corresponding to the table's columns. As an example we will create three columns using the values in the figure on the following page. Note that the Allow Nulls column in the first row is unchecked.

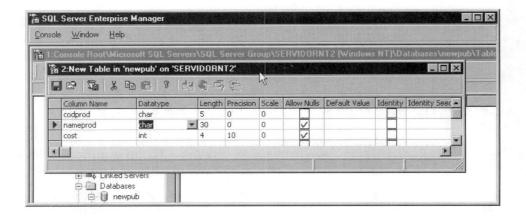

Click with the right mouse button on any column and choose Properties.

In the Indexes/Keys tab of the Properties dialog box, click on the New button.

In the Column Name field, select the column (or columns) that will form the index. In this example we selected codprod.

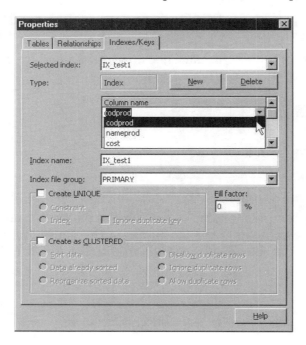

The name of the index can be changed. Just enter another name in the Index Name field.

In the Index File Group field you can select a different group of files to create the index.

If you want to create an index of the unique type, check the Create UNIQUE field and select whether the field will be limited by the index or by a constraint. If you want to create an index of the clustered type, check the Create as CLUSTERED box and select one of its options.

To finish, just close the dialog box. Note that in this table we created one index based on one of the fields, and that we did not create a primary key.

Creating an Index in an Existing Table

Now we are going to create another index for the test1 table we have just created.

To create a new index in an existing table, expand the database and then expand the Tables folder.

Click on the name of the table with the right mouse button and select Design Table.

Click with the right mouse button on any column and then select Properties. The Properties dialog box appears.

In the Indexes/Keys tab, click on New.

In the Column Name field, select the column or group of columns that will be part of the index. In this example, we will create an index called **name** (enter it in the Index Name field), based on the Nameprod column, and then choose the Create as CLUSTERED option.

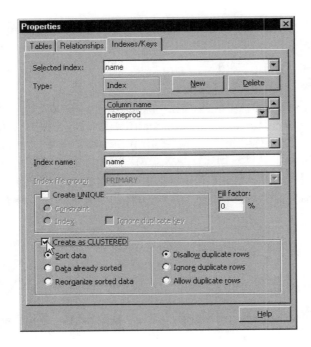

Creating an Index with the Wizard

To use a wizard for index creation, click with the right mouse button on the database's folder and select Tools.

Expand the Database item, and double-click on Create Index Wizard. Follow the wizard's steps, as detailed below.

In the first screen, select the database and the table where the index will be created. Press Next.

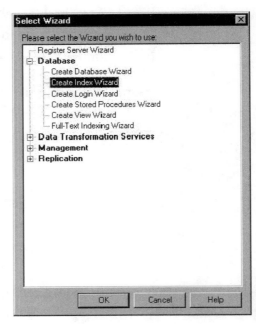

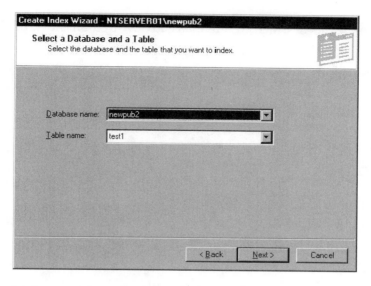

In the next step the wizard shows the existing indexes. Just press Next. In the dialog box that follows, select the column or columns that will form the index.

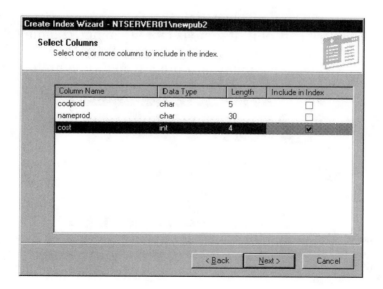

In this case we select the column Cost and press Next.

In this step you can specify a fixed value for the fill factor option, or change the index type to unique. You can also specify the creation of a clustered index. Since we have already created an index of this type for this table, that option is disabled. Press Next.

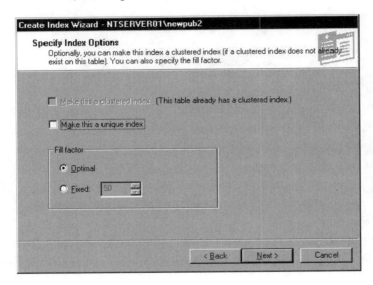

In the last step you can change the name of the index and verify the columns that are part of it. If there is more than one column selected, you can change the order of columns using the Move Up and Move Down buttons. To create the index, just press the Finish button.

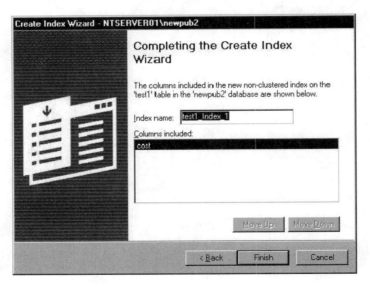

Reconstructing an Index

An index is physically written inside the database in an index page. The index pages are created sequentially through pointers that indicate the place in the next page. When the key fields, and consequently the index, change, the index pages are fragmented. We recommend that you reconstruct the index using the CREATE INDEX command and the WITH DROP_EXISTING option that uses the existing data order to speed up the process.

Viewing an Index

To view the existing indexes in a table, use the system stored sp_helpindex <table_name> procedure. It performs a query in the sysindexes system table, which contains information on all the indexes. This procedure must be run in the Query Analyzer. For example, to run this procedure for the Customers table in the Northwind database, open the Query Analyzer, select the Northwind database, and then run the command **exec sp_helpindex customers**, as shown in the next figure.

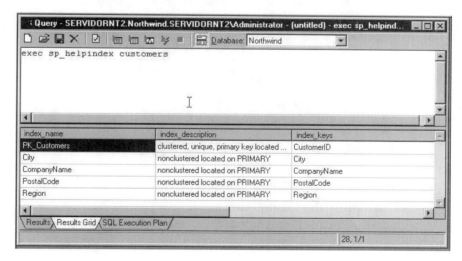

Deleting an Index

After creating an index, you can delete it if you are not going to use it. Temporary or unnecessary indexes can be deleted with the following steps:

Expand the database and the Tables folder.

In the detail panel, click on the right mouse button on the table from which you want to remove the index and select Design Table in the quick menu.

Click on any column with the right mouse button and select Properties. The Properties dialog box appears.

In the Indexes/Keys tab, select the index to be deleted in the Selected Index list box and press the Delete button.

The next screen shows this operation being executed for the Orders table of the Northwind database.

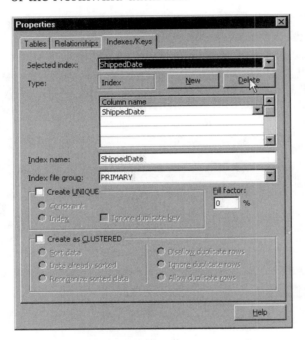

If we press the Delete button, the ShippedDate index would be eliminated. To cancel this operation, just close the dialog box.

Summary

In this chapter you have seen the types of indexes maintained by the SQL Server. You saw how to create indexes using the Create Index Wizard and the Properties dialog box, and how to view and delete them. In the next chapter we will learn how to create database views.

Chapter 8

Views

A view is a virtual table with its contents defined by a database query. The view is not a physical table, but a set of instructions that returns a set of data. The next figure shows two tables that serve as the basis for the creation of a view.

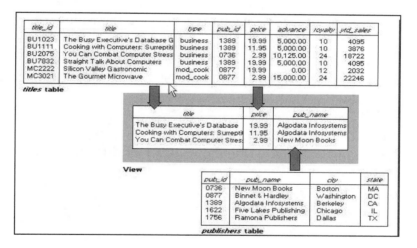

The use of views is particularly useful when you want to focus on a certain kind of information maintained by the database. Imagine a corporate database accessed by several users in different departments. The information that the sale team handles certainly is quite different from that used by the accounting and marketing departments. Using views can provide the user with just the information he or she needs, whether it comes from one or several tables in the database.

Views allow different users to see the same information with a different focus. They allow the combination of information to fulfill the needs of certain users, and they can even be exported to other applications.

Creating a View

A view can be created with the Transact-SQL CREATE VIEW command or by using the Enterprise Manager view editor.

When creating a view, always keep in mind the following considerations:

➤ A view can only be created in the database that is being used.

➤ It is not possible to associate triggers, rules, and defaults to a view.

➤ A view can use data from another view.

➤ A view can be referenced by a stored procedure.

➤ It is not possible to create an index for a view.

➤ If more than one column of the view has the same name, they must be referenced by an alias and preceded by the name of the table to which they belong.

➤ The columns of a view are identical to the columns of the source table.

We will create a view in the Northwind database to serve as a followup for a customer whose order has already been shipped. Such a view will use fields from the Orders and Customers tables. Its structure will be the following:

Fields OrderId, and ShippedDate from Orders table, and fields Company-Name, ContactName, and Phone of the Customers table.

Expand the Northwind database, click on the SQL Server Views folder, and right-click on New SQL Server View.

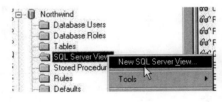

Click on the Add Table button; it's the last button in the toolbar and has a plus sign. When the dialog box appears showing the database's tables, select Orders and click on the Add button.

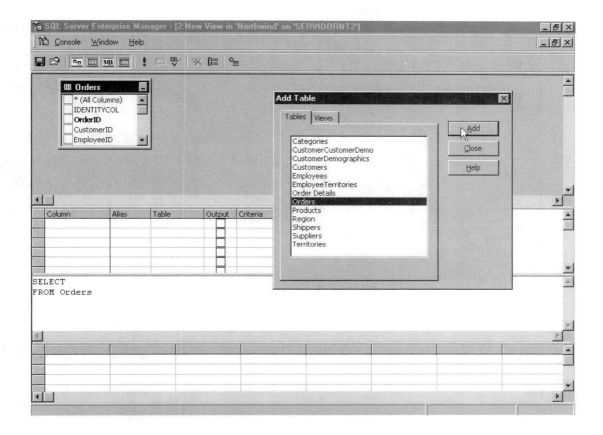

Repeat this operation with the Customers table. You will note that the tables are linked, because they are related by the customer_id field. Press the Close button to close the dialog box.

The next step is to select the columns that will be displayed by the view in both tables. Click on the bottom border of both tables and increase the viewing area of the fields. Select the field view. Select the fields shown in the figure on the following page. The selection order of the fields is important, since it defines the order in which the columns appear. Select the fields in the following order: OrderID, ShippedDate, CompanyName, ContactName, Phone.

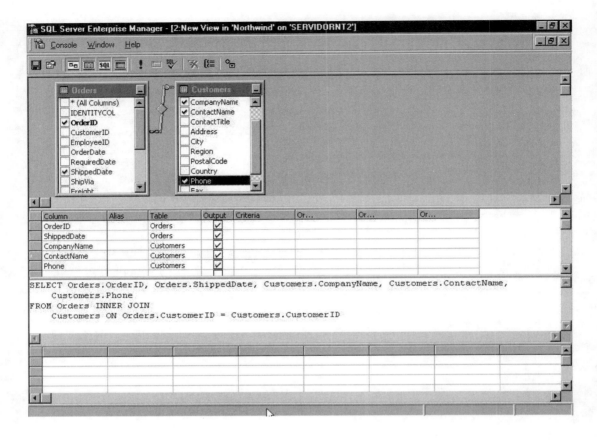

Note that as each column is selected, the SELECT command needed for its execution is written in the central panel.

Now you execute the query by pressing the Run button (the button with the exclamation mark in the toolbar). The result of the view appears in the bottom panel, as shown in the following figure.

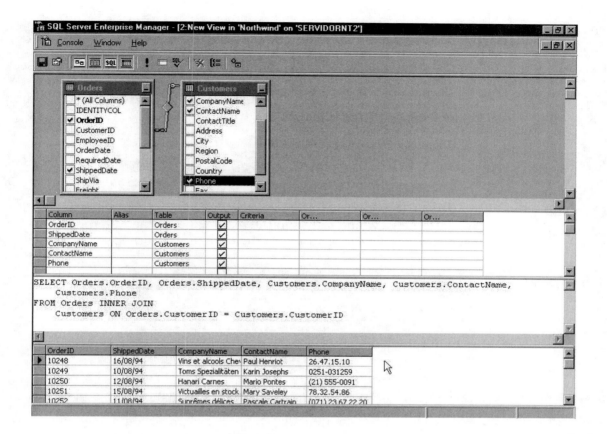

Saving a View

To save the view, press the Save button (the one on the left end in the toolbar), enter a name for the view (we'll call it **viewtest1** in this example), and press OK. The new view will be displayed with the other views in the detail panel. Close the view editor by clicking on the Close (x) button.

After a view is created, it can be examined, edited, or deleted in the quick menu, which is activated by right-clicking on the name of the view. These operations are detailed in the following sections.

Examining a View

On the user's side, a view is a table just like any other. Therefore, to see its contents just choose the Open SQL Server View option and select Return All Rows to see all the rows, or select Return Top and specify how many rows you want to see.

To close the view and return to the main panel of the Enterprise Manager, click on the Close button in the upper right corner.

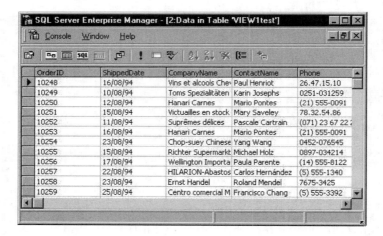

Editing a View

The Design SQL Server View option opens the view editor. There you can make all the changes you need. Among these changes are permanently deleting a column and changing the display order of the columns.

Preventing the Display of a Column

To prevent displaying some of the columns, you must uncheck in the top panel the column you don't want to display. The figure on the next page shows the ContactName column unchecked. To see the view without the column, press the Run button. The panel at the bottom shows the result.

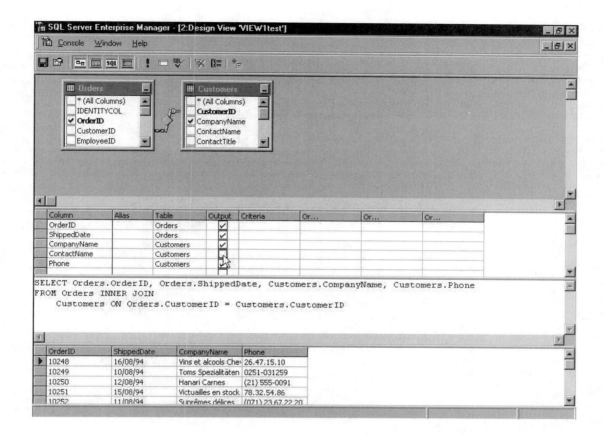

You can prevent the display of columns and maintain all of them inside the list of selected columns. However, if you save the view with a column unchecked, the next time you load the view, the column will not be part of it anymore.

Changing the Order of Columns

To change the order of the columns, you can use drag and drop to move the column to a new position. For example, to make the Phone column appear in the third column, select the column name, click the gray button to the left of the name, and drag it above the line of the CompanyName column as shown below.

To see the change you need to run the view. Here is the result:

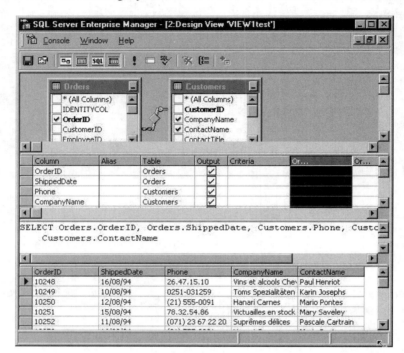

Inserting New Columns

To insert a new column in the view, check the desired column in the top panel. The new column will always be inserted in the last position. You can move it to another place in the view by using the previous technique.

Adjusting Panels

You can change the size of the panels by clicking and dragging the lines that separate them. To prevent the display of a panel, or to display it after it has been hidden, click with the right mouse button on any panel, select Show Panes, and check or uncheck the panel you want to remove or display.

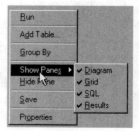

Renaming a View

Only those views created by the user can be renamed. You can rename a view by using the quick menu that appears after you click with the right mouse button on the name of the view you want to change or by pressing the F2 key after the view is selected in the detail panel.

Deleting a View

When a view is deleted, the tables that serve as its origin are not affected. Only its definition is deleted. To delete a view, click with the right mouse button on the name of the view you want to delete and then press the Del key after the view is selected in the detail panel. This brings up a dialog box in which you can confirm the deletion of the table.

Summary

In this chapter you saw how views are useful tools to offer a different picture of the same information to different users. You saw how to create, change, rename, and delete a view. In the next chapter we will discuss a more advanced subject: stored procedures.

Stored Procedures

A stored procedure is basically a program written in Transact-SQL that is stored in a SQL Server database. The SQL commands, variables, and logic flow form a stored procedure. It can be manually run or be invoked by other programs.

Using stored procedures is quite useful in a client/server environment, both for performance and maintenance. Since one stored procedure can be used by several programs, maintaining the system is easier because one change is reflected immediately to all users. Once the stored procedure is run in the server, subsequent accesses are quick, because the execution plan is maintained in the memory. As with other languages, the stored procedures of SQL Server 7 accept input parameters and can return several values as output parameters to the program that invoked them. A stored procedure can make a call to another stored procedure. It can also return a status value indicating whether it was run with success or the cause of the failure.

Note that although stored procedures return output parameters, they are different from functions, as they do not return a value in place of their name and cannot be used in expressions.

A stored procedure can be created with the Transact-SQL CREATE PROCEDURE command, and can be changed with the ALTER PROCEDURE command.

Structure of a Stored Procedure

The creation of a stored procedure requires the specification of the procedure's name, its parameters, and the body containing the Transact-SQL commands that will be run. The following example shows a stored procedure receiving as a parameter the title of a book and returning the number of these books sold in the year. An explanation of the code follows.

```
1. CREATE PROCEDURE get_sales_for_title
2. @title varchar(80),
3. @ytd_sales int OUTPUT AS
4. SELECT @ytd_sales = ytd_sales
5. FROM titles
6. WHERE title = @title
7. RETURN
8. GO
```

Line	Meaning
1	Creates a procedure called get_sales_for_title
2	Creates an input parameter called @title
3	Creates an output parameter called @ytd_sales
4-6	The body of the procedure
7	Finishes the execution of the procedure

Types of Stored Procedures

Stored procedures can be divided into local, stored in the local server, or remote, stored in another server. They can also be classified into stored procedures defined by the user or system stored procedures that are procedures previously created that are part of the server. At the end of this chapter is a list of the system stored procedures.

Components of a Stored Procedure

Now let's take a look at the components of a stored procedure. These include parameters and return codes.

Parameters

With parameters you can establish communication between a stored procedure and the outside world. When a program executes a stored procedure, it can pass values to it in the form of parameters. These values can be used by the procedure to perform its task. For example, you can pass a product code that will be used by a SELECT command to filter a query. A stored procedure can contain up to 255 parameters and a return code.

Names and Data Types

Parameters must have an exclusive name and start with the @ symbol. You must also include the data type definition. In the next example, a parameter called code is created with the Varchar type and size 8.

```
CREATE PROCEDURE test1
@code varchar(8)
```

Direction of the Parameter

All the parameters created are considered input parameters, i.e., they receive data from the program that invoked the stored procedure. By adding the word OUTPUT to the definition of the parameter, the procedure can return the present value of the parameter to the program that invoked it.

```
CREATE PROCEDURE test1
@code varchar(8)
@totalcode int OUTPUT
```

Return Codes

Stored procedures can return an integer type value called a return code to indicate whether its execution was successful. This must be created as an output parameter with the option OUTPUT, and must be returned to the program that executed the procedure through the RETURN command. The user can use positive return values and create the codes according to his needs. For example:

Value	Meaning
0	Stored procedure completed with success
1	Input parameter was not specified
2	Invalid parameter contents

Take a look at this example:

```
CREATE PROCEDURE test2
@code varchar(8) = NULL,
AS
IF @code IS NULL
BEGIN
PRINT "ERROR: Parameter not entered."
RETURN(1)
END
```

Reserved Values

The zero value indicates that the procedure was completed with success. The negative values, from –99 to –1, indicate the reason for the failure. Just the first 14 values are used.

Value	Meaning
0	Procedure executed with success
−1	Missing object
−2	Data type error
−3	Process found a deadlock
−4	Permission error
−5	Syntax error
−6	Miscellaneous error
−7	Resource error
−8	Non-fatal internal error
−9	System limits reached
−10	Fatal internal error
−11	Fatal internal error
−12	Table or index corrupted
−14	Hardware error found

Creating a Stored Procedure

A stored procedure is created with the CREATE PROCEDURE command. The actual creation process can be accomplished with the Enterprise Manager, the Query Analyzer, or the Stored Procedures Wizard. With the exception of the CREATE commands, virtually any SQL command can be included in a stored procedure. These are the commands that are not allowed:

CREATE DEFAULT   CREATE TRIGGER

CREATE PROCEDURE   CREATE VIEW

CREATE RULE

When a stored procedure calls another stored procedure, the second stored procedure can access all the objects that were created by the first one. When a remote stored procedure is executed, the changes made by it in the remote server cannot be rolled back. You can create a temporary stored procedure by adding # and ## before the name of the procedure.

As an example we will create a stored procedure in the Northwind database. First expand the folder of that database and click with the right mouse button on the Stored Procedures folder. In the quick menu, select New Stored Procedure. A dialog box opens in which you can enter the commands of the stored procedure.

Notice the stored procedure that is created in the following figure. This stored procedure will show the contents of the Phone and CompanyName columns of the Customers table. The name of the stored procedure can be specified inside quotes or brackets.

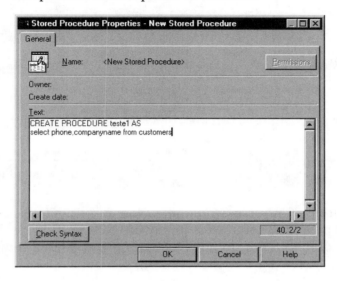

Press the OK button to save the stored procedure. This will bring up a list of the stored procedures for the Northwind database.

Running a Stored Procedure

A stored procedure can be run with the EXECUTE or EXEC commands. In addition to return codes, the stored procedure can return data sets created by the SELECT command and error messages due to incorrect processing of SQL Server 7. Messages generated by the PRINT command can also be returned.

Using the Query Analyzer, select the procedure's database in the Database field, then enter the name of the procedure and press the Run button. In this case, the EXECUTE command is optional. Here's the result of the stored procedure we have just created:

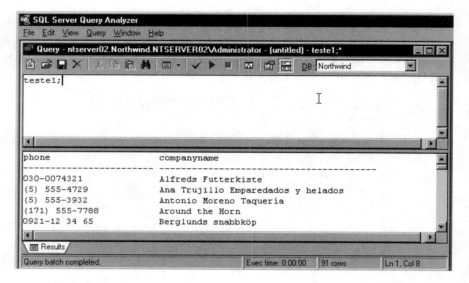

The execution of a system stored procedure is quite similar. Just specify
its name and all the parameters it may use. The next figure shows the
execution of the system stored procedure sp_helpdb that returns information about the database in the server.

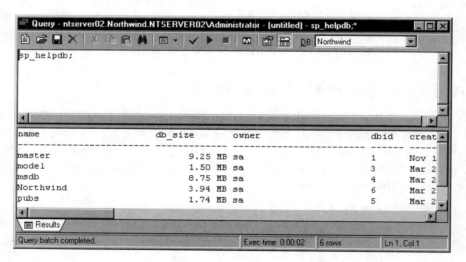

Creating a Stored Procedure with Parameters

Including parameters in a stored procedure is quite simple. All you have
to do is to specify the name of the parameter and its data type. When

more than one parameter is specified, they must be separated by commas. As an example we will create a procedure called au_state in the Pubs database that returns the authors who live in the state used as the parameter. Here is the code for this procedure:

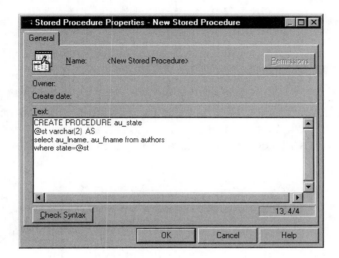

Execute the command **exec au_state CA** to return all the authors in California.

Changing a Stored Procedure

To change a stored procedure you must use the ALTER PROCEDURE command followed by the name of the stored procedure and the changes needed. In the next example we will change the au_state stored procedure to include an additional column.

```
ALTER PROCEDURE au_state
@st varchar(2) AS
SELECT au_lname, au_fname, state from authors
where state=@st
```

To save on typing, copy the text for the creation of the procedure, insert it in the typing area, and then make the necessary changes. The execution of this procedure with the CA parameter will return the new column, as shown on the next page.

```
au_lname          au_fname          state
--------------    --------------    -----
White             Johnson           CA
Green             Marjorie          CA
Carson            Cheryl            CA
.
.
```

Using a Standard Value as the Parameter

A standard value can be entered as a parameter in the CREATE PROCEDURE command. This value is used when the user does not indicate a specific value as parameter. Change the au_state procedure using the ALTER PROCEDURE command and use a standard value as the state parameter.

```
ALTER PROCEDURE au_state
@st varchar(2)='UT' AS
SELECT au_lname, au_fname, state from authors
where state=@st
```

Here is the result of the execution of the procedure when no parameter is specified:

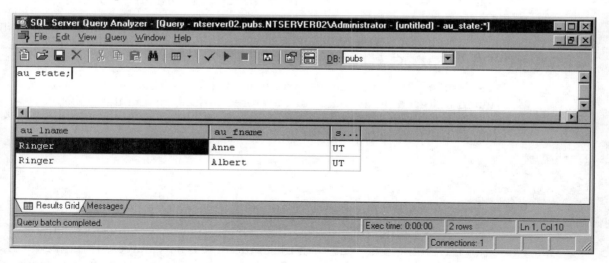

Recompiling a Stored Procedure

A stored procedure is automatically compiled the first time it is executed. When a new index is created that benefits the stored procedure, the procedure will not be automatically recompiled. This recompilation occurs only when the contents of a table used by the stored procedure are changed. To force the recompilation you can use the system stored procedure sp_recompile.

Example: `stored procedure_recompile au_state`

Deleting a Stored Procedure

A stored procedure can be deleted with the DROP PROCEDURE command, shown below, or through the Enterprise Manager. To delete a stored procedure, select the name of the procedure in the detail panel and press the Del key, or use the Delete option in the quick menu.

Example: `DROP PROCEDURE test1`

System Stored Procedures

SQL Server 7 has more than 100 special stored procedures that execute administrative tasks. These system stored procedures can be executed from any database. They are stored in the Master database. These procedures are easily identified, as their names start with the prefix "sp_". If a user creates a stored procedure with this prefix and the name of a system stored procedure, it will not be executed. The system stored procedures are grouped in the following categories:

Category	Description
Catalog Procedures	Implement ODBC data dictionary functions
Cursor Procedures	Implement cursor functionality
Distributed Queries Procedures	Manage distributed queries
SQL Server Agent Procedures	Set events
Replication Procedures	Manage replication
Security Procedures	Manage security resources
System Procedures	Perform maintenance functions
Web Assistant Procedures	Used by the Web Assistant Wizard
General Extended Procedures	Manage the interface with external programs
SQL Mail Extended Procedures	Execute e-mail operations with SQL
SQL Server Profiler Extended Procedures	Support operations of the SQL Server Profiler
OLE Automation Procedures	Support the OLE automation operations
Data Transformation Services Procedures	Support DTS operations

Following is a list of the system stored procedures by category. The names of many of these stored procedures are self-explanatory. A complete description of these stored procedures can be found in the online help.

Catalog Procedures

sp_column_privileges	sp_special_columns
sp_columns	sp_sproc_columns
sp_databases	sp_statistics
sp_fkeys	sp_stored_procedures
sp_pkeys	sp_table_privileges
sp_server_info	sp_tables

Cursor Procedures

sp_cursor_list	sp_describe_cursor_tables
sp_describe_cursor_columns	

Distributed Queries Procedures

sp_addlinkedserver	sp_indexes
sp_addlinkedsrvlogin	sp_linkedservers
sp_catalogs	sp_primarykeys
sp_column_privileges_ex	sp_serveroption
sp_columns_ex	sp_table_privileges_ex
sp_droplinkedsrvlogin	sp_tables_ex
sp_foreignkeys	

SQL Server Agent Procedures

sp_add_alert	sp_help_jobschedule
sp_add_category	sp_help_jobserver
sp_add_job	sp_help_jobstep
sp_add_jobschedule	sp_help_notification
sp_add_jobserver	sp_help_operator
sp_add_jobstep	sp_helphistory
sp_add_notification	sp_help_targetserver
sp_add_operator	sp_help_targetservergroup
sp_add_targetservergroup	sp_helptask
sp_add_targetsvrgrp_member	sp_manage_jobs_by_login
sp_addtask	sp_msx_defect
sp_apply_job_to_targets	sp_msx_enlist

SQL Server Agent Procedures

sp_delete_alert	sp_post_msx_operation
sp_delete_category	sp_purge_jobhistory
sp_delete_job	sp_purgehistory
sp_delete_jobschedule	sp_reassigntask
sp_delete_jobserver	sp_remove_job_from_targets
sp_delete_jobstep	sp_resync_targetserver
sp_delete_notification	sp_start_job
sp_delete_operator	sp_stop_job
sp_delete_targetserver	sp_update_alert
sp_delete_targetservergroup	sp_update_category
sp_delete_targetsvrgrp_member	sp_update_job
sp_droptask	sp_update_jobschedule
sp_help_alert	sp_update_jobstep
sp_help_category	sp_update_notification
sp_help_downloadlist	sp_update_operator
sp_help_job	sp_update_targetservergroup
sp_help_jobhistory	sp_updatetask

Replication Procedures

sp_add_agent_parameter	sp_enumcustomresolvers
sp_add_agent_profile	sp_enumfullsubscribers
sp_addarticle	sp_generatefilters
sp_adddistpublisher	sp_getmergedeletetype
sp_adddistributiondb	sp_get_distributor
sp_adddistributor	sp_grant_publication_access
sp_addmergearticle	sp_help_agent_default
sp_addmergefilter	sp_help_agent_parameter
sp_addmergepublication	sp_help_agent_profile
sp_addmergepullsubscription	sp_help_publication_access
sp_addmergepullsubscription_agent	sp_helparticle
sp_addmergesubscription	sp_helparticlecolumns
sp_addpublication	sp_helpdistpublisher
sp_addpublication_snapshot	sp_helpdistributiondb
sp_addpublisher	sp_helpdistributor
sp_addpullsubscription	sp_helpmergearticle
sp_addpullsubscription_agent	sp_helpmergearticleconflicts
sp_addsubscriber	sp_helpmergeconflictrows
sp_addsubscriber_schedule	sp_helpmergedeleteconflictrows

Replication Procedures

sp_addsubscription
sp_addsynctriggers
sp_article_validation
sp_articlecolumn
sp_articlefilter
sp_articlesynctranprocs
sp_articleview
sp_browsereplcmds
sp_changearticle
sp_changedistpublisher
sp_changedistributiondb
sp_changedistributor_password
sp_changedistributor_property
sp_changemergearticle
sp_changemergefilter
sp_changemergepublication
sp_changemergepullsubscription
sp_changemergesubscription
sp_changepublication
sp_changesubscriber
sp_changesubscriber_schedule
sp_changesubstatus
sp_change_subscription_properties
sp_deletemergeconflictrow
sp_distcounters
sp_drop_agent_parameter
sp_drop_agent_profile
sp_droparticle
sp_dropdistributiondb
sp_dropdistributor
sp_dropmergearticle
sp_dropmergefilter
sp_dropmergepublication
sp_dropmergepullsubscription
sp_dropmergesubscription
sp_droppublication
sp_droppullsubscription
sp_dropsubscriber
sp_dropsubscription

sp_helpmergefilter
sp_helpmergepublication
sp_helpmergepullsubscription
sp_helpmergesubscription
sp_helppublication
sp_helppublication_snapshot
sp_helppullsubscription
sp_helpreplicationdb
sp_helpreplicationdboption
sp_helpreplicationoption
sp_helpsubscriber
sp_helpsubscriberinfo
sp_helpsubscription
sp_helpsubscription_properties
sp_link_publication
sp_mergedummyupdate
sp_mergesubscription_cleanup
sp_publication_validation
sp_refreshsubscriptions
sp_reinitmergepullsubscription
sp_reinitmergesubscription
sp_reinitpullsubscription
sp_removedbreplication
sp_replcmds
sp_replcounters
sp_repldone
sp_replflush
sp_replicationdboption
sp_replicationoption
sp_replication_agent_checkup
sp_replshowcmds
sp_repltrans
sp_revoke_publication_access
sp_script_synctran_commands
sp_scriptdelproc
sp_scriptinsproc
sp_scriptupdproc
sp_subscription_cleanup
sp_table_validation

Replication Procedures

sp_dumpparamcmd

Security Procedures

sp_addalias	sp_droprole
sp_addapprole	sp_droprolemember
sp_addgroup	sp_dropserver
sp_addlinkedsrvlogin	sp_dropsrvrolemember
sp_addlogin	sp_dropuser
sp_addremotelogin	sp_grantdbaccess
sp_addrole	sp_grantlogin
sp_addrolemember	sp_helpdbfixedrole
sp_addserver	sp_helpgroup
sp_addsrvrolemember	sp_helplogins
sp_adduser	sp_helpntgroup
sp_approlepassword	sp_helpremotelogin
sp_change_users_login	sp_helprole
sp_changedbowner	sp_helprolemember
sp_changegroup	sp_helprotect
sp_changeobjectowner	sp_helpsrvrole
sp_dbfixedrolepermission	sp_helpsrvrolemember
sp_defaultdb	sp_helpuser
sp_defaultlanguage	sp_password
sp_denylogin	sp_remoteoption
sp_dropalias	sp_revokedbaccess
sp_dropapprole	sp_revokelogin
sp_dropgroup	sp_setapprole
sp_droplinkedsrvlogin	sp_srvrolepermission
sp_droplogin	sp_validatelogins
sp_dropremotelogin	

System Procedures

sp_addextendedproc	sp_helpdb
sp_addmessage	sp_helpdevice
sp_addtype	sp_helpextendedproc
sp_addumpdevice	sp_helpfile
sp_altermessage	sp_helpfilegroup
sp_autostats	sp_help_fulltext_catalogs

System Procedures

sp_attach_db	sp_help_fulltext_catalogs_cursor
sp_attach_single_file_db	sp_help_fulltext_columns
sp_bindefault	sp_help_fulltext_columns_cursor
sp_bindrule	sp_help_fulltext_tables
sp_bindsession	sp_help_fulltext_tables_cursor
sp_certify_removable	sp_helpindex
sp_configure	sp_helplanguage
sp_create_removable	sp_helpserver
sp_createstats	sp_helpsort
sp_datatype_info	sp_helptext
sp_dbcmptlevel	sp_helptrigger
sp_dboption	sp_indexoption
sp_depends	sp_lock
sp_detach_db	sp_monitor
sp_dropdevice	sp_processmail
sp_dropextendedproc	sp_procoption
sp_dropmessage	sp_recompile
sp_droptype	sp_refreshview
sp_dsninfo	sp_rename
sp_enumdsn	sp_renamedb
sp_executesql	sp_serveroption
sp_getbindtoken	sp_setnetname
sp_fulltext_catalog	sp_spaceused
sp_fulltext_column	sp_tableoption
sp_fulltext_database	sp_unbindefault
sp_fulltext_service	sp_unbindrule
sp_fulltext_table	sp_updatestats
sp_help	sp_validname
sp_helpconstraint	sp_who

Web Assistant Procedures

sp_dropwebtask	sp_makewebtask
sp_enumcodepages	sp_runwebtask

General Extended Procedures

xp_cmdshell	xp_revokelogin
xp_enumgroups	xp_snmp_getstate

General Extended Procedures

xp_findnextmsg

xp_grantlogin

xp_loginconfig

xp_logininfo

xp_logevent

xp_msver

xp_snmp_raisetrap

xp_sprintf

xp_sqlinventory

xp_sscanf

xp_sqlmaint

SQL Mail Extended Procedures

xp_deletemail

xp_findnextmsg

xp_readmail

xp_sendmail

xp_startmail

xp_stopmail

SQL Server Profiler Extended Procedures

xp_sqltrace

xp_trace_addnewqueue

xp_trace_deletequeuedefinition

xp_trace_destroyqueue

xp_trace_enumqueuedefname

xp_trace_enumqueuehandles

xp_trace_eventclassrequired

xp_trace_generate_event

xp_trace_getappfilter

xp_trace_getconnectionidfilter

xp_trace_getcpufilter

xp_trace_getdbidfilter

xp_trace_getdurationfilter

xp_trace_geteventfilter

xp_trace_geteventnames

xp_trace_getevents

xp_trace_gethostfilter

xp_trace_gethpidfilter

xp_trace_getindidfilter

xp_trace_getntdmfilter

xp_trace_getntnmfilter

xp_trace_getobjidfilter

xp_trace_getqueueautostart

xp_trace_getqueuedestination

xp_trace_getuserfilter

xp_trace_getwritefilter

xp_trace_loadqueuedefinition

xp_trace_pausequeue

xp_trace_restartqueue

xp_trace_savequeuedefinition

xp_trace_setappfilter

xp_trace_setconnectionidfilter

xp_trace_setcpufilter

xp_trace_setdbidfilter

xp_trace_setdurationfilter

xp_trace_seteventclassrequired

xp_trace_seteventfilter

xp_trace_sethostfilter

xp_trace_sethpidfilter

xp_trace_setindidfilter

xp_trace_setntdmfilter

xp_trace_setntnmfilter

xp_trace_setobjidfilter

xp_trace_setqueueautostart

xp_trace_setqueuecreateinfo

xp_trace_setqueuedestination

xp_trace_setreadfilter

xp_trace_setserverfilter

SQL Server Profiler Extended Procedures	
xp_trace_getqueueproperties	xp_trace_setseverityfilter
xp_trace_getreadfilter	xp_trace_setspidfilter
xp_trace_getserverfilter	xp_trace_settextfilter
xp_trace_getseverityfilter	xp_trace_setuserfilter
xp_trace_getspidfilter	xp_trace_setwritefilter
xp_trace_gettextfilter	

OLE Automation Extended Stored Procedures	
sp_OACreate	sp_OAMethod
sp_OADestroy	sp_OASetProperty
sp_OAGetErrorInfo	sp_OAStop
sp_OAGetProperty	Object Hierarchy Syntax

Summary

This chapter provided a brief introduction to stored procedures, a subject that deserves special attention in SQL Server 7. In the next chapter we will learn how to work with triggers, a kind of stored procedure that is automatically activated when certain events occur.

Triggers

Most applications developed to manage a desktop database or legacy corporate databases are also responsible for managing the system's business rules. For example, when a specified minimum quantity of a product is reached in an inventory control system, the program must trigger a routine that requires the purchase of a new lot and the issuance of a control report. If the database is accessed by a tool that allows changes or by another system that does not perform this control, the product inventory can fall below the minimum quantity with no notification.

One of the attractive features of the SQL Server 7 is a control mechanism called a database trigger. A trigger is just a block of Transact-SQL commands that is automatically executed when an INSERT, DELETE, or UPDATE statement is executed in a table.

The main application of a trigger is the creation of validation methods and access restrictions to the database, such as security routines. Instead of leaving the control for the application, the table itself starts executing those controls through the triggers, making the handling of the database much more secure. Among the applications of a trigger are:

➤ Creating the contents of a column derived from other columns
➤ Creating validation mechanisms involving queries in multiple tables
➤ Creating logs to register the use of a table
➤ Updating other tables when there are additions or other changes in the current table

Components of a Trigger

A trigger is composed of two parts:

➤ A SQL command to activate the trigger. The INSERT, DELETE, and UPDATE commands can activate a trigger. The same trigger can be invoked when more than one action occurs. In other words, a trigger can be invoked when an INSERT command is executed, or when an UUPDATE or DELETE command is executed.

➤ An action executed by the trigger. The trigger executes the PL/SQL block.

Limitations of Triggers

Here are some limitations and considerations about the use of the triggers:

➤ A trigger can execute the commands contained in its body or activate stored procedures and other triggers in order to execute certain tasks.

➤ Any SET command can be specified inside a trigger. It remains active during the execution of the trigger.

➤ You cannot create a trigger for a view. However, when the view is used, the triggers of the base table normally are activated.

➤ When a trigger is executed, the results are returned to the application that called it. To avoid returning the results, do not use the SELECT command that returns results or execute the attribution of contents to the variables.

➤ The TRUNCATE TABLE command cannot be intercepted by a trigger of the delete type. The WRITETEXT command does not activate a trigger.

➤ The Transact-SQL commands listed below cannot be used inside a trigger:

ALTER DATABASE	ALTER PROCEDURE	ALTER TABLE
ALTER TRIGGER	ALTER VIEW	CREATE DATABASE
CREATE DEFAULT	CREATE INDEX	CREATE PROCEDURE
CREATE RULE	CREATE SCHEMA	CREATE TABLE
CREATE TRIGGER	CREATE VIEW	DENY
DISK INIT	DISK RESIZE	DROP DATABASE
DROP DEFAULT	DROP INDEX	DROP PROCEDURE
DROP RULE	DROP TABLE	DROP TRIGGER
DROP VIEW	GRANT	LOAD DATABASE
LOAD LOG	RESTORE DATABASE	RESTORE LOG
REVOKE	RECONFIGURE	TRUNCATE TABLE
UPDATE STATISTICS		

Creating a Trigger

A trigger can be created through the Enterprise Manager or the Query Analyzer. In both cases you need to enter the SQL commands. First let's look at the simplified syntax of the SQL command. See the reference guide in Appendix A for the complete syntax.

```
CREATE TRIGGER trigger_name ON table_name
FOR  [INSERT/,DELETE/,UPDATE]
AS commands
```

ON table_name indicates the table or schema in which the trigger is being created.

FOR must be followed by the type of command or commands that activate the trigger.

AS starts the body of the trigger with the commands that will be executed.

In this chapter we'll create two tables with the structure shown in the following figure. These tables will be created in the Newpub2 database.

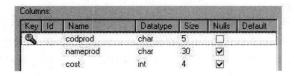

One table is called Test1 and the other table is called Test2. All the triggers will be created in the Test1 table.

Creating a Trigger with the Enterprise Manager

Expand the database and the folder where the table is located. Then click with the right mouse button on the name of the table in which you want to create the trigger. Select the Task option in the quick menu and select Manage Triggers. This procedure is also valid for changing or eliminating the trigger.

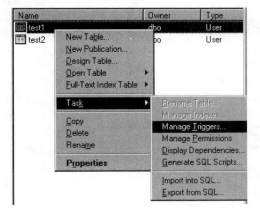

This step brings up the Trigger Properties dialog box.

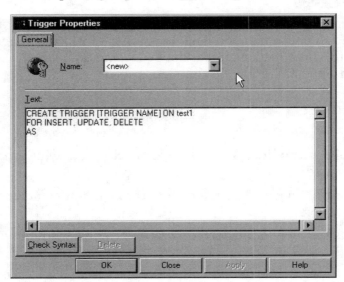

This dialog box shows a central panel with the basic structure of the trigger. You must replace the contents inside the brackets [trigger name] with the name of the trigger that will be created. Note in the figure on the following page that the name of the trigger appears in the appropriate place.

In the second line you choose the type of trigger action, that is, the command that will activate it. The default is INSERT, DELETE, and UPDATE. After the word AS you specify the block of commands.

The first trigger to be created will display a message in the screen saying that a record was inserted in the table. This will show that the trigger is really activated by the INSERT command. Enter the PRINT statement as shown in the next screen and press the OK button to save the trigger.

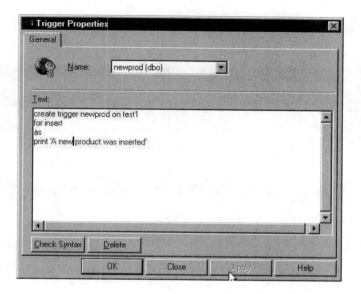

Now we are going to test the functioning of this trigger using the Query Analyzer. We will insert a line in the Test1 table. After loading the program, select the Newpub2 database and enter the following command:

INSERT test1 values (1,"prod01",10)

Examine the result in the following figure:

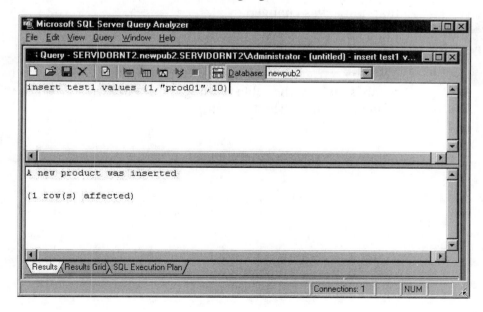

Now we are going to insert a new record and list the contents of the table:

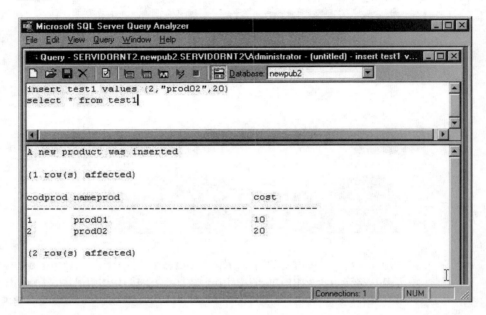

In the following section we will create two additional triggers. One will display a message when a line is deleted and the other one will indicate that a line was changed.

Creating a Trigger with the Query Analyzer

Creating a trigger is just as easy with the Query Analyzer. Just select the database where the table is using the Database field, enter the text of the trigger, and press the Run button.

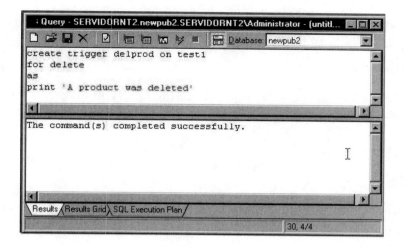

If no error occurs, a message is displayed indicating the command was completed with success. If any syntax error occurs, an error message is displayed. In this case, return to the top panel and correct the command. To test the trigger, let's eliminate the record for prod01.

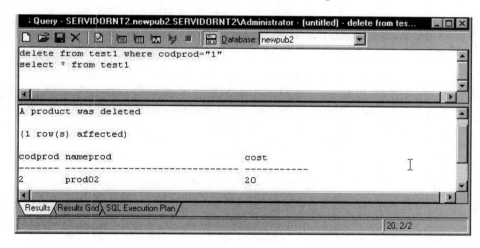

Note that the SELECT command returned only the remaining record in the table. Reinsert the record for prod01 in the table.

Now let's create a trigger that is activated when the UPDATE command is executed. The code for the trigger is the following:

```
CREATE TRIGGER updprod ON test1
FOR  UPDATE
AS
print "a product was updated"
```

Now execute the following code in the Query Analyzer to increase by 20 percent the value of the Cost field of the codprod 2 record:

```
update test1
set cost=cost*1.2
where codprod="2"
select * from test1
```

and see the result:

```
one product was updated
(1 row(s) affected)

codprod nameprod        cost
------- -------------   -----
1       prod01          10
2       prod02          24
```

The Inserted and Deleted Tables

When a trigger is executed, the SQL Server 7 creates two temporary tables that only exist when the trigger is activated. One is called Inserted and the other is Deleted. When an INSERT or UPDATE command is executed, the records that are created or changed are copied to the Inserted table. When a DELETE command is executed, the deleted lines are copied to the Deleted table.

These tables are useful when you want to have the lines added, deleted, or altered during the process of executing the trigger. They are particularly useful for copying lines from one table to another.

To show the existence of this table we will change the updprod trigger as illustrated in the next figure. After activating the Trigger Properties dialog box, select the name of the trigger in the Name field and insert the SELECT statement at the end of the trigger's text.

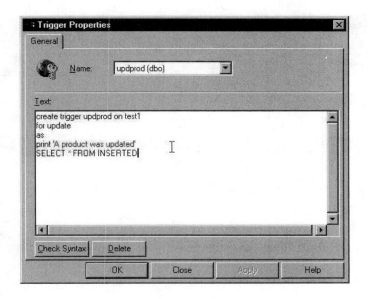

Press OK to save the changes. After executing the following example, change the updprod trigger and eliminate this line.

The following code updates the record with prod02 and shows the result through the selection of the lines of the Inserted table, which shows just the altered record and Test1. The trigger shows the message "A product was updated" and the contents of the Inserted table.

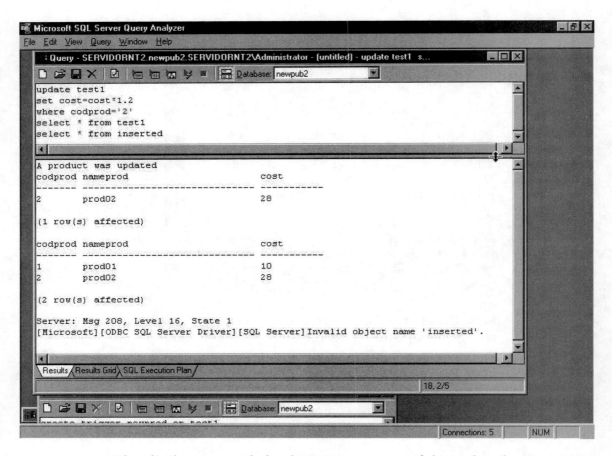

This display was made by the SQL statement of the updprod trigger. Note that an error occurs when we try to display the data of the Inserted table after the trigger is executed, since the Inserted table does not exist anymore.

Changing a Trigger

A trigger can be changed directly with the ALTER TRIGGER command, as shown below. Another option is to eliminate the trigger and create it again. This operation can also be performed in the Trigger Properties dialog box.

Syntax: `ALTER TRIGGER trigger_name`

Creating Line Replication with Triggers

Using the temporary tables of triggers we can create a mechanism to perform an instant replication from one table to another. We can insert, change, or delete a record in another table at the very moment the operation is being executed in the current table.

We will create three triggers to replicate the operations of the Test1 table to the Test2 table. The first trigger will replicate the insertion of a record. Its name will be insreplic. The code of the trigger is the following. Use one of the methods previously described to create the triggers.

```
CREATE TRIGGER [insreplic] ON test1
FOR insert AS
insert into test2
select codprod,nameprod,cost from inserted
```

In this trigger we used the INSERT INTO and SELECT commands to obtain the fields of the Inserted table.

The next trigger replicates a deletion. We use the DELETE FROM command and the WHERE clause to filter the record that will be deleted by searching for it in the Deleted table, which in this case contains only the record that was just deleted.

```
CREATE TRIGGER [delrepl] ON test1
FOR DELETE
as
delete from test2
where test2.codprod in (select codprod from deleted)
```

The next trigger replicates the updates made in Test1. In it we update the Cost column from Test2 with the contents of the Cost column of the Inserted table (remember that INSERT and UPDATE use the same Inserted table). The WHERE clause is also used to update just the record with the code found in the Inserted table.

```
CREATE TRIGGER [updrep] ON test1
FOR update
AS
update test2
set cost=(select cost from inserted)
where test2.codprod in (select codprod from inserted)
```

After creating the triggers it's time to test them. First, let's see how the two tables execute these SELECT commands:

```
select * from test1
select * from test2
```

This is the result you should obtain in the Query Analyzer:

```
codprod nameprod           cost
------- ----------------   -------
1       prod01             10
2       prod02             28

(2 row(s) affected)


codprod nameprod                       cost
------- ----------------------------   -----------

(0 row(s) affected)
```

Now we will add the following code to the Test1 table and see how it affects the two tables:

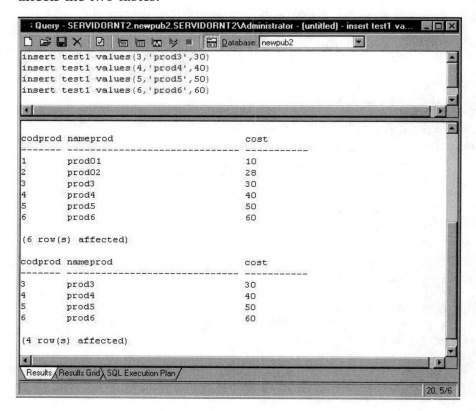

Note that Test2 has the same four lines inserted in Test1.

Now let's test the replication of a change. Change the value of the Cost field for prod6 from 60 to 555, and run the code shown in the top panel of the next figure. Note that the replication has worked properly.

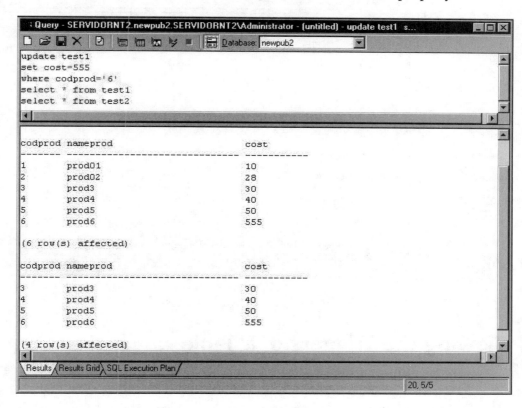

The last test replicates the exclusion of a line. We will eliminate the product with codprod 4.

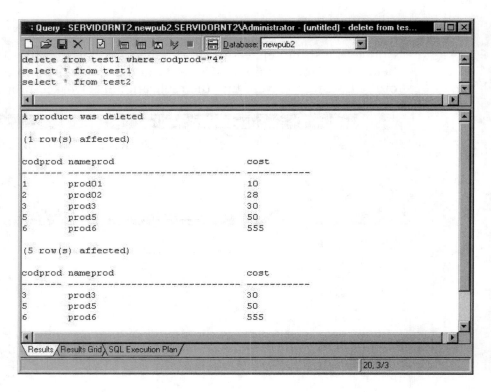

Once more the replication was successful.

Viewing the Triggers of a Table

Through the stored procedure sp_helptrigger you can find out the types of triggers defined to a table in the current database.

Syntax: `sp_helptrigger [@tabname =]` *'table'* `[,[@triggertype =]` *'type'*`]`

[@tabname =] *'table'* is the name of the table where the trigger was created.

[@triggertype =] *'type'* is the type of the trigger from which you want more information. The types allowed in this parameter are DELETE, INSERT, and UPDATE.

Example: `sp_helptrigger test1`

To view the text of the trigger, use the stored procedure sp_helptext. It returns the text of the specified object. This object can be a trigger, stored procedure, view, rule, or default.

Syntax: `sp_helptext [@objname =] 'name'`

[@objname =] '*name*' is the name of the object about which you want more information.

Notice the two stored procedures applied to the table Test1 and one of the triggers.

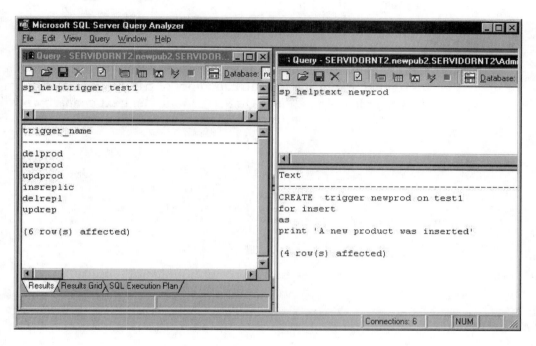

Deleting a Trigger

In order to delete a trigger, first expand the Databases folder, expand the database in which the table containing the trigger belongs, and then click Tables.

In the details pane, right-click the table in which the trigger exists, point to Task, and then click Manage Triggers.

In the Name list, select the name of the trigger to delete, and select Delete.

You can also use the SQL DROP TRIGGER statement:

Syntax: `DROP TRIGGER` *trigger_name*

This removes the trigger's structure from the database and removes the privileges granted to other users. If the table containing the trigger is eliminated, the trigger will also be removed from the database.

You can also use the Trigger Properties dialog box to delete a trigger. Select the trigger's name in the Name box, press the Delete button, and confirm the deletion.

Summary

This chapter discussed some of the functionality that triggers offer to the developer. Exploring the full capability of triggers is one of the great challenges in learning about SQL Server 7. In the next chapter we will talk about the replication features offered by SQL Server 7.

Replication

Replication is a very important technology in the corporate database environment. Replication enables you to distribute data and stored procedures throughout the organization. The data in a database can be duplicated and copied to several places inside the company. These distributed databases can be synchronized to always have the same value, such as a price list synchronized across all branches.

Replication Model

The SQL Server adopts the model of replication based on the "publish and subscribe" model introduced with version 6.0. Publishers, distributors, subscribers, articles, and publications compose this model, in addition to the subscriptions of push and pull type. This model allows the replication to heterogeneous databases through the use of ODBC or OLE DB.

Types of Replication

SQL Server supports three types of replication: snapshot, transactional, and merge.

Snapshot

Snapshot replication makes a photograph of the database that is replicated to its subscribers, who receive a complete copy of the data rather than just the changes. This replication is perfect when there is not a constant updating of the database, and for users who do not update the tables.

Transactional

Transactional replication allows the replication of tables and stored procedures. It allows the filtering of data that will be published. This replication uses a log file to store the changes made in an article (table, for example) since the last publication, monitoring the INSERT, UPDATE, and DELETE commands. The changes are stored in the distribution database and then are sent to the subscribers.

Merge

Replication of the merge type controls the changes made in a source database and synchronizes the values between the editor (publisher) and the subscribers. The changes made in the target database update the source database and vice versa.

To publish some piece of data you need to create a publication by selecting the tables and stored procedures, as well as its availability to the subscribers. The objects included in a publication, such as tables or row groups, are called *articles*. A stored procedure can be an article from a merge-type replication.

Subscribing a Publication

To receive a publication you need to subscribe to it. You have to specify a database that will receive the publication. There are two types of publication: pull and push.

A subscription of the type *push* is executed when the publisher (editor) is managed in a centralized way. In this case, a copy of the publication is dispatched or pushed to the subscriber.

The subscription of the type *pull* is executed when the subscriber is administered in a decentralized way. It pulls a copy of the publication from the editor. Once configured, the publication and target tables must be synchronized for the publication control process to be correctly executed.

The following section describes the step-by-step creation of a transactional replication. We will create a replication of the Northwind database.

Transactional Replication Example

Open the Enterprise Manager and double-click on the server name. Select Replicate Data in the right panel.

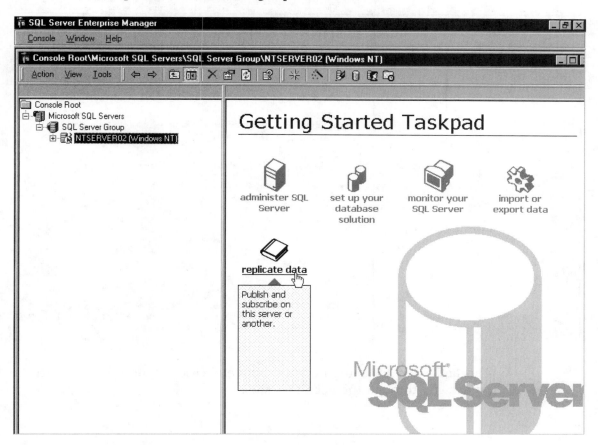

In the next screen, select Configure Replication.

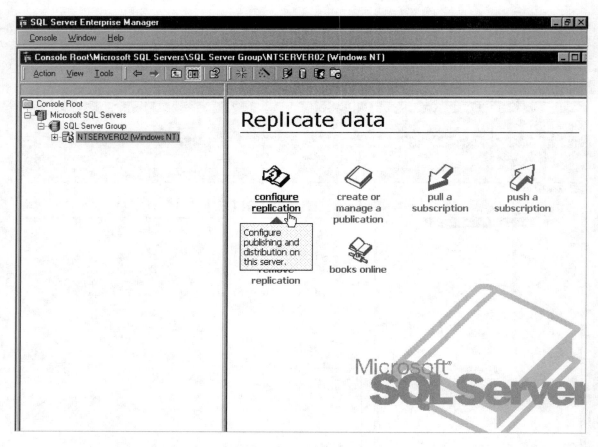

This activates the Configure Publishing and Distribution Wizard, which guides you through the necessary steps.

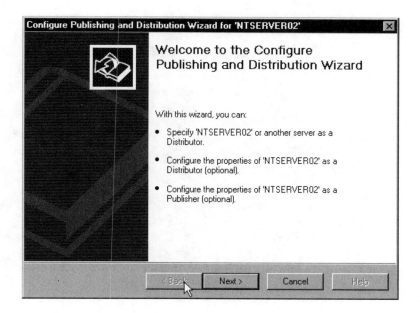

Click on Next. Then choose the distribution database, which in this example will remain in the local server.

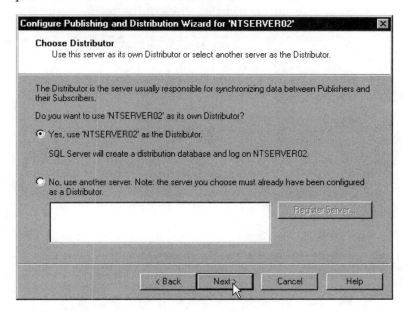

Click on Next. A screen with the configurations is displayed. We will use the default settings provided.

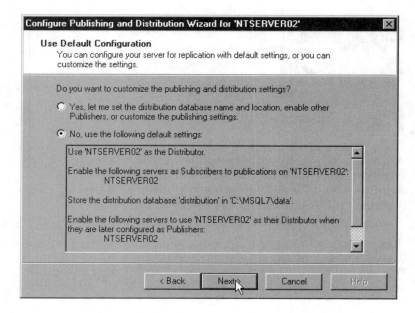

Accept the default values and click on Next. The wizard will complete the task and allow you to specify the publishing and distribution database. Press the Finish button to begin the configuration process.

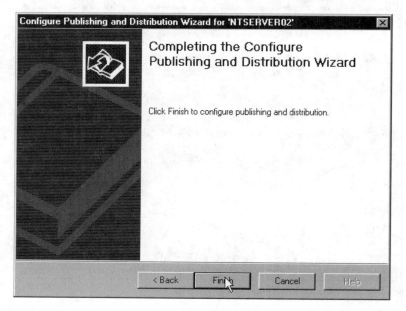

A dialog box shows the progress of the process, as shown below:

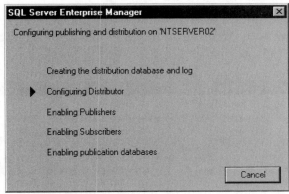

A message confirming the execution of the task appears at the end. Press the OK button to continue. If the SQL Server Agent is not configured to start when the computer is turned on, a dialog box appears asking you to configure it. When finished, press the Close button.

Defining the Publications

Click on the Create or Manage Publication item in the right panel. The Create and Manage Publications dialog box is displayed.

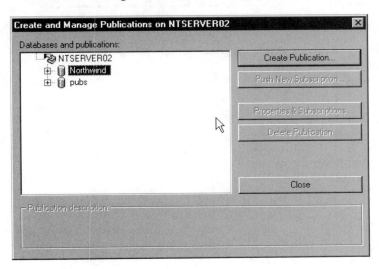

Select the Northwind database and click on the Create Publication button. The Create Publication Wizard is activated.

Press the Next button in the first screen that appears. In the second step you can select the type of publication you want from the available options. Select Transactional Publication and press Next.

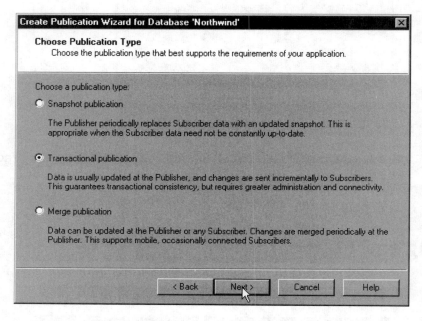

You will be asked about immediate-updating subscriptions. Accept the default value to avoid immediate-updating subscriptions and press Next.

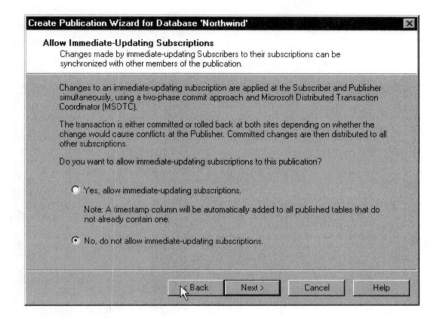

SQL 7 then asks you to specify the subscribers that will be allowed. It permits subscribers that are not running SQL 7. In this example, select All Subscribers and then press Next.

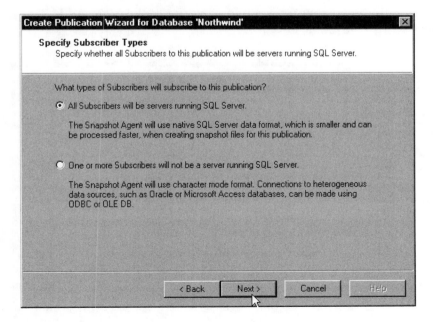

Now you need to select the articles, or objects, that will be published. All the available tables will be displayed. In this example we will choose all of them. Therefore, press the Publish All and Next buttons.

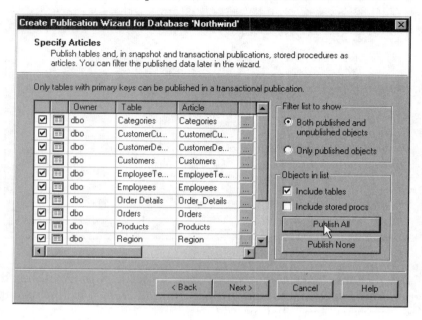

In the next step enter a name for the replication. Add **_Tran** to the name Northwind and press Next.

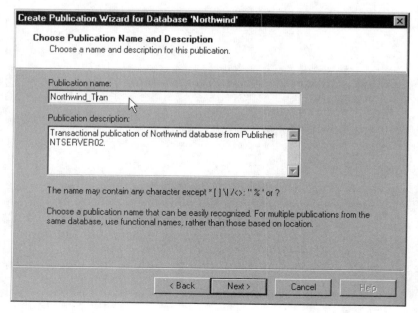

In the next step you can customize the replication or publish it without filters. Click on Yes and press the Next button.

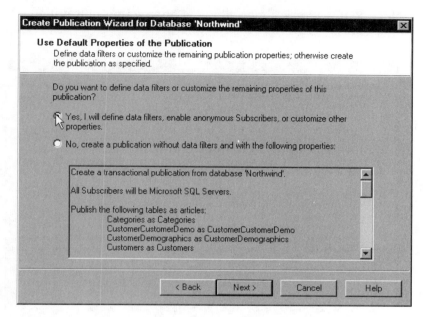

In the next dialog box, select No and press the Next button.

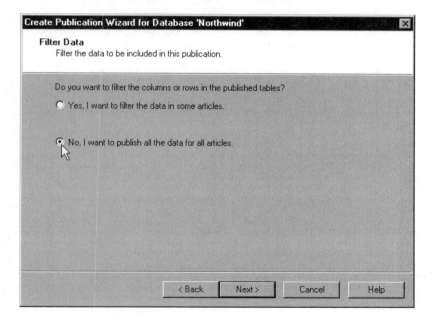

Select either Yes or No, depending on whether you want to publish all the data or entire tables. Click on Next.

Next, SQL will ask about allowing anonymous subscribers. Select Yes and click on Next.

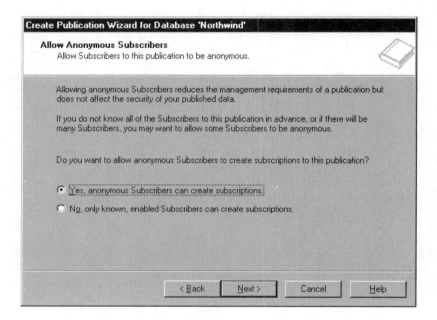

The next screen sets the Snapshot Agent. Specify that you want an immediate snapshot and click on the Next button.

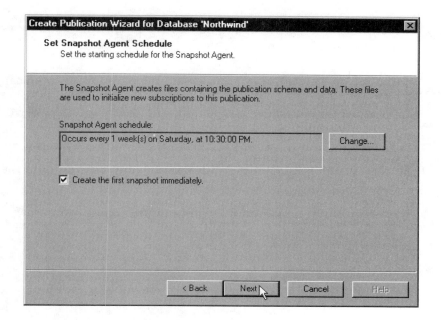

Accept the defaults suggested.

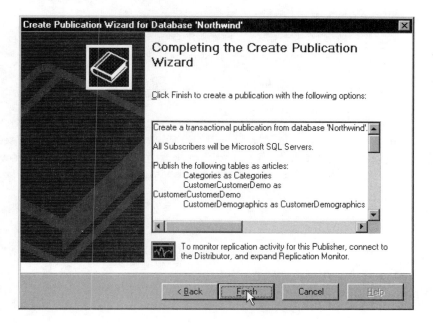

Press Finish. The final wizard screen is shown with a summary of what will be done. Click on OK to close.

Dispatching the Publication

The next step consists of dispatching the publication. Now we will configure the subscriptions for the publication and create another database that will be filled out with the initial snapshot that we have just created.

In the Create and Manage Publications dialog box, click on the Push New Subscription button.

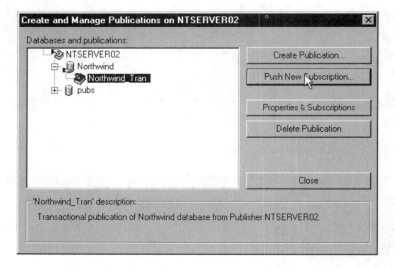

The Push Subscription Wizard is activated. Click on the Next button of the first screen that appears. Then click on Subscribers and select your server from the list. In our example, it is NTSERVER02. If you are following this example, select the name of your server.

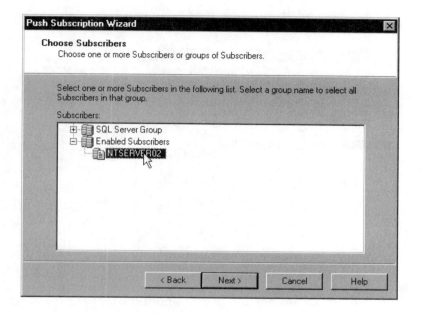

Click on Next and select the target database. You can either enter a name, as shown below:

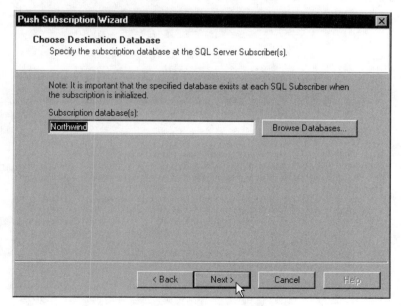

or click on Browse Databases, which brings up a dialog box:

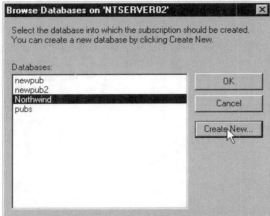

In this example we need to create another database. To do that, click on Create New. Enter **NWinTran** in the Name field.

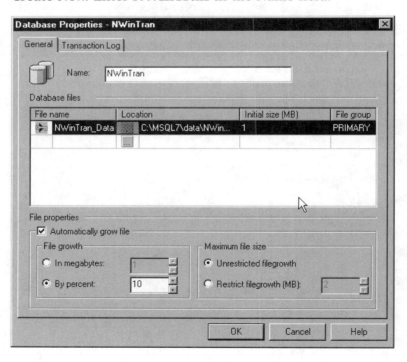

Press OK to return to the previous screen. Select the database just created, and press OK.

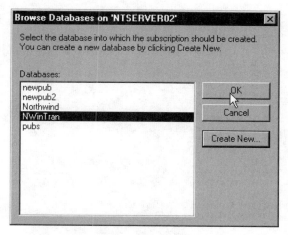

Press Next in the dialog box that appears. In the dialog box that follows you can decide when the publication will be updated. Let's select Continuously and press Next.

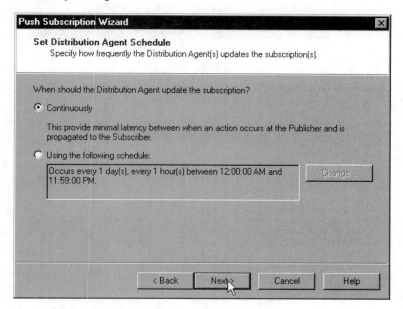

Since we have just created the subscription database, we will choose to start the initialization process immediately. Then press Next.

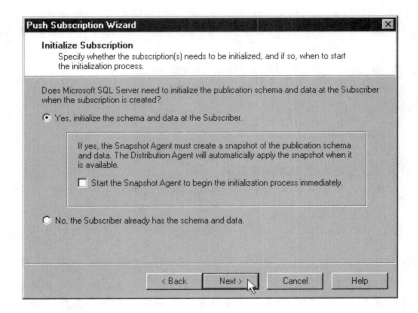

The SQL Server Agent must be loaded for this operation to work. The following figure shows its status.

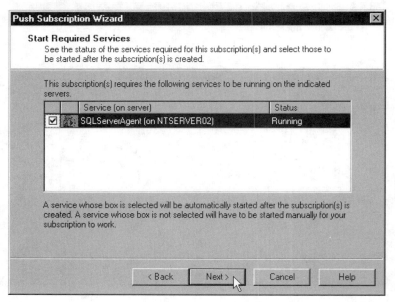

Click on Next, and then click on Finish. After a moment a message is displayed informing you of the operation's progress.

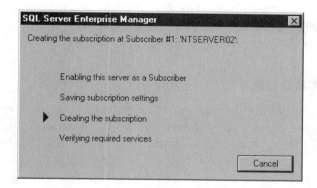

Click on the Close button.

Checking the Replication

You can see the status of the replication by clicking on the Replication Monitor item in the Enterprise Manager database tree and expanding its items until you find the publication, as shown in the next screen.

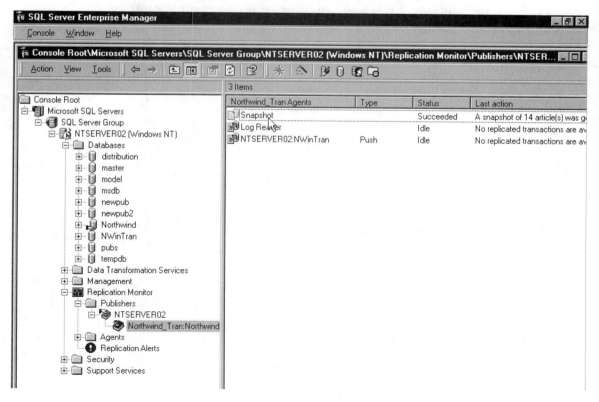

If you click on some of the text in the right panel, you will get more information on the state of the operation performed.

Testing the Replication

Let's use the Query Analyzer to test the replication. After opening it and connecting to the server, we will update the price of a product and see what happens. Then, update the contents of the Products table with the following script:

```
Begin transaction
Update Northwind..Products
Set Unitprice=24
Where ProductId=14
Commit transaction
```

After that create a new query and execute it:

```
Select ProductID, ProductName, UnitPrice from Northwind..products where ProductID=14
Select ProductID, ProductName, UnitPrice from NWinTran..products where ProductID=14
```

You will see that the product value is the same in both tables.

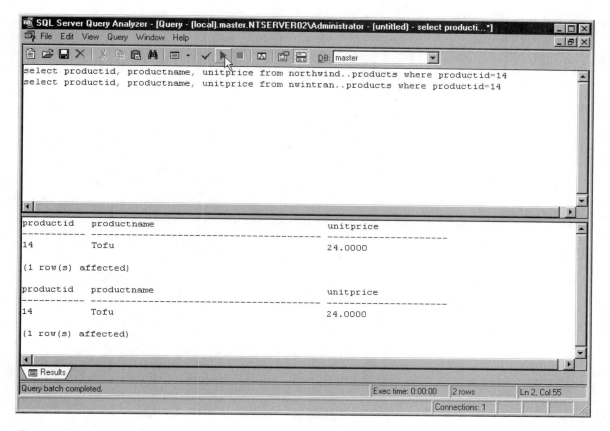

Summary

Although it's an elaborate process, replication itself is a simple concept. This chapter gave an example of transactional replication. The next chapter shows how to create a merge-type replication.

Merge Replication

In this chapter we show how to create a merge-type replication in which the changes made to a source database or a target database can be updated on a reciprocal basis. If you have already performed the steps to create a transactional replication, you can skip down to the Defining the Replication section. In this first section we will configure a replication from the beginning.

Open the Enterprise Manager and click on the server name. In the right panel, select Replication Data. In the next screen that appears, select Configure Replication. This opens the Configure Publishing and Distribution Wizard. If you have previously created the replication, a different screen appears. If this occurs, close it and go to the Defining the Replication section.

The opening screen of the wizard welcomes you and guides you through the steps needed to configure your publication. Click on Next. In the next screen, select the distribution database, which in this example will remain in the local server.

Click on Next; a screen with the configurations is displayed, as shown on the next page. We will use the default provided by clicking on the Next button.

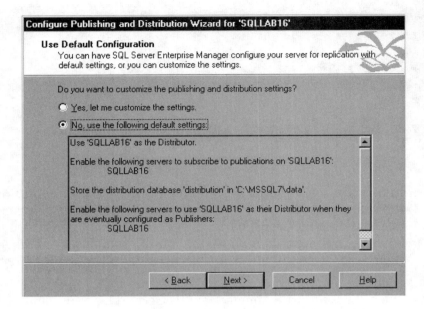

The wizard will complete the task and allow you to specify the publishing and distribution database. Then press the Finish button. The dialog box shows the progress of this operation. When it is finished, press the Close button.

Defining the Replication

In the screen with the menu containing the replication tasks, click on the item Create or Manage a Publication.

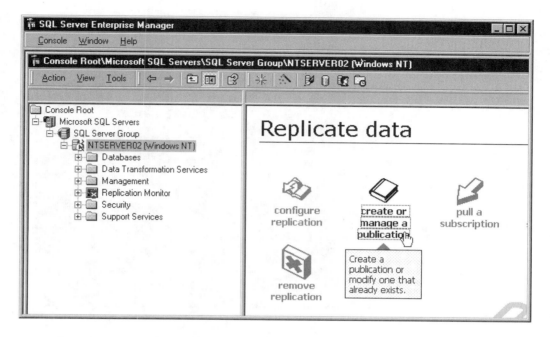

The Create and Manage Publications dialog is displayed. Select the Northwind database and click on the Create Publication button.

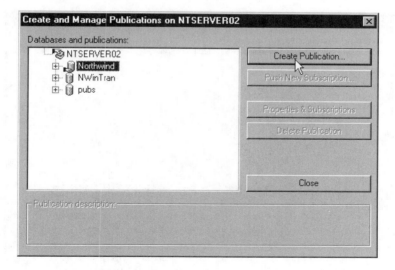

This activates the Create Publication Wizard. Press Next to go to the second screen. If you have created another publication, a dialog box asks if you want to use one of them as a template. In this case, select No and press Next.

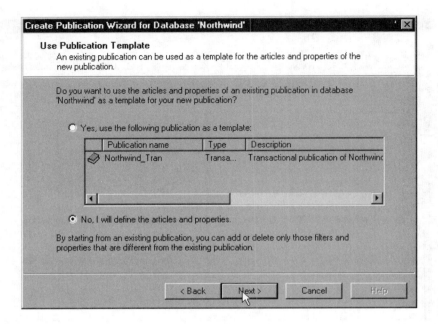

You can select the type of publication you wish among the options given. In this example, we select Merge Publication and press Next.

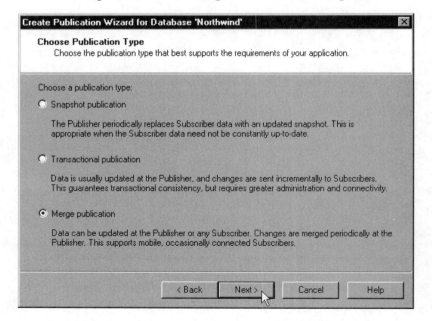

SQL 7 allows the use of subscribers who are not in a SQL 7 database. However, in this example we will choose All Subscribers, indicating that all the subscribers belong to a SQL Server database.

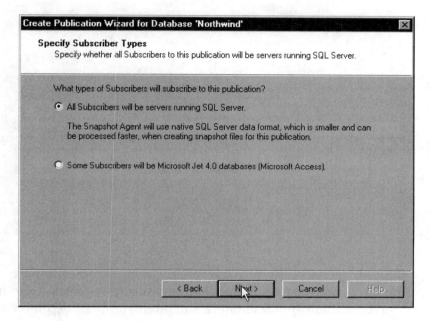

Press the Next button to proceed. The next step is used to define the articles, or objects, that will be published. All the available tables are displayed. In this example, we will select all of them. To do that, press Publish All and then Next.

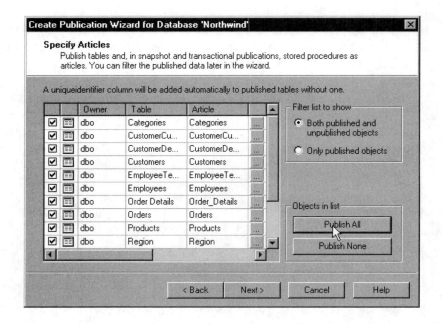

In a merge replication SQL Server requires all tables to have unique identifiers. It will create unique identifiers for those tables without them. SQL
Server will notify you about this and tell you that the tables' sizes have
increased because of it. Press OK.

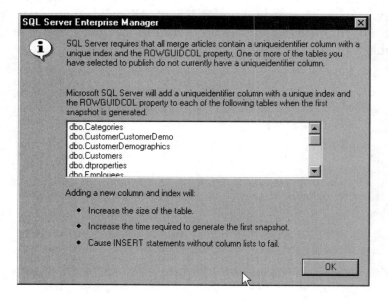

In the next step enter a name for the replication. We add **_Merge** to the name Northwind and then press Next to proceed.

Next you have the option of customizing the replication or publishing it without any filters. Click on Yes and press the Next button.

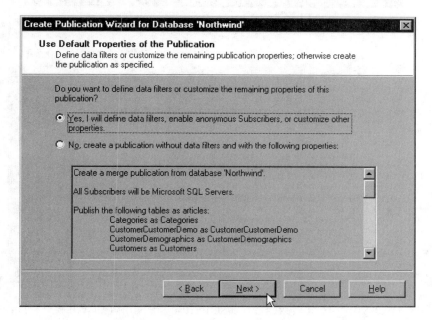

Then select No and press the Next button.

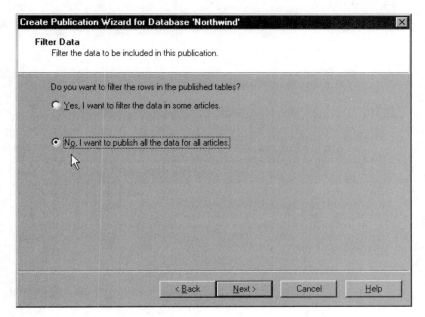

Now we will allow anonymous subscribers by selecting the option Yes and pressing the Next button. The schedule screen of the Snapshot Agent displays.

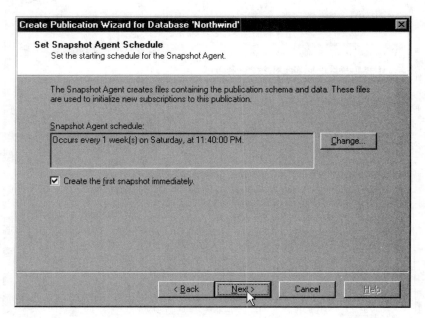

After you press Next in the schedule screen you will see a screen showing the options you chose. Press the Finish button; the creation process starts immediately.

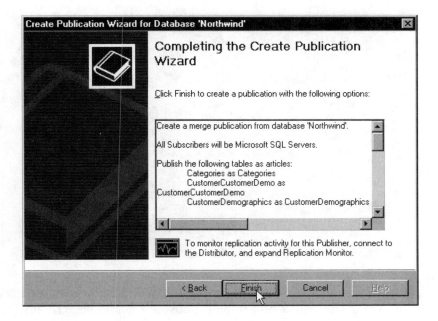

A box showing the task's progress is displayed.

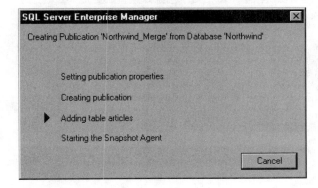

Then a window alerts you that the process is complete.

Dispatching the Publication

When you press either the Close or OK buttons, the Create and Manage Publications dialog box appears. Select Northwind_Merge and click the Push New Subscription button.

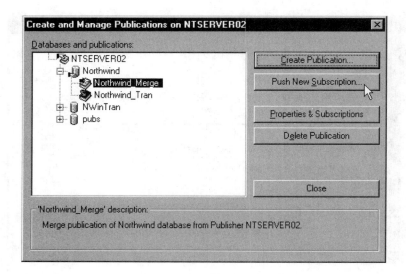

This activates the Push Subscription Wizard. In the first screen, just click on Next. Then click on Enabled Subscribers and select your server in the list.

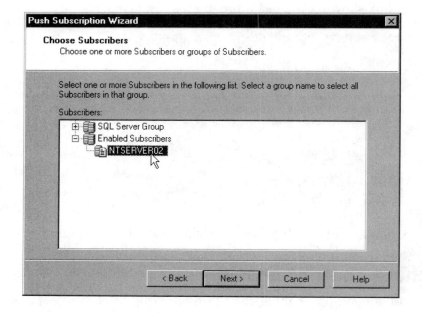

After selecting the subscriber server, click on Next and select the target database.

In this example we need to create another database. To do that, click on Browse Databases to display the following dialog and click on Create New.

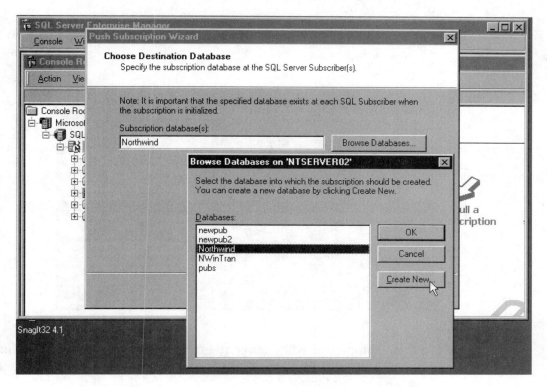

Enter **NwindMerge** as the name of the new database and press the OK button. This returns you to the previous screen. Select this database, and then press OK.

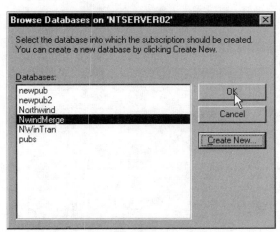

Press Next to bring up a new dialog box. Here you can decide whether the publication will be updated. To change the frequency of updates, use the Change button.

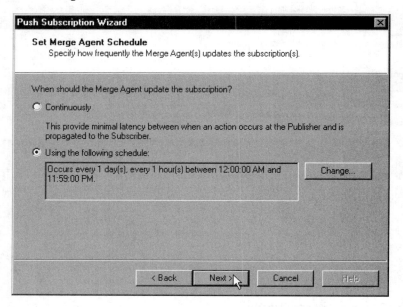

In this example we will change the frequency to 1 minute. Click on the Change button to display a dialog box, and change the field Occurs Every from Hours to Minutes.

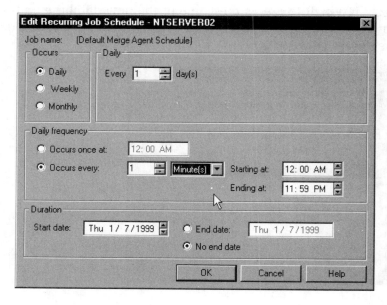

Then click on OK. Click on Next to accept the change.

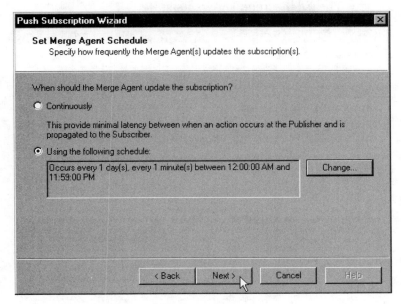

Since we have just created the subscription database, we will start the process of initialization immediately. Select Yes and press Next.

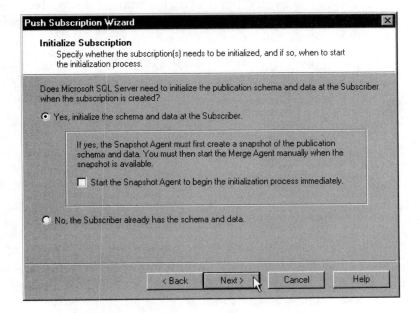

Press Next to proceed. In the next step the SQL Server Agent must be loaded. The next screen shows its state.

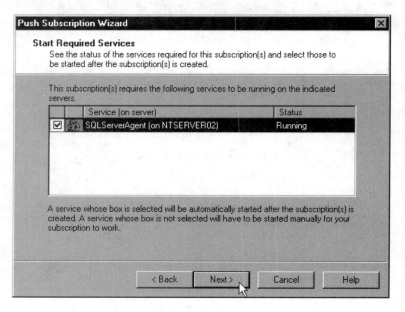

If the column status does not display the word "Running," the SQL Server Agent must be activated before you continue. Click on Next and then click on Finish. A message will indicate that the process is complete. To finish the process, click on the Close button.

To return to the Create and Manage Publications dialog box, press the Close button.

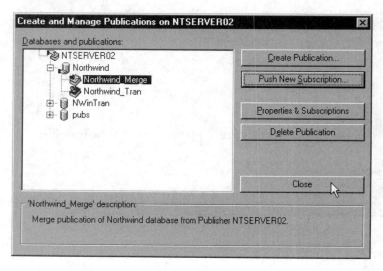

Checking the Replication

To see the status of the replication, click on the item Replication Monitor and expand its items until you find the publication that was created, as shown below.

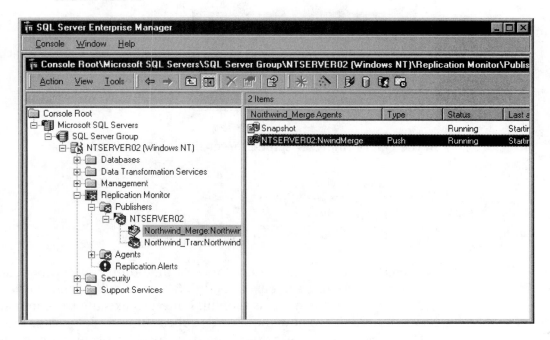

Testing the Replication

To test the replication we will make some changes in the Publishers database and see if they are correctly made. To do that, we will use the Query Analyzer and run some brief code. After each execution we will see what happens in the current table and use the Conflict Solver to eliminate the conflicts.

Using the Query Analyzer

The Query Analyzer must be opened from the SQL 7 menu. In this example, select Use Windows NT Authentication. Press OK.

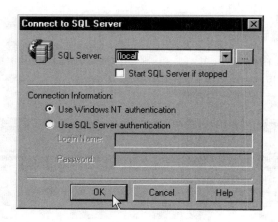

In the Query Analyzer screen, enter the following code:

```
begin tran
        update northwind..products
            set unitprice=20 where productid=1
        update nwindmerge..products
            set unitprice=21 where productid=1
commit tran
```

This code indicates that the unit price of the product with productid 1 be increased to 20 in the publisher and to 21 in the subscriber, causing a conflict between them. Press the Run button to execute the commands. Now it's time to see how the records appear in both databases. If we execute the following code, we will see that the price of the products in both databases is the same.

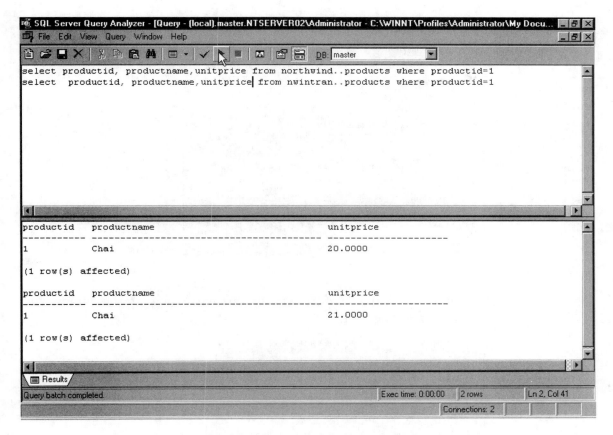

This shows that the Northwind database overwrote the value of the product in the NwindMerge database.

To solve this conflict, use the Enterprise Manager. Select the server used and click with the right mouse button on the NwindMerge database.

In the menu that appears, click on All Tasks and View Replication Conflicts.

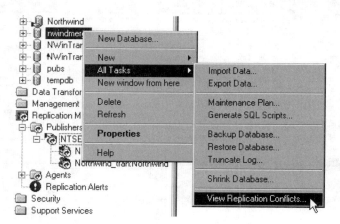

The dialog box of the Conflict Manager appears, showing the data in the database. Press Connect.

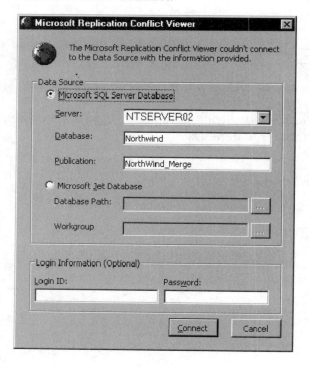

The next screen shows that the table dbo.Products has some problems.

To fix this problem, click on the View button. The next screen displays the reason for the conflict.

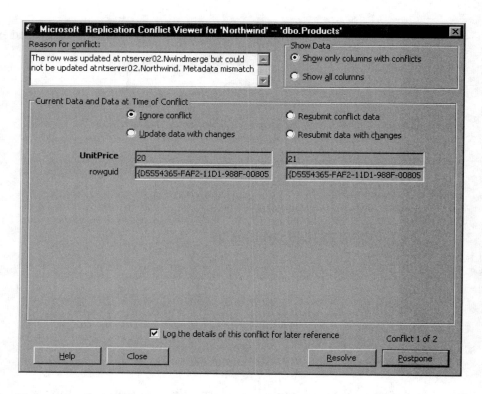

Note that the publisher won the dispute for the updating. Now we can select who is going to win. The changes made are replicated across all the topology. In this case we will keep the changes made by the publisher database. To do that, press the Resolve button. Note the conflict in the Reason for Conflict area.

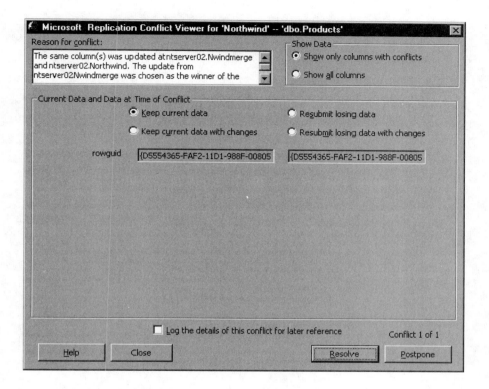

Close the dialog box by pressing the Close button.

Summary

As you have seen, replication is a matter that involves planning and considering how the users use the system in order to provide the best replication. In the next chapter we will discuss data warehouses and their place in the decision support system, one of the strengths of SQL Server 7.

Data Warehousing and OLAP

A data warehouse is used as the basis of a decision support system. It was created to solve some of the problems arising when an organization tries to execute the strategic analysis, using the same database that executes the online transaction processing (OLTP).

A typical OLTP system is characterized by a great number of users who simultaneously add and change data. The database represents the state of a certain business, such as the reservation system of an airline, at a certain moment in time.

However, the great amount of data maintained in many OLTP systems can overwhelm an organization. As the databases grow larger with more complex data, the answer time can quickly deteriorate due to the competition for the available resources.

A typical OLTP system has many users who add data to the database, while a smaller number of users generate reports from the database. As the volume of data increases, the reports take more time to be generated.

However, when the users need to analyze their data, many problems may arise:

➤ As users do not understand the complex relationships among the tables, they cannot generate ad hoc queries.

➤ Because the application database can be segmented across several servers, it is difficult for the users to find the tables.

➤ Security restrictions prevent users from accessing data with the detail level they require.

➤ The database administrators prevent ad hoc queries to OLTP systems, keeping analytical users from performing queries that may decrease the performance of the mission-critical databases of production.

Data warehousing and online analytical processing (OLAP) provide the keys to solve these problems.

Data warehousing is an approach for storing data in which the heterogeneous sources of data (generally spread out in several OLTP databases) are migrated for data storage that is homogeneous and separate. The data warehouses provide these benefits for analytical users:

➤ The data is adequately organized for analytical queries and not for transaction processing.

➤ The differences among the data structures in several heterogeneous databases can be solved.

➤ The rules for data transformation can be applied to validate and consolidate the data when they are moved from the OLTP database to the data warehouse.

➤ The security and performance issues can be resolved without the need for changes in the production systems.

Eventually the organizations may want to maintain the storage of smaller and more topic-oriented data, called data marts. In contrast to a data warehouse, which generally encapsulates all the company's analysis data, a *data mart* usually is a subset of corporate data oriented to the smaller set of users or business functions.

What is a Data Warehouse?

A data warehouse can help the decision support applications and the online analytical processing (OLAP), because it provides data that are:

➤ Consolidated and consistent

➤ Oriented to the subject

➤ Historical

➤ Read only

Consolidated and Consistent Data

A data warehouse consolidates the operational data from a variety of sources with consistent conventions of naming, measures, physical attributes, and semantics.

For example, in many organizations applications use similar data in different formats: the dates can be stored in the Julian or Gregorian formats, true/false data can be represented as one/zero, on/off, true/false, or positive/negative. Different applications also can use different terms to describe the same data type. An application can use the term "balance," while another will use "total amount" to represent the amount of money in a bank account.

The data must be stored in the data warehouse in an exclusive format that is acceptable and agreed to by the business analysts, regardless of the variations of external operational sources. This consolidation allows an organization's data, such as data from legacy mainframes, spreadsheet data, or even data from the Internet, to be consolidated in the data warehouse and to be efficiently cross-referenced, providing the analysts a better understanding of the business.

Subject-Oriented Data

The operational data sources of an entire organization tend to contain a great amount of data about several business-related functions, such as client records, information about products, and so on. However, much of that information is mixed in with data that is not relevant to the business or executive reports, and is organized in a way that makes it difficult to query the data. A data warehouse organizes only the main business information from operational sources, so that it is easily available to the business analysts.

Historical Data

The OLTP system data represents the current value at any moment in time. The OLTP systems often contain only the current data. For example, the order entry application always shows the current value of the inventory; it does not show the inventory from yesterday or two hours ago. Any future query to the inventory can return a different answer.

However, the data stored in a data warehouse is accurate at some point in the past, because the data stored represents the historical information. The data in a data warehouse generally represents the data along a period of time, perhaps ten or more years. Actually, the data warehouses store snapshots of a business's operational data, generated along a certain period of time. They are accurate in a specific moment and generally do not change.

Read-Only Data

As the data stored in a data warehouse represents a point in time, deletions, insertions, and updates (except for those involved in the data loading process) do not apply to a data warehouse. After the data is moved to the data warehouse, it generally does not change, unless it is incorrect. Usually the only operation that occurs in a data warehouse after it is configured is loading the query to data.

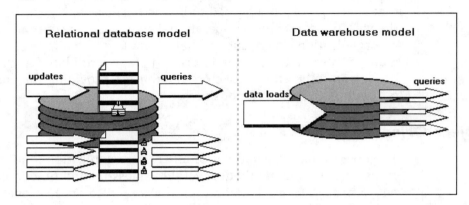

As the data does not change after loading, the design of a data warehouse can be optimized in the queries through an effective use of the indexes, precalculated data, and denormalization of the physical database. When the data does not need to be changed, the OLAP tools can be used to manage the queries with relation to the static data in the warehouse and the dynamic data. For example, a team working on the corporate budget would use the data warehouse data for the figures of the previous year together with the dynamic data, such as budget and forecasts for the current year.

Data Warehousing and OLAP

Although used interchangeably, the terms "data warehousing" and "online analytical processing (OLAP)" are different system components often called decision support components.

A *data warehouse* is a database containing data that generally represents the business history of an organization. The historic data of a data warehouse is used in analysis activities that support business decisions at several levels. The data in a data warehouse is organized to support the analysis, instead of processing transactions in real time, such as in the online transaction processing (OLTP) systems.

OLAP is a technology that processes the data in a data warehouse in multidimensional structures, providing quick answers to complex analytical queries. The purpose of OLAP is to organize and summarize great quantities of data, so it can be quickly analyzed and evaluated, using online tools such as the Microsoft® PivotTable® and graphical representations. The answer to a query to historical data often takes subsequent queries, as the analyst researches answers or explores possibilities. The OLAP system provides the speed and flexibility to support the analyst in real time.

Introducing the Microsoft Decision Support Services

The Microsoft Decision Support Services is a new middle-tier server for online analytical processing (OLAP). The Decision Support Services system includes a powerful server that builds multidimensional cubes of data for analysis and provides quick access of the client to the cube's information. The Microsoft® PivotTable® Service, the client OLE DB 2.0, is used by Microsoft Excel and applications from other vendors to recover multidimensional data from the server and present it to the user.

The Decision Support Services organizes the data from a data warehouse in multidimensional cubes with precalculated summary information to provide quick answers to complex analytical queries.

Among the main resources of the Decision Support Services are:

➤ Unmatched ease of use, provided by the user interface and by the wizards

➤ A data model that is flexible and robust for the cube's definition and storage

➤ The automated solution for the "syndrome of data explosion" that devastates the traditional OLAP technologies

➤ Scalable architecture capable of supporting several OLAP data warehouse servers

➤ Cooperative and smart client/server cache for quick answers to queries and reduction of network traffic

➤ APIs largely supported and documented and open architecture to support client applications

Ease of Use

Integrated Management Console

The Microsoft Decision Support Services includes a graphical administration tool called OLAP Manager. This is a snap-in component of the Microsoft Management Console (MMC). As such, it provides a common structure and a user interface to define, access, and manage OLAP servers and databases. You can use several snap-in components from the MMC; for example, you can install the SQL Server Enterprise Manager and other snap-in components together with the OLAP Manager.

Cube Wizard

You can build all the necessary structures to create an OLAP cube with this easy-to-use wizard. The wizard guides you through the process to create and implement the OLAP, from the mapping of data sources and creation of dimensions to the definition of the measures and population of cubes.

Cube Editor

You can edit the existing cube's structures and create new structures, using simple drag and drop operations. The Cube Editor complements the Cube Wizard, allowing you to examine the cubes you created with the wizard or to quickly create new cubes. The editor integrates three distinct views of the cube:

➤ The **Tree View** panel display a hierarchic view of dimensions, dimension levels, measures, and calculated measures of the cube.

➤ The **Schema** panel displays the real tables of the data warehouse, the dimension tables, and the relationship between them that define the cube's schema. You can change the cube's schema in this panel.

➤ The **Browse** panel displays the data in your cube. You can switch to the data view to check the ongoing work while making changes in the cube's structure. The example data will be generated while the new cube's structure is still being processed; the real data will appear when the cube's structure has not changed since the last cube's processing.

Dimension Wizard

You can create a shared dimension to be used by any cube or a private dimension to be used in only one cube in a quick and easy way with the

Dimension Wizard. You can map columns of the database's dimension table to dimension levels, or you can use the time dimension incorporated to create several time dimensions based on one data and hour column in the database. You can use the Dimension Wizard with flat schemas (single dimension tables) or star or snowflake schemas (multiple dimension tables).

Browsing Cube Data

You can view a cube's data without leaving the OLAP Manager. You don't need to switch to another application in order to check your cube's projects.

Usage Analysis Wizard

The Usage Analysis Wizard helps you to understand how a cube is being used, displaying information registered in the query, such as data, user, answer time, and frequency in a tabular and graphical format.

Usage-Based Optimization Wizard

The Usage-Based Optimization Wizard is used to adjust the cube's performance, based on the real use of the cube by its users. You can guide the wizard to create aggregations to improve performance, based on any combination of users, number of times a query was executed, answer time for the query, storage means where data reside, or the data range.

Tutorial and General Material

The online tutorial can help you master the OLAP Manager in about one hour. Designed for beginners and advanced users of OLAP, this tutorial guides you through the steps to create a basic cube, as well as more advanced operations, such as the creation of partitions and virtual cubes. The tutorial is an excellent tool to learn the OLAP and the operations and resources of the OLAP Manager.

You can also find information on the OLAP and Decision Support Services in the right panel of the OLAP Manager.

Data Storage and Aggregation Wizard

This wizard creates aggregations appropriate to the intended use of your cube and specifies the storage means of the cube's information. The options that are available in this wizard allow you to optimize the exchange between answer time and storage requirement, according to the needs of your application and users.

Virtual Cube Wizard

The Virtual Cube Wizard associates cubes and selects dimensions and measures from them, in order to create a virtual cube. A virtual cube also allows one query to be routed to several cubes, including those cubes that are being executed in different servers. A virtual cube appears for the users as if it were a real cube, but it does not require additional storage space; it is similar to a view of a relational database that associates tables.

OLE DB Data Source Locator Integration

The Decision Support Services uses the Microsoft Data Source Locator component to help the selection of OLE DB or ODBC data sources.

Flexible Data Model

Multiple Data Storage Options

The Microsoft Decision Support Services allow you to determine the storage method that is more appropriate to your system:

➤ **MOLAP:** A cube's basic data is stored together with the aggregation data in a multidimensional structure. The MOLAP storage provides excellent performance and data compression.

➤ **ROLAP:** A cube's basic data is stored together with the aggregation data in a relational database. The ROLAP storage allows you to maximize your investment in relational technology and tools for the management of corporate data.

➤ **HOLAP:** A cube's basic data is stored in a relational database; the aggregation data is stored in a high-performance multidimensional structure. The additional options of HOLAP include virtual cubes and partitions. The HOLAP storage offers the benefits of MOLAP for aggregations, without the need of basic detailed data.

Partitioned Storage

You can partition a logic cube in physically separate sections. You can store each partition in a different view, in a different physical location, and with an aggregation level that is appropriate to the partition's data.

The result is that you can adjust the performance and characteristics of the data management in your system.

Partition Incorporation

After partitioning a cube, you can recombine the partitions into one physical cube. One use for the partition incorporation is to migrate part of the cube's data to other storage devices, so data is used less.

Virtual Cubes

You can associate physical cubes to logical virtual cubes, the way tables can be associated to views in a relational database. A virtual cube provides access to data in the combined cubes, without the need to build a new cube. This allows you to maintain the best design for each individual cube.

Scalability

Partitions

You can spread a cube across several servers, dividing it into partitions. Then the Microsoft Decision Support Services can recover data in parallel in order to attend the queries. The partitioning allows you to manage your storage strategy, to increase the scale with several servers and the performance.

Incremental Updates

A cube can be updated by processing just the data that has changed instead of processing the entire cube. You can also perform quick updates in the OLAP cubes while they are being used.

Support for Oracle 7.3 and 8.0

These versions of Oracle can be used as sources of data warehouses and targets for the storage of ROLAP cubes.

LAN, WAN, Internet, and Mobile Scenarios

The smart cache management integrates the DSS analysis server to the client Microsoft PivotTable Service, minimizing the traffic of the LAN and WAN connections. The PivotTable Service contains an efficient multidimensional calculation engine to further minimize the network traffic and allow the analysis of multidimensional local data when the client is not connected to the server.

Microsoft ActiveX® controls, Active Server Page scripting, and the ADO APIs provide a wide range of solutions for the OLAP query of data in the Web.

Cube Security

Access to the cube is based on the Microsoft Windows NT® security and is managed through the assignment of roles to the cubes.

Windows NT Support for the DEC Alpha Platform

Besides the Intel® platform, the Windows NT for the Digital Equipment Corporation Alpha platform supports all client/server technologies of the Decision Support Services.

Client Support for Windows 95 and Windows 98

The PivotTable Service runs on Microsoft Windows® 95 and Windows 98, supporting the client applications available to these platforms.

Calculated Members

You can use the Cube Editor to create calculated measures and calculated dimension members, combining MDX expressions, mathematical formulas, and user-defined functions. The Calculated Member Builder provides an interface to add MDX expression models to the expression for calculated members. This resource allows you to define new measures and dimensions based on a rich expression syntax that is easier to use.

Server Architecture

The Microsoft Decision Support Services provides server capacities for the creation and management of multidimensional OLAP data and to provide data to clients through the Microsoft® PivotTable® Service. The server operations include the creation of multidimensional data cubes from relational databases of data warehouses and the storage of the cubes in multidimensional structures, in relational databases, and in combinations of both. The metadata of a cube's multidimensional structures are stored in a repository of a relational database.

A user interface is provided through the snap-in for the Microsoft Management Console (MMC). The interfaces are provided to allow customized applications written with Microsoft Visual Basic® 5.0 to interact with the object model that controls the server, as well as the snap-in of the user interface.

The basic server architecture is shown below:

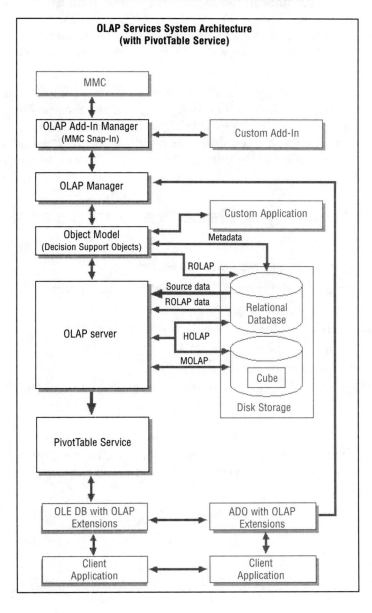

Client Architecture

The Microsoft PivotTable Service communicates with the DSS Analysis server and provides interfaces to be used by the client applications that access the OLAP data in the server. The client applications connect to the PivotTable Service using the interfaces OLE DB 2.0 for C++ or the object model ADO 2.0 for automation languages such as Microsoft Visual Basic®. The PivotTable Service communicates with the server through a proprietary protocol.

The PivotTable Service can also create local cube files containing a cube's data in the server or from OLE DB relational databases. The local cubes can be stored as multidimensional files in the client computer as ROLAP cubes in the relational database, from which they are extracted. The local cubes can be used offline with the PivotTable Service for portable analysis.

Creating and Building a Data Warehouse and OLAP System

The steps to build a data warehouse include:

➤ Determining the requirements of the business, users, and technicians
➤ Creating and building the database
➤ Extracting and loading the data warehouse
➤ Creating and building the OLAP database
➤ Creating and processing aggregations
➤ Querying and maintaining the data warehouse and OLAP databases

Summary

This chapter introduced data warehousing and the OLAP system. The next chapter gives a practical example of using the OLAP manager.

OLAP Manager Practical Example

In this chapter we will develop a cube to query the FoodMart database. The cube will be developed based on its use by the company's marketing department, which wants to evaluate sales from several points of view. Before creating the cube itself, some preparation must be done.

This tutorial uses the FoodMart database found in the FoodMart folder on the companion CD, which should be installed. Follow the instructions in Appendix B to install the CD before you begin this project.

Configuring the DSN

Before continuing we need to configure the connection with the data source we will use in this example. To do that, follow these steps:

From the Start button, activate the Control Panel and double-click on the ODBC Data Sources icon, as shown in the following figure.

Then click on the System DSN tab, highlight FoodMart, and press Add.

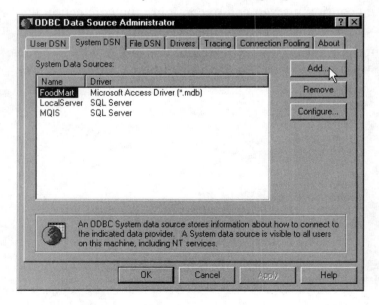

Then choose the Access driver (*.mdb) that must be displayed with the name FoodMart.

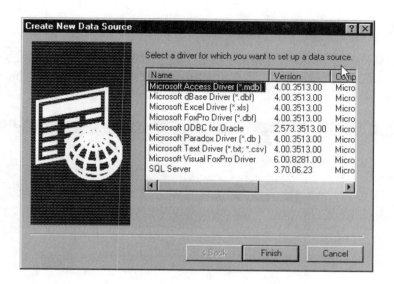

A dialog box displays when you press Finish. Enter a name for the data source. In this example, use **Foodmart** and press the Select button to enter the location of the FoodMart.mdb database. This should already be installed in the \Olap Services\sample folder.

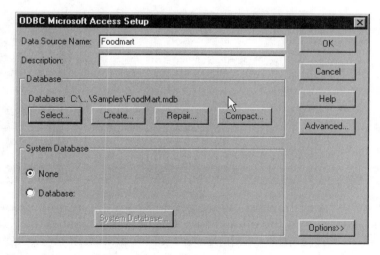

Press the OK button in this dialog box to complete the data source creation.

Loading the OLAP Manager

To load the OLAP Manager, select Start|Programs|Microsoft SQL Server 7.0|OLAP Services|Olap Manager. The working screen of the OLAP Manager is displayed.

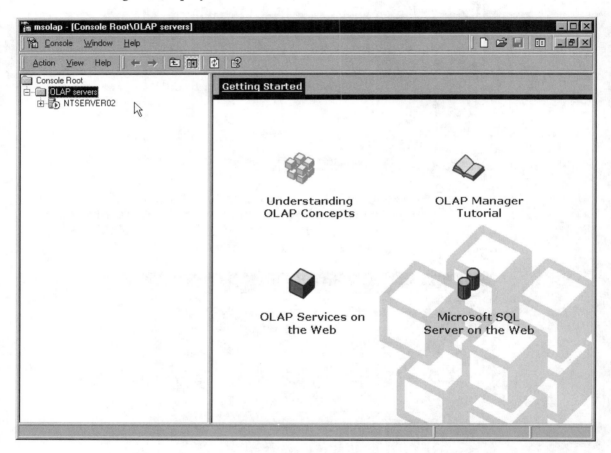

Before we start the process we need to create a new database structure and connect it to the data source we have just created. Click on the plus sign (+) next to the OLAP Servers folder and click on the server used with the right mouse button. In the menu that appears, click on Connect. Then enter the name **Foodmart** in the Database Name field in the dialog box that appears, and press the OK button.

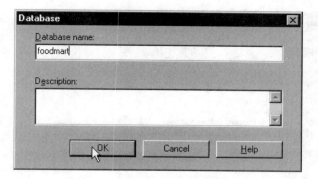

When the FoodMart database is expanded by clicking on the plus sign, notice that it has three folders: Cubes, Virtual Cubes, and Library.

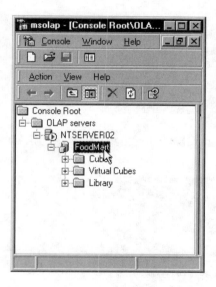

Configuring the Data Source

In the next step we configure the data source. In the tree view of the OLAP Manager, open the Library folder and click with the right mouse button on Data Sources. Then select New Data Source in the menu that appears. In the next screen choose Microsoft OLE DB Provider for ODBC Drivers and press the Next button.

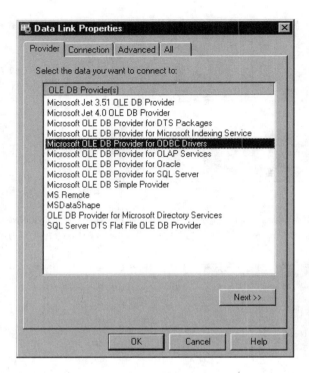

Then click on the Connection tab and select FoodMart in the Use Data Source Name field.

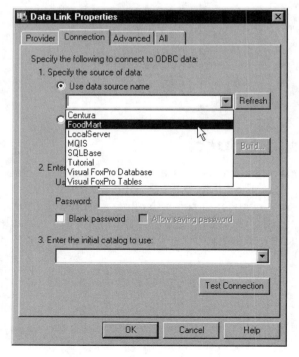

After choosing the FoodMart item, press the Test Connection button; an OK message is displayed. Then close the dialog box by pressing the OK button.

Creating Shared Dimensions

To create a new dimension, click with the right mouse button on the Shared Dimensions folder and then select New Dimension in the popup menu that appears. This brings up the Dimension Wizard.

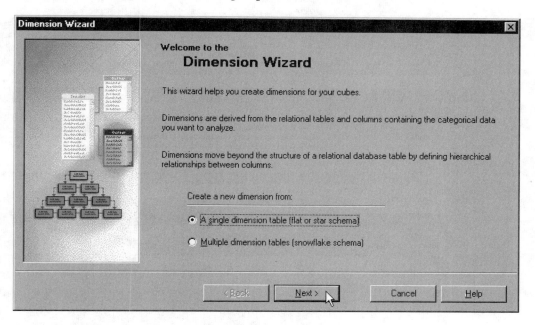

We will create a single dimension. Make sure the button next to Single Dimension Table is selected and click on Next. Then click on the Food-mart database. After expanding it, select the time_by_day table, and press Next.

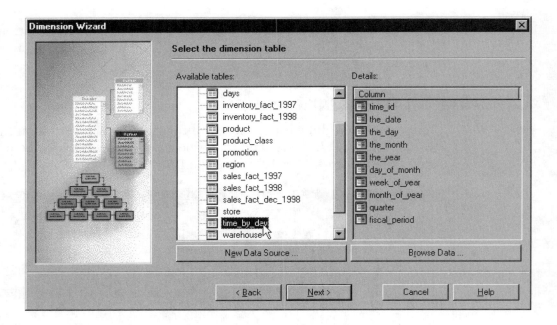

Then we define the dimension type. Choose Time Dimension and press Next.

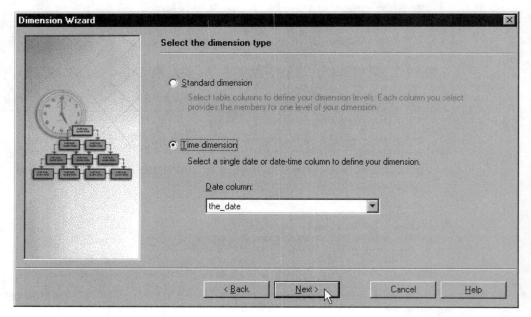

Here, we define the time dimension levels. In this example, we choose Year, Quarter, Month, to create a dimension with subdivisions for year, quarter, and month, and press Next.

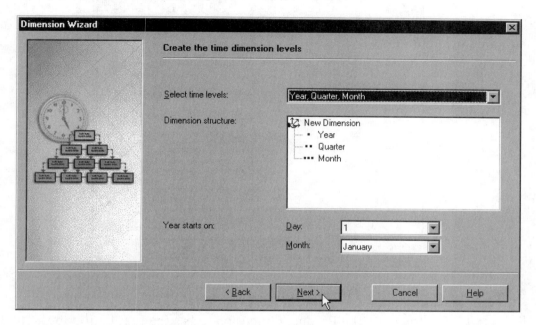

Then we enter the name of the dimension in the last step. Enter **Time1** and press the Finish button. The wizard opens the Dimension Editor illustrated on the following page:

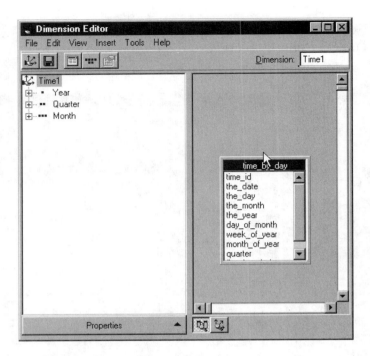

Creating a Product Dimension

To create the Product dimension, press the first button in the tool bar. This activates the Dimension Wizard. Select Multiple Dimension Tables and press the Next button.

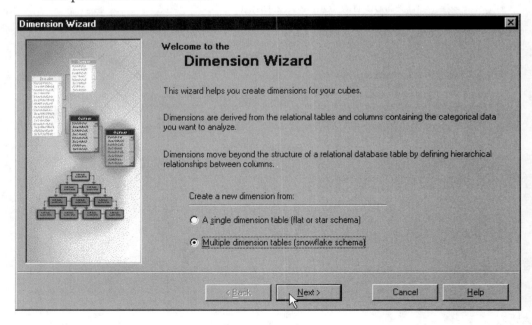

Then select the Product and Product_class tables by double-clicking on them. Press Next.

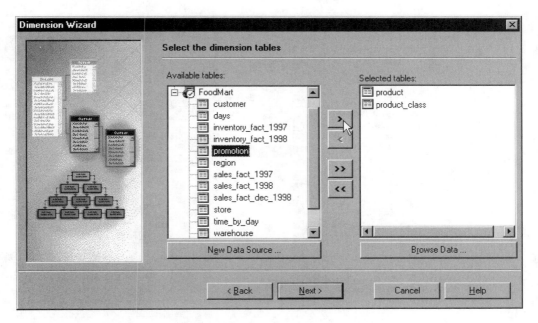

The two tables are displayed with the link that exists between them. Press Next to proceed.

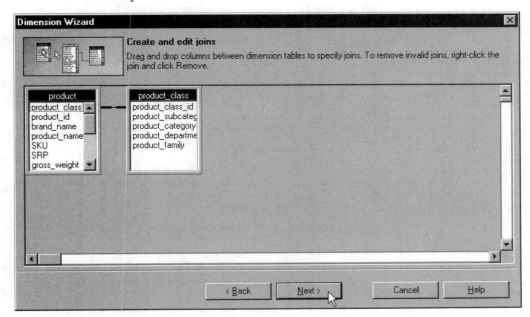

Choose the levels of the dimension that will be formed by the product_category, product_subcategory, and brand_name columns, and press Next.

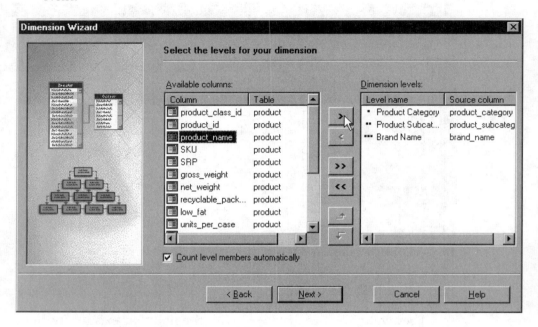

In the last step, enter the name **product1** for this dimension, and press the Finish button.

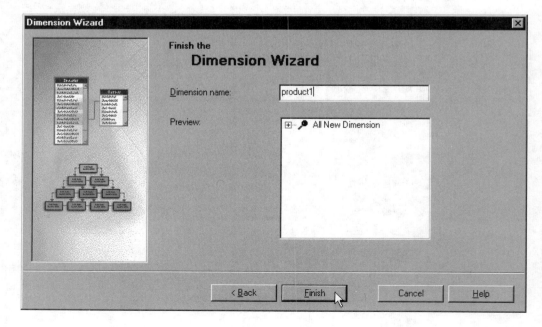

Creating the Store Dimension

There is another dimension in this cube, called the Store dimension. Follow these steps to create it:

Click on the New Dimension button.

In the first screen of the Dimension Wizard, choose the Single Dimension item, and press Next.

Select the FoodMart database and the Store table, and press Next.

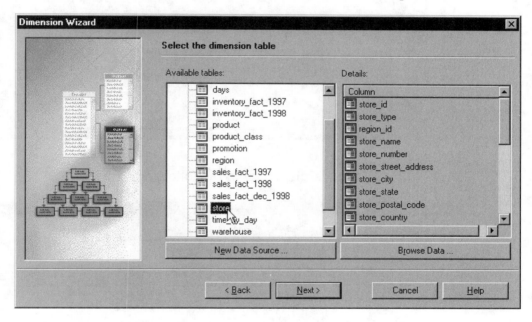

In the next screen that appears, click on Next to keep the Standard Dimension default option.

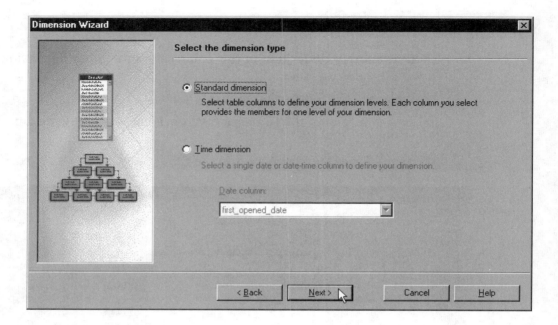

Now select the levels shown in the following figure:

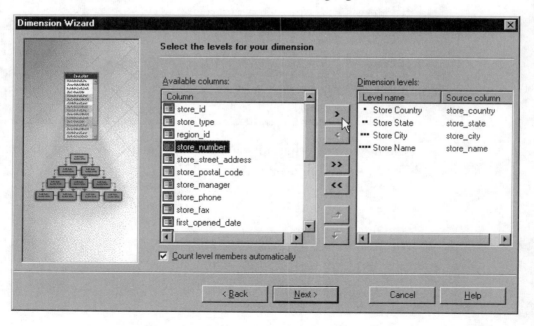

In the last step enter **Store1** as the name of the dimension and press OK.

After closing the Dimension Wizard, press File and Exit. Check to see that all of these are created below the Shared Dimensions folder.

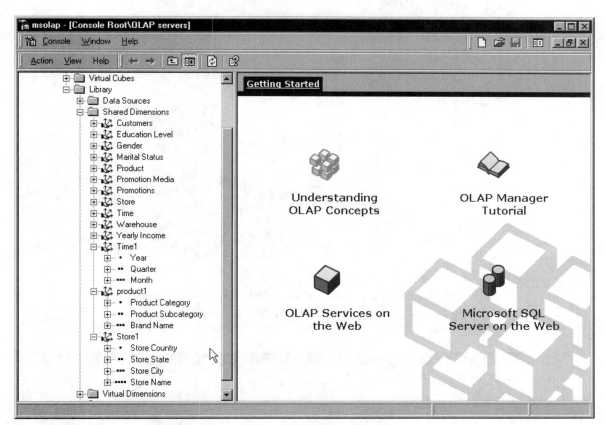

Building the Cube

Now we are going to create a cube that will be used by the marketing department to analyze the company's sales.

To create this cube, click with the right mouse button on the Cubes folder, select New Cube, and choose the wizard. In the first screen, which is simply an informational screen, press Next. Then choose sales_fact_1997 in the FoodMart database. This contains information about sales in 1997.

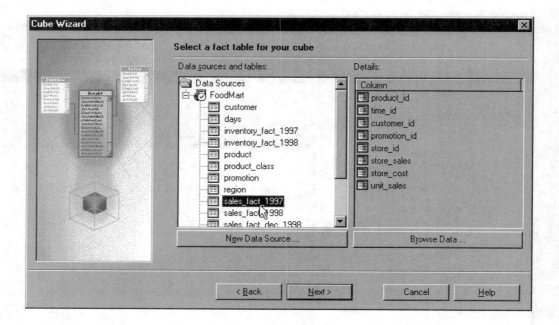

After pressing Next, select the numeric columns that will be used in the next step. The following figure shows the selected columns. They are store_sales (sales), store_cost (costs), and unit_sales (unit sales).

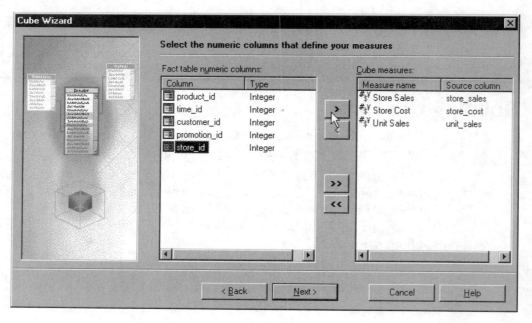

Press Next and select the dimensions for the cube. Since we want to use all three of the dimensions, click on the first button with double arrows to select all of them.

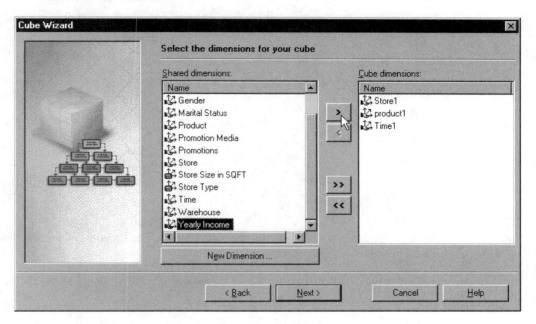

Creating a Dimension Quickly

Before completing the cube's creation, you can add new dimensions at any time. Just press the New Dimension button to activate the wizard again. In this section, we will create a dimension called Promotion, following these steps:

Choose the Single Dimension table and press Next.

Select either the Tutorial database or the Promotion table in the Food-Mart database. Then press Next.

Select Standard Dimension and press Next.

Choose the media_type and promotion_name columns, and press Next.

Enter **promotion1** as the name of the dimension, and press Next.

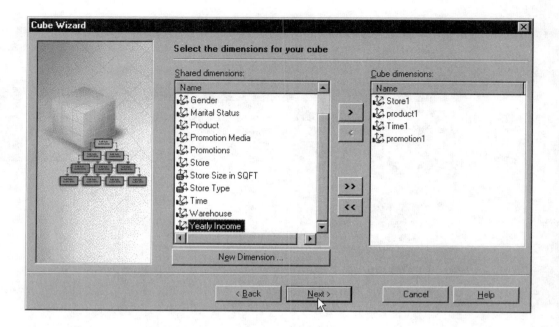

In the last step enter **Sales1** as the cube's name and press the Finish button.

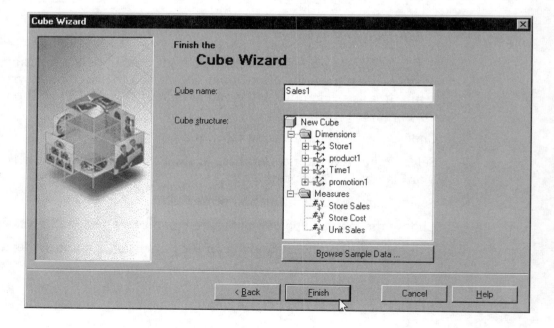

All dimensions will now be available below the Shared Dimensions folder.

Editing the Cube

The Cube Editor should open automatically. If not, expand the FoodMart database tree, click on the Sales cube with the right mouse button, and select the Edit Cube option. The Cube Editor will open, displaying a graphical interface formed by two panels.

The left panel of the Cube Editor is the cube tree view. At the right is the schema panel with a graphical display of the cube's structure. The fact table is shown with a yellow title bar and the dimension tables are shown with blue title bars.

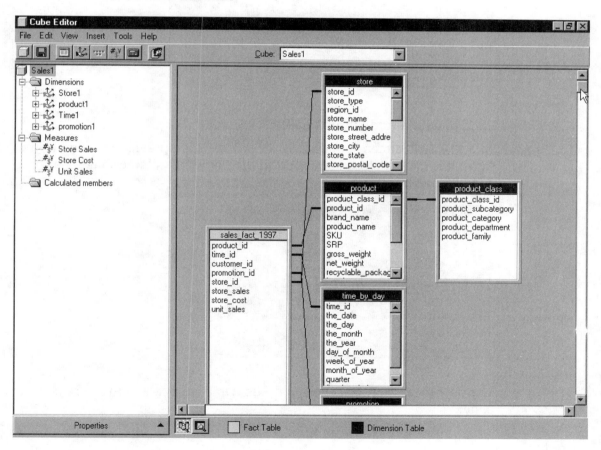

Adding New Dimensions

Using the Cube Editor we will add a dimension containing the demographic data of the clients. To add new dimensions, activate the Insert menu and the Tables option. In the dialog box that appears, select the Customer table in the FoodMart database.

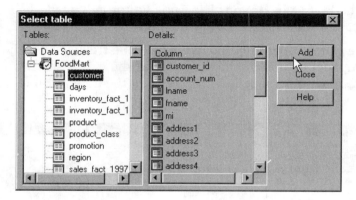

Then press the Add button and the Close button.

To add a new dimension, double-click in the state-province column of the Customer table. Select Dimension in the Map The Column dialog box, and press OK.

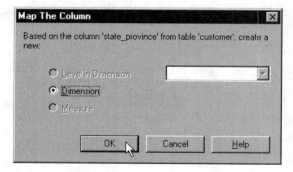

The new dimension is displayed in the database tree and in the schema panel.

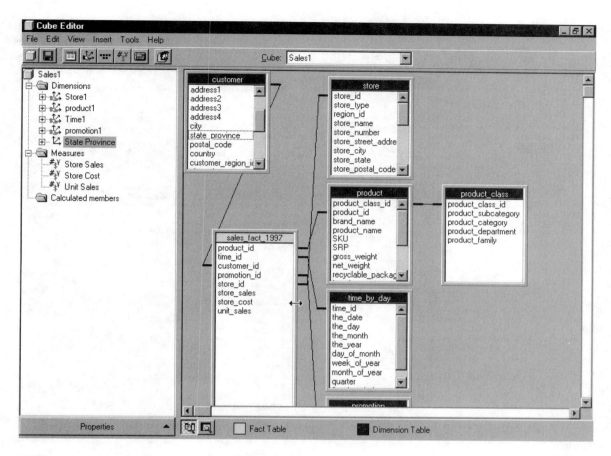

Changing the Name of a Dimension

To change the name of a dimension, right-click on it in the database tree and then choose Rename, or activate the Edit menu and select the Rename option. Select state_province in the tree, and use the Edit|Rename option.

Enter **customer1** as the new name for the dimension. To add another item, click and drag the City column of the Customer table in the schema panel to the Customer table of the view tree. The Customer dimension will then be composed of State Province and City.

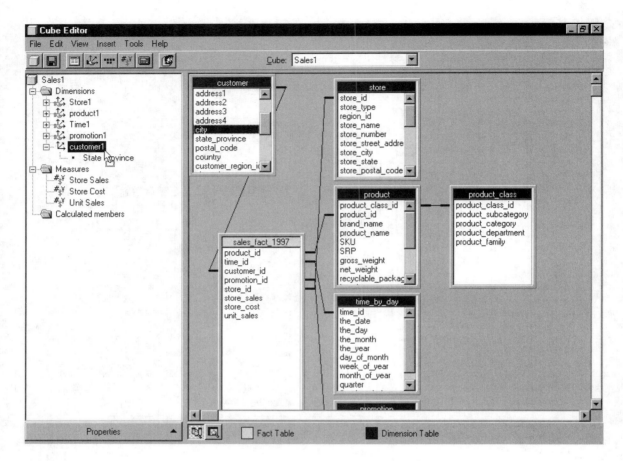

Adding Roles

A role defines the users or user groups that can access the data in the cube you create. In this section, we will create a role that allows several users to access the cube. To create a role, activate the Tools menu and the Manage Roles option. In the dialog box that appears, press the New Role button.

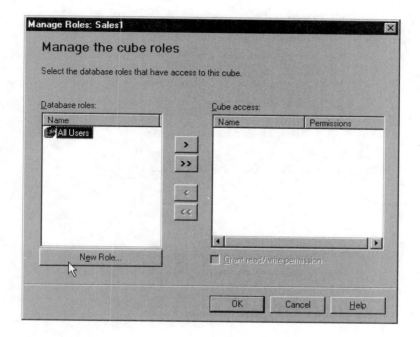

Enter the name of the role in the Role Name box; in this example, use
Marketing1. Then select the users that can use the cube by pressing the
Groups and Users button. Here, you can select the users that will have
access, or you can simply enter your user name if you do not want to
grant access to others. Select all the users of the database (in this example, the database is NTSERVER02).

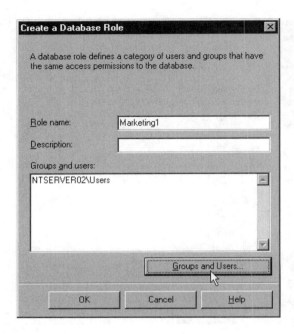

That's all. Press OK to proceed to the last screen, shown below.

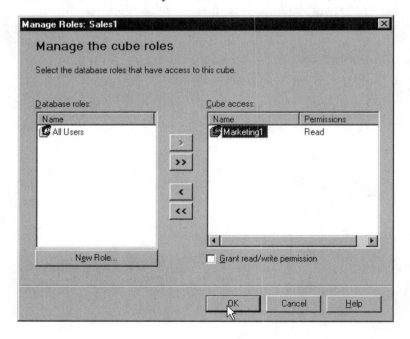

When you press the OK button, the role creation is complete.

Designing Aggregations

To get the best performance in queries you should execute the Storage Design Wizard before starting the query process.

Select Tools|Storage Design. This activates the Storage Design Wizard. Press next in the first screen.

The type of storage we will use is MOLAP. Select it and press Next.

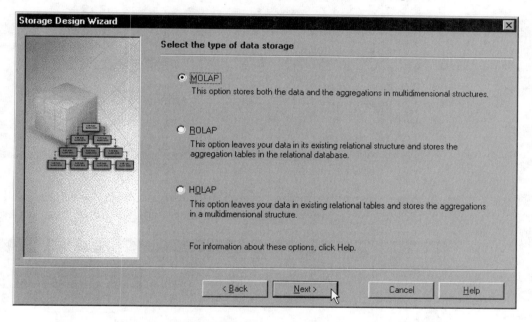

In the next step, set the aggregation options by selecting Performance Gain Reaches and entering **40**. This indicates to the DSS that it must improve the performance by up to 40 percent, no matter how much disk space is used.

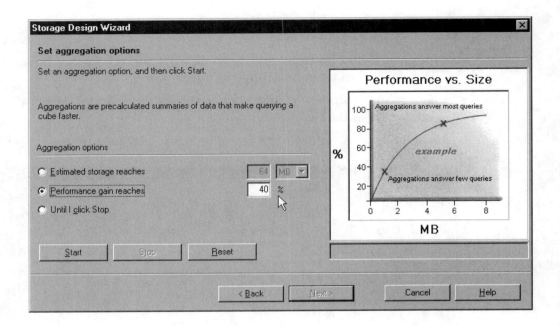

Press Start to begin the process. In a few moments, a window will show the number of aggregations executed to achieve the requested percentage.

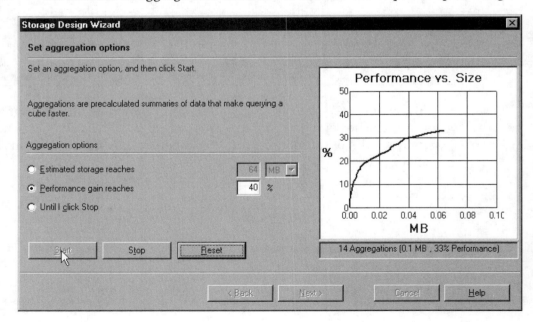

Then press Next and select the default option to save the aggregations when the Finish button is pressed. The process starts and a panel shows its progress.

When it finishes, press Next, choose the default option (Process Now), and press Finish.

The cube processing task begins and its progress is shown in a panel.

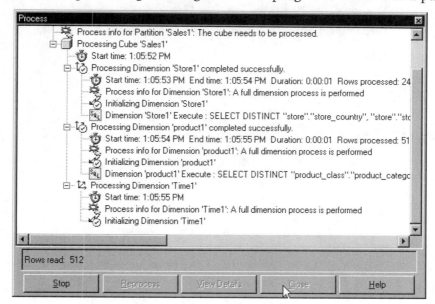

When a message appears saying the process is over, press the Close button. If it fails, press the View Details button to see what happened.

Navigating with the Cube

Finally we can navigate by the cube. You perform this task with the Browse Data option, which can be activated in the quick menu by clicking with the right mouse button on the name of the cube, Sales in this example.

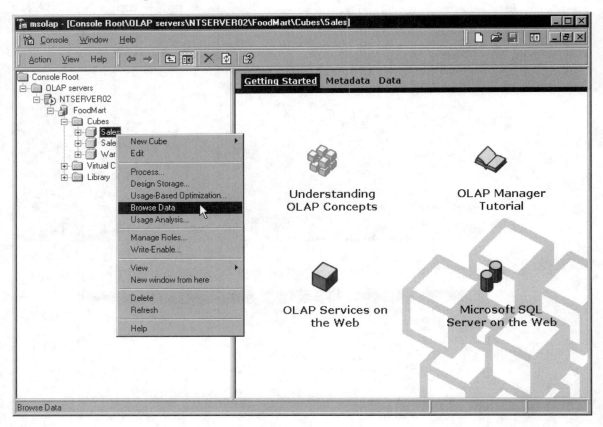

The Cube Browser appears. It has two main parts: At the top is the dimension panel and at the bottom is the grid.

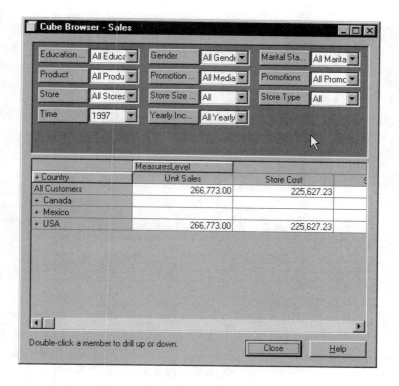

You can filter the data that is displayed by clicking on the selecting list that appears next to the name of the dimension and selecting a specific item.

You can also change the dimension in the grid, replacing one dimension with another dimension you select in the dimension panel. To do this, just click and drag the desired dimension in the dimension panel above the dimension you want to replace in the grid. As an example, we will drag the Product dimension above the MeasureLevel dimension. The screen on the next page shows the results.

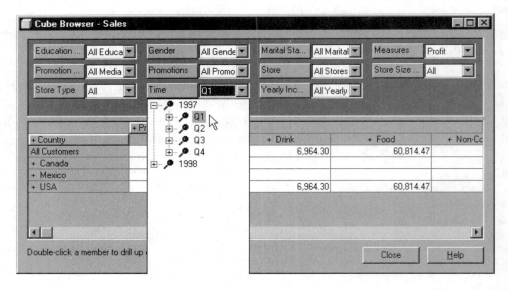

If you want to add a dimension to the grid, drag the dimension and drop it in an area that has no other dimension.

To filter the displayed data, select the filtering level in the selection list. The next screen shows how to select a filter for the first quarter of 1997.

To expand a category, double-click on it.

Summary

Working with cubes is a task that requires thorough knowledge of the database, particularly of the user's information needs. The steps to prepare the cube are vital to the correct design of a model that satisfies the users. However, once the cube is completed, its operation is extremely simple and any user of a spreadsheet will be using the cube with ease in just a few minutes.

Data Transformation Services, an important component of SQL Server 7.0, is discussed in the next chapter.

Data Transformation Services

One of the most interesting modules of SQL Server 7.0 is the Data Transformation Services (DTS). With the DTS you can convert data from the SQL Server to other data formats that are compatible with OLE DB, ODBC, and text files. The use of the OLE DB allows native access to data in OLE DB providers, such as Access, Excel, and the SQL Server itself. You can also access data sources such as Oracle, Sybase, DB2, and other sources that have an ODBC provider, as well as export data to create pivot tables in an Excel spreadsheet. The DTS is a basic element for the creation of databases for decision support, thus helping with data gathering and transformation.

Concepts

Importing and Exporting Data

Importing or exporting means converting data between applications that use different data formats so the local or external application can work with the information.

Transforming Data

Data transformation is the set of operations performed on a data source before it is written to its target location. For example, a column in a table can be the result of the transformation and calculations applied to several columns and rows from one or more tables.

Architecture

A DTS package is, in essence, a detailed description of the operations that must be performed to import, export, or transform a piece of data. A DTS package can include the copying of tables among databases and the transforming of data from one format to another using ODBC, ActiveX,

SQL commands, or even external programs that can be part of a DTS package.

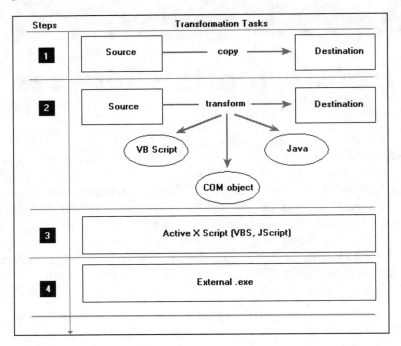

By using different technologies and the COM architecture, you can easily create the basic structure of the data warehouses.

Ways to Create a DTS Package

A DTS package can be created in two ways, either with the DTS Package Designer or with a wizard. The Data Transformation Services Package Designer is a graphical tool designed for more advanced users to consolidate, transform, and integrate heterogeneous data that comes from several sources. Through the use of the DTS Package Designer you can define the workflow and the data flow, and save them in the SQL Server repository.

The DTS Import and Export Wizards are similar to other wizards that interact with the user.

The functionality of the DTS is limited by the capacities of the OLE DB drivers or the data sources. Through the use of the wizards you can import, export, and transform data from the following sources:

➤ dBase and Paradox
➤ ASCII texts with a fixed field size
➤ ODBC data sources
➤ SQL Server databases
➤ Excel spreadsheets
➤ Access and FoxPro files
➤ OLE DB data sources specified by the user

Among the operations performed by the wizards are:

➤ Executing ActiveX, JScript, PerlScript, and VBScript scripts
➤ Copying an entire table or the result of a SQL query
➤ Building a query inside the wizard
➤ Changing the name, data type, size, precision, scale, and acceptance of Null values of one column during the copy from the source to the target
➤ Saving the DTS package in a SQL Server database, and programming its execution

Creating a DTS Package

In this section, we will see an example of how to create a DTS package using the DTS Package Designer. This task consists of transforming the NorthWind database into a database called DWStar. You can follow along with the steps for the procedure or simply examine the steps through the screens shown in this section. The first step is to create a database called NWStar that is the same size as the NorthWind database. Then follow these steps:

Start the Enterprise Manager and connect to your server by clicking on the plus sign next to SQL Server Group, and then clicking on the name of the server, NTSERVER02 in this example.

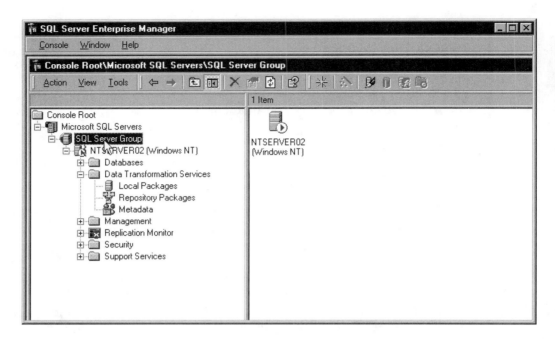

Right-click on the Data Transformation Services folder and on Local Packages. In the menu that appears, select New Package. The DTS package tool appears.

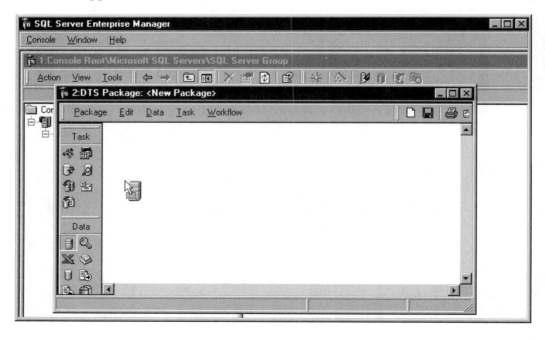

Then click and drag SQL Server 7 (the server icon in the left of the work area window below the word Data in the toolbar) to create a connection. This will open the Connection Properties dialog box.

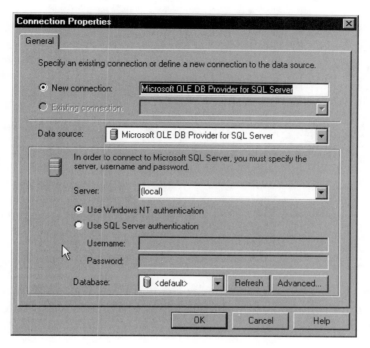

In the New Connection field, enter **DWStar** as shown in the screen on the following page. Select Use Windows NT Authentication. Click on Refresh to update the list of databases and select NWStar in the Database field.

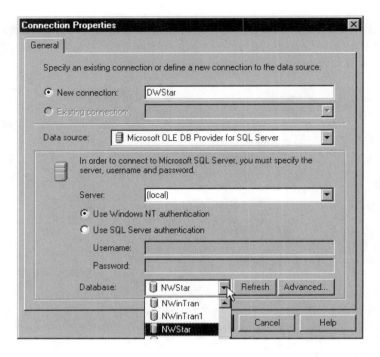

Press the OK button. The work area will show that we now have a connection. Each dimension that we want to fill out or populate must have its own connection.

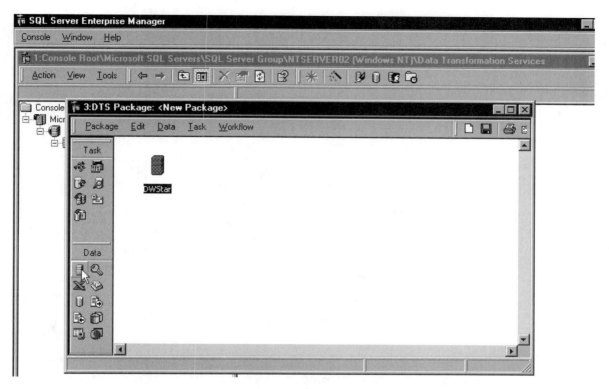

In this example we will create five connections. To create the second connection, click and drag the SQL Server 7 icon to the work area. When the Connection Properties dialog box appears, enter **NorthWind** in the New Connection field, check Use Windows NT Authentication, click on Refresh, and select Northwind from the database list.

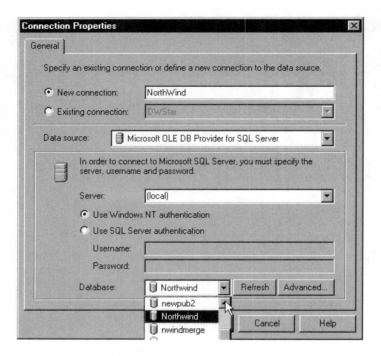

Press the OK button to complete the creation. We will use a different method to add the remaining connections. Instead of creating a new connection, we will use an existing connection. To do this, press or drag the SQL Server 7 icon to the work area. In the Connection Properties dialog box, check the Existing Connection item, and select NorthWind in the drop-down list.

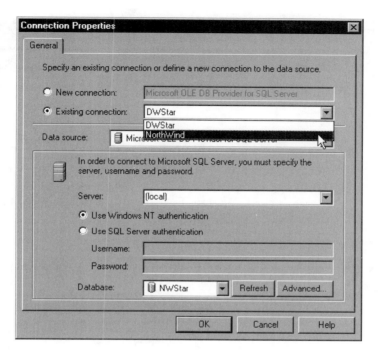

Press the OK button again to have the connection displayed in your work area. Repeat this process to create additional NorthWind connections for a total of five connections. Use this procedure to create a second DWStar connection. Your work should appear similar to that shown in the figure on the following page.

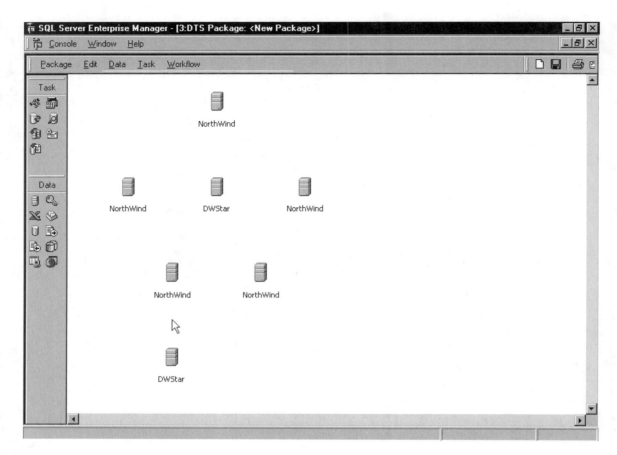

Transforming Data

The next step of the process consists of creating links for the data flow. Click on the NorthWind icon at the top of the screen. Then, keep the Ctrl key pressed while clicking on the central DWStar icon, as shown in the next figure. Click with the right button on the DWStar icon and select Workflow|Transform Data.

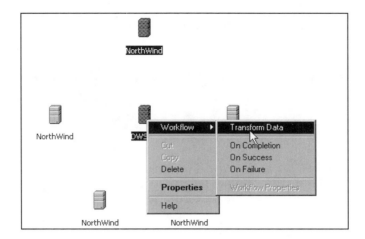

An arrow will connect the icons.

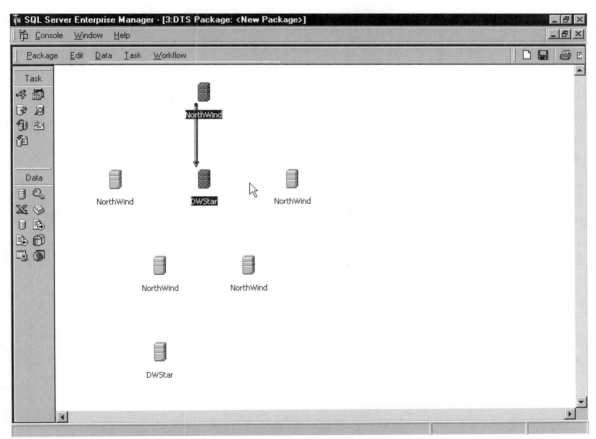

Repeat this procedure with three other NorthWind connections, as shown below.

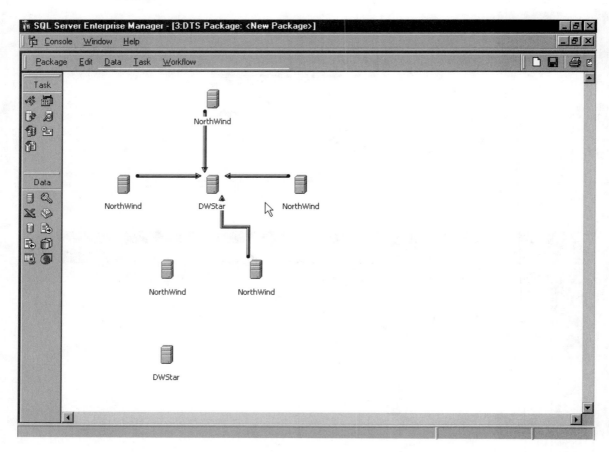

Now we will create another link between the remaining Northwind and DWStar icons, as shown in the next figure.

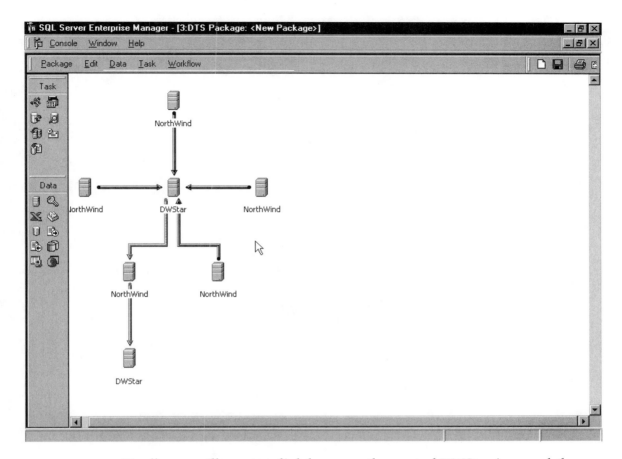

Finally, we will create a link between the central DWStar icon and the unlinked NorthWind icon.

This time, click on the first DWStar icon and then keep the Ctrl key pressed and click on NorthWind. Right-click on the NorthWind icon, and select Workflow|On Success.

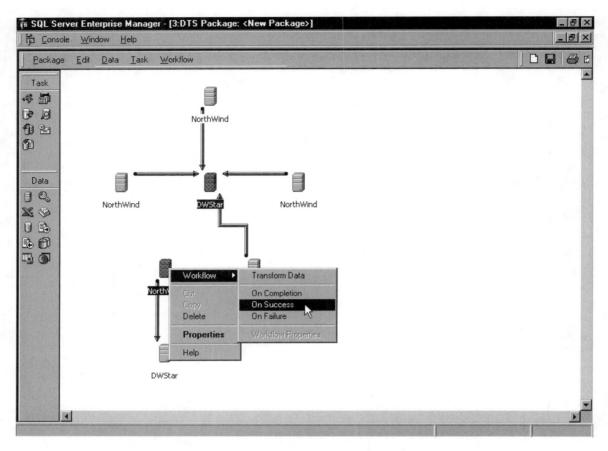

Note that the arrow line assumes a different format.

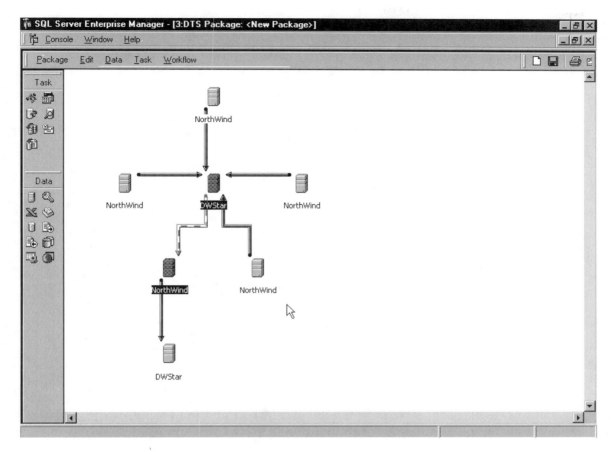

Double-click on the line linking the NorthWind icon at the top of the screen to the DWStar icon in the middle of the screen. In the dialog box that appears, enter **Load Time Dimension** in the Description box and select the SQL Query item. In the SQL Query field, enter the Time Dimension query. This query can be found at the end of this chapter, along with the other queries.

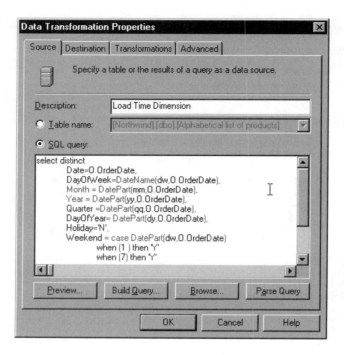

After entering the query's contents, click on the Destination tab. In the Table Name field, select NWStar.DBO.Time in the list. (If this table was not previously created, open a window with the Create New button. Replace the name of the table with **Time** in the first line of the command, and the table will be created.)

Then click on the Transformations tab and select all the columns displayed in the Source and Destination tables.

Select Copy Column in the New Transformation box, and press the OK button. The columns are mapped showing their correspondence.

Click on OK to finish.

Customer Dimension

Now we will create the Customer Dimension. Double-click on the line linking the NorthWind icon on the left side of the work area and the central DWStar icon.

In the Description field, enter **Load Customer Dimension**. Then check the SQL Query item and enter the contents of the customer dimension provided at the end of this chapter.

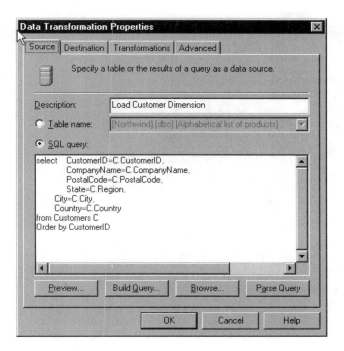

Select the Destination tab and NWStar.DBO.Customer or create a new table by clicking on the Create New button, and providing the name in the appropriate location of the Create Table command.

In the Transformations tab, select all the fields of the Source and Destination tables. Select Copy Column in the New Transformation box and press OK to map the columns.

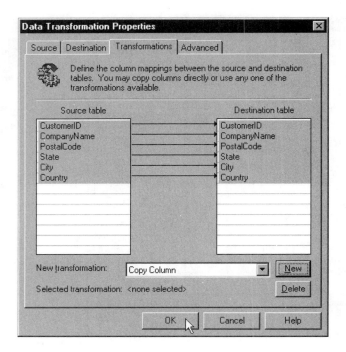

The Geography Dimension

Now we will create the Geography Dimension. Double-click on the line that links the right NorthWind icon and the DWStar icon. In the dialog box that appears, enter **Load Geography Dimension** in the Description field. Check the SQL Query item and enter the contents of the appropriate query (found at the end of this chapter).

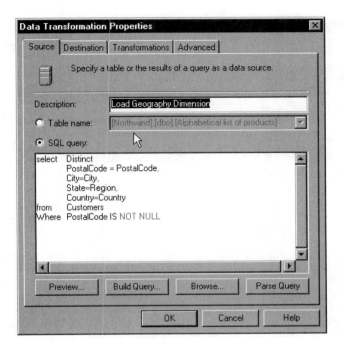

Click on the Transformations tab. (If this table was not previously created, open a window with the Create New button. Replace the name of
the table with **Geography** in the first line of the command, and the
table will be created.)

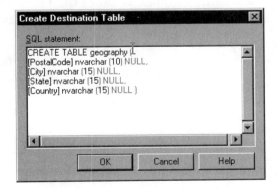

Select all the fields in the Source and Destination tables. Then select
Copy Column in the New Transformation box and press OK.

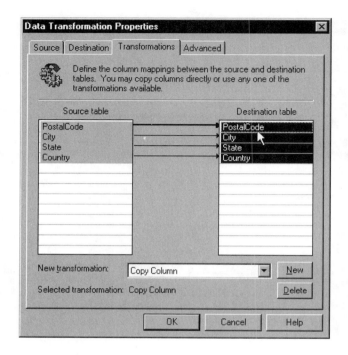

The columns were mapped showing their correspondence.

The Products Dimension

This dimension is created with a double-click on the line linking the NorthWind icon at the bottom right of the screen and the DWStar icon in the middle of the screen.

In the Description item, enter **Load Products Dimension**. Select the SQL Query item and enter the corresponding query listed at the end of the chapter.

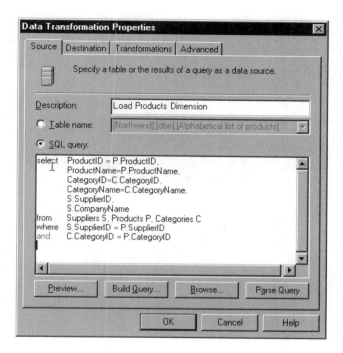

In the Destination tab, select NWStar.DBO.Products in the Table Name box. (You can create the table if it does not exist by clicking the Create New button.)

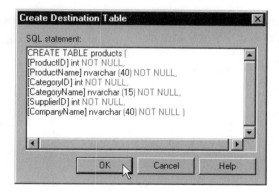

In the Transformations tab, select all the fields of the Source and Destination tables. Select Copy Column in the New Transformation box. Press the OK button.

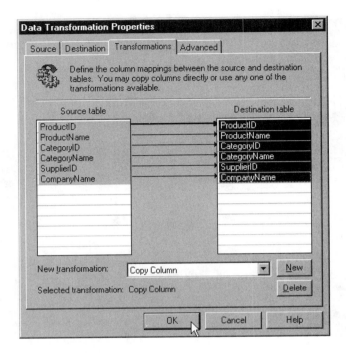

Press the OK button to finish.

The Orders Fact Table

Next we will create a link between the DWStar icon at the bottom of the screen and the NorthWind icon near it.

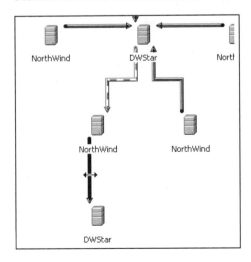

Double-click on the line that links the icons; the Data Transformation Properties dialog box will appear. On the Source tab, enter **Load Orders Fact Table** in the Description field, select SQL Query, and enter the Orders Fact Table code found at the end of the chapter in the SQL Query window.

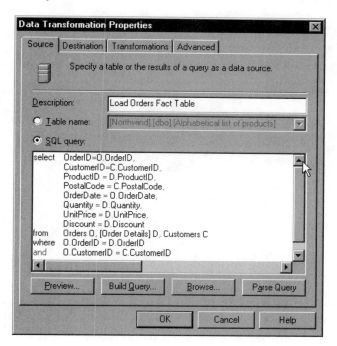

In the Destination tab, select or create NWStar.DBO.Orders (you can create the table if it does not exist by clicking the Create New button).

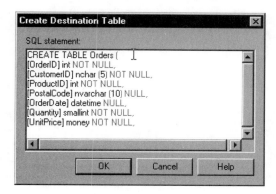

In the Transformations tab, select all the fields of the Source and Destination tables. Select Copy Column in the New Transformation box. Press the OK button.

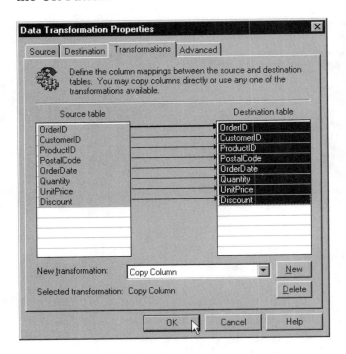

We are almost finished. All we need to do is save the DTS package. To do that, click on the Save Package button on the toolbar.

Enter **Transform NorthWind** as the package name in the Save DTS Package dialog box, and press the OK button.

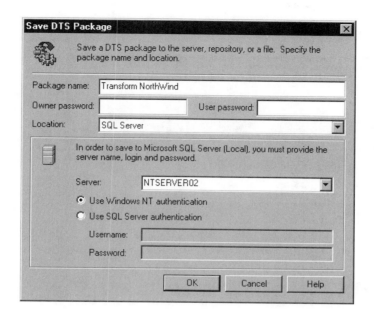

Executing a DTS Package

Press the Execute button on the toolbar.

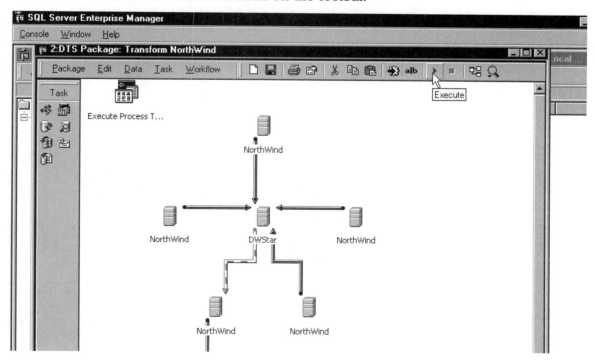

Observe as the package is being executed.

If there is anything wrong, the execution status will indicate an error.

We have just transformed a database. In this example we created an exact copy of the first database in the second database, using the SQL Server itself as the source. See the figure on the following page.

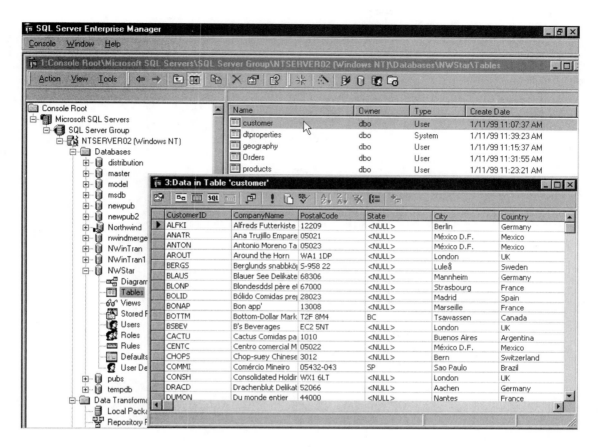

This same procedure can be used to gather data from an Oracle, Sybase, or DB2 database and to create a new SQL database or any other database with a format supported by the product.

Following are the queries to enter in the SQL Query field for each respective query.

```
****************** Queries to DWStar schema ***********************************

-- Time Dimension
select distinct
            Date=O.OrderDate,
            DayOfWeek=DateName(dw,O.OrderDate),
            Month = DatePart(mm,O.OrderDate),
            Year = DatePart(yy,O.OrderDate),
            Quarter =DatePart(qq,O.OrderDate),
            DayOfYear= DatePart(dy,O.OrderDate),
            Holiday='N',
```

```
                        Weekend = case DatePart(dw,O.OrderDate)
                            when (1 ) then 'Y'
                            when (7) then 'Y'
                            else 'N'
                            end,
                        YearMonth = DateName(month, O.OrderDate) + '_' +
                                        DateName(year,O.OrderDate),
                        WeekOfYear=DatePart(wk,O.OrderDAte)
                        from Orders O

-- Customer Dimension
select                  CustomerID=C.CustomerID,
                        CompanyName=C.CompanyName,
                        PostalCode=C.PostalCode,
                        State=C.Region,
                        City=C.City,
                        Country=C.Country
from                    Customers C
Order by                CustomerID

-- Geography Dimension
select                  Distinct
                        PostalCode = PostalCode,
                        City=City,
                        State=Region,
                        Country=Country
from                    Customers
Where                   PostalCode IS NOT NULL

-- Products Dimension
select                  ProductID = P.ProductID,
                        ProductName=P.ProductName,
                        CategoryID=C.CategoryID,
                        CategoryName=C.CategoryName,
                        S.SupplierID,
                        S.CompanyName
from                    Suppliers S, Products P, Categories C
where                   S.SupplierID = P.SupplierID
and                     C.CategoryID = P.CategoryID

-- Orders Fact Table
select                  OrderID=O.OrderID,
                        CustomerID=C.CustomerID,
                        ProductID = D.ProductID,
                        PostalCode = C.PostalCode,
                        OrderDate = O.OrderDate,
                        Quantity = D.Quantity,
```

```
                  UnitPrice = D.UnitPrice,
                  Discount = D.Discount
from              Orders O, [Order Details] D, Customers C
where             O.OrderID = D.OrderID
and               O.CustomerID = C.CustomerID
order by          OrderID, ProductID
```

Summary

This chapter introduced the Data Transformation Services, and demonstrated the creation of DTS dimensions. The next chapter shows how to export data using the DTS Export Wizard.

DTS Practical Example

In this chapter we will see how to export data from SQL Server to other types of file using the Export Wizard.

Using the Export Wizard

First, expand the database tree and click with the right mouse button on the Data Transformation Services folders. Then click All Tasks|Export Data. Press the Next button in the first screen of the wizard. In the second screen, choose Microsoft OLE DB Provider for SQL Server in the Source field. Check the Use Windows NT Authentication item, and select the Pubs database in the Database field.

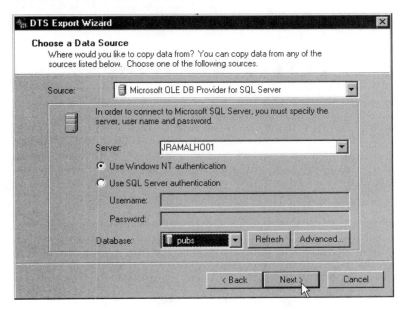

Press Next. In the Destination field, select Microsoft Excel 8.0 (Excel 97). In the File Name field, select the name of the spreadsheet that will receive the data. In this example we have created a blank spreadsheet named testimport.xls in the MSSQL7\Data directory. Press Next.

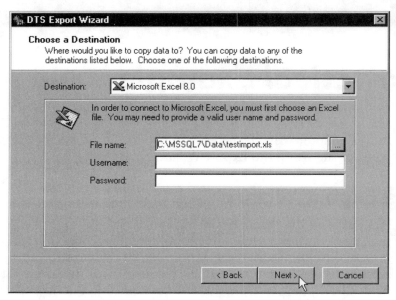

In our example we want to copy all the tables of the database. Optionally, we could create a query to filter the tables and rows to be copied. Select Copy Table(s) from the Source Database and press Next.

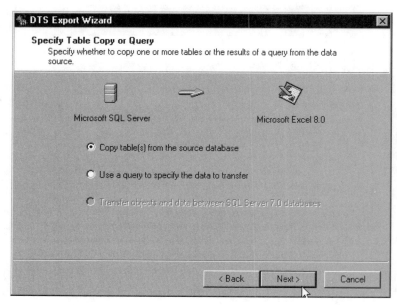

In this example, we will select the Authors, Titles, and Titleauthor tables.

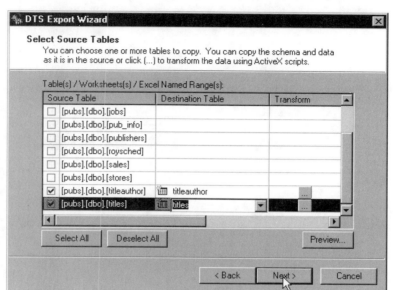

Press Next. (If you want to transform some of the columns during the copy, just press the button in the Transform column. We won't show that process in this example.)

In the Column Mappings and Transformations dialog box, shown on the following page, you can change the characteristics of the table that will be created in the destination location. In the Transformations tab you can specify a script in VBScript, JavaScript, or PerlScript to transform or process columns in the original table.

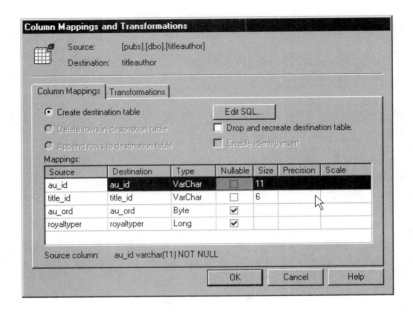

Now let's come back to the original process. After pressing Next in the dialog box where you selected the tables, another screen appears asking if you want to execute the export operation now. Select Run Immediately and press Next.

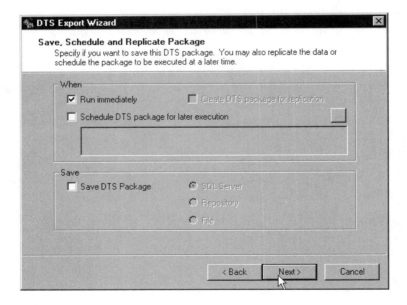

The last screen of the wizard shows a summary of what will be done. Just press the Finish button to complete the process. The results are shown in the following screen.

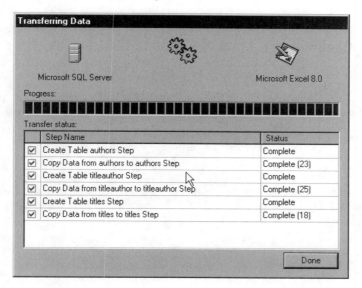

Notice in the figure on the following page that in the workbook of the Excel spreadsheet specified as the destination location there are three pages, one for each table.

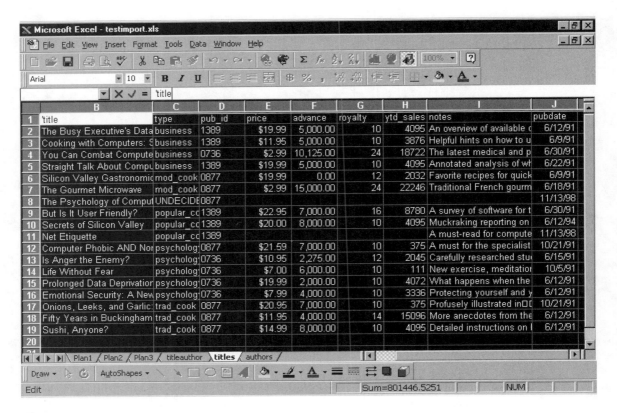

Summary

This chapter demonstrated how to export data using the Export Wizard. The next chapter describes some of the graphical tools that come with SQL Server.

Tools

Overview

SQL Server 7.0 comes with a set of graphical tools that simplify or speed up the execution of the administrative tasks. These tools are described below:

- ➤ Microsoft Management Console
- ➤ SQL Server Client Network Utility
- ➤ SQL Server Enterprise Manager
- ➤ SQL Server Network Utility
- ➤ Performance Monitor
- ➤ SQL Server Profiler
- ➤ SQL Server Query Analyzer
- ➤ SQL Server Service Manager
- ➤ SQL Server Setup
- ➤ Version Upgrade Wizard

Below is a brief description of each of these tools. Some of them have already been discussed in earlier chapters, but others will be detailed here.

Microsoft Management Console

The Microsoft Management Console (MMC) is the basic interface for managing a BackOffice server. It is located behind several tools such as the SQL Server Enterprise Manager or OLAP Manager.

SQL Server Client Network Utility

The SQL Server Client Network Utility is a tool designed to manage the client configuration for network connections defined by the user and for the DB-Library and Net-Libraries.

277

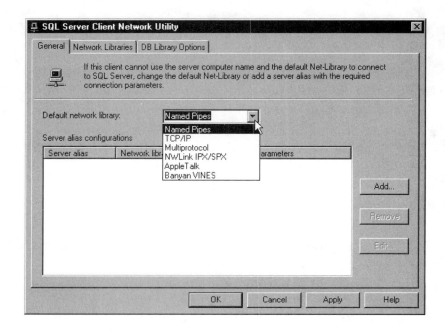

You can configure the following items in the General tab:

Option	Function
Default Network Library	Specifies the default library for communication with the SQL Server
Server Alias Configurations	Indicates the aliases of the client computers
Network Library	Indicates the network library that is used
Connection Parameters	Indicates possible parameters associated to the connection address
Add	Allows the addition of a new network connection
Remove	Allows the removal of a connection
Edit	Allows the editing of a connection

SQL Server Enterprise Manager

Our old friend, the SQL Server Enterprise Manager, is the main tool for the management of the SQL Server 7 servers. Among the tasks it performs are:

➤ Creating, viewing, and maintaining a database's contents through the creation of tables, stored procedures, indexes, rules, and diagrams

➤ Importing and exporting data

➤ Transforming data

➤ Executing administrative tasks

Here is the Enterprise Manager:

SQL Server Network Utility

This program configures the connection with the SQL Server when the communication protocol between the server and its clients is not working properly.

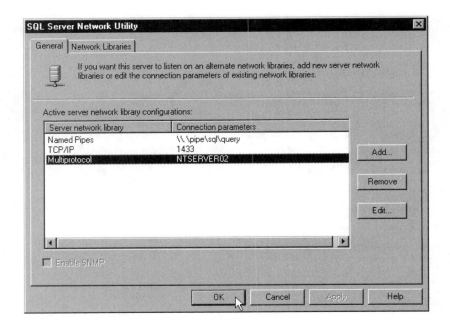

Performance Monitor

The Performance Monitor offers an instant analysis of the activities of the database, and is an excellent tool for diagnosing problems that the system may present.

SQL Server Profiler

The SQL Server Profiler continuously records the activities of the server. The data can be sent to the screen through graphics or to a file or table that will be analyzed later.

SQL Server Query Analyzer

The Query Analyzer allows the execution of SQL commands and scripts and permits the user to graphically view the steps for the execution of a query. This tool also analyzes indexes and proposes changes to improve the performance. We saw it in detail earlier in this book.

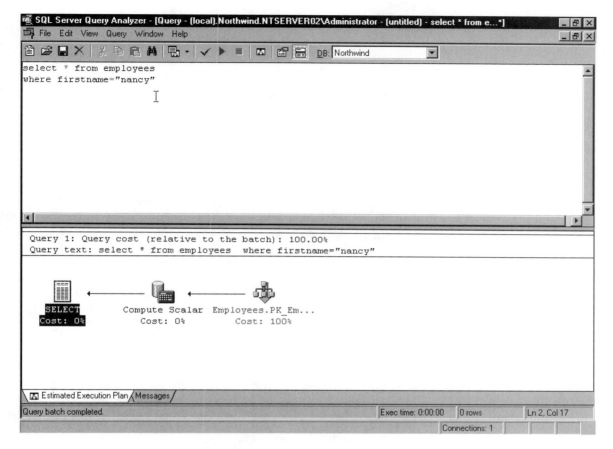

SQL Server Service Manager

The SQL Server Service Manager is a small tool used to start or stop the SQL Server (MSSQLServer), SQL Server Agent, and the Microsoft Distributed Transaction Coordinator (MSDTC). The SQL Server Service Manager appears as an icon on the task bar.

SQL Server Setup

SQL Server Setup is used to install and configure the server. After it is installed, it can be used for several tasks including fine-tuning the security options, reconstructing the master database, and exchanging network options.

Version Upgrade Wizard

The Upgrade Wizard helps with the migration of the database from SQL Server 6.5 to version 7.

The rest of this chapter discusses in detail some of the tools that have not yet been covered in this book.

SQL Server Profiler

The SQL Server Profiler helps you monitor server events such as login attempts, connection and disconnection from the server, execution of batch scripts of the Transact-SQL language, and deadlocks.

With the Server Profile you can create traces to gather information about the server and its events. This information can be stored in special files or database tables, or can be directly viewed by the Server Profile.

Registering a Server

A server must be registered in order to be monitored by the Server Profiler. To perform this task, activate the Register SQL Server option in the Tools menu, as shown below. Then, in the Registered SQL Server Properties dialog box that appears, select the name of the server and press OK.

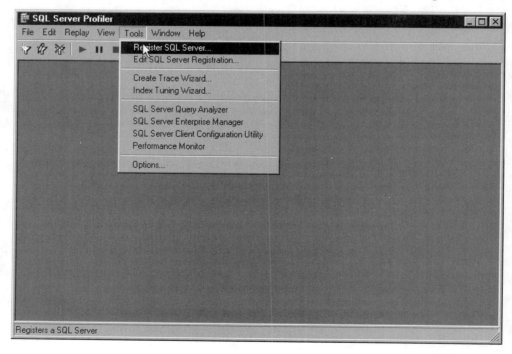

Creating a Trace

A trace is composed of the data captured by the events being monitored. To create a trace, activate the New Trace option from the File menu. In the Trace Properties dialog box, enter **Test1** in the Trace Name field.

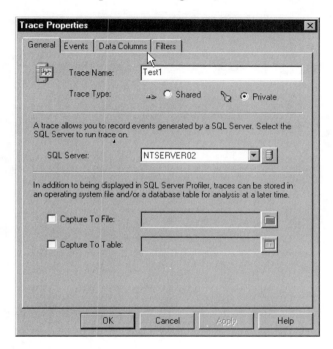

The following chart shows adjustments you can make in the General tab:

Option	Function
Trace Name	Specifies the name of the trace
Trace Type Shared	Grants access to any user
Trace Type Private	Grants access only to the user that created the trace
SQL Server	Specifies the server that is monitored
Capture To File	Captures the trace to a file in the operating system
Capture To Table	Captures the trace to a table in the database

Press OK to start the trace. The screen on the next page shows the result.

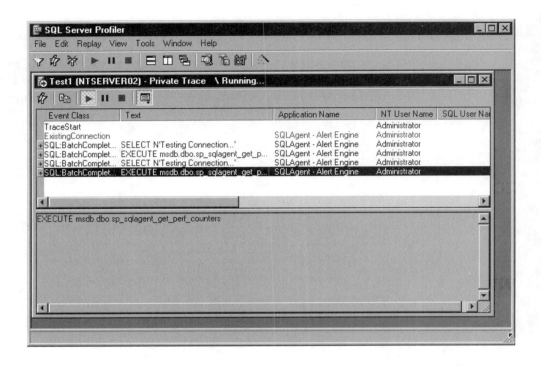

Filters

Filters are criteria that determine the events to be monitored by the trace. To specify the filter, select File|Open and click on Trace Definition. In the dialog box that appears, click on the Filters tab and select a criterion in the Trace Event Criteria list.

Starting a Trace

To start a trace, select File|Run Traces. In the dialog box that appears, click on Selected Traces in one or more traces, since several traces can be simultaneously executed.

Saving a Trace

A trace can be saved using File|Open|Trace Definition. Specify a name for the trace in the Trace Properties dialog box and select Capture to Table. Then enter the names for the database, owner, and table.

SQL Server Service Manager

The Service Manager must appear as default in the taskbar. To start an instance of the SQL Server, double-click on the Service Manager icon and execute the following procedures:

In the Server field, select the name of the server you want to initialize or enter the complete name of the remote server.

In the Services field, select MSSQLServer.

Double-click on Start/Continue.

With the Pause button you can temporarily stop the SQL Server. To reactivate its execution, just press Start/Continue. To stop the execution of the server, press the Stop button.

Performance Monitor

The Performance Monitor is an X-ray of the activities of local or remote servers. With it you can check the state (or behavior) of objects such as processors, memory, cache, threads, and processes. These objects can be associated with counters that show statistics about them.

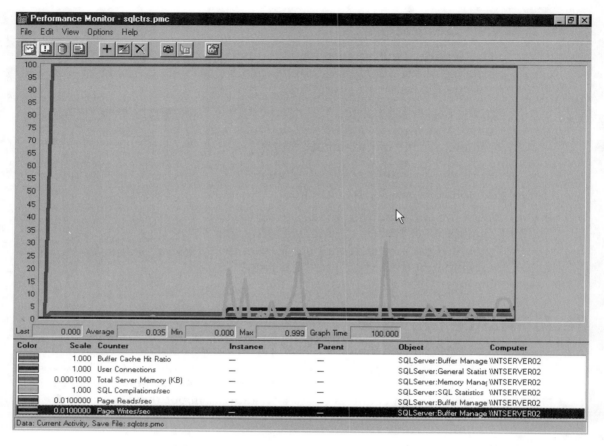

The Performance Monitor is comprised of four windows called Chart, Alert, Log, and Report, which can be displayed with the respective options in the View menu.

The statistics recorded are lost if they are not saved before quitting the program. You can save the adjustments made to one of the windows by clicking on the Save Settings option in the File menu. To save adjustments to all the windows, select Save Workspace in the File menu.

To include the analysis of new objects, use the Add to Chart option of the Edit menu. In the dialog box that appears, select one of the available options in the Object field, as shown in the following figure.

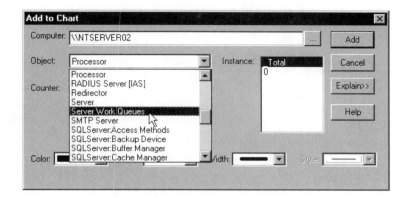

Summary

This chapter gave a broad overview of some SQL Server tools that have not been previously discussed in this text. These tools can help you perform administrative tasks. Next is a discussion of backing up and restoring data.

Backing Up and Restoring

SQL Server 7 has two tools designed to execute a backup copy of the database and its components. These tools are very important for the continuity of a database's operation when there is a hardware failure, an inadvertent deletion of a table, or even a loss of the server.

Making a backup involves copying the database to a safe location. A backup copy must be done whenever possible to another machine in the network, tape, or other magnetic means. The backup copies everything that is inside the database, including the transaction log.

The transaction log is a serial record of all the changes made to a database. This log is used in the restoration process to redo all the changes that have occurred in the database since the last backup.

The restoration of a database, when successful, returns the database to the status it had when the latest backup was executed. If during the execution of the backup copy some transaction was not completed, it will be undone to guarantee the consistency of the database.

Types of Backup

The SQL Server 7 allows two types of backup: complete and differential. The complete backup, as the name implies, is an exact photograph of the database. The differential backup is a copy of the changes made in the database since the last complete backup. By using these two types of backup you can create safe backup mechanisms to optimize the disk space and time. For example, you can make a complete backup early in the morning and a differential backup at noon and at the end of the day.

SQL Server provides the ability to create and recover a backup through the use of Transact-SQL commands, such as BACKUP DATABASE or RESTORE DATABASE, or through the Enterprise Manager or Backup Wizard. In this chapter we will cover the use of the Enterprise Manager and the Backup Wizard.

Creating a Backup with the Enterprise Manager

To perform a backup with the Enterprise Manager, right-click on the Databases folder to activate the quick menu.

Select All Tasks|Backup Database.

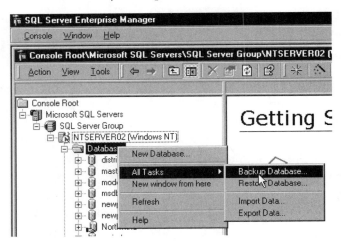

Initially we will create a backup for the Newpub2 database.

The first step is selecting the database. In the Database field, select the name of the database that will be copied. Master is selected as default. Select Newpub2 and press the OK button. (If you have not created this database, just follow along in the book.)

In the second step of the process, select the destination location for the backup. To do that, press the Add button in the Destination panel to bring up the Choose Backup Destination dialog box. The default is MSSQL7\BACKUP directory. Ideally the backup should be located in another network machine or another drive in the current machine. To select another location, click on the Browse button (the button with three dots) and select another folder. In this example, we will accept the default directory as the target location.

If your machine has tape units, they would appear as an option in the destination location dialog box.

These steps are shown on the following page.

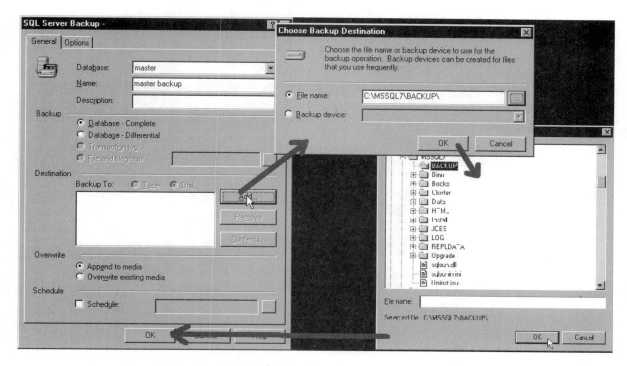

In addition to selecting the destination location, you must name the backup file. As an example, we will use **newpub back01**. Then press the OK button.

The backup process is started. It can take from a few seconds to several hours, depending on the size of the database.

Changing the Database

Now we'll make some changes to the Newpub2 database.

First let's create a dummy table called Test3, which contains just one column called codprod. Then we'll eliminate the record in which codprod has a value of 6 in the Test2 table.

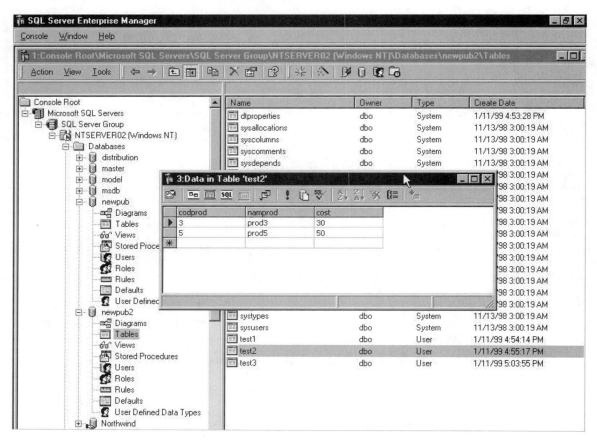

Now the database is changed. Since we already have a complete copy of it, there's no need to create a complete backup.

Restoring the Backup

To recover a complete backup, right-click on the Databases folder and select All Tasks|Restore Database. A dialog box appears, as shown in the following figure.

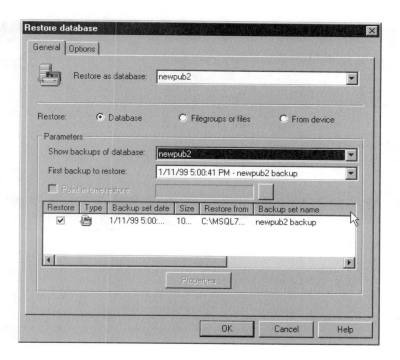

In the Restore as Database field, select newpub2. In the Parameters panel, select the Newpub2 database in the Show Backups of Database field. Press the OK button.

A dialog box shows the progress of the restore process.

Now comes the final test. We will open the Tables folder and check the contents of the Test2 table. The next screen shows the result.

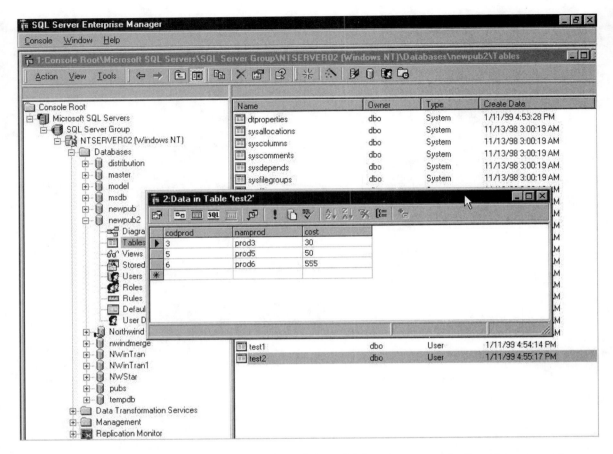

Note that there is no Test3 table, which was created after the execution of the first backup, and that the line with codprod 6 is back in the Test2 table.

Scheduling a Backup

The backup can be made immediately or scheduled so it does not affect work. To schedule a backup, select the Schedule item in the SQL Server Backup dialog box.

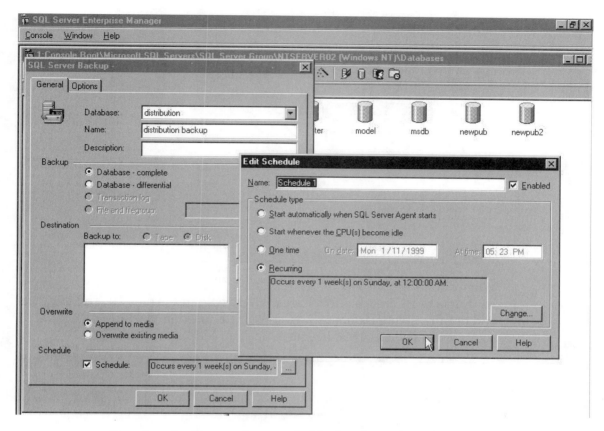

Pressing the Browse button (with the three dots) brings up the Edit Schedule dialog box in which you can select when the backup will start. You can schedule one execution of the backup at a predetermined time by checking the One Time option and entering the day and hour. Or you can schedule periodic backups with the Recurring option. It shows a default frequency that can be changed with the Change button. You can also specify that the backup start as soon as the SQL Server Agent is started or during CPU idle times.

Creating a Differential Backup

A differential backup allows the creation of a backup using just the data that changed since the last backup. This reduces the information stored by the backup files, saving time and space. For example, you can perform a complete backup on Mondays and differential backups on the other days of the week. If you have any problem overnight, just recover the backup from the previous day. We will create two differential backups.

Before creating the first one, let's include another line in the Test1 table.
Enter **7**, **prod7**, **777**.

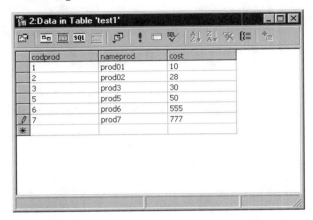

When you insert this line in the Test1 table, the Test2 table will be automatically updated, because of the trigger we created in Chapter 10. This time we
will use the Create Database Backup Wizard. Click on the Tools menu and
select Wizards. Select Management|Backup Wizard and press OK.

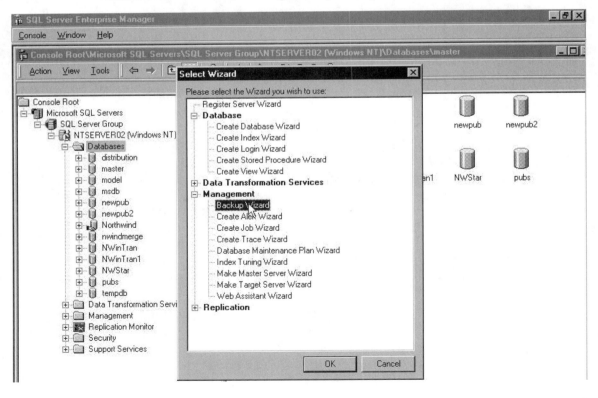

The first screen of the wizard displays informative data. Press Next in this screen. In the next step, select the database to be copied from the list displayed in the Databases Name field.

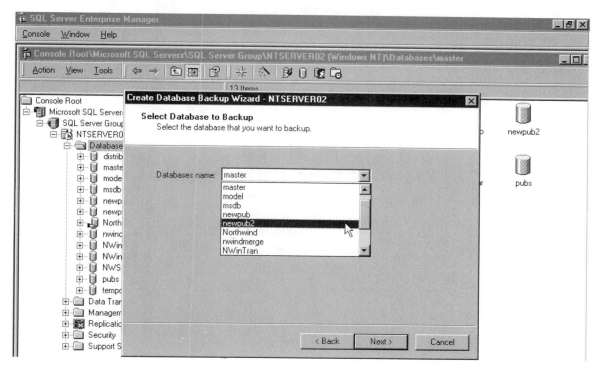

In the example we will select Newpub2 and press Next. The next step is used to confirm or enter a name for the backup and an optional description. Enter **backup newpub2 i01** as the backup name and **differential backup** as the description. Then press Next. The next step determines the type of backup that will be performed.

The first option, Database Backup, copies the entire database. The second option, Differential Database, copies just the data that is new or has changed. The last option copies only the transaction log. Select the Differential Database option and press the Next button.

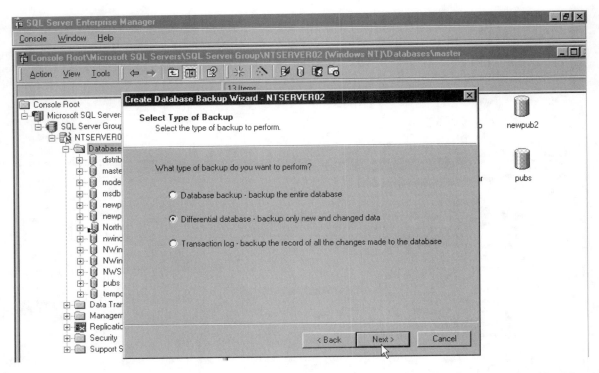

In this step you select the target location for the backup. Here we'll add the backup to the file that was already created with the Append option.

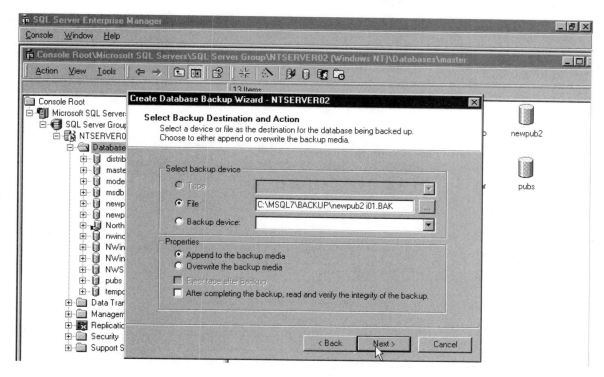

After pressing the Next button, a final dialog box appears, which displays a summary of the operations. Press the Finish button in this dialog box.

To test the differential backup, let's include a record in the Test1 table with the following contents:

```
Codprod=8
Nameprod=prod8
Cost=888
```

Let's also eliminate the record with codprod 5.

Then we will create another differential backup following the steps given above for using the Backup Wizard and entering the name **newpub2 differential 2**.

Restoring a Backup

You can use a similar process to recover both a differential and a complete backup. Select All Tasks|Restore Database.

In the Restore Database dialog box, select the database to be restored. Here we'll select Newpub2.

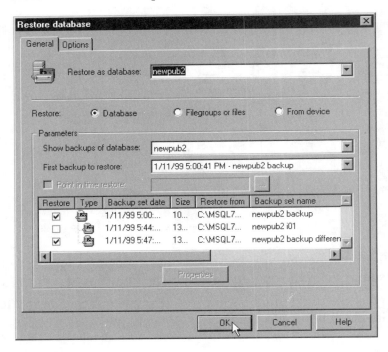

Observe in the Backup Set Name column that three backups were performed. The first one is the initial complete backup. The other two are differential backups that were performed later.

Restoring the Complete Backup

You can restore just the complete backup (the first one in the list) so all the changes made, such as the inclusion of records 7 and 8 and the elimination of record 5, are cancelled. In this case the selection to be made is shown in the following figure:

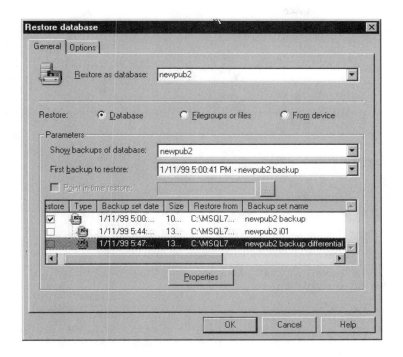

Press the OK button to complete the restoration. Notice the contents of the Test1 table:

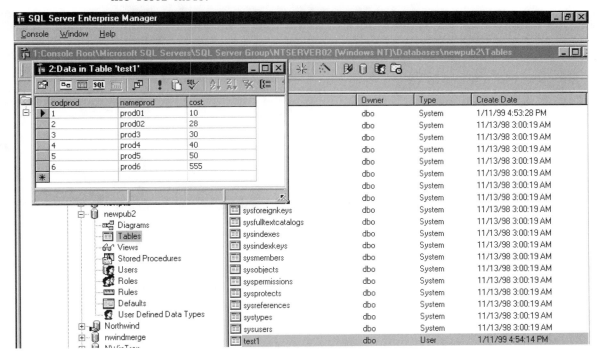

Restoring the Differential Backup

To restore a differential backup, first select the backup you want to recover. Checking the box in the Restore column of the differential backup automatically selects the complete backup, since in this operation the program recovers the complete backup and then the differential backup. After selecting this backup, press the OK button.

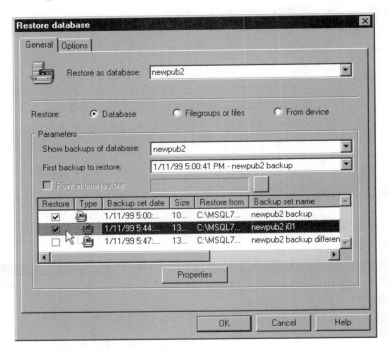

Notice the contents of the Test1 table:

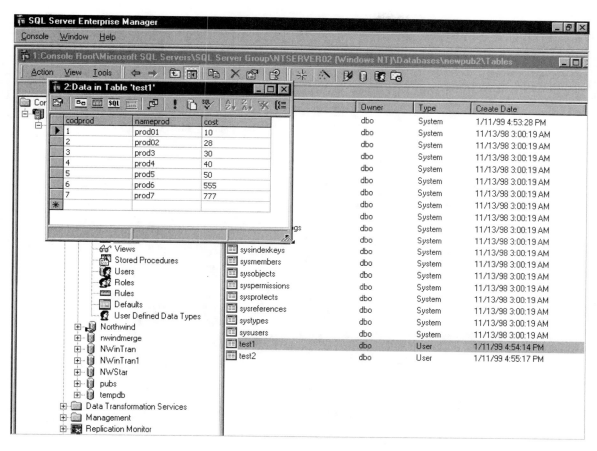

It shows the codprod line 7 that was inserted after the last complete backup.

Now we will perform the restoration of the second differential backup by checking its Restore box and pressing the OK button.

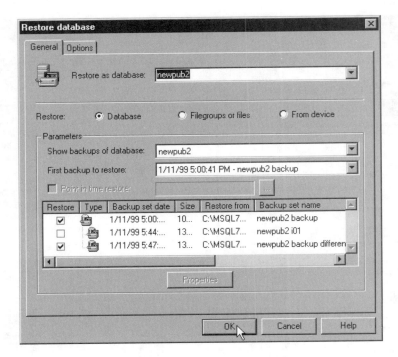

Note that now the codprod record 5 does not appear anymore and the record 8 was recovered.

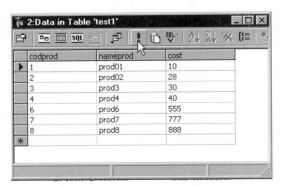

Summary

This chapter showed how simple the backup and recovery operations in a database are due to the interface adopted by SQL Server 7.

With this chapter we close the tutorial part of this book. This section showed you the most relevant aspects of SQL Server 7 and gave you a practical overview. Next you will find the reference guide for the Transact-SQL language. It offers a quick introduction to the syntax and functionality of commands and functions.

Transact-SQL Reference Guide

ABS

Returns the absolute, positive value of the given expression.

Syntax

ABS(*numeric_expression*)

Arguments

numeric_expression

An expression of the exact numeric or approximate numeric data type category, except for the **bit** data type.

ACOS

Returns the angle (in radians), whose cosine is the input argument. Also called arc cosine.

Syntax

ACOS(*float_expression*)

Arguments

float_expression

An expression of the type **float** or **real**, with a value between –1 and 1. Values outside this range return NULL.

ALL

Compares a scalar value with a single-column set of values. Returns **TRUE** when the comparison specified is **TRUE** for all pairs (*scalar_expression*, *x*) where *x* is a value in the single-column set. Returns **FALSE** otherwise.

Syntax

scalar_expression { = | <> | != | > | >= | !> | < | <= | !< } ALL (*subquery*)

Arguments

scalar_expression

Any valid Microsoft® SQL Server™ expression.

307

{ = | <> | != | > | >= | !> | < | <= | !< }
>A comparison operator.

subquery
>A subquery whose result set has one column. The column data type must be the same data type as the data type of *scalar_expression*.
>
>A restricted SELECT statement (the ORDER BY clause, the COMPUTE clause, and the INTO keyword are not allowed).

ALTER DATABASE

>Changes file definitions and size settings for a database.

Syntax

```
ALTER DATABASE database
{ ADD FILE <filespec> [, ...n] [TO FILEGROUP filegroup_name]
| ADD LOG FILE <filespec> [, ...n]
| REMOVE FILE logical_file_name
| ADD FILEGROUP filegroup_name
| REMOVE FILEGROUP filegroup_name
| MODIFY FILE <filespec>
| MODIFY FILEGROUP filegroup_name filegroup_property
}
<filespec> ::=
(NAME = 'logical_file_name'
[, FILENAME = 'os_file_name' ]
[, SIZE = size]
[, MAXSIZE = { max_size | UNLIMITED } ]
[, FILEGROWTH = growth_increment] )
```

Arguments

database
>The name of the database being changed.

ADD FILE
>Specifies a file or filegroup is being added.

TO FILEGROUP
>Specifies the filegroup to add the specified file to.

filegroup_name
>The name of the filegroup to add the specified file to.

ADD LOG FILE
>Specifies that a log file be added to the specified database.

REMOVE FILE
>Removes the description of the file from the database system tables and deletes the physical file. The file cannot be removed unless it is empty.

ADD FILEGROUP

Specifies that a filegroup is to be added.

filegroup_name

The name of the filegroup to add or drop.

REMOVE FILEGROUP

Removes the filegroup from the database and deletes all the files in the filegroup. The filegroup cannot be removed unless it is empty.

MODIFY FILE

Specifies the given file should be modified, including the FILENAME, SIZE, FILEGROWTH, and MAXSIZE options. Only one of these properties can be changed at a time. NAME must be specified in <filespec> to identify the file to be modified. If SIZE is specified, the new size must be larger than the current size of the file. FILENAME can only be specified for files in the tempdb database, and the new name does not take effect until SQL Server is restarted.

MODIFY FILEGROUP *filegroup_name filegroup_property*

Specifies the given filegroup property be applied to the filegroup. The values for *filegroup_property* are:

READONLY

Specifies the filegroup is read-only. Updates to objects in it are not allowed. The primary filegroup cannot be made read-only. Only users who have exclusive access to the database can mark a filegroup read-only.

READWRITE

Reverses the READONLY property. Updates are enabled for the objects in the filegroup. Only users who have exclusive access to the database can mark a filegroup read-write.

DEFAULT

Specifies the filegroup is the default filegroup for the database. Only one filegroup in a database can be the default filegroup. When you make one filegroup the default filegroup, the default property is removed from the filegroup that had been the default. CREATE DATABASE makes the primary filegroup the initial default filegroup. New tables and indexes are created in the default filegroup if no filegroup is specified in the CREATE TABLE, ALTER TABLE, or CREATE INDEX statements.

NAME

Specifies logical name for the file.

'*logical_file_name*'

The name used in Microsoft SQL Server when referencing the file. Must be unique in the server.

FILENAME

> Specifies an operating system filename. When used with MODIFY FILE, FILENAME can only be specified for files in the tempdb database. The new tempdb filename takes effect only after SQL Server has been stopped and restarted.

'*os_file_name*'

> The path and file name used by the operating system for the file. The file must reside in the server in which SQL Server is installed.

SIZE

> Specifies the size of the file.

size

> The size of the file. The MB and KB suffixes can be used to specify megabytes or kilobytes. The default is MB. The minimum value for *size* is 512 KB, and the default if *SIZE* is not specified is 1 MB. When specified with ADD FILE, *size* is the initial size for the file. When specified with MODIFY FILE, *size* is the new size for the file, and must be larger than the current size of the file.

MAXSIZE

> Specifies maximum size to which the file is allowed to grow.

max_size

> The maximum size to which the file can grow. The MB and KB suffixes can be used to specify megabytes or kilobytes. The default is MB. If *max_size* is not specified, the file will grow until the disk is full. The Microsoft Windows NT® event log warns an administrator when a disk is about to become full.

UNLIMITED

> Specifies that the file grows until the disk is full.

FILEGROWTH

> Specifies file growth increment.

growth_increment

> The amount of space added to the file each time new space is needed. A value of 0 indicates no growth. The value can be specified in MB, KB, or %. When % is specified, the growth increment size is the specified percentage of the size of the file at the time the increment occurs. If a number is specified without MB, KB, or %, the default is MB. The default value if FILEGROWTH is not specified is 10%, and the minimum value is 64 K. The size specified is rounded to the nearest 64 K.

ALTER PROCEDURE

Alters a previously created procedure (created by executing the CREATE PROCEDURE statement) without changing permissions and without affecting any dependent stored procedures or triggers. For more information about the parameters used in the ALTER PROCEDURE statement, see the CREATE PROCEDURE statement.

Syntax

```
ALTER PROC[EDURE] procedure_name [;number]
[
{@parameter data_type } [= default] [OUTPUT]
]
[, ...n]
[WITH
{
RECOMPILE
| ENCRYPTION
| RECOMPILE, ENCRYPTION
}
]
[FOR REPLICATION]
AS
sql_statement [...n]
```

Arguments

procedure_name

> The name of the procedure to change. Procedure names must conform to the rules for identifiers.

;number

> An existing optional integer used to group procedures of the same name so that they can be dropped together with a single DROP PROCEDURE statement.

@parameter

> A parameter in the procedure.

data_type

> The data type of the parameter.

default

> A default value for the parameter.

OUTPUT

> Indicates that the parameter is a return parameter.

n

> A placeholder indicating up to 1,024 parameters can be specified.

{RECOMPILE | ENCRYPTION | RECOMPILE, ENCRYPTION}

> RECOMPILE indicates that Microsoft SQL Server does not cache a plan for this procedure and the procedure is recompiled each time it is executed.

> ENCRYPTION indicates that SQL Server encrypts the syscomments table entry that contains the text of the ALTER PROCEDURE statement.

FOR REPLICATION

Specifies that stored procedures created for replication cannot be executed on the subscribing server, and is used when creating a filter stored procedure that is executed only by replication. This option cannot be used with the WITH RECOMPILE option.

AS

The actions the procedure is to take.

sql_statement

Any number and type of Transact-SQL statements to be included in the procedure. Some limitations do apply.

n

A placeholder indicating that multiple Transact-SQL statements can be included in the procedure.

ALTER TABLE

Modifies a table definition by adding or removing columns and constraints, or by disabling or enabling constraints.

Syntax

```
ALTER TABLE table
{
[WITH CHECK | WITH NOCHECK]
{ [ALTER COLUMN column_name
{
[ new_data_type [ (precision[, scale] ) ]
[ NULL | NOT NULL ] ]
| [ {ADD | DROP} ROWGUIDCOL ]
}
]
| ADD
{ [ <column_definition> ]
| column_name AS computed_column_expression
| [ <table_constraint> ]
}[, ...n]
| DROP
{ [CONSTRAINT] constraint
| COLUMN column
}[, ...n]
| {CHECK | NOCHECK} CONSTRAINT
{ALL | constraint[, ...n]}
| {ENABLE | DISABLE} TRIGGER
{ALL | trigger[, ...n]}
}
}
<column_definition> ::= { column_name data_type }
```

```
[ NULL | NOT NULL ]
[ IDENTITY [(seed[, increment] )
[NOT FOR REPLICATION] ] ]
[ ROWGUIDCOL ]
[ <column_constraint> ::=
[CONSTRAINT constraint_name]
{ { PRIMARY KEY | UNIQUE }
[CLUSTERED | NONCLUSTERED]
[WITH [FILLFACTOR = fillfactor]
[[,] {SORTED_DATA
| SORTED_DATA_REORG}]]
[ON {filegroup | DEFAULT} ]
| [FOREIGN KEY]
REFERENCES ref_table
[ ( ref_column ) ]
[NOT FOR REPLICATION]
| DEFAULT constant_expression [WITH VALUES]
| CHECK [NOT FOR REPLICATION]
(logical_expression)
}
] [ ...n]
<table_constraint> ::= [CONSTRAINT constraint_name]
{ [ { PRIMARY KEY | UNIQUE }
[ CLUSTERED | NONCLUSTERED]
{ ( column[, ...n] ) }
[ WITH [FILLFACTOR = fillfactor]
[[,] {SORTED_DATA
| SORTED_DATA_REORG} ]
]
[ON {filegroup | DEFAULT} ]
]
| FOREIGN KEY
[(column[,...n])]
REFERENCES ref_table [(ref_column[, ...n])]
[NOT FOR REPLICATION]
| DEFAULT constant_expression
[FOR column]
| CHECK [NOT FOR REPLICATION]
(logical_expression)
}
```

Arguments

table

> The name of the table to be altered. If the table is not in the current database or owned by the current user, the database and owner can be explicitly specified.

WITH CHECK | WITH NOCHECK

> Specifies whether the data in the table is or is not validated against a newly added or reenabled FOREIGN KEY or CHECK constraint. If not specified, WITH

CHECK is assumed for new constraints, and WITH NOCHECK is assumed for reenabled constraints. If you do not want to verify new CHECK or FOREIGN KEY constraints against existing data, use WITH NOCHECK. This option is not recommended except in rare cases; the constraints are evaluated in all future updates and constraint violations that were suppressed when the constraint was added may cause future updates to fail, even if the constraint protected column is not changed.

ALTER COLUMN

Specifies that the given column is to be changed or altered. ALTER COLUMN is not allowed if the sp_dbcmptlevel setting is 65 or earlier. The altered column cannot be:

➤ text
➤ image
➤ ntext
➤ timestamp
➤ The ROWGUIDCOL for the table
➤ A computed column or be used in a computed column
➤ A replicated column
➤ Used in an index, unless the column is a **varchar** or **varbinary** data type, the data type is not changed, and the new size is equal to or larger than the old size
➤ Used in a CHECK, FOREIGN KEY, UNIQUE, or PRIMARY KEY constraint (except that altering the length of a variable-length column used in a constraint is allowed)
➤ Associated with a default

column_name

The name of the column to be altered, added, or dropped. For new columns, *column_name* can be omitted for columns created with a **timestamp** data type. The name timestamp is used if no *column_name* is specified for a **timestamp** data type column.

new_data_type

The new data type for the altered column. Criteria for the *new_data_type* of an altered column are:

➤ The previous *data_type* must implicitly convert to the *new_data_type*.
➤ The *new_data_type* cannot be **timestamp**.
➤ ANSI null defaults are always on for ALTER COLUMN; if not specified, the column is nullable.
➤ ANSI padding is always on for ALTER COLUMN.
➤ The altered column must have a valid identity type for an identity column.
➤ The current setting for SET ARITHABORT is used except when converting an identity, in which case SET ARITHABORT is always ON.

precision

The precision for the specified data type.

scale

The scale for the specified data type.

[{ADD | DROP} ROWGUIDCOL]

Specifies the ROWGUIDCOL property is being added to or dropped from the specified column. ROWGUIDCOL is a keyword indicating that the column is a row global unique identifier column. Only one **uniqueidentifier** column per table can be designated as the ROWGUIDCOL column. The ROWGUIDCOL property can be assigned only to a **uniqueidentifier** column.

The ROWGUIDCOL property does not enforce uniqueness of the values stored in the column. It also does not automatically generate values for new rows inserted into the table. To generate unique values for each column, either use the NEWID function on INSERT statements or specify the NEWID function as the default for the column.

ADD

Specifies that one or more column definitions, computed column definitions, or table constraints are being added.

computed_column_expression

An expression that defines the value of a *computed column*. A computed column is a virtual column that is not physically stored in the table. It is computed from an expression using other columns in the same table. For example, a computed column could have the definition: cost AS price * qty. The expression can be a noncomputed column name, constant, function, variable, and any combination of these connected by one or more operators. The expression cannot be a subquery.

Computed columns can be used in select lists, WHERE clauses, ORDER BY clauses, or any other locations where regular expressions can be used, with these exceptions:

➤ A computed column cannot be used as a key column in an index or as part of any PRIMARY KEY, UNIQUE, FOREIGN KEY, or DEFAULT constraint definition.

➤ A computed column cannot be the target of an INSERT or UPDATE statement.

Note Because each row in a table may have different values for columns involved in a computed column, the computed column may not have the same result for each row.

DROP [CONSTRAINT] *constraint* | COLUMN *column*

> Specifies that *constraint* or *column* is removed from the table. Multiple columns and constraints can be listed. A column to be dropped cannot be:
>
> ➤ A replicated column
> ➤ Used in an index
> ➤ Used in a CHECK, FOREIGN KEY, UNIQUE, or PRIMARY KEY constraint
> ➤ Associated with a default defined with the DEFAULT keyword, or bound to a default object
> ➤ Bound to a rule

n

> A placeholder indicating that the preceding item can be repeated *n* number of times.

CHECK | NOCHECK

> Specifies that *constraint* is enabled or disabled. When disabled, future inserts or updates to the column are not validated against the constraint conditions. This option can only be used with FOREIGN KEY and CHECK constraints.

ALL

> Specifies that all constraints are disabled with the NOCHECK option, or enabled with the CHECK option.

{ENABLE | DISABLE} TRIGGER

> Specifies that *trigger* is enabled or disabled. When a trigger is disabled it is still defined for the table; however, when INSERT, UPDATE, and DELETE statements are executed on the table, the actions in the trigger are not performed until the trigger is reenabled.

ALL

> Specifies that all triggers in the table are enabled or disabled.

trigger

> Specifies the name of the trigger to disable or enable.

column_name data_type

> The data type for the new column. *data_type* can be any Microsoft SQL Server-based or user-defined data types. If a column is added with a **uniqueidentifier** data type, it can be added with a DEFAULT constraint that uses the NEWID() function to supply the unique identifier values in the new column for each existing row in the table.

NULL | NOT NULL

> Specifies whether the column can accept null values. Columns that do not allow null values can be added with ALTER TABLE. When a new column is added to a table, either the column must allow null values or the column must be added with a default constraint.

If the new column allows null values and no default is specified, the new column contains a null value for each row in the table. If the new column allows null values and a default constraint is added with the new column, the WITH VALUES option can be used to store the default value in the new column for each existing row in the table.

If the new column does not allow null values, a DEFAULT constraint must be added with the new column, and the new column automatically loads with the default value in the new columns in each existing row.

IDENTITY

Specifies that the new column is an identity column. When a new row is added to the table, SQL Server provides a unique, incremental value for the column. Identity columns are commonly used in conjunction with PRIMARY KEY constraints to serve as the unique row identifier for the table. The IDENTITY property can be assigned to a **tinyint, smallint, int, decimal(p,0)**, or **numeric(p,0)** columns. Only one identity column can be created per table. DEFAULT constraints and bound defaults cannot be used with an identity column. Either both the seed and increment must be specified, or neither. If neither is specified, the default is (1,1).

seed

The value that is used for the first row loaded into the table.

increment

The incremental value that is added to the identity value of the previous row that was loaded.

NOT FOR REPLICATION

Specifies that the IDENTITY property should not be enforced when a replication login, such as sqlrepl, inserts data into the table.

CONSTRAINT

Specifies the beginning of a PRIMARY KEY, UNIQUE, FOREIGN KEY, CHECK, or DEFAULT constraint definition.

constraint_name

The name of the new constraint. Constraint names must follow the rules for identifiers, except that the name cannot begin with a number sign (#). If *constraint_name* is not supplied, a system-generated name is assigned to the constraint.

PRIMARY KEY

A constraint that enforces entity integrity for a given column or columns through a unique index. Only one PRIMARY KEY constraint can be created per table.

UNIQUE

A constraint that provides entity integrity for a given column or columns through a unique index.

CLUSTERED | NONCLUSTERED

Specifies that a clustered or nonclustered index is created for the PRIMARY KEY or UNIQUE constraint. PRIMARY KEY constraints default to CLUSTERED; UNIQUE constraints default to NONCLUSTERED.

If a clustered constraint or index already exists on a table, CLUSTERED cannot be specified in ALTER TABLE. If a clustered constraint or index already exists on a table, PRIMARY KEY constraints default to NONCLUSTERED.

WITH FILLFACTOR = *fillfactor*

Specifies how full SQL Server should make each index page used to store the index data. User-specified *fillfactor* values can be from 1 through 100. If a value is not specified, the default is 0. A lower *fillfactor* creates the index with more space available for new index entries without having to allocate new space. For more information, see CREATE INDEX.

SORTED_DATA | SORTED_DATA_REORG

Options that eliminate the sort performed when a clustered index is created. The data in the column(s) used for the index must already be stored in a sorted order or an error is returned. For more information, see CREATE INDEX.

ON {*filegroup* | DEFAULT}

Specifies the storage location of the index that is created for the constraint. If *filegroup* is specified, the index is created in the named filegroup. If DEFAULT is specified, the index is created in the default filegroup. If ON is not specified, the index is created in the *filegroup* that contains the table. If ON is specified when adding a clustered index for a PRIMARY KEY or UNIQUE constraint, the entire table is moved to the specified filegroup when the clustered index is created.

FOREIGN KEY...REFERENCES

A constraint that provides referential integrity for the data in the column. FOREIGN KEY constraints require that each value in the column exists in the specified column in the referenced table.

ref_table

The name of the table that is referenced by the FOREIGN KEY constraint.

ref_column

A column or list of columns in parentheses that is referenced by the new FOREIGN KEY constraint.

DEFAULT

A constraint that specifies the value provided for the column. DEFAULT constraints can be used to provide values for a new column in the existing rows of data. DEFAULT constraints cannot be added to columns that have a **timestamp** data type, an IDENTITY property, an existing DEFAULT constraint, or a bound default. If the column has an existing default, the default must be dropped before the new default can be added.

WITH VALUES

Specifies that the value given in DEFAULT *constant_expression* is stored in the new column added to existing rows. Only applies when a DEFAULT constraint is specified as part of an ADD column clause in an ALTER TABLE statement when the added column allows null values. If WITH VALUES is not specified, the value NULL is stored in the new column added to existing rows.

constant_expression

A literal value, a NULL, or a system function that is used as the default value for the column.

CHECK

A constraint that enforces domain integrity by limiting the possible values that can be entered in a column or columns.

logical_expression

A logical expression that is used in a CHECK constraint and returns TRUE or FALSE. The *logical_expression* used with CHECK constraints cannot reference another table, but can reference other columns in the same table for the same row.

column[, ...*n*]

A column or list of columns in parentheses used in a new constraint.

FOR *column*

Specifies the column to be used with a table level's DEFAULT constraint.

ALTER TRIGGER

Alters the definition of a trigger created previously by the CREATE TRIGGER statement. For more information about the parameters used in the ALTER TRIGGER statement, see the CREATE TRIGGER statement.

Syntax

```
ALTER TRIGGER trigger_name
ON table
[WITH ENCRYPTION]
{
{FOR {[,] [DELETE] [,] [UPDATE] [,][INSERT]}
[NOT FOR REPLICATION]
AS
sql_statement [...n]
}
|
{FOR {[,] [INSERT] [,] [UPDATE]}
[NOT FOR REPLICATION]
AS
IF UPDATE (column)
[{AND | OR} UPDATE (column) [, ...n]]
```

```
sql_statement [...n]
   }
}
```

Arguments

trigger_name

>The name of the existing trigger to alter.

table

>The table on which the trigger is executed.

WITH ENCRYPTION

>Encrypts the syscomments entries that contain the text of the ALTER TRIGGER statement.

Note If a previous trigger definition was created using WITH ENCRYPTION or RECOMPILE, these options are only enabled if they are included in ALTER TRIGGER.

FOR {[,] [DELETE] [,] [UPDATE] [,][INSERT]} | {[,] [INSERT] [,] [UPDATE]}

>Specifies which data modification statements, when attempted on this table, activate the trigger. At least one option must be specified. Any combination of these, in any order, is allowed in the trigger definition. If more than one option is specified, separate the options with commas.

Note If the ALTER TRIGGER statement specifies {INSERT, UPDATE, DELETE} | {INSERT, DELETE} trigger information different from the original CREATE TRIGGER statement, the ALTER TRIGGER statement overrides the behavior specified in CREATE TRIGGER. For example, if an UPDATE trigger is altered to an INSERT trigger and a different INSERT trigger already exists, then an additional INSERT trigger is created.

NOT FOR REPLICATION

>Indicates that the trigger should not be executed when a replication login such as sqlrepl modifies the table involved in the trigger.

AS

>The actions the trigger is to take.

sql_statement

>The trigger condition or conditions and action or actions.

n

>A placeholder indicating that multiple Transact-SQL statements can be included in the trigger.

IF UPDATE (*column*)

>   Tests for an INSERT or UPDATE action to a specified column; not used with DELETE operations.

{AND | OR}

>   Specifies another column to test for either an INSERT or UPDATE action.

column

>   The name of the column to test for either an INSERT or UPDATE action.

ALTER VIEW

Alters a previously created view (created by executing CREATE VIEW) without affecting dependent stored procedures or triggers and without changing permissions. For more information about the parameters used in the ALTER VIEW statement, see the CREATE VIEW statement.

Syntax

```
ALTER VIEW view_name [(column [, ...n])]
[WITH ENCRYPTION]
AS
select_statement
[WITH CHECK OPTION]
```

Arguments

view_name

>   The view to change.

column

>   The name of one or more columns, separated by commas, to be part of the given view.

Tip Column permissions are maintained only when columns have the same name before and after ALTER VIEW is performed.

Note In the columns for the view, the permissions for a column name apply across a CREATE VIEW or ALTER VIEW statement, regardless of the source of the underlying data. For example, if permissions are granted on the title_id column in a CREATE VIEW statement, an ALTER VIEW statement can rename the title_id column (for example, to qty) and still have the permissions that are associated with the view using title_id.

n

>   A placeholder indicating *column* can be repeated *n* number of times.

ENCRYPTION

> Encrypts the syscomments entries that contain the text of the CREATE VIEW statement.

AS

> The actions the view is to take.

select_statement

> The SELECT statement that defines the view.

CHECK OPTION

> Forces all data modification statements executed against the view to adhere to the criteria set within the *select_statement* defining the view.

Remarks

For more information about ALTER VIEW, see Remarks in CREATE VIEW.

APP_NAME

Returns the program name for the current session if one has been set by the program.

Syntax

```
APP_NAME()
```

Return Type: nvarchar(128)

ASCII

Returns the ASCII code value, an integer, of the leftmost character of a character expression.

Syntax

```
ASCII(character_expression)
```

Arguments

character_expression

> An expression of the type **char** or **varchar**.

Return Type: int

ASIN

Returns the angle (in radians) whose sine is the input argument. Also called arc sine.

Syntax

```
ASIN(float_expression)
```

Arguments

float_expression

> An expression of the type **float**. The value must be between −1 and 1. Values outside this range return NULL and report a domain error.

Return Type: float

ATAN

Returns the angle (in radians) whose tangent is the given float expression. Also called arc tangent.

Syntax

ATAN(*float_expression*)

Arguments

float_expression

> An expression of the type **float**.

Return Type: float

ATN2

Returns the angle (in radians), also called arc tangent, whose tangent is between the two given float expressions.

Syntax

ATN2(*float_expression*, *float_expression*)

Arguments

float_expression

> An expression of the **float** data type.

Return Type: float

AVG

Returns the average of the values in a group. Null values are ignored.

Syntax

AVG([ALL | DISTINCT] *expression*)

Arguments

ALL

> Applies the aggregate function to all values. ALL is the default.

DISTINCT

> Specifies that AVG be performed only on each unique instance of a value, regardless of how many times the value occurs.

expression

> An expression of the exact numeric or approximate numeric data type category, except for the **bit** data type. Aggregate functions and subqueries are not permitted.

Return Type: Returns a value of the same type as *expression*.

BACKUP

Backs up an entire database, transaction log, or one or more files or filegroups.

Syntax

Backing up an entire database:

```
BACKUP DATABASE {database_name | @database_name_var}
TO <backup_device> [, ...n]
[WITH
[BLOCKSIZE = {blocksize | @blocksize_variable}]
[[,] DESCRIPTION = {text | @text_variable}]
[[,] DIFFERENTIAL]
[[,] EXPIREDATE = {date | @date_var}
| RETAINDAYS = {days | @days_var}]
[[,] FORMAT | NOFORMAT]
[[,] {INIT | NOINIT}]
[[,] MEDIADESCRIPTION = {text | @text_variable}]
[[,] MEDIANAME = {media_name | @media_name_variable}]
[[,] [NAME = {backup_set_name | @backup_set_name_var}]
[[,] {NOSKIP | SKIP}]
[[,] {NOUNLOAD | UNLOAD}]
[[,] [RESTART]
[[,] STATS [= percentage]]
]
```

Backing up specific files or filegroups:

```
BACKUP DATABASE {database_name | @database_name_var}
<file_or_filegroup> [, ...m]
TO <backup_device> [, ...n]
[WITH
[BLOCKSIZE = {blocksize | @blocksize_variable}]
[[,] DESCRIPTION = {text | @text_variable}]
[[,] EXPIREDATE = {date | @date_var}
| RETAINDAYS = {days | @days_var}]
[[,] FORMAT | NOFORMAT]
[[,] {INIT | NOINIT}]
[[,] MEDIADESCRIPTION = {text | @text_variable}]
[[,] MEDIANAME = {media_name | @media_name_variable}]
[[,] [NAME = {backup_set_name | @backup_set_name_var}]
[[,] {NOSKIP | SKIP}]
[[,] {NOUNLOAD | UNLOAD}]
[[,] [RESTART]
```

```
[[, ] STATS [= percentage]]
]
```

Arguments

DATABASE

> Specifies the complete backup of the database. If a list of files and filegroups is specified, then only those files and filegroups are backed up.

> **Note** During a full database or differential backup, SQL Server backs up enough of the log to produce a consistent database when the database is restored.

{*database_name* | *@database_name_var*}

> The database from which the log, partial database, or complete database is being backed up. If supplied as a variable (*@database_name_var*), this name can be specified either as a string constant (*@database_name_var* = database name) or as a variable of character string data type, except for the **ntext** or **text** data types.

<backup_device>

> Specifies the permanent or temporary backup device to use for the backup operation. Can be one or more of the following:

{*backup_device_name*} | {*@backup_device_name_var*}

> The logical name, which must follow the rules for identifiers, of the backup device(s) (created by sp_addumpdevice) to which the database is backed up. If supplied as a variable (*@backup_device_name_var*), the backup device name can be specified either as a string constant (*@backup_device_name_var* = backup device name) or as a variable of character string data type, except for the **ntext** or **text** data types.

{ DISK | TAPE | PIPE } = '*temp_backup_device*' | *@temp_backup_device_var*

> Allows backups to be created on the named disk, tape, or pipe device. When using a temporary disk backup device, the temporary disk backup devices must not exist prior to specifying the BACKUP statement. When using a tape backup device, specify WITH FORMAT to ensure that the backup device is a valid Microsoft Tape format data set.

With disk and tape, specify the complete path and filename. For example, DISK = 'c:\mssql7\backup\mybackup.dat' or TAPE = \\.\TAPE0. With pipe, specify the name of the named pipe that will be used by the client application. If supplied as a variable (*@temp_backup_name_var*), the temporary backup device name can be specified as a string constant or as a variable of character string data type, except for the **ntext** or **text** data types.

Pipe files have been added to allow third-party vendors a flexible and powerful way to connect their own software. For typical Transact-SQL use, pipe files are not used.

If you are using a network server with a UNC name or using a redirected drive letter, specify a device type of disk.

Tip When specifying multiple files, logical filenames (or variables) and temporary filenames (or variables) can be mixed. However, all devices must be of the same type (disk, tape, or pipe).

n

A placeholder indicating that multiple backup devices may be specified. The maximum number of backup devices is 32.

BLOCKSIZE = {*blocksize* | *@blocksize_variable*}

Specifies the physical block size, in bytes.

For DISK, BLOCKSIZE is ignored.

For TAPE, BLOCKSIZE only applies if the tape is being overwritten by using FORMAT. When using tape media, the backup operation selects an appropriate block size. Explicitly stating a block size overrides the backup operation's selection of a block size.

For PIPE, the backup operation uses 65,536 bytes unless BLOCKSIZE is specified.

DESCRIPTION = {*text* | *@text_variable*}

Specifies the free-form text describing the backup set. Can be a maximum of 255 characters.

DIFFERENTIAL

Specifies the database backup should consist only of the portions of the database that have changed since the last full backup. A differential database backup usually takes up less space than a full database. Use this option so all individual log backups since the last full database backup do not need to be applied.

The DIFFERENTIAL option is specified for full database backups only.

Note During a full database or differential backup, SQL Server backs up enough of the log to produce a consistent database when the database is restored.

EXPIREDATE = {*date* | *@date_var*}

Specifies the date when the backup set expires and can be overwritten. If supplied as a variable (*@date_var*), this date can be specified as a string constant (*@date_var* = date), a variable of character string data type (except for the **ntext** or **text** data types), a **smalldatetime**, or **datetime** variable, and it must follow the configured **datetime** format for the system. This option is used for DISK and TAPE devices only and is effective only when specified with all backup sets on the media.

RETAINDAYS = {*days* | *@days_var*}

Specifies the number of days that must elapse before this backup media set can be overwritten. If supplied as a variable (*@days_var*), it must be specified as an integer. This option is used for disk and tape devices only and is effective only when specified with INIT. Specifying SKIP overrides this option.

Tip If EXPIREDATE or RETAINDAYS is not specified, expiration is determined by the media retention configuration setting of sp_configure. These options only prevent SQL Server from overwriting a file. Tapes can still be erased using other methods, and disk files can still be deleted through the operating system.

FORMAT

Specifies that the media header should be written on all volumes used for this backup operation and rewrites the backup device. Any existing media header is overwritten. The FORMAT option also invalidates the entire media contents, ignoring any existing password.

Tip Use FORMAT carefully. Initializing one backup device or medium renders the entire backup set contained unusable.

By specifying FORMAT, the backup operation implies SKIP and INIT; SKIP and INIT do not need to be explicitly stated.

NOFORMAT

Specifies the media header should not be written on all volumes used for this backup operation and does not rewrite the backup device unless INIT is specified.

INIT

Specifies the backup set should be the first file on the disk or tape device and preserves the media header. If INIT is specified, any existing data on that device is overwritten.

The backup media is not overwritten if either of the following conditions is met:

➤ All backup sets on the media have not yet expired. For more information, see the EXPIREDATE and RETAINDAYS options.

➤ The backup set name given in the BACKUP statement, if provided, does not match the name on the backup media. For more information, see the NAME option.

Use the SKIP option to override these checks.

Note If the backup media is password-protected or encrypted, SQL Server does not write to the media. To overwrite media that is either password-protected or encrypted, specify the WITH FORMAT option.

NOINIT

Specifies the backup set is appended to the current DISK or TAPE device. NOINIT is the default.

MEDIADESCRIPTION = {*text* | *@text_variable*}

Specifies the free-form text description, maximum of 255 characters, describing the media set.

MEDIANAME = {*media_name* | *@media_name_variable*}

Specifies the media name, a maximum of 128 characters, for the entire backup media set. If MEDIANAME is specified, it must match the previously specified media name already existing on the backup volume(s). If not specified or if the SKIP option is specified, there is no verification check of the media name.

Note If FORMAT is specified, MEDIANAME specifies the media name that is written. In addition, tapes shared between SQL Server database backups and Microsoft Windows NT backups must have a non-null MEDIANAME.

NAME = {*backup_set_name* | *@backup_set_name_var*}

Specifies the name of the backup set. Names are limited to 128 characters. If NAME is not specified, it is blank.

NOSKIP

Instructs the BACKUP statement to check the expiration date and name of all backup sets on the media before allowing them to be overwritten.

SKIP

Disables the backup set expiration and name checking, which is usually performed by the BACKUP statement to prevent overwrites of backup sets.

NOUNLOAD

Specifies the tape is not unloaded automatically from the tape drive after a backup. NOUNLOAD remains set until UNLOAD is specified. This option is used only for tape devices.

UNLOAD

Specifies that the tape is automatically rewound and unloaded when the backup is finished. UNLOAD is set by default when a new user session is started. It remains set until that user specifies NOUNLOAD. This option is used only for tape devices.

RESTART

Specifies that SQL Server restarts the backup operation that was interrupted. The RESTART option saves time because it restarts the backup operation at the point it was interrupted. To RESTART a specific backup operation that was interrupted, repeat the entire BACKUP statement and add the RESTART option. Using the RESTART option is not required, but can save time.

Tip This option can only be used for backups directed to tape media and for backups that span multiple tape volumes. A restart operation never occurs on the first volume of the backup.

STATS [= *percentage*]

Displays a message every time another *percentage* completes, and is used to gauge progress. If *percentage* is omitted, SQL Server displays a message after every 10% completed.

<file_or_filegroup>

Specifies the logical names of the files or filegroups to include in the database backup. Multiple files or filegroups may be specified.

FILE = {*logical_file_name* | *@logical_file_name_var*}

Names one or more files to include in the database backup.

FILEGROUP = {*logical_filegroup_name* | *@logical_filegroup_name_var*}

Names one or more filegroups to include in the database backup.

BEGIN...END

Encloses a series of Transact-SQL statements so that a group of Transact-SQL statements can be executed. BEGIN...END blocks can be nested.

Syntax

```
BEGIN
{
sql_statement
| statement_block
}
END
```

Arguments

{*sql_statement* | *statement_block*}

Any valid Transact-SQL statement or statement grouping as defined with a statement block. To define a statement block, use the control-of-flow language keywords BEGIN and END. Although all Transact-SQL statements are valid within a BEGIN...END block, certain Transact-SQL statements should not be grouped together within the same batch (statement block).

Result Type: Boolean

BEGIN DISTRIBUTED TRANSACTION

Specifies the start of a Transact-SQL distributed transaction managed by Microsoft Distributed Transaction Coordinator (MS DTC).

Syntax

```
BEGIN DISTRIBUTED TRAN[SACTION]
[transaction_name | transaction_variable]
```

Arguments

transaction_name

A user-defined transaction name used to track the distributed transaction within MS DTC utilities.

transaction_variable

The name of a user-defined variable containing a transaction name used to track the distributed transaction within MS DTC utilities. The variable must be declared with a **char**, **varchar**, **nchar**, or **nvarchar** data type.

Remarks

The server executing the BEGIN DISTRIBUTED TRANSACTION statement is the transaction originator and controls the completion of the transaction. When a subsequent COMMIT TRANSACTION or ROLLBACK TRANSACTION statement is issued for the connection, the controlling server requests that MS DTC manage the completion of the distributed transaction across the servers involved.

There are two ways remote SQL servers are enlisted in a distributed transaction:

➤ A connection already enlisted in the distributed transaction makes a remote stored procedure call referencing a remote server.

➤ A connection already enlisted in the distributed transaction executes a distributed query referencing a remote server.

For example, a BEGIN DISTRIBUTED TRANSACTION is issued on ServerA, then the connection calls a stored procedure on ServerB and another stored procedure on ServerC, and the stored procedure on ServerC executes a distributed query against ServerD; all four SQL servers are involved in the distributed transaction. ServerA is the originating, controlling server for the transaction.

The connections involved in Transact-SQL distributed transactions do not get a transaction object they can pass to another connection for it to explicitly enlist in the distributed transaction. The only way for a remote server to enlist in the transaction is to be the target of a remote stored procedure call or a distributed query.

The sp_configure remote proc trans option controls whether calls to remote stored procedures in a local transaction automatically cause the local transaction to be promoted to a distributed transaction managed by MS DTC. The connection-level SET option REMOTE_PROC_TRANSACTIONS can be used to override the server default established by sp_configure remote proc trans. With this option set on, a remote stored procedure call causes a local transaction to be promoted to a distributed transaction. The connection that creates the MS DTC transaction becomes the originator for the transaction. COMMIT TRANSACTION initiates an MS DTC coordinated commit. If the sp_configure remote proc trans option is set on, remote stored procedure calls in local transactions are automatically protected as part of distributed transactions without having to rewrite applications to specifically issue BEGIN DISTRIBUTED TRANSACTION instead of BEGIN TRANSACTION.

When a distributed query is executed in a local transaction, the transaction is automatically promoted to a distributed transaction if the target OLE DB data source supports ITransactionLocal. If the target OLE DB data source does not support ITransactionLocal, only read-only operations are allowed in the distributed query.

BEGIN TRANSACTION

Marks the starting point of an explicit, local transaction. BEGIN TRANSACTION increments @@TRANCOUNT by 1.

Syntax

```
BEGIN TRAN[SACTION] [transaction_name | @tran_name_variable]
```

Argument

transaction_name

The name assigned to the transaction. *transaction_name* must conform to the rules for identifiers. Use transaction names only on the outermost pair of nested BEGIN...COMMIT or BEGIN...ROLLBACK statements.

@tran_name_variable

The name of a user-defined variable containing a valid transaction name. The variable must be declared with a **char**, **varchar**, **nchar**, or **nvarchar** data type.

Remarks

BEGIN TRANSACTION represents a point where the data referenced by a connection is known to be logically and physically consistent. If errors are encountered, all data modifications made after BEGIN TRANSACTION can be rolled back to return the data to this known state of consistency. Each transaction lasts until it either completes without errors and COMMIT TRANSACTION is issued to make the modifications a permanent part of the database, or errors are encountered and all modifications are erased with a ROLLBACK TRANSACTION statement.

BEGIN TRANSACTION starts a local transaction for the connection issuing the statement. Depending on the current transaction isolation level settings, many resources acquired to support the Transact-SQL statements issued by the connection are locked by the transaction until it is completed with either a COMMIT TRANSACTION or ROLLBACK TRANSACTION statement. Transactions left outstanding for long periods of time can prevent other users from accessing these locked resources.

Naming multiple transactions in a series of nested transactions with a *transaction_name* has little effect on the transaction. Only the first (outermost) transaction name is registered with the system. A rollback to any other name (other than a valid *savepoint_name*) generates an error. None of the statements executed before the rollback are in fact rolled back at the time this error occurs. The statements are only rolled back when the outer transaction is rolled back.

BREAK

Exits the innermost WHILE loop. Any statements following the END keyword are ignored. BREAK is often, but not always, activated by an IF test.

BULK INSERT

Copies a data file into a database table in a user-specified format.

Syntax

```
BULK INSERT [['database_name'.]['owner'].]{'table_name' FROM data_file}
[WITH
(
[ BATCHSIZE [ = batch_size]]
[[,] CHECK_CONSTRAINTS]
[[,] CODEPAGE [ = ACP | OEM | RAW | code_page]]
[[,] DATAFILETYPE [ =
{'char' | 'native'| 'widechar' | 'widenative'}]]
[[,] FIELDTERMINATOR [ = 'field_terminator']]
[[,] FIRSTROW [ = first_row]]
[[,] FORMATFILE [ = 'format_file_path']]
[[,] KEEPIDENTITY]
[[,] KEEPNULLS]
[[,] LASTROW [ = last_row]]
[[,] MAXERRORS [ = max_errors]]
[[,] ORDER ({column [ASC | DESC]} [, ...n])]
[[,] ROWTERMINATOR [ = 'row_terminator']]
[[,] TABLOCK]
)
]
```

Arguments

'database_name'

The name of the database in which the specified table resides. If not specified, this is the current database.

'owner'

The name of the table owner. *owner* is optional if the user performing the bulk copy operation owns the specified table. If *owner* is not specified and the user performing the bulk copy operation does not own the specified table, Microsoft SQL Server returns an error message, and the bulk copy operation is canceled.

'*table_name*'

The name of the table to bulk copy data into.

data_file

The full path of the data file that contains the data to be copied into the specified table. BULK INSERT can copy data from a disk (including network, floppy disk, hard disk, and so on).

BATCHSIZE [= *batch_size*]

Specifies the number of rows in a batch. Each batch is copied to the server as one transaction. SQL Server commits, or rolls back in the case of failure, the transaction for every batch. By default, all data in the specified data file is one batch.

CHECK_CONSTRAINTS

Specifies that any constraints on *table_name* are checked during the bulk copy operation. By default, constraints are ignored.

CODEPAGE [= ACP | OEM | RAW | *code_page*]

Specifies the code page of the data in the data file. CODEPAGE is relevant only if the data contains **char**, **varchar**, or **text** columns with character values greater than 127 or less than 32.

CODEPAGE Value	Description
ACP	Columns of **char**, **varchar**, or **text** data type are converted from the ANSI/Microsoft Windows code page (ISO 1252) to the SQL Server code page.
OEM (default)	Columns of **char**, **varchar**, or **text** data type are converted from the system OEM code page to the SQL Server code page.
RAW	This is the fastest option because no conversion from one code page to another occurs.
<value>	Specific code page number, for example, 850.

DATAFILETYPE [= {'char' | 'native' | 'widechar' | 'widenative'}]

Specifies that BULK INSERT performs the copy operation using the specified default.

DATAFILETYPE Value	Description
char (default)	Performs the bulk copy operation from a data file containing character data. \t (tab character) is the default field separator. \n (newline character) is the default row terminator.
native	Performs the bulk copy operation using the native (database) data types of the data. The data file to be loaded was created by BCP OUT from SQL Server.

DATAFILETYPE Value	Description
widechar	Performs the bulk copy operation from a data file containing Unicode characters. \t (tab character) is the default field separator. \n (newline character) is the default row terminator.
widenative	Performs the same as **native**, except **char**, **varchar**, and **text** columns are stored as Unicode in the data file. The data file to be loaded was created by BCP OUT from SQL Server. This option offers a higher performance alternative to the **widechar** option, and is intended for transferring data from one SQL Server to another using a data file. Use this option when you are transferring data that contains ANSI extended characters and you want to take advantage of the performance of native mode.

FIELDTERMINATOR [= 'field_terminator']

Specifies the field terminator to be used for **char** and **widechar** data files. The default is \t (tab character).

FIRSTROW [= first_row]

Specifies the number of the first row to copy. The default is 1, indicating the first row in the specified data file.

FORMATFILE [= 'format_file_path']

Specifies the full path of a format file describing the contents of the data file, containing stored responses from a previous use of the bcp Utility on the same table. The format file describes the format of the data file in detail, and should be used in cases where: the data file contains greater or fewer columns than the table; the columns are in a different order; the column delimiters vary; or there are other changes in the format of the data. Format files are normally created by using the bcp Utility and modified with a text editor as needed.

KEEPIDENTITY

Used to indicate that identity columns are present in the file being imported. If KEEPIDENTITY is not given, the file being imported should not contain values for these columns because SQL Server automatically assigns unique values based on the seed and increment values specified during table creation. If KEEPIDENTITY is specified, SQL Server takes the values for the identity columns from the data file.

KEEPNULLS

Specifies that empty columns should retain a null value during the bulk copy operation, rather than have any default values for the columns inserted.

LASTROW [= last_row]

Specifies the number of the last row to copy. The default is 0, indicating the last row in the specified data file.

MAXERRORS [= *max_errors*]

> Specifies the maximum number of errors that can occur before the bulk copy operation is canceled. Each row that cannot be imported by the bulk copy operation is ignored and counted as one error. If *max_errors* is not specified, the default is 10.

ORDER ({*column* [ASC | DESC]} [, ...*n*])

> Specifies how the data in the data file is sorted. Bulk copy performance is improved if the data being loaded is sorted according to the clustered index on the table. If the data file is sorted in a different order, or there is no clustered index on the table, the ORDER clause is ignored. The names of the columns supplied must be valid columns in the destination table. By default, the bulk insert operation assumes the data file is unordered.

n

> A placeholder indicating that multiple columns can be specified.

ROWTERMINATOR [= '*row_terminator*']

> Specifies the row terminator to be used for **char** and **widechar** data files. The default is \n (newline character).

TABLOCK

> Specifies that a table-level lock is acquired for the duration of the bulk copy operation. This option significantly improves performance, because holding a lock only for the duration of the bulk copy operation reduces lock contention on the table. A table can be loaded by multiple clients concurrently if the table has no indexes and TABLOCK is specified. By default, locking behavior is determined by the table option Table Lock on Bulk Load.

Permissions

BULK INSERT permissions default to members of the sysadmin fixed database role, the database owner, and table owner, who can transfer them to other users.

CASE

Evaluates a list of conditions and returns one of multiple possible result expressions.

CASE has two formats:

> ➤ The simple CASE function compares an expression to a set of simple expressions to determine the result.

> ➤ The searched CASE function evaluates a set of Boolean expressions to determine the result.

Both formats support an optional ELSE argument.

Syntax

Simple CASE function:

```
CASE input_expression
WHEN when_expression THEN result_expression
[, ...n]
[
ELSE else_result_expression
]
END
```

Searched CASE function:

```
CASE
WHEN Boolean_expression THEN result_expression
[, ...n]
[
ELSE else_result_expression
]
END
```

Arguments

input_expression

> The expression that is evaluated when using the simple CASE format. *input_expression* is any valid Microsoft SQL Server expression.

WHEN *when_expression*

> A simple expression to which *input_expression* is compared when using the simple CASE format. *when_expression* is any valid SQL Server expression. The data types of *input_expression* and each *when_expression* must be either the same or an implicit conversion.

THEN *result_expression*

> The expression that is returned when *input_expression* equals *when_expression* or *Boolean_expression* evaluates to TRUE. *result_expression* is any valid SQL Server expression.

n

> A placeholder indicating that multiple WHEN *when_expression* THEN *result_expression* clauses, or multiple WHEN *Boolean_expression* THEN *result_expression* clauses can be used.

ELSE *else_result_expression*

> The expression that is returned if no comparison operation evaluates to TRUE. If this argument is omitted and no comparison operation evaluates to true, CASE returns NULL. *else_result_expression* is any valid SQL Server expression. The data types of *else_result_expression* and any *result_expression* must be either the same or an implicit conversion.

WHEN *Boolean_expression*

> The Boolean expression that is evaluated when using the searched CASE format. *Boolean_expression* is any valid Boolean expression.

CAST and CONVERT

> Explicitly converts an expression of one data type to another. CAST is a synonym for CONVERT.

Syntax

Using CAST:

```
CAST(expression AS data_type)
```

Using CONVERT:

```
CONVERT (data_type[(length)], expression [, style])
```

Arguments

expression

> Any valid Microsoft SQL Server expression.

data_type

> The target system-supplied data type. User-defined data types cannot be used.

length

> An optional parameter of **nchar**, **nvarchar**, **char**, **varchar**, **binary**, or **varbinary** data types.

style

> The style of date format you want when converting **datetime** or **smalldatetime** data to character data (**nchar**, **nvarchar**, **char**, **varchar**, **nchar**, or **nvarchar** data types) or the string format when converting **float**, **real**, **money**, or **smallmoney** data to character data (**nchar**, **nvarchar**, **char**, **varchar**, **nchar**, or **nvarchar** data types).

> In the table, the two columns on the left represent the *style* values for **datetime** or **smalldatetime** conversion to character data. Add 100 to a *style* value to get a four-place year that includes the century (yyyy).

Without Century (yy)	With Century (yyyy)	Standard	Output
-	0 or 100 (*)	Default	mon dd yyyy hh:miAM (or PM)
1	101	USA	mm/dd/yy
2	102	ANSI	yy.mm.dd
3	103	British/French	dd/mm/yy
4	104	German	dd.mm.yy
5	105	Italian	dd-mm-yy
6	106	-	dd mon yy

Without Century (yy)	With Century (yyyy)	Standard	Output
7	107	-	mon dd, yy
8	108	-	hh:mm:ss
-	9 or 109 (*)	Default + milliseconds	mon dd yyyy hh:mi:ss:mmmAM (or PM)
10	110	USA	mm-dd-yy
11	111	Japan	yy/mm/dd
12	112	ISO	yymmdd
-	13 or 113 (*)	Europe default + milliseconds	dd mon yyyy hh:mm:ss:mmm(24h)
14	114	-	hh:mi:ss:mmm(24h)
-	20 or 120 (*)	ODBC canonical	yyyy-mm-dd hh:mi:ss(24h)
-	21 or 121 (*)	ODBC canonical (with milliseconds)	yyyy-mm-dd hh:mi:ss.mmm(24h)

* The default values (*style* 0 or 100, 9 or 109, 13 or 113, 20 or 120, and 21 or 121) always return the century (yyyy).

When converting to character data from **smalldatetime**, the styles that include seconds or milliseconds show zeroes in these positions. You can truncate unwanted date parts when converting from **datetime** or **smalldatetime** values by using an appropriate **char** or **varchar** data type length.

In the following table, the column on the left represents the *style* values for **float** or **real** conversion to character data.

style Value	Output
0 (default)	Six (6) digits maximum. In scientific notation, when appropriate.
1	Always eight (8) digits. Always scientific notation.
2	Always sixteen (16) digits. Always scientific notation.

In the following table, the column on the left represents the *style* value for **money** or **smallmoney** conversion to character data.

style Value	Output
0 (default)	No commas every 3 digits to the left of the decimal point. Two (2) digits to the right of the decimal point. For example, 4235.98.
1	Commas every 3 digits to the left of the decimal point. Two (2) digits to the right of the decimal point. For example, 3,510.92.
2	No commas every 3 digits to the left of the decimal point. Four (4) digits to the right of the decimal point. For example, 4235.9819.

Return Values

Given by the *data_type* parameter.

Remarks

Implicit conversions are those conversions that occur without specifying either the CAST or CONVERT function. Explicit conversions are those conversions that require the CAST (CONVERT) function to be specified.

CEILING

A mathematical function that returns the smallest integer greater than or equal to the given numeric expression.

Syntax

CEILING(*numeric_expression*)

Arguments

numeric_expression

An expression of the exact numeric or approximate numeric data type category, except for the **bit** data type.

Return Type: Same as input type

CHAR

A string function that converts an **int** ASCII code to a character.

Syntax

CHAR(*integer_expression*)

Arguments

integer_expression

An integer from 0 through 255. NULL is returned if the integer expression is not in this range.

Return Type: char(1)

CHARINDEX

Returns the starting position of the specified *pattern* in an expression.

Syntax

CHARINDEX('*pattern*', *expression* [, *start_location*])

Arguments

'*pattern*'

An expression containing the sequence of characters to be found. *pattern* is an expression of the short character data type category.

expression

An expression, usually a column that is searched for the specified pattern. *expression* is of the character string data type category.

start_location

The character position to start searching for *pattern* in *expression*. If *start_location* is not given, is a negative number, or is zero, the search starts at the beginning of *expression*.

Return Type: integer

CHECKPOINT

Forces all dirty pages (those database pages that have been updated since the last checkpoint) in the current database to be written to disk. Manual checkpoints, caused by executing the CHECKPOINT statement, supplement automatic checkpoints, which occur at intervals calculated by Microsoft SQL Server on the basis of the configurable value for maximum acceptable recovery time. The configurable value for maximum acceptable recovery time is set by using the Recovery Interval of sp_configure.

Syntax

```
CHECKPOINT
```

CLOSE

Closes an open cursor by releasing the current result set and freeing any cursor locks held on the rows the cursor is positioned on. CLOSE leaves the data structures accessible for reopening, but fetches and positioned updates are not allowed until the cursor is reopened. CLOSE must be issued on an open cursor; it is not allowed on cursors that have only been declared or are already closed.

Syntax

```
CLOSE { { [GLOBAL] cursor_name } | cursor_variable_name }
```

Arguments

GLOBAL

Specifies *cursor_name* refers to a global cursor.

cursor_name

The name of an open cursor. If both a global and a local cursor exist with *cursor_name* as their name, then *cursor_name* refers to the global cursor if GLOBAL is specified. If GLOBAL is not specified, *cursor_name* refers to the local cursor.

cursor_variable_name

The name of a cursor variable associated with an open cursor.

COL_LENGTH

Returns the defined length of a column.

Syntax

```
COL_LENGTH('table', 'column')
```

Arguments

'*table*'

> The name of the table for which to determine column length information. *table* is an expression of type **nvarchar**.

'*column*'

> The name of the column for which to determine length. *column* is an expression of type **nvarchar**.

Return Type: integer

COL_NAME

Returns the name of a database column, given the corresponding table identification number and column identification number.

Syntax

```
COL_NAME(table_id, column_id)
```

Arguments

table_id

> The identification number of the table containing the database column. *table_id* is of type **int**.

column_id

> The identification number of the column. *column_id* parameter is of type **int**.

Return Type: sysname

COLUMNPROPERTY

Returns information about a column or procedure parameter.

Syntax

```
COLUMNPROPERTY(id, column, 'property')
```

Arguments

id

> The ID of the table or procedure.

column

> The name of the column or parameter.

'*property*'

> The information to be returned for the object with *id*. The following table shows the values that can be used for *property*:

property Value	Description	Value Returned
'AllowsNull'	The column or parameter allows null values.	1 = **true** 0 = **false** NULL = Column or parameter not found
'IsComputed'	The column is a computed column.	1 = **true** 0 = **false** NULL = Not a valid column
'IsCursorType'	The procedure parameter is of type CURSOR.	1 = **true** 0 = **false** NULL = Column or parameter not found
'IsFulltextIndexed'	The column has been registered for full-text indexing.	1 = **true** 0 = **false** NULL = Not a valid column or ID
'IsIdentity'	Whether or not the column uses the identity property.	1 = **true** 0 = **false** NULL = Column or parameter not found
'IsIdNotForRepl'	The column checks for the IDENTITY_INSERT setting. If IDENTITY NOT FOR REPLICATION is specified, the IDENTITY_INSERT setting is not checked.	1 = **true** 0 = **false** NULL = Column or parameter not found
'IsOutParam'	The procedure parameter is an output parameter.	1 = **true** 0 = **false** NULL = Column or parameter not found
'IsRowGuidCol'	The column has the **uniqueidentifier** data type and is defined with the ROWGUIDCOL property.	1 = **true** 0 = **false** NULL = Column or parameter not found
'Precision'	The precision for the column or parameter data type. The precision of the specified column data type.	NULL = Column or parameter not found
'Scale'	The scale for the column or parameter data type.	NULL= Column or parameter not found
'UsesAnsiTrim'	The ANSI padding setting was ON when the table was initially created.	1 =**true** 0=**false** NULL= Column or parameter not found, or it is not a binary or string data type

Return Type: int

COMMIT TRANSACTION

Marks the end of a successful implicit or user-defined transaction. If @@TRANCOUNT is 1, COMMIT TRANSACTION makes all data modifications performed since the start of the transaction a permanent part of the database, frees the resources held by the connection, and decrements @@TRANCOUNT to 0. If @@TRANCOUNT is greater than 1, COMMIT TRANSACTION decrements @@TRANCOUNT by 1.

Syntax

```
COMMIT [ TRAN[SACTION] [transaction_name | @tran_name_variable] ]
```

Arguments

transaction_name

Ignored by Microsoft SQL Server. *transaction_name* specifies a transaction name assigned by a previous BEGIN TRANSACTION. *transaction_name* must conform to the rules for identifiers. *transaction_name* can be used as a readability aid by indicating to programmers which nested BEGIN TRANSACTION the COMMIT TRANSACTION is associated with.

@tran_name_variable

The name of a user-defined variable containing a valid transaction name. The variable must be declared with a **char**, **varchar**, **nchar**, or **nvarchar** data type.

Remarks

It is the responsibility of Transact-SQL programmers to issue COMMIT TRANSACTION only at a point when all data referenced by the transaction is logically correct.

If the transaction being committed was a Transact-SQL distributed transaction, COMMIT TRANSACTION triggers MS DTC to use a two-phase commit protocol to commit all the servers involved in the transaction. If a local transaction spans two or more databases on the same server, SQL Server uses an internal two-phase commit to commit all the databases involved in the transaction.

When used in nested transactions, commits of the inner transactions do not free resources or make their modifications permanent. The data modifications are made permanent and resources freed only when the outer transaction is committed. Each COMMIT TRANSACTION issued when @@TRANCOUNT is greater than 0 simply decrements @@TRANCOUNT by 1. When @@TRANCOUNT is finally decremented to 0, the entire outer transaction is committed. Because *transaction_name* is ignored by SQL Server, issuing a COMMIT TRANSACTION referencing the name of an outer transaction when there are outstanding inner transactions only decrements @@TRANCOUNT by 1.

Issuing a COMMIT TRANSACTION when @@TRANCOUNT is 0 results in an error that there is no corresponding BEGIN TRANSACTION.

You cannot roll back a transaction after a COMMIT TRANSACTION statement is issued because the data modifications have been made a permanent part of the database.

COMMIT WORK

Marks the end of a transaction.

Syntax

```
COMMIT [WORK]
```

Remarks

This statement functions identically to COMMIT TRANSACTION, except that COMMIT TRANSACTION accepts a user-defined transaction name. With or without specifying the optional WORK keyword, this COMMIT syntax is compatible with SQL-92.

CONTAINS

Searches columns containing character-based data types for precise or "fuzzy" (less precise) matches to single words and phrases, the proximity of words within a certain distance of one another, and weighted matches. CONTAINS can search for:

➤ A word or phrase.

➤ The prefix of a word or phrase.

➤ A word that is near another word.

➤ A word that is derived from another (for example, the word "drive" is the inflectional stem of "drives," "drove," "driving," and "driven").

➤ A word that has a higher designated weighting than another word.

Syntax

```
CONTAINS
( {column | *}, '<contains_search_condition>'
)
<contains_search_condition> ::=
{
<simple_term>
| <prefix_term>
| <proximity_term>
| <generation_term>
| <isabout_term>
| (<contains_search_condition>)
}
[ {
{AND | AND NOT | OR} <contains_search_condition>
}
] [...n]
<isabout_term> ::=
ISABOUT
( {
<generation_term>
| <prefix_term>
| <proximity_term>
| <simple_term>
}
[WEIGHT (weight_value)]
)
<generation_term> ::=
FORMSOF (INFLECTIONAL, <simple_term>)
<prefix term> ::=
word * | "phrase * "
<proximity_term> ::=
{<simple_term> | <prefix_term>} {NEAR() | ~}
<simple_term> ::=
word | " phrase "
```

Arguments

column

The name of a specific column that has been registered for full-text searching. Columns of the character string data types are valid full-text searching columns.

*

Specifies that all columns in the table that have been registered for full-text searching should be used to search for the given <contains_search_condition>(s). If more than one table is in the FROM clause when using CONTAINS and the *, then * must be qualified by the table name.

<contains_search_condition>

Specifies some text to search for in the specified *column*.

<simple_term>

Specifies a match for an exact word (one or more characters without spaces or punctuation) or phrase (one or more consecutive words that may have spaces between them). "blue berry," "blueberry," and "Microsoft SQL Server" are all examples of a valid <simple_term>. Phrases should be enclosed in double quotation marks (""). Words in a phrase must appear in the same order as specified in the <contains_search_condition> as they appear in the database column. The search for characters in the word or phrase is case insensitive. When searching for a single word, do not use these noise words: "a," "and," "the," and so on. SQL Server includes a standard list of noise words. Noise words in full-text indexed columns are not stored in the full-text index. If a noise word is used in a single word search, SQL Server returns an error message indicating that only noise words are present in the query.

Assume that one particular row's value in the testing column contains the text, "This is a test." Another row contains the value "test documents" in the testing column. Since "this," "is," and "a" are all noise words, they are not stored in the full-text index. The WHERE clause which uses CONTAINS (WHERE CONTAINS (testing, ' "this is a test" ')) is equivalent to the WHERE clause which also uses CONTAINS (WHERE CONTAINS(testing, 'test'). Both rows (the rows containing the text of "This is a test" and "test documents" in the testing column) are returned in the query result set.

<prefix_term>

Specifies a match of words or phrases beginning with the specified text. Enclose a <prefix_term> in double quotation marks ("") and an asterisk (*) before the ending quotation mark. All text starting with the <simple_term> specified before the asterisk is matched. The asterisk matches zero, one, or more characters (of the root word(s) in the word or phrase). When using a phrase as a <prefix_term>, each word contained in a phrase is considered to be a separate prefix. Therefore, a query specifying a <prefix_term> of "local wine *" matches any rows with the text of "local winery," "locally-grown wine," and so on.

<proximity_term>

Specifies a match of words or phrases that must be close to one another. <proximity_term> operates similarly to the AND operator: Both require that more than one word or phrase exist in the column being searched. As the words in <proximity_term> appear closer together, the better the match.

<isabout_term>

Specifies that the matching rows (returned by the query) match a list of words and phrases, each optionally given a weighting value.

AND | AND NOT | OR

Specifies a logical operation between two <contains_search_condition>s. When a <contains_search_condition> contains parenthesized groups, these parenthesized groups are evaluated first. After evaluating parenthesized groups, these rules apply when using these logical operators with <contains_search_conditions>s:

➤ NOT is applied before AND.

➤ NOT can only occur after AND, as in AND NOT. The OR NOT operator is not allowed. NOT cannot be specified before the first term (for example, CONTAINS(*mycolumn*, 'NOT "phrase_to_search_for" ').

➤ AND is applied before OR.

➤ Boolean operators of the same type (AND, OR) are associative and can therefore be applied in any order.

n

A placeholder indicating that multiple <contains_search_conditions> can be specified.

ISABOUT

Specifies the <isabout_term> keyword.

<generation_term>

Specifies a match of words when the included <simple_terms> include variants of the original word for which to search.

WEIGHT (*weight_value*)

Specifies a weight value which is a number between 0.0 and 1.0. Each component in the <isabout_term> may include a *weight_value*. *weight_value* is a way to change how various portions of a query affect the rank value assigned to each row matching the query. Weighting forces a different measurement of the ranking of a value because all the components of the <isabout_term> are used together to determine the match. A row is returned if there is a match on any one of the ISABOUT parameters, whether or not a weight value is assigned. To determine values for each returned row which indicates the degree of matching between the returned rows, see CONTAINSTABLE.

INFLECTIONAL

Specifies that both plural and singular forms of nouns and the various tenses of verbs are to be matched.

word

A string of characters without spaces or punctuation.

phrase

One or more *word*s with spaces between each *word*.

NEAR() | ~

Indicates that the word or phrase on the left-hand side of the NEAR() or ~ operator should be close to the word or phrase on the right-hand side of the NEAR() or ~ operator. It is possible to chain multiple <proximity_terms>. For example,

```
A NEAR() B NEAR() C
```

means word or phrase A should be near word or phrase B, which should be near word or phrase C.

Microsoft SQL Server ranks the distance between the left-hand and right-hand word(s) or phrase(s). A low rank value (for example, 0) indicates a large distance between the two. If the specified words or phrases are far apart from each other, the query is considered to be satisfied; however, the query has a very low (zero) rank value. However, if the <contains_search_condition> consists only of one or more NEAR() proximity terms, then SQL Server does not return rows with a rank value of zero. For more information about ranking, see CONTAINSTABLE.

CONTAINSTABLE

Returns a table of zero, one, or more rows for those columns containing character-based data types for precise or "fuzzy" (less precise) matches to single words and phrases, the proximity of words within a certain distance of one another, and weighted matches. CONTAINSTABLE can search for this information in the FROM clause of a query:

➤ A word or phrase.
➤ The prefix of a word or phrase.
➤ A word that is near another word.
➤ A word that is derived from another (for example, the word "drive" is the inflectional stem of "drives," "drove," "driving," and "driven").
➤ A word that has a higher designated weighting than another word.

Syntax

```
CONTAINSTABLE (table, {, column | *}, '<contains_search_condition>')
<contains_search_condition> ::=
{
```

```
<simple_term>
| <prefix_term>
| <proximity_term>
| <generation_term>
| <isabout_term>
| (<contains_search_condition>)
}
[ {
{AND | AND NOT | OR} <contains_search_condition>
}
] [...n]
<isabout_term> ::=
ISABOUT
( {
<generation_term>
| <prefix_term>
| <proximity_term>
| <simple_term>
}
[WEIGHT (weight_value)]
)
<generation_term> ::=
FORMSOF (INFLECTIONAL, <simple_term>)
<prefix term> ::=
word * | "phrase * "
<proximity_term> ::=
{<simple_term> | <prefix_term>} {NEAR() | ~}
<simple_term> ::=
word | " phrase "
```

Arguments

table

> The name of the table that has been marked for full-text querying. *table* can be a one-part database object name or a multi-part database object name.

column

> The name of the column to search which resides within the specified *table*, which must be marked for full-text querying. Columns of the character string data types are valid full-text searching columns.

*

> Specifies that all columns in the table that have been registered for full-text searching should be used to search for the given <contains_search_condition>(s).

<contains_search_condition>

> Specifies some text to search for in the specified *column*. For more information about <contains_search_condition>, see CONTAINS.

Remarks

CONTAINSTABLE can also specify selection criteria. The table returned has a column named KEY that contains "full-text key" values. Each full-text indexed table has a column whose values are guaranteed to be unique and the values returned in the KEY column are the "full-text key" values of the rows that match the selection criteria specified in the <contains_search_condition>.

The table produced by CONTAINSTABLE can have one or more property columns. Microsoft SQL Server supports the RANK property, which is a value (between 0 and 1,000) for each row that indicates how well a row matches the selection criteria.

Permissions

Execute permissions are available only by users with the appropriate SELECT privileges on the table and/or the referenced table's columns.

CONTINUE

Restarts a WHILE loop. Any statements after the CONTINUE keyword are ignored. CONTINUE is often, but not always, activated by an IF test. For more information, see WHILE.

COS

A mathematical function that returns the trigonometric cosine of the given angle (in radians) in the given expression.

Syntax

COS(*float_expression*)

Arguments

float_expression

> An *expression* of type **float**.

Return type: float

COT

A mathematical function that returns the trigonometric cotangent of the specified angle (in radians) in the given **float** expression.

Syntax

COT(*float_expression*)

Arguments

float_expression

> An *expression* of type **float**.

Return Type: float

COUNT

An aggregate returning the number of items in a group.

Syntax

```
COUNT({[ALL | DISTINCT] expression] | *})
```

Arguments

ALL

Applies the aggregate function to all values. ALL is the default.

DISTINCT

Specifies that COUNT returns the number of unique non-null values.

expression

An expression of any type except **uniqueidentifier**, **text**, **image**, or **ntext**. Aggregate functions and subqueries are not permitted.

*

Specifies that all rows should be counted to return the total number of rows in a table. COUNT(*) takes no parameters and cannot be used with DISTINCT. COUNT(*) does not require an *expression* parameter because, by definition, it does not use information about any particular column. COUNT(*) returns the number of rows in a specified table without eliminating duplicates. It counts each row separately, including rows that contain null values.

Tip Distinct aggregates, such as AVG(DISTINCT *column_name*), COUNT(DISTINCT *column_name*), MAX(DISTINCT *column_name*), MIN(DISTINCT *column_name*), and SUM(DISTINCT *column_name*), are not supported when using CUBE or ROLLUP. If used, Microsoft SQL Server returns an error message and aborts the query.

Return Type: int

CREATE DATABASE

Creates a new database and the files used to store the database, or attaches a database from the files of a previously created database.

Syntax

```
CREATE DATABASE database_name
[ ON [PRIMARY]
[ <filespec> [, ...n] ]
[, <filegroup> [, ...n] ]
]
[ LOG ON { <filespec> } ]
[ FOR LOAD | FOR ATTACH ]
```

```
<filespec> ::=
( [ NAME = logical_file_name, ]
FILENAME = 'os_file_name'
[, SIZE = size]
[, MAXSIZE = { max_size | UNLIMITED } ]
[, FILEGROWTH = growth_increment] ) [, ...n]
<filegroup> ::=
FILEGROUP filegroup_name <filespec> [, ...n]
```

Arguments

database_name

> The name of the new database. Database names must be unique within a server and conform to the rules for identifiers.

ON

> Specifies that the disk files used to store the data portions of the database (data files) are explicitly defined. The keyword is followed by a comma-delimited list of <filespec> items defining the data files for the primary filegroup. This list can be followed by an optional, comma-delimited list of <filegroup> items defining user filegroups and their files.

PRIMARY

> Specifies that the associated <filespec> list defines the files in the primary filegroup. The primary filegroup contains all of the database system tables. It also contains all objects not assigned to user filegroups. The first <filespec> entry in the primary filegroup creates the primary file, which is the file containing the logical start of the database and system tables. A database can have only one primary file. If the PRIMARY keyword is not specified, the first file listed in the CREATE DATABASE statement becomes the primary file.

n

> A placeholder to indicate that multiple files can be specified for the new database.

LOG ON

> Specifies that the disk files used to store the database log (log files) are explicitly defined. The keyword is followed by a comma-delimited list of <filespec> items defining the log files. If the LOG ON clause is not specified, a single log file is automatically created with a system-generated name and a size that is 25 percent of the sum of the sizes of all the data files for the database.

FOR LOAD

> This clause is supported for compatibility with older versions of Microsoft SQL Server. The database is created with the database option DBO Use Only turned on, and the status is set to Loading. This is not needed in SQL Server version 7.0 because the RESTORE statement can re-create a database as part of the restore operation.

FOR ATTACH

Specifies that you are attaching a database from an existing set of operating system files. There must be a <filespec> entry specifying the first primary file. The only other <filespec> entries needed are those for any files that have a different path than when the database was first created or last attached. A <filespec> entry must be specified for these files. The database being attached must have been created using the same code page and sort order as the SQL Server. Use the system stored procedure sp_attach_db instead of using CREATE DATABASE FOR ATTACH directly. Use CREATE DATABASE FOR ATTACH only when you must specify more than 16 <filespec> items.

NAME

Specifies the logical name for the file defined by the <filespec>. The NAME parameter is not required when FOR ATTACH is specified.

logical_file_name

The name used to reference the file in any SQL statements executed after the database is created. *logical_file_name* must be unique in the database and conform to the rules for identifiers.

FILENAME

Specifies the operating system filename for the file defined by <filespec>.

'os_file_name'

The path and file name used by the operating system when it creates the physical file defined by the <filespec>. The path in *os_file_name* must specify a folder on the server in which SQL Server is installed.

SIZE

Specifies the size of the file defined in <filespec>.

size

The initial size of the file defined in <filespec>. The MB and KB suffixes can be used to specify megabytes or kilobytes; the default is MB. The minimum value for *size* is 512 KB. The default if *size* is not specified is 1MB. The size specified for the primary file must be at least as large as the primary file of the model database.

MAXSIZE

Specifies the maximum size to which the file defined in <filespec> can grow.

max_size

The maximum size to which the file defined in <filespec> can grow. The MB and KB suffixes can be used to specify megabytes or kilobytes; the default is MB. If *max_size* is not specified, the file will grow until the disk is full.

Note The Microsoft Windows NT event log warns the SQL Server administrator if a disk is about to become full.

UNLIMITED

Specifies that the file defined in <filespec> grows until the disk is full.

FILEGROWTH

Specifies the growth increment of the file defined in <filespec>. The FILEGROWTH setting for a file cannot exceed the MAXSIZE setting.

growth_increment

The amount of space added to the file each time new space is needed. A value of 0 indicates no growth. The value can be specified in MB, KB, or %. If a number is specified without MB, KB, or %, the default is MB. When % is specified, the growth increment size is the specified percentage of the size of the file at the time the increment occurs. The default value if FILEGROWTH is not specified is 10%, and the minimum value is 64 K. The size specified is rounded to the nearest 64 K.

Remarks

You can use a single CREATE DATABASE statement to create a database and the files that store the database.

SQL Server implements the CREATE DATABASE statement in two steps:

➤ SQL Server uses a copy of the model database to initialize the database and its catalog

➤ SQL Server then fills the rest of the database with empty pages, except for pages that have internal data recording how the space is used in the database.

Any user-defined objects in the model database are therefore copied to all newly created databases. You can add to the model database any objects (such as tables, views, stored procedures, data types, and so on) that you want to have in all your databases.

There are three types of files used to store a database:

➤ The primary file contains the startup information for the database. The primary file is also used to store data. Every database has one primary file.

➤ Secondary files hold all of the data that does not fit in the primary data file. Databases need not have any secondary data files if the primary file is large enough to hold all of the data in the database. Other databases may be large enough to need multiple secondary data files, or they may use secondary files on separate disk drives to spread the data across multiple disks.

➤ Log files hold the log information used to recover the database. There must be at least one log file for each database, although there may be more than one. The minimum size for a log file is 512 K.

Every database has at least two files, a primary file and a log file.

Although *os_file_name* can be any valid operating system filename, the name more clearly reflects the purpose of the file if you use the following recommended extensions:

File Type	Recommended Filename Extension
Primary data file	.mdf
Secondary data file	.ndf
Log file	.ldf

Each database has an *owner* who has the ability to perform special activities in the database. The owner is the user who creates the database. The database owner can be changed through sp_changedbowner.

Each new database inherits the database option settings from the model database (unless FOR ATTACH is specified). For example, the database option Select Into/Bulkcopy is set to OFF in model and any new databases you create. If you use sp_dboption to change the options for the Bmodel database, these option settings will be in effect for any new databases you create. If FOR ATTACH is specified on the CREATE DATABASE statement, the new database inherits the database option settings of the original database.

The master database should be backed up after a user database is created.

When a SIZE parameter is not supplied in <filespec> for a primary file, SQL Server uses the size of the primary file in the model database.

When a SIZE parameter is not specified in <filespec> for a secondary or log file, SQL Server makes the file 1 MB.

When a simple CREATE DATABASE database_name statement is specified with no additional parameters, the database is made the same size as the model database.

All databases have at least a primary filegroup. All system tables are allocated in the primary filegroup. A database can also have user-defined filegroups. If an object is created with an ON *filegroup* clause specifying a user-defined filegroup, then all the pages for the object are allocated from the specified filegroup. The pages for all user objects created without an ON *filegroup* clause or with an ON DEFAULT clause are allocated from the default file group. When a database is first created, the primary filegroup is the default filegroup. You can specify a user-defined filegroup as the default filegroup using ALTER DATABASE:

```
ALTER DATABASE database_name MODIFY FILEGROUP filegroup_name DEFAULT
```

To display a report on a database or on all the databases on a SQL Server, execute sp_helpdb. For a report on the space used in a database, use sp_spaceused. For a report on the filegroups in a database, use sp_helpfilegroup, and use sp_helpfile for a report of the files in a database.

Earlier versions of SQL Server used DISK INIT statements to create the files for a database before the CREATE DATABASE statement was executed. For backward compatibility with earlier versions of SQL Server, the CREATE DATABASE statement can also create a new database on files or devices that were created with the DISK INIT statement.

Permissions

CREATE DATABASE permission defaults to the system administrator. The system administrator can grant CREATE DATABASE permissions to other logins. CREATE DATABASE permission must be explicitly granted; it is not granted by the GRANT ALL statement.

CREATE DATABASE permission is usually limited to a few logins to maintain control over disk usage on the computer running SQL Server.

CREATE DEFAULT

Creates an object called a *default*. When bound to a column or a user-defined data type, a default specifies a value to be inserted into the column to which the object is bound (or into all columns, in the case of a user-defined data type) when no value is explicitly supplied during an insert. Defaults, a backward compatibility feature, perform some of the same functions as default constraints. Default constraints, created using the DEFAULT keyword of ALTER or CREATE TABLE, are the preferred, standard way to restrict column data because the constraint definition is stored with the table and automatically dropped when the table is dropped. A default is beneficial, however, when the default is used multiple times for multiple columns.

Syntax

```
CREATE DEFAULT default
AS constant_expression
```

Arguments

default

> The name of the default. Default names must conform to the rules for identifiers. Specifying the default owner name is optional.

constant_expression

> An expression that contains only constant values (it cannot include the names of any columns or other database objects). Any constant, built-in function, or mathematical expression can be used. Enclose character and date constants in single quotation marks ('); monetary, integer, and floating-point constants do not require quotation marks. Binary data must be preceded by 0x, and monetary data must be preceded by a dollar sign ($). The default value must be compatible with the data type of the column.

Remarks

When creating defaults using the CREATE DEFAULT statement:

> ➤ A default can be created only in the current database. Within a database, default names must be unique by owner. After a default has been created, use sp_bindefault to bind it to a column or to a user-defined data type.

➤ If the default is not compatible with the column to which it is bound, Microsoft SQL Server generates an error message when trying to insert the default value. For example, N/A cannot be used as a default for a **numeric** column.

➤ If the default value is too long for the column to which it is bound, the value is truncated.

➤ CREATE DEFAULT statements cannot be combined with other Transact-SQL statements in a single batch.

➤ To display definitions and binding information, execute sp_helptext. Find the value of a default by using sp_helptext with the default name as the parameter.

➤ A default must be dropped before creating a new one of the same name, and the default must be unbound by executing sp_unbindefault before it is dropped.

➤ If a column has both a default and a rule associated with it, the default value must not violate the rule. A default that conflicts with a rule is never inserted, and SQL Server generates an error message each time it attempts to insert the default.

Once bound to a column, a default value is inserted when:

➤ A value is not explicitly inserted.

➤ Either the DEFAULT VALUES or DEFAULT keywords are used with INSERT to insert default values. For more information and examples, see INSERT.

➤ If NOT NULL is specified when creating a column and a default is not created for it, an error message is generated whenever a user fails to make an entry in that column. This table illustrates the relationship between the existence of a default and the definition of a column as NULL or NOT NULL. The entries in the table show the result.

Column definition	No entry, no default	No entry, default	Enter NULL, no default	Enter NULL, default
NULL	NULL	default	NULL	NULL
NOT NULL	error	default	error	error

➤ To rename a default, use sp_rename. For a report on a default, use sp_help.

Permissions

CREATE DEFAULT permission defaults to members of the db_owner fixed database role, who can transfer it to other users.

CREATE INDEX

Creates an index on a given table. This statement either changes the physical ordering of the table or provides the optimizer with a logical ordering of the table to increase query efficiency. When an index is created for the primary key, use the table- and column-level primary key constraints by specifying the PRIMARY KEY keywords provided with either the CREATE TABLE or ALTER TABLE statements.

Only the table owner can create indexes on that table. The owner of a table can create an index at any time, whether or not there is data in the table. Indexes can be created on tables in another database by specifying a qualified database name.

Syntax

```
CREATE [UNIQUE] [CLUSTERED | NONCLUSTERED]
INDEX index_name ON table (column [, ...n])
[WITH
[PAD_INDEX]
[[,] FILLFACTOR = fillfactor]
[[,] IGNORE_DUP_KEY]
[[,] DROP_EXISTING]
[[,] STATISTICS_NORECOMPUTE]
]
[ON filegroup]
```

Arguments

UNIQUE

Creates a unique index (one in which no two rows are permitted to have the same index value). Microsoft SQL Server checks for duplicate values when the index is created (if data already exists) and checks each time data is added with an INSERT or UPDATE statement. If duplicate key values exist, the CREATE INDEX statement is canceled and an error message giving the first duplicate is returned. A unique index cannot be created on a single column or multiple columns (composite index) where the complete key (all columns of that key) is NULL in more than one row; these are treated as duplicate values for indexing purposes.

When a unique index exists, UPDATE or INSERT statements that would generate duplicate key values are rolled back, and SQL Server displays an error message. This is true even if the UPDATE or INSERT statement changes many rows but causes only one duplicate. If an attempt is made to enter data for which there is a unique index and the IGNORE_DUP_KEY option is specified, only the rows violating the UNIQUE index fail. When processing an UPDATE statement, IGNORE_DUP_KEY has no effect. (For more information, see the IGNORE_DUP_KEY option, later in this topic.)

SQL Server does not allow the creation of a unique index on columns that already include duplicate values, whether or not IGNORE_DUP_KEY is set. If attempted, SQL Server displays an error message; duplicates must be eliminated before a unique index can be created on the column(s).

CLUSTERED

Creates an object where the physical order of rows is the same as the indexed order of the rows, and the bottom (leaf) level of the clustered index contains the actual data rows. Because nonclustered indexes are rebuilt when a clustered index is created, create the clustered index before creating any nonclustered indexes.

If CLUSTERED is not specified, a nonclustered index is created.

Note Because the leaf level of a clustered index and its data pages are the same by definition, creating a clustered index and using the ON *filegroup* clause effectively moves a table from the file on which the table was created to the new filegroup. Before creating tables or indexes on specific filegroups, verify which filegroups are available and that they have enough empty space for the index. It is vital that the filegroup have at least 1.2 times the space required for the entire table.

NONCLUSTERED

Creates an object that specifies the logical ordering of a table. With a nonclustered index, the physical order of the rows is not the same as their indexed order. The leaf level of a nonclustered index contains references to row index entries. That is, each index entry contains an indexed value and a reference to the row with that value. If the table does not have a clustered index, the reference is the row's disk address. If the table does have a clustered index, the reference is the search key in the clustered index.

Each table can have as many as 249 nonclustered indexes (regardless of how they are created: implicitly with constraints or explicitly with CREATE INDEX). Each index can provide access to the data in a different sort order.

index_name

The name of the index. Index names must be unique within a table but need not be unique within a database. Index names must follow the rules of identifiers.

Note A computed column, as created in a CREATE TABLE statement, cannot be used as a key column or as part of any PRIMARY KEY, UNIQUE, FOREIGN KEY, or CHECK constraint definition.

table

The table that contains the column or columns to be indexed. Specifying the database and table owner names are optional.

column

The column or columns to which the index applies. Specify two or more column names to create a composite index on the combined values in the specified columns. List the columns to be included in the composite index (in sort-priority order) inside the parentheses after *table*.

Note Columns consisting of the **ntext**, **text**, **image**, or **bit** data types or computed columns cannot be specified as columns for an index.

Composite indexes are used when two or more columns are best searched as a unit or if many queries reference only columns in the index. As many as 16 columns can be combined into a single composite index. All the columns in a composite index must be in the same table. The maximum allowable size of the combined index values is 900 bytes. (That is, the sum of the lengths of the columns that make up the composite index cannot exceed 900 bytes.)

Note Although composite indexes of two or more columns can be used as an index expression, SQL Server built-in functions such as UPPER cannot be used in the index expression.

n

A placeholder indicating that multiple *columns* can be specified for any particular index.

PAD_INDEX

Specifies the space to leave open on each interior node. By default, SQL Server ensures that each index node accommodates at least two rows of the index maximum size. If the setting specified for PAD_INDEX falls below this two-row index maximum size, then SQL Server internally overrides the specified setting to allow a minimum of two rows of the index maximum size. The PAD_INDEX setting is useful only when FILLFACTOR is also specified, because PAD_INDEX uses the same percentage specified by FILLFACTOR.

Note The number of items on an interior index page is never less than two, regardless of how low the value of FILLFACTOR.

FILLFACTOR = *fillfactor*

Specifies how full SQL Server should make the leaf level of each index page during index creation. When an index page fills up, SQL Server must take time to split the index page to make room for new rows, which is quite time-consuming. For update-intensive tables, a properly chosen FILLFACTOR value yields better update performance than an improper FILLFACTOR value. The value of the original FILLFACTOR is stored with the index in sysindexes.

When FILLFACTOR is specified, SQL Server rounds up on the number of rows to be placed on each page. For example, issuing CREATE CLUSTERED INDEX ... FILLFACTOR = 33 creates a clustered index. Assume that SQL Server calculates that 5.2 rows in 33% of the space on a page. SQL Server rounds so that 6 rows are placed on each page.

Note Using an explicit FILLFACTOR setting applies only when the index is first created. SQL Server does not dynamically keep the specified percentage of empty space in the pages.

User-specified FILLFACTOR values can be from 1 through 100. If no value is specified, the default value is 0. When FILLFACTOR is set to 0, only the leaf pages are filled. Space is left in nonleaf pages for at least two entries where an entry is an index pointer in an index page. Change the default FILLFACTOR setting by executing sp_configure.

Use a FILLFACTOR of 100 only when there are no INSERT or UPDATE statements. If FILLFACTOR is 100, SQL Server creates indexes with leaf pages 100 percent full. A FILLFACTOR of 100 makes sense only for read-only tables. An INSERT or UPDATE made after the creation of an index with a 100 percent FILLFACTOR causes page splits for each INSERT and possibly each UPDATE. The default FILLFACTOR algorithm assumes that there is at least enough space for one more entry in an internal page.

Setting FILLFACTOR to 100 completely fills the leaf pages; therefore, the leaf pages have no space for additional items. Setting FILLFACTOR to 100 fills index node pages except for space for two entries.

Smaller FILLFACTOR values (except 0) cause SQL Server to create new indexes with pages that are not completely full. For example, a FILLFACTOR of 10 can be a reasonable choice when creating an index on a table that is known to contain a small portion of the data that it will eventually hold. Smaller FILLFACTOR values also cause each index to take more storage space.

When FILLFACTOR is set to any value other than 0 or 100, space is left in nonleaf pages for one entry (two for non-unique clustered indexes), and space is left in leaf pages so that no leaf page is more full than the percentage specified by FILLFACTOR, as shown in the following table.

FILLFACTOR	Internal Page	Leaf Page
0%	Two free entries	100% full
1 - 99%	Two free entries	<= FILLFACTOR % full
100%	Two free entries	100% full

Tip Creating a clustered index with FILLFACTOR affects the amount of storage space the data occupies because SQL Server redistributes the data when it creates the clustered index.

IGNORE_DUP_KEY

Controls what happens when attempting to insert a duplicate key in a unique clustered index. It is meaningful only when the INSERT statement affects multiple rows. SQL Server issues a warning and does not insert the row containing the duplicate. If IGNORE_DUP_KEY is set and an INSERT statement that creates duplicate keys is executed, the row causing the duplicates is ignored.

Note If IGNORE_DUP_KEY is not specified, no rows are inserted by the INSERT.

A unique index cannot be created on a column that already includes duplicate values, whether or not IGNORE_DUP_KEY is set. If attempted, SQL Server displays an error message and lists the duplicate values. Eliminate the duplicate values before creating a unique index on the column.

The IGNORE_DUP_KEY index option controls what happens when a duplicate key is created with the INSERT statement. The table shows when these options can be used.

Index Type	Options
Clustered	IGNORE_DUP_KEY allowed.
Unique clustered	IGNORE_DUP_KEY allowed.
Nonclustered	Not allowed.
Unique nonclustered	IGNORE_DUP_KEY allowed.

DROP_EXISTING

Specifies that the given table's clustered index should be dropped and rebuilt. Then, all existing nonclustered indexes are updated. Because nonclustered indexes must go through the clustered index to gain access to rows in a table, the DROP_EXISTING option prevents two UPDATE operations of the nonclustered indexes: the first update after the drop of the clustered index and the second update after the clustered index is re-created.

If the same index name and columns as the original index are provided, SQL Server will not sort the rows. If a different index name and columns from the original index are provided, SQL Server sorts the rows. If the leaf level of the index is not sorted, the CREATE INDEX statement fails.

Note When executing a CREATE INDEX statement with the DROP_EXISTING option, SQL Server assumes that the index is consistent (there is no corruption in the index). The rows in the specified index should be sorted by the specified key referenced in the CREATE INDEX statement.

STATISTICS_NORECOMPUTE

Specifies that out-of-date index statistics are not automatically recomputed. To restore automatic statistics updating, execute UPDATE STATISTICS without the NORECOMPUTE option.

Tip Disabling automatic recomputation of distribution statistics may prevent the SQL Server optimizer from picking optimal execution plans for queries involving the table.

ON *filegroup*

Creates the specified index on the given *filegroup*. The filegroup must have already been created by executing either CREATE DATABASE or ALTER DATABASE.

Remarks

When creating indexes using the CREATE INDEX statement:

➤ Space is allocated to tables and indexes in increments of one extent (eight 8 K pages) at a time. Each time an extent is filled, another is allocated. Indexes on very small or empty tables will use single page allocations until eight pages have been added to the index and then will switch to extent allocations. For a report on the amount of space allocated and used by an index, use sp_spaceused.

➤ Creating a clustered index requires space available in your database equal to approximately 1.2 times the size of the data. This is space in addition to the space used by the existing table; the data is duplicated in order to create the clustered index, and the old, nonindexed data is deleted when the index is complete. When using the DROP_EXISTING option, the space needed for the clustered index is the amount of space equal to the existing index's space requirements.

Note Because the maximum allowable index size is 900 bytes, large **char**, **varchar**, **binary**, and **varbinary** columns (greater than 900 bytes) or **nchar** or **nvarchar** columns (greater than 450 characters) cannot be used in an index.

➤ If CREATE INDEX is performed in the context of an explicit transaction, allocation locks are taken and held until the explicit transaction is committed. Because allocation locks are taken and held until the explicit transaction is committed, large index creation operations may consume large amounts of memory for obtaining these locks, or the index creation may fail if lock space is exhausted. If the same CREATE INDEX statement is performed using an implicit transaction, it does not fail because allocation locks are not held for implicit transactions.

➤ Indexes can be created on a temporary table. When the table is dropped or the session ends, all indexes and triggers are dropped.

➤ To display a report on an object's indexes, execute sp_helpindex.

➤ Entire filegroups affected by a CREATE INDEX statement since the last filegroup backup must be backed up as a unit.

➤ If CREATE INDEX is executed during a database or transaction log backup, SQL Server aborts the BACKUP statement and the backup operation fails.

Permissions

CREATE INDEX permission defaults to the table owner and is not transferable.

CREATE PROCEDURE

Creates a stored procedure (a saved collection of Transact-SQL statements) that can take and/or return user-supplied parameters. Stored procedures increase performance and consistency when performing repetitive tasks because stored procedures are compiled the first time they are executed. When executed again, subsequent run time is much shorter than for the equivalent set of stand-alone statements because the execution plan is cached and resides in memory. Procedures can be created for permanent use or for temporary use within a user's session (local temporary procedure) or for temporary use within all users' sessions (global temporary procedure). Stored procedures can also control access and update databases by executing business logic between the user request and the actual database statement(s).

Syntax

```
CREATE PROC[EDURE] procedure_name [;number]
[
{@parameter data_type} [VARYING] [= default] [OUTPUT]
]
[, ...n]
[WITH
{
RECOMPILE
| ENCRYPTION
| RECOMPILE, ENCRYPTION
}
]
[FOR REPLICATION]
AS
sql_statement [...n]
```

Arguments

procedure_name

The name of the new stored procedure. Procedure names must conform to the rules for identifiers and must be unique within the database and its owner.

Local or global temporary procedures can be created by preceding *procedure_name* with a single number sign (*#procedure_name*) for local temporary procedures and a double number sign (*##procedure_name*) for global temporary procedures. The complete name, including # or ##, cannot exceed 128 characters. Stored procedures can also be created for autoexecution. Autoexecution stored procedures are run automatically when Microsoft SQL Server starts. Specifying the procedure owner name is optional.

;number

> An optional integer used to group procedures of the same name so they can be dropped together with a single DROP PROCEDURE statement. When grouping is used with a procedure whose name was created using delimited identifiers, the number should not be included as part of the identifier; use the appropriate delimiter only around *procedure*. For example, if the procedures were created using quoted identifiers (""), then surround the procedure name with quotes. For example, "detailproc". If the procedures were created using bracketed delimiters ([and]), then surround the procedure name with [and]. For example, [detailproc]. Use the same procedure name for procedures in the same group. Procedures used in the same application are often grouped this way. For example, the procedures used with the application *orders* might be named orderproc;1, orderproc;2, and so on. The statement DROP PROCEDURE orderproc drops the entire group. After procedures have been grouped, individual procedures within the group cannot be dropped.

@parameter

> A parameter in the procedure. One or more parameters can optionally be declared in a CREATE PROCEDURE statement. The value of each declared parameter must be supplied by the user when the procedure is executed (unless a *default* for the parameter has been defined). A stored procedure can have a maximum of 1,024 parameters.

> The first character of a parameter name must be the at sign (@) and conform to the rules for identifiers. Parameters are local to the procedure; the same parameter names can be used in other procedures. By default, parameters can take the place only of constants; they cannot be used in place of table names, column names, or the names of other database objects. For more information, see EXECUTE.

> Parameters are nullable, by default. If a NULL parameter value is passed and that parameter is used (in a CREATE or ALTER TABLE statement) where the column referenced does not allow NULLs (inserting into a non-NULL column), SQL Server generates an error. To prevent passing a NULL parameter value to a non-NULL column, either add programming logic to the procedure or use a default value (with the DEFAULT keyword of CREATE or ALTER TABLE) for the column.

data_type

> The data type of the parameter. All data types, including **text** and **image**, may be used as a parameter for a stored procedure. However, the **cursor** data type may only be used on OUTPUT parameters and cannot be used for input parameters. When specifying a data type of **cursor**, the VARYING and OUTPUT keywords must also be specified.

Note There is no limit on the maximum number of output parameters that can be of **cursor** data type.

VARYING

Specifies the result set supported as an output parameter (constructed dynamically by the stored procedure and whose contents can vary). Applies only to cursor parameters.

default

A default value for the parameter. If a default is defined, a user can execute the procedure without specifying a value for that parameter. The default must be a constant. It can include wildcard characters (%, _, [], and [^]) if the procedure uses the parameter with the LIKE keyword. The default can be NULL. The procedure definition can specify that some action be taken if the parameter value is NULL.

OUTPUT

Indicates that the parameter is a return parameter. The value of this option can be returned to EXEC[UTE]. Use return parameters to return information to the calling procedure. Text parameters cannot be used as OUTPUT parameters. An output parameter using the OUTPUT keyword can be a cursor placeholder.

n

A placeholder indicating that up to 1,024 parameters may be specified.

{RECOMPILE | ENCRYPTION | RECOMPILE, ENCRYPTION}

RECOMPILE indicates that SQL Server does not cache a plan for this procedure and the procedure is recompiled each time it is executed. Use the RECOMPILE option when using atypical or temporary values without overriding the execution plan that is cached in memory.

When created, a stored procedure is resolved, which allows the procedure to be associated with a particular table. When that table is dropped at a later date, all stored procedures associated with that table should be dropped and re-created to be resolved again.

The WITH RECOMPILE option does not perform the resolution process; therefore, using WITH RECOMPILE with new tables since the procedure was originally created is not useful. Executing the WITH RECOMPILE option allows SQL Server to rebuild the query plan that SQL Server uses each time the procedure is executed.

Note If any constraints are added or altered, any stored procedures referencing the table are automatically recompiled.

ENCRYPTION indicates that SQL Server encrypts the syscomments table entry containing the text of the CREATE PROCEDURE statement.

Note During an upgrade, SQL Server uses the encrypted comments stored in syscomments to re-create encrypted procedures.

FOR REPLICATION

This option is mutually exclusive of the WITH RECOMPILE option. Specifies that stored procedures created for replication cannot be executed on the subscribing server and is used when creating a filter stored procedure that is executed only by replication.

AS

Specifies the actions the procedure is to take.

sql_statement

Any number and type of Transact-SQL statements to be included in the procedure. Some limitations do apply.

n

A placeholder indicating that multiple Transact-SQL statements may be included in this procedure.

Remarks

When creating procedures using the CREATE PROCEDURE statement:

➤ The maximum size of a stored procedure is 128 KB.

➤ When defining a user-defined stored procedure, a stored procedure can be created only in the current database (except for temporary procedures, which are always created in tempdb). The CREATE PROCEDURE statement cannot be combined with other Transact-SQL statements in a single batch.

Note A user-defined stored procedure may exist in any database, including master or any user-defined database. However, when a user-defined stored procedure meets all of the following conditions, then this user-defined stored procedure is more correctly identified as a user-defined system stored procedure:

➤ Exists in the master database.
➤ Is owned by a member of the db_owner fixed database role.
➤ Starts with sp_ as the first three characters of the procedure name.

➤ If the first three characters of the procedure name are sp_, SQL Server searches the master database for the procedure. If no qualified procedure name is provided, SQL Server searches for the procedure as if the owner name is dbo. To resolve the stored procedure name as a user-defined stored procedure with the same name as a system stored procedure, provide the fully qualified procedure name.

➤ SQL Server saves the settings of both SET QUOTED_IDENTIFIER and SET ANSI_NULLS when a stored procedure is created or altered. These original settings are restored when the stored procedure is executed. Therefore, any client session settings for SET QUOTED_IDENTIFIER and SET ANSI_NULLS are restored after stored procedure execution. Within the stored procedure, any changes to SET ANSI_NULLS do not take effect until the stored procedure completes execution.

Other SET options, such as SET ARITHABORT, SET ANSI_WARNINGS, or SET ANSI_PADDINGS, are not saved when a stored procedure is created or altered. If the logic of the stored procedure is dependent on a particular setting, include a SET statement at the start of the procedure to ensure the proper setting. When a SET statement is executed from a stored procedure, the setting remains in effect only until the stored procedure completes. The setting is then restored to the value it had when the stored procedure was called. This allows individual clients freedom to set the options wanted without impacting the logic of the stored procedure.

Note Whether SQL Server interprets an empty string (NULL) as either a single space or as a true empty string is controlled by the setting of sp_dbcmptlevel. If the setting of sp_dbcmptlevel is less than or equal to 65, then SQL Server interprets empty strings as single spaces. If the setting of sp_dbcmptlevel is equal to 70, then SQL Server interprets empty strings as empty strings.

CREATE RULE

Creates an object called a *rule*. When bound to a column or a user-defined data type, a rule specifies the acceptable values that can be inserted into that column. Rules, a backward compatibility feature, perform some of the same functions as CHECK constraints. CHECK constraints, created using the CHECK keyword of ALTER or CREATE TABLE, are the preferred, standard way to restrict the values in a column (multiple constraints can be defined on a column or multiple columns). A column or user-defined data type can have only one rule bound to it. However, a column can have a rule and one or more CHECK constraints associated with it. When this is true, all restrictions are evaluated.

Syntax

```
CREATE RULE rule
AS condition_expression
```

Arguments

rule

> The name of the new rule. Rule names must conform to the rules for identifiers. Specifying the rule owner name is optional.

condition_expression

> The condition(s) defining the rule. A rule can be any expression that is valid in a WHERE clause, and it can include such elements as arithmetic operators, relational operators, and predicates (for example, IN, LIKE, BETWEEN). A rule cannot reference columns or other database objects. Built-in functions that do not reference database objects can be included.

> A *condition_expression* includes one variable. The at sign (@) precedes each local variable. The expression refers to the value that is entered with the UPDATE or INSERT statement. Any name or symbol can be used to represent the value when writing the rule, but the first character must be @.

Remarks

When creating rules using the CREATE RULE statement:

➤ The CREATE RULE statement cannot be combined with other Transact-SQL statements in a single batch. Rules do not apply to data already existing in the database at the time the rules are created, and rules cannot be bound to system data types. A rule can be created only in the current database. After creating a rule, execute sp_bindrule to bind the rule to a column or to a user-defined data type.

➤ The rule must be compatible with the data type of the column. A rule cannot be bound to a **text**, **image**, or **timestamp** column. Be sure to enclose character and date constants with single quotation marks (') and to precede binary constants with 0x. For example, "@value LIKE A%" cannot be used as a rule for a numeric column. If the rule is not compatible with the column to which it has been bound, Microsoft SQL Server returns an error message when inserting a value (not when the rule is bound).

➤ A rule bound to a user-defined data type is activated only when attempting to insert a value into or to update a database column of the user-defined data type. Because rules do not test variables, do not assign a value to a user-defined data type variable that would be rejected by a rule bound to a column of the same data type.

➤ To get a report on a rule, use sp_help. To display the text of a rule, execute sp_helptext with the rule name as the parameter. To rename a rule, use sp_rename.

➤ It is necessary to drop a rule (using DROP RULE) before creating a new one with the same name, and the rule must be unbound (using sp_unbindrule) before it is dropped. Use sp_unbindrule to unbind a rule from a column.

➤ A new rule can be bound to a column or data type without unbinding the previous one; the new rule overrides the previous one. Rules bound to columns always take precedence over rules bound to user-defined data types. Binding a rule to a column replaces a rule already bound to the user-defined data type of that column. But binding a rule to a data type does not replace a rule bound to a column of that user-defined data type. The table shows the precedence in effect when binding rules to columns and to user-defined data types where rules already exist.

New Rule Bound to:	User-defined Data Type	Column
User-defined data type	Old rule replaced	No change
Column	Old rule replaced	Old rule replaced

➤ If a column has both a default and a rule associated with it, the default must fall within the domain defined by the rule. A default that conflicts with a rule is never inserted. SQL Server generates an error message each time it attempts to insert such a default.

Note Whether SQL Server interprets an empty string (NULL) as either a single space or as a true empty string is controlled by the setting of sp_dbcmptlevel. If the setting of sp_dbcmptlevel is less than or equal to 65, then SQL Server interprets empty strings as single spaces. If the setting of sp_dbcmptlevel is equal to 70, then SQL Server interprets empty strings as empty strings.

Permissions

CREATE RULE permissions default to the members of the db_owner fixed database role, who can transfer them to other users.

CREATE SCHEMA

Creates a schema that can be thought of as a conceptual container object, which is the definition of the database without any data in it.

Syntax

```
CREATE SCHEMA
[AUTHORIZATION owner]
[schema_element [schema_element2[...schema_elementn]]]
```

Arguments

AUTHORIZATION *owner*

Specifies the ID of the schema object owner. This identifier must be a valid security account in the database.

schema_element = {*table_definition* | *view_definition* | *grant_statement*}

table_definition = CREATE TABLE statement

Creates a table within this defined schema.

view_definition = CREATE VIEW statement

> Creates a view for this schema.

grant_statement = GRANT statement

> Grants permissions to a user or group of users.

Remarks

Often database developers find it useful to keep a script or procedure which creates the database schema for creating a copy of the database for testing or installation. Database administrators can set up a database and use the CREATE SCHEMA statement to set up all of the objects and permissions in a single batch.

CREATE SCHEMA provides a way to create database objects such as tables and views and to grant permissions on the objects, all within a single batch. The created objects do not need to appear in logical order. For example, a GRANT statement can grant permission to an object before the object itself has been created.

In another example, a CREATE VIEW statement can appear before the CREATE TABLE statement is created as long as all necessary objects are in the same CREATE SCHEMA statement. Also, the CREATE TABLE statement can declare foreign keys to tables that have not yet been created. Because objects are created at the same time, it is possible to create two tables that have mutually dependent foreign keys.

There are other ways to achieve the same results (DDL in transaction or add foreign key after creating both tables), and there are no restrictions to the objects created with CREATE SCHEMA other than that they are created under the current database user. In Microsoft SQL Server, using the owner qualifier on database objects or on a separate database is usually preferable to using the CREATE SCHEMA statement.

The tables and view can be specified in any order. For example, a view can appear before the table on which it is defined.

CREATE TABLE

Creates a new table.

Syntax

```
CREATE TABLE table_name
( { <column_definition>
| column_name AS computed_column_expression
| <table_constraint>
} [, ...n]
)
[ON {filegroup | DEFAULT} ]
[TEXTIMAGE_ON {filegroup | DEFAULT} ]
<column_definition> ::= { column_name data_type }
[ NULL | NOT NULL ]
[ IDENTITY [(seed, increment )
[NOT FOR REPLICATION] ] ]
[ ROWGUIDCOL ]
```

```
[ <column_constraint> ::=
[CONSTRAINT constraint_name]
{ { PRIMARY KEY | UNIQUE }
[CLUSTERED | NONCLUSTERED]
[WITH [FILLFACTOR = fillfactor]
[[,] {SORTED_DATA
| SORTED_DATA_REORG}]]
[ON {filegroup | DEFAULT} ]
| [FOREIGN KEY]
REFERENCES ref_table
[ ( ref_column ) ]
[NOT FOR REPLICATION]
| DEFAULT constant_expression
| CHECK [NOT FOR REPLICATION]
(logical_expression)
}
] [ ...n]
<table_constraint> ::= [CONSTRAINT constraint_name]
{ [ { PRIMARY KEY | UNIQUE }
[ CLUSTERED | NONCLUSTERED]
{ ( column[, ...n] ) } }
[ WITH [FILLFACTOR = fillfactor]
[[,] {SORTED_DATA
| SORTED_DATA_REORG} ]
]
[ON {filegroup | DEFAULT} ]
]
| FOREIGN KEY
[(column[, ...n])]
REFERENCES ref_table [(ref_column[, ...n])]
[NOT FOR REPLICATION]
| CHECK [NOT FOR REPLICATION]
(search_conditions)
}
```

Arguments

table_name

> The name of the new table. Table names must conform to the rules for identifiers and the combination of *owner.table_name* must be unique within the database. The length of the name for a local temporary table (when the name is prefixed with a single number sign (#)) cannot exceed 116 characters. For all other tables, *table_name* can contain up to 128 characters.

column_name

> The name of a column in the table. Column names must conform to the rules for identifiers and must be unique in the table. *column_name* can be omitted for columns created with a **timestamp** data type; the name **timestamp** is used if *column_name* is not specified for a **timestamp** column.

computed_column_expression

An expression defining the value of a *computed column*. A computed column is a virtual column not physically stored in the table. It is computed from an expression using other columns in the same table. For example, a computed column could have the definition: cost AS price * qty. The expression can be a noncomputed column name, constant, function, variable, and any combination of these connected by one or more operators. The expression cannot be a subquery.

Computed columns can be used in select lists, WHERE clauses, ORDER BY clauses, or any other locations where regular expressions can be used, with the following exceptions:

➤ A computed column cannot be used as a key column in an index or as part of any PRIMARY KEY, UNIQUE, FOREIGN KEY, or DEFAULT constraint definition.

➤ A computed column cannot be the target of an INSERT or UPDATE statement.

Note Because each row in a table may have different values for columns involved in a computed column, the computed column may not have the same result for each row.

ON {*filegroup* | DEFAULT}

Specifies the filegroup in which the table is stored. If *filegroup* is specified, the table is stored in the named filegroup. The filegroup must exist within the database. If DEFAULT is specified or if ON is not specified at all, the table is stored in the default filegroup.

ON {*filegroup* | DEFAULT} can also be specified in a PRIMARY KEY or UNIQUE constraint. These constraints create indexes. If *filegroup* is specified, the index is stored in the named filegroup. If DEFAULT is specified, the index is stored in the default filegroup. If no filegroup is specified in a constraint, the index is stored in the same filegroup as the table.

TEXTIMAGE_ON

Keywords indicating that the **text**, **ntext**, and **image** columns are stored on the specified filegroup. TEXTIMAGE ON is not allowed if there are no **text**, **ntext**, or **image** columns in the table. If TEXTIMAGE_ON is not specified the **text**, **ntext**, and **image** columns are stored in the same filegroup as the table.

data_type

Specifies the data type of the column. System or user-defined data types are acceptable. User-defined data types are created with sp_addtype before they can be used in a table definition.

The NULL/NOT NULL assignment for a user-defined data type can be overridden during the CREATE TABLE statement. However, the length specification cannot be changed; you cannot specify a length for a user-defined data type in a CREATE TABLE statement.

NULL | NOT NULL

Keywords that determine whether or not NULL values are allowed in the column.

IDENTITY

A keyword indicating that the new column is an identity column. When a new row is added to the table, Microsoft SQL Server provides a unique, incremental value for the column. Identity columns are commonly used in conjunction with PRIMARY KEY constraints to serve as the unique row identifier for the table. The IDENTITY property can be assigned to a **tinyint**, **smallint**, **int**, **decimal(p,0)**, or **numeric(p,0)** columns. Only one identity column can be created per table. Bound defaults and DEFAULT constraints cannot be used with an identity column. You must specify either both the seed and increment, or neither. If neither are specified, the default is (1,1).

seed

The value that is used for the very first row loaded into the table.

increment

The incremental value that is added to the identity value of the previous row that was loaded.

NOT FOR REPLICATION

Indicates that the IDENTITY property should not be enforced when a replication login such as sqlrepl inserts data into the table.

ROWGUIDCOL

A keyword indicating that the new column is a row global unique identifier column. Only one **uniqueidentifier** column per table can be designated as the ROWGUIDCOL column. The ROWGUIDCOL property can be assigned only to a **uniqueidentifier** column.

The ROWGUIDCOL property does not enforce uniqueness of the values stored in the column. It also does not automatically generate values for new rows inserted into the table. To generate unique values for each column, either use the NEWID function on INSERT statements or use the NEWID function as the default for the column.

CONSTRAINT

An optional keyword indicating the beginning of a PRIMARY KEY, UNIQUE, FOREIGN KEY, CHECK, or DEFAULT constraint definition. Constraints are special properties that enforce data integrity and create special types of indexes for the table and its columns.

constraint_name

> The name of a constraint. Constraint names must be unique within a database.

PRIMARY KEY

> A constraint that enforces entity integrity for a given column or columns through a unique index. Only one PRIMARY KEY constraint can be created per table.

UNIQUE

> A constraint that provides entity integrity for a given column or columns through a unique index. A table can have multiple UNIQUE constraints.

CLUSTERED | NONCLUSTERED

> Keywords to indicate that a clustered or a nonclustered index is created for the PRIMARY KEY or UNIQUE constraint. PRIMARY KEY constraints default to CLUSTERED and UNIQUE constraints default to NONCLUSTERED.

> You can only specify CLUSTERED for one constraint in a CREATE TABLE statement. If you specify CLUSTERED for a UNIQUE constraint and also specify a PRIMARY KEY constraint, the PRIMARY KEY defaults to NONCLUSTERED.

WITH [FILLFACTOR = *fillfactor*]

> Specifies how full SQL Server should make each index page used to store the index data. User-specified *fillfactor* values can be from 1 through 100. If you don't specify a value, the default is 0. A lower *fillfactor* creates the index with more space available for new index entries without having to allocate new space.

WITH [SORTED_DATA | SORTED_DATA_REORG]

> Options that eliminate the sort performed when a clustered index is created. The data in the column(s) used for the index must already be stored in a sorted order or an error is returned.

FOREIGN KEY...REFERENCES

> A constraint that provides referential integrity for the data in the column or columns. FOREIGN KEY constraints require that each value in the column exists in the corresponding referenced column(s) in the referenced table. FOREIGN KEY constraints can only reference columns that are primary or unique constraints in the referenced table.

ref_table

> The name of the table referenced by the FOREIGN KEY constraint.

(*ref_column*[, ...])

> A column or list of columns referenced by the FOREIGN KEY constraint.

DEFAULT

> A constraint that specifies the value provided for the column when a value is not explicitly supplied during an insert. DEFAULT values can be applied to any columns except those defined as **timestamp**, or those with the IDENTITY property. DEFAULT values are removed when the table is dropped. Only a literal

value, such as a character string; a system function, such as SYSTEM_USER(); or a NULL can be used as a default value.

constant_expression

A literal value, a NULL, or a system function used as the default value for the column.

CHECK

A constraint that enforces domain integrity by limiting the possible values that can be entered into a column or columns.

NOT FOR REPLICATION

Keywords used to prevent the CHECK constraint from being enforced during the distribution process used by replication. When tables are subscribers to a replication publication, users should not update the subscription table directly; they should instead update the publishing table and let replication distribute the data back to the subscribing table. A CHECK constraint can be defined on the subscription table to prevent users from modifying it. Unless the NOT FOR REPLICATION clause is added, however, the CHECK constraint would also prevent the replication process from distributing modifications from the publishing table to the subscribing table. The NOT FOR REPLICATION clause means the constraint is enforced on user modifications, but not for the replication process.

The NOT FOR REPLICATION CHECK constraint is applied to both the before and after image of an updated record to prevent records from being added to or deleted from the replicated range. All deletes and inserts are checked; if they fall within the replicated range, they are rejected.

When used with an identity column, SQL Server allows the table not to have its identity column values reseeded when a replication user updates the identity column.

logical_expression

A logical expression that returns TRUE or FALSE.

column

A column or list of columns in parentheses used in table constraints to indicate the columns that are used in the constraint definition.

n

A placeholder indicating that the preceding item can be repeated *n* number of times.

Remarks

SQL Server can have as many as 2 billion tables per database and 1,024 columns per table. The number of rows and total size of the table are limited only by the available storage. The maximum number of bytes per row is 8,092. If you create tables with **varchar**, **nvarchar**, or **varbinary** columns whose total defined width exceeds 8,092 bytes, the table is created but a warning message appears. Trying to insert more than

8,092 bytes into such a row or to update a row so that its total row size exceeds 8,092 produces an error message and the statement fails.

The table is created in the current database unless a different database is explicitly specified in the CREATE TABLE statement with the optional database name. (Cross-database creation of tables and indexes is allowed as long as the creator is listed in the sysusers table of the other database and has CREATE TABLE permission in that database. However, cross-database creation of views, rules, defaults, stored procedures, and triggers is not allowed.)

Temporary Tables

You can create local and global temporary tables. Local temporary tables are visible only in the current session; global temporary tables are visible to all sessions.

Signify a local temporary table by prefixing *table_name* with a single number sign (*#table_name*) and prefix global temporary table names with a double number sign (*##table_name*).

SQL statements reference the temporary table using the value specified for *table_name* in the CREATE TABLE statement:

```
CREATE TABLE #MyTempTable (INT PRIMARY KEY)
INSERT INTO #MyTempTable VALUES (1)
```

If a local temporary table is created in a stored procedure or application that can be executed at the same time by several users, SQL Server has to be able to distinguish the tables created by the different users. SQL Server does this by internally appending a numeric suffix to each local temporary table name. The full name of a temporary table as stored in the sysobjects table consists of the *table_name* specified in the CREATE TABLE statement and the system-generated numeric suffix. To allow for the suffix, the *table_name* value specified for a local temporary name cannot exceed 116 characters.

Temporary tables are automatically dropped when they go out of scope, unless they have already been explicitly dropped using DROP TABLE:

➤ A local temporary table created in a stored procedure is automatically dropped when the stored procedure completes. The table can be referenced by any nested stored procedures executed by the stored procedure that created the table. The table cannot be referenced by the process that called the stored procedure that created the table.

➤ All other local temporary tables are automatically dropped at the end of the current session.

➤ Global temporary tables are automatically dropped when the session that created the table ends and all other tasks have stopped referencing them. The association between a task and a table is only maintained for the life of a single Transact-SQL statement. This means that a global temporary table is dropped at the completion of the last Transact-SQL statement that was actively referencing the table when the creating session ended.

When creating local or global temporary tables, the CREATE TABLE syntax supports constraint definitions with the exception of FOREIGN KEY constraints. If a FOREIGN KEY constraint is specified in a temporary table, the statement returns a warning message indicating that the constraint was skipped, and the table is created without the FOREIGN KEY constraints. Temporary tables cannot be referenced in FOREIGN KEY constraints.

PRIMARY KEY Constraints

➤ A table can contain only one PRIMARY KEY constraint.

➤ If CLUSTERED or NONCLUSTERED is not specified for a PRIMARY KEY constraint, CLUSTERED is used if there are no clustered indexes specified for UNIQUE constraints.

➤ All columns defined within a PRIMARY KEY constraint must be defined as NOT NULL. If nullability is not specified, all columns participating in a PRIMARY KEY constraint have their nullability set to NOT NULL.

UNIQUE Constraints

➤ If CLUSTERED or NONCLUSTERED is not specified for a UNIQUE constraint, NONCLUSTERED is used by default.

➤ A table can contain up to 249 unique constraints.

FOREIGN KEY Constraints

➤ When a non-null value is entered into the column of a FOREIGN KEY constraint, the value must exist in the referenced column; otherwise, a foreign key violation error message is returned.

➤ FOREIGN KEY constraints can reference only tables within the same database on the same server. If you want cross-database referential integrity or custom messaging, implement this functionality through triggers. For more information about creating triggers, see CREATE TRIGGER.

➤ FOREIGN KEY constraints can reference another column in the same table (a self-reference).

➤ The number of columns and data types of each column specified in a FOREIGN KEY constraint must match the columns in the REFERENCES clause.

➤ A table can contain a maximum of 63 FOREIGN KEY constraints.

➤ FOREIGN KEY constraints are not enforced on temporary tables.

➤ A table can reference up to 63 different tables in its FOREIGN KEY constraints.

➤ FOREIGN KEY constraints can only reference columns in PRIMARY KEY or UNIQUE constraints in the referenced table.

DEFAULT Constraints

➤ A column can have only one DEFAULT constraint.

➤ A DEFAULT constraint can contain constant values, functions, SQL-92 niladic functions, or NULL. The following table shows the niladic functions and the values they return for the default during an INSERT statement.

SQL-92 Niladic Function	Value Returned
CURRENT_TIMESTAMP	Current date and time
CURRENT_USER	Name of user performing insert
SESSION_USER	Name of user performing insert
SYSTEM_USER	Name of user performing insert
USER	Name of user performing insert

➤ *constant_expression* in a DEFAULT constraint cannot refer to another column in the table, and it cannot refer to other tables, views, or stored procedures.

➤ DEFAULT constraints cannot be created on columns with a **timestamp** data type or columns with an IDENTITY property.

➤ DEFAULT constraints cannot be created for columns with user-defined data types if the user-defined data type has a *bound* default.

CHECK Constraints

➤ A column can have any number of CHECK constraints, and the condition can include multiple logical expressions combined with AND and OR. Multiple CHECK constraints for a column are validated in the order they are created.

➤ The search condition must evaluate to a Boolean expression and cannot reference another table.

➤ A column-level CHECK constraint can only reference the constrained column, and a table-level CHECK constraint can only reference columns in the same table.

CHECK CONSTRAINTS and RULES serve the same function of validating the data during INSERT and DELETE statements.

➤ When a rule and one or more CHECK constraints exist for a column or columns, all restrictions are evaluated.

General Constraint Information

➤ An index created for a constraint cannot be dropped with the DROP INDEX statement; the constraint must be dropped with the ALTER TABLE statement. An index created for and used by a constraint can be rebuilt with the DBCC DBREINDEX statement.

➤ Constraint names must follow the rules for identifiers, except that the name cannot begin with a number sign (#). If *constraint_name* is not supplied, a system-generated name is assigned to the constraint. The *constraint_name* appears in any error message about constraint violations.

➤ When a constraint is violated in an INSERT, UPDATE, or DELETE statement, the statement is terminated. However, the transaction (if the statement is part of an explicit transaction) continues to be processed. You can use the ROLLBACK TRANSACTION statement with the transaction definition by checking the @@error global variable.

If a table has FOREIGN KEY or CHECK constraints and triggers, the constraint conditions are evaluated before the trigger is executed.

For a report on a table and its columns, use sp_help or sp_helpconstraint. To rename a table, use sp_rename. For a report on the views and stored procedures that depend on a table, use sp_depends.

Space is generally allocated to tables and indexes in increments of one extent at a time. When the table or index is created, it is allocated pages from mixed extents until it has enough pages to fill a uniform extent. After it has enough pages to fill a uniform extent, another extent is allocated each time the currently allocated extents become full. For a report on the amount of space allocated and used by a table, execute sp_spaceused.

Nullability Rules Within a Table Definition

The nullability of a column determines whether or not that column can allow a null value (NULL) as the data in that column. NULL is not 0 or blank. It means no entry has been made or an explicit NULL was supplied, and it usually implies that the value is either unknown or not applicable.

When creating or altering a table with the CREATE TABLE or ALTER TABLE statements, database and session settings influence and possibly override the nullability of the data type used in a column definition. It is recommended that you always explicitly define a column as NULL or NOT NULL or, if using a user-defined data type, allow the column to use the data type's default nullability.

When not explicitly specified, column nullability follows these rules:

➤ If the column is defined with a user-defined data type:
  ➤ SQL Server uses the nullability specified when the data type was created. Use sp_help to get the data type's default nullability.
➤ If the column is defined with a system-supplied data type:
  ➤ If the system-supplied data type has only one option, it takes precedence. **timestamp** data types must be NOT NULL.
  ➤ If the setting of sp_dbcmptlevel is 65 or lower, **bit** data types default to NOT NULL if the column does not have an explicit NULL or NOT NULL.
  ➤ If any session settings are ON (turned on with the SET statement), then:
    ➤ If ANSI_NULL_DFLT_ON is ON, NULL is assigned.
    ➤ If ANSI_NULL_DFLT_OFF is ON, NOT NULL is assigned.
  ➤ If any database settings are configured (changed with sp_dboption), then:
    ➤ If 'ANSI null default' is TRUE, NULL is assigned.
    ➤ If 'ANSI null default' is FALSE, NOT NULL is assigned.
➤ When not explicitly defined (neither of the ANSI_NULL_DFLT options are set) for the session and the database is set to the default ('ANSI null default' is FALSE), then the SQL Server default of NOT NULL is assigned.

Note The SQL Server ODBC driver and SQL Server OLE DB provider both default to having ANSI_NULL_DFLT_ON set to ON. ODBC and OLE DB users can configure this in ODBC data sources, or with connection attributes or properties set by the application.

CREATE TRIGGER

Creates a trigger, which is a special kind of stored procedure that is automatically executed when a user attempts the specified data modification statement on the specified table. Triggers are often used for enforcing business rules and data integrity. Referential integrity can be defined by using foreign key constraints (using the FOREIGN KEY keywords) in the CREATE TABLE statement. If constraints exist on the trigger table, they are checked prior to trigger execution. If either primary or foreign key constraints are violated, the trigger is not executed (fired). Microsoft SQL Server allows the creation of multiple triggers for any given INSERT, UPDATE, or DELETE statement.

Syntax

```
CREATE TRIGGER trigger_name
ON table
[WITH ENCRYPTION]
{
{FOR {[,] [DELETE] [,] [INSERT] [,] [UPDATE]}}
[WITH APPEND]
[NOT FOR REPLICATION]
AS
sql_statement [ ...n]
}
|
{FOR {[,] [INSERT] [,] [UPDATE]}}
[WITH APPEND]
[NOT FOR REPLICATION]
AS
IF UPDATE (column)
[{AND | OR} UPDATE (column)]
[ ...n]
sql_statement [ ...n]
}
}
```

Arguments

trigger_name

      The name of the trigger. A trigger name must conform to the rules for identifiers and must be unique within the database. Providing the trigger owner name is optional.

table

The table on which the trigger is executed; sometimes called the trigger table. Providing the owner name of the table is optional. Views cannot be specified.

WITH ENCRYPTION

Encrypts the syscomments entries that contain the text of CREATE TRIGGER.

{[,] [DELETE] [,] [INSERT] [,] [UPDATE] } | {[,] [INSERT] [,] [UPDATE]}

Keywords that specify which data modification statements, when attempted against this table, activate the trigger. At least one option must be specified. Any combination of these in any order is allowed in the trigger definition. If more than one option is specified, separate the options with commas.

WITH APPEND

Specifies that an additional trigger of an existing type should be added. Use of this optional clause is needed only when sp_dbcmptlevel sets the compatibility level setting less than or equal to 65. If sp_dbcmptlevel sets the compatibility level setting greater than or equal to 70, then the WITH APPEND optional clause is not needed to add an additional trigger of an existing type (this is the default behavior of CREATE TRIGGER with the compatibility level setting of sp_dbcmptlevel greater than or equal to 70).

NOT FOR REPLICATION

Indicates that the trigger should not be executed when a replication process modifies the table involved in the trigger.

AS

The actions the trigger is to take.

sql_statement

The trigger condition(s) and action(s). Trigger conditions specify additional criteria that determine whether the attempted DELETE, INSERT, or UPDATE statements can cause the trigger action(s) to be carried out.

The trigger actions specified in the Transact-SQL statements go into effect when the user action (DELETE, INSERT, or UPDATE) is attempted.

Triggers can include any number and kind of Transact-SQL statements but should not include the SELECT statement. A trigger is designed to check or change data based on a data modification statement; it should not return data to the user. The Transact-SQL statements in a trigger often include control-of-flow language. A few special tables are used in CREATE TRIGGER statements:

➤ Deleted and Inserted are logical (conceptual) tables. They are structurally similar to the table on which the trigger is defined (that is, the table on which the user action is attempted) and hold the old values or new values of the rows that may be changed by the user action. For example, to retrieve all values in the Deleted table, use:

```
SELECT *
FROM deleted
```

➤ In a DELETE, INSERT, or UPDATE trigger, SQL Server does not allow **text**, **ntext**, or **image** column references in the Inserted and Deleted tables if the compatibility level of sp_dbcmptlevel is equal to 70. The **text**, **ntext**, and **image** values in the Inserted and Deleted tables cannot be accessed. To retrieve the new value in either an INSERT or UPDATE trigger, join the Inserted table with the original update table. A compatibility level of 60 or 65 allows **text** or **image** column references in either Inserted or Deleted to appear as NULL values.

n

A placeholder indicating that multiple Transact-SQL statements can be included in the trigger. For the IF UPDATE (*column*) statement, multiple columns can be included by repeating the UPDATE (*column*) clause.

IF UPDATE (*column*)

Tests for an INSERT or UPDATE action to a specified column and is not used with DELETE operations. More than one column can be specified. Because the table name is specified in the ON clause, do not include the table name before the column name in an IF UPDATE clause. To test for an INSERT or UPDATE action for more than one column, specify a separate UPDATE(*column*) clause following the first one.

Note The IF UPDATE (*column*) clause functions identically to a regular IF, IF...ELSE, or WHILE statement and can use the BEGIN...END block.

column

The name of the column to test for either an INSERT or UPDATE action. This column can be of any data type supported by SQL Server.

Remarks

When creating triggers using the CREATE TRIGGER statement:

➤ SQL Server provides declarative referential integrity (DRI) through the table creation statements (ALTER TABLE and CREATE TABLE); however, DRI does not provide cross-database referential integrity. To enforce referential integrity (rules about the relationships between the primary and foreign keys of tables), use primary and foreign key constraints (the PRIMARY KEY and FOREIGN KEY keywords of ALTER TABLE and CREATE TABLE).

Note Whether SQL Server interprets an empty string (NULL) as either a single space or as a true empty string is controlled by the setting of sp_dbcmptlevel. If the setting of sp_dbcmptlevel is less than or equal to 65, SQL Server interprets empty strings as single spaces. If the setting of sp_dbcmptlevel is equal to 70, SQL Server interprets empty strings as empty strings.

Trigger Limitations

➤ CREATE TRIGGER must be the first statement in the batch and can apply to only one table.

➤ A trigger is created only in the current database; however, a trigger can reference objects outside the current database.

➤ If the trigger owner name is specified (to qualify the trigger), qualify the table name in the same way.

➤ The same trigger action can be defined for more than one user action (for example, INSERT and UPDATE) in the same CREATE TRIGGER statement.

➤ Any SET statement can be specified inside a trigger. The SET option chosen remains in effect during the execution of the trigger and then reverts to its former setting.

➤ When a trigger fires, results are returned to the calling application, just like stored procedures. To eliminate having results returned to an application due to a trigger firing, do not include either SELECT statements that return results or statements that perform variable assignment in a trigger. It is recommended that a trigger not include SELECT statements that return results to the user, since special handling for these returned results would have to be written into every application in which modifications to the trigger table are allowed. If variable assignment must occur in a trigger, use a SET NOCOUNT statement at the beginning of the trigger to eliminate the return of any result sets.

➤ A trigger cannot be created on a view.

➤ A TRUNCATE TABLE statement is not caught by a DELETE trigger. Although a TRUNCATE TABLE statement is, in effect, like a DELETE without a WHERE clause (it removes all rows), it is not logged and thus cannot execute a trigger. Since permission for the TRUNCATE TABLE statement defaults to the table owner and is not transferable, only the table owner should be concerned about inadvertently circumventing a DELETE trigger with a TRUNCATE TABLE statement.

➤ The WRITETEXT statement, whether logged or unlogged, does not activate a trigger.

➤ These Transact-SQL statements are not allowed in a trigger:

ALTER DATABASE	ALTER PROCEDURE	ALTER TABLE
ALTER TRIGGER	ALTER VIEW	CREATE DATABASE
CREATE DEFAULT	CREATE INDEX	CREATE PROCEDURE
CREATE RULE	CREATE SCHEMA	CREATE TABLE
CREATE TRIGGER	CREATE VIEW	DENY
DISK INIT	DISK RESIZE	DROP DATABASE
DROP DEFAULT	DROP INDEX	DROP PROCEDURE
DROP RULE	DROP TABLE	DROP TRIGGER
DROP VIEW	GRANT	LOAD DATABASE

LOAD LOG	RESTORE DATABASE	RESTORE LOG
REVOKE	RECONFIGURE	TRUNCATE TABLE
UPDATE STATISTICS		

CREATE VIEW

Creates a virtual table that represents an alternative way of looking at the data in one or more tables. Views can be used as security mechanisms by granting permission on a view but not on the underlying (base) tables.

Syntax

```
CREATE VIEW view_name [(column [, ...n])]
[WITH ENCRYPTION]
AS
select_statement
[WITH CHECK OPTION]
```

Arguments

view_name

The name of the view. View names must follow the rules for identifiers. Specifying the view owner name is optional.

column

The name to be used for a column in a view. Naming a column in CREATE VIEW is always legal but only necessary when a column is derived from an arithmetic expression, a function, or a constant, when two or more columns may otherwise have the same name (usually because of a join), or when a column in a view is given a name different from the column from which it is derived. Column names can also be assigned in the SELECT statement.

If *column* is not specified, the view columns acquire the same names as the columns in the SELECT statement.

Note In the columns for the view, the permissions for a column name apply across a CREATE VIEW or ALTER VIEW statement, regardless of the source of the underlying data. For example, if permissions are granted on the title_id column in a CREATE VIEW statement, an ALTER VIEW statement can name the title_id column with a different column name, such as qty, and still have the permissions associated with the view using title_id.

n

A placeholder indicating that multiple columns can be specified.

WITH ENCRYPTION

Encrypts the syscomments entries that contain the text of the CREATE VIEW statement.

AS

The actions the view is to take.

select_statement

The SELECT statement that defines the view. It can use more than one table and other views. To select from the objects referenced in the SELECT clause of a view being created, it is necessary to have the appropriate permissions.

A view need not be a simple subset of the rows and columns of one particular table. A view can be created using more than one table and/or other views with a SELECT clause of any complexity.

There are, however, a few restrictions on the SELECT clauses in a view definition. A CREATE VIEW statement cannot:

➤ Include ORDER BY, COMPUTE, or COMPUTE BY clauses.

➤ Include the INTO keyword.

➤ Reference a temporary table.

Since the *select_statement* portion of the CREATE VIEW statement syntax uses the SELECT statement, it is valid to use <join_hints> as specified in the FROM clause. For more information, see FROM and SELECT.

Functions can be used in the *select_statement*.

This *select_statement* can be multiple SELECT statements separated by UNION to create a query using partitioned data. For partitioned data to be used in ALTER VIEW or CREATE VIEW, constraint values must be able to be verified. If constraint checking has been disabled, reenable constraint checking with either the WITH CHECK option or CHECK *constraint_name* options of ALTER TABLE. It is not necessary to have constraints to use partitioned data. However, query optimization generates less optimal plans without constraints.

WITH CHECK OPTION

Forces all data modification statements executed against the view to adhere to the criteria set within the *select_statement* defining the view. When a row is modified through a view, the WITH CHECK OPTION guarantees that the data remains visible through the view after the modification has been committed.

Remarks

When creating views using the CREATE VIEW statement:

➤ A view can be created only in the current database. A view can reference a maximum of 1,024 columns.

➤ When querying through a view, Microsoft SQL Server checks to make sure that all the database objects referenced anywhere in the statement exist, that they are valid in the context of the statement, and that data modification statements do not violate any data integrity rules. A check that fails returns an error message. A successful check translates the action into an action against the underlying table(s).

➤ If a view depends on a table (or view) that has been dropped, SQL Server produces an error message if anyone tries to use the view. If a new table (or view) is created, even if the table structure does not change from the previous base table, to replace the one dropped, the view again becomes usable. If the new table (or view) structure changes, then the view must be dropped and re-created.

➤ When creating a view, the name of the view is stored in the sysobjects table. Information about the columns defined in a view is added to the syscolumns table, and information about the view dependencies is added to the sysdepends table. In addition, the text of the CREATE VIEW statement is added to the syscomments table. This is similar to a stored procedure, but when a view is executed for the first time, only its query tree is stored in procedure cache. Each time a view is accessed, its execution plan is recompiled.

➤ Updateable views can modify and reference only one base table at a time.

➤ SQL Server saves the settings of SET QUOTED_IDENTIFIER and SET ANSI_NULLS when a view is created. These original settings are restored when the view is used. Therefore, any client session settings for SET QUOTED_IDENTIFIER and SET ANSI_NULLS is ignored.

CURRENT_TIMESTAMP

A system function that returns the current date and time. This function is equivalent to GETDATE.

Syntax

```
CURRENT_TIMESTAMP
```

Return Type: datetime

CURRENT_USER

A system function that returns the current user. This function is equivalent to USER_NAME.

Syntax

```
CURRENT_USER
```

Return Type: sysname

CURSOR_STATUS

A scalar function that allows the caller of a stored procedure to determine whether or not the procedure has returned a cursor and result set for a given parameter.

Syntax

```
CURSOR_STATUS
(
{'local', 'cursor_name'}
| {'global', 'cursor_name'}
```

```
| {'variable', 'cursor_variable'}
)
```

Arguments

'local'

Specifies a constant that indicates the source of the cursor is a local cursor name.

'cursor_name'

The name of the cursor. A cursor name must conform to the rules for identifiers.

'global'

Specifies a constant that indicates the source of the cursor is a global cursor name.

'variable'

Specifies a constant that indicates the source of the cursor is a local variable.

'cursor_variable'

The name of the cursor variable. A cursor variable must be defined using the **cursor** data type.

Return Type: smallint

Return Value	Cursor Name	Cursor Variable
1	The result set of the cursor has at least one row: For insensitive and keyset cursors, the result set has at least one row. For dynamic cursors, the result set can have zero, one, or more rows.	The cursor allocated to this variable is open. For insensitive and keyset cursors, the result set has at least one row. For dynamic cursors, the result set can have zero, one, or more rows.
0	The result set of the cursor is empty.*	The cursor allocated to this variable is open, but the result set is definitely empty.*
-1	The cursor is closed.	The cursor allocated to this variable is closed.
-2	Not applicable.	Can be that no cursor was assigned to this OUTPUT variable by the previously called procedure. A cursor was assigned to this OUTPUT variable by the previously called procedure but it was in a closed state upon completion of the procedure. Therefore, the cursor is deallocated and not returned to the calling procedure. There is no cursor assigned to a declared cursor variable.
-3	A cursor with the specified name does not exist.	A cursor variable with the specified name does not exist; if one exists, it has not yet had a cursor allocated to it.

* Dynamic cursors never return this result.

DATABASEPROPERTY

Returns the named database property value given a database and property name.

Syntax

```
DATABASEPROPERTY('database', 'property')
```

Arguments

'*database*'

> The name of the database for which to return the named property information. *database* is **nvarchar(128)**.

'*property*'

> The name of the database property to return. *property* is **varchar(128)**. *property* can be one of the following values:

property Value	Description	Value Returned
IsAnsiNullDefault	Database follows SQL-92 rules for allowing null values.	1 = True 0 = False NULL = Value not found
IsAnsiNullsEnabled	All comparisons to a null evaluate to unknown.	1 = True 0 = False NULL = Value not found
IsAnsiWarningsEnabled	Error or warning messages are issued when standard error conditions occur.	1 = True 0 = False NULL = Value not found
IsAutoClose	Database shuts down cleanly and frees resources after the last user exits.	1 = True 0 = False NULL = Value not found
IsAutoShrink	Database files are candidates for automatic periodic shrinking.	1 = True 0 = False NULL = Value not found
IsBulkCopy	Database allows non-logged operations.	1 = True 0 = False NULL = Value not found
IsCloseCursorsOn-CommitEnabled	Cursors open when a transaction is committed are closed.	1 = True 0 = False NULL = Value not found
IsDboOnly	Database is in DBO-only access mode.	1 = True 0 = False NULL = Value not found
IsDetached	Database was detached by a detach operation.	1 = True 0 = False NULL = Value not found
IsEmergencyMode	Emergency mode to allow suspect database to be usable.	1 = True 0 = False NULL = Value not found
IsFulltextEnabled	Database is full-text enabled.	1 = True 0 = False NULL = Value not found
IsInLoad	Database is going through the loading process.	1 = True 0 = False NULL = Value not found
IsInRecovery	Database is recovering.	1 = True 0 = False NULL = Value not found
IsInStandBy	Database is online as read-only, with restore log allowed.	1 = True 0 = False NULL = Value not found
IsLocalCursorsDefault	Cursor declarations default to LOCAL.	1 = True 0 = False NULL = Value not found
IsNotRecovered	Database failed to recover.	1 = True 0 = False NULL = Value not found

property Value	Description	Value Returned
IsNullConcat	Null concatenation operand yields NULL.	1 = True 0 = False NULL = Value not found
IsOffline	Database is offline.	1 = True 0 = False NULL = Value not found
IsQuotedIdentifiers- Enabled	Double quotation marks can be used on identifiers.	1 = True 0 = False NULL = Value not found
IsReadOnly	Database is in read-only access mode.	1 = True 0 = False NULL = Value not found
IsRecursiveTriggers- Enabled	Recursive firing of triggers is enabled.	1 = True 0 = False NULL = Value not found
IsShutDown	Database encountered a problem at startup.	1 = True 0 = False NULL = Value not found
IsSingleUser	Database is in single-user access mode.	1 = True 0 = False NULL = Value not found
IsSuspect	Database is suspect.	1 = True 0 = False NULL = Value not found
IsTruncLog	Database truncates its log on checkpoints.	1 = True 0 = False NULL = Value not found
Version	Version number of the specified database if the database is open.	Version number = Database is open NULL = Database is closed.

Return Type: integer

DATALENGTH

A system function that returns the number of bytes used to represent any expression.

Syntax

DATALENGTH(*expression*)

Arguments

expression

An expression of any type.

Return Type: int

DATEADD

Returns a new **datetime** value based on adding an interval to a specified date.

Syntax

DATEADD(*datepart, number, date*)

Arguments

datepart

A parameter used with DATEADD, DATEDIFF, DATENAME, and DATEPART. The table lists date parts and abbreviations recognized by Microsoft SQL Server.

Date Part	Abbreviation
year	yy
quarter	qq
month	mm
day of year	dy
day	dd
week	wk
hour	hh
minute	mi
second	ss
millisecond	ms

number

The value used to increment *datepart*.

date

An expression returning a **datetime** or **smalldatetime** value, or a character string in a date format.

If the year is given with two digits, <50 is interpreted as the next century (20xx) and >=50 is interpreted as this century (19xx). So "25" is "2025" and "50" is "1950."

Return Type: The return type of DATEADD is **smalldatetime** if the *date* argument is **smalldatetime**; it is **datetime** otherwise.

DATEDIFF

Returns the number of *datepart* "boundaries" crossed between two specified dates.

Syntax

```
DATEDIFF(datepart, startdate, enddate)
```

Arguments

datepart

A parameter used with DATEADD, DATEDIFF, DATENAME, and DATEPART. The table lists date parts and abbreviations recognized by Microsoft SQL Server.

Date Part	Abbreviation
year	yy
quarter	qq
month	mm
day of year	dy
day	dd
week	wk
hour	hh
minute	mi
second	ss
millisecond	ms

startdate

The beginning date for the calculation. *startdate* is an expression returning a **datetime** or **smalldatetime** value, or a character string in a date format.

Because **smalldatetime** is accurate only to the minute, when a **smalldatetime** value is used with either *datename* or *datepart*, seconds and milliseconds are always 0.

If the year is given with two digits, <50 is interpreted as the next century (20xx) and >=50 is interpreted as this century (19xx). So "25" is "2025" and "50" is "1950."

startdate is subtracted from *enddate*. If *startdate* is later than *enddate*, a negative value is returned.

enddate

The ending date for the calculation. *enddate* is an expression returning a **datetime** or **smalldatetime** value, or a character string in a date format.

Return Type: integer

DATENAME

Returns a character string representing the specified date part of the specified date.

Syntax

```
DATENAME(datepart, date)
```

Arguments

datepart

A parameter used with DATEADD, DATEDIFF, DATENAME, and DATEPART. See DATEDIFF for the date parts and abbreviations recognized by Microsoft SQL Server.

The date part *weekday* or *dw* returns the day of the week (Sunday, Monday, and so on) when used with DATENAME. It returns a corresponding number (Sunday = 1, Saturday = 7) when used with DATEPART.

date

An expression returning a **datetime** or **smalldatetime** value, or a character string in a date format.

Because **smalldatetime** is accurate only to the minute, when a **smalldatetime** value is used with DATENAME, seconds and milliseconds are always 0.

If the year is given with two digits, <50 is interpreted as the next century (20xx) and >=50 is interpreted as this century (19xx). So "25" is "2025" and "50" is "1950."

Return Type: nvarchar

DATEPART

Returns an integer representing the specified date part of the specified date.

Syntax

DATEPART(*datepart*, *date*)

Arguments

datepart

A parameter used with DATEADD, DATEDIFF, DATENAME, and DATEPART. See DATEDIFF for the date parts and abbreviations recognized by Microsoft SQL Server.

The week date part (*wk*) respects and reflects changes made to SET DATEFIRST. January 1 of any year defines the starting number for the week date part (*wk*). For example, DATEPART (wk, 'Jan 1, xxxx')=1 where xxxx is any year.

The weekday date part (*dw*) returns the day of the week (Sunday, Monday, and so on) when used with DATENAME. It returns a corresponding number (Sunday = 1, Saturday = 7) when used with DATEPART.

Note The number produced by the weekday *datepart* depends on the value of SET DATEFIRST, which sets the first day of the week.

date

An expression returning a **datetime** or **smalldatetime** value, or a character string in a date format.

Because **smalldatetime** is accurate only to the minute, when a **smalldatetime** value is used with DATEPART, seconds and milliseconds are always 0.

If the year is given with two digits, <50 is interpreted as the next century (20xx) and >=50 is interpreted as this century (19xx). So "25" is "2025" and "50" is "1950."

Return Type: int

DAY

Returns an integer representing the day part of the specified date.

Syntax

DAY(*date*)

Arguments

date

An expression of type **datetime** or **smalldatetime**.

Return Type: int

DB_ID

Returns the database identification number.

Syntax

DB_ID(['*database_name*'])

Arguments

'*database_name*'

The database name used to return the corresponding database identification number. *database_name* is **nvarchar**.

Return Type: smallint

DB_NAME

Returns the database name.

Syntax

DB_NAME(*database_id*)

Arguments

database_id

The ID of the database to be returned. *database_id* is **smallint**. If no ID is specified, the name of the current database is returned.

Return Type: nvarchar(128)

DEALLOCATE

Removes a cursor reference. When the last cursor reference is deallocated, the data structures comprising the cursor are released by Microsoft SQL Server.

Syntax

```
DEALLOCATE { { [GLOBAL] cursor_name } | cursor_variable_name}
```

Arguments

cursor_name

> The name of an already-declared cursor. If both a global and a local cursor exist with *cursor_name* as their name, then *cursor_name* refers to the global cursor if GLOBAL is specified. If GLOBAL is not specified, *cursor_name* refers to the local cursor.

cursor_variable_name

> The name of a cursor variable.

DECLARE @local_variable

Variables are declared in the body of a batch or procedure with the DECLARE statement and given or assigned values with either a SET or SELECT statement. Cursor variables can be declared with this statement and used with other cursor-related statements. After declaration, all variables are initialized as NULL.

Syntax

```
DECLARE
{
{@local_variable data_type}
| {cursor_variable_name CURSOR}
} [, ...n]
```

Arguments

@local_variable

> The name of a variable. Variable names must begin with an at sign (@). Local variable names must conform to the rules for identifiers.

data_type

> Any system-supplied or user-defined data type. A variable cannot be of **text**, **ntext**, or **image** data type.

cursor_variable_name

> The name of a cursor variable. A cursor name cannot be the same name as a variable of any type (the name cannot start with @). *cursor_variable_name* must conform to the naming specifications of *@local_variable*.

CURSOR

> Specifies that the variable is a local cursor variable.

n

> A placeholder indicating that multiple variables can be specified and assigned values.

Remarks

Variables are often used in a batch or procedure as counters for WHILE, LOOP, or for an IF...ELSE block.

Variables can be used only in expressions, not in place of object names or keywords. To construct dynamic SQL statements, use EXECUTE.

The scope of a local variable is the batch, stored procedure, or statement block in which it is declared. For more information about using local variables in statement blocks, see BEGIN...END.

A cursor variable that currently has a cursor assigned to it can be referenced as a source in a:

➤ CLOSE statement

➤ DEALLOCATE statement

➤ FETCH statement

➤ OPEN statement

➤ Positioned DELETE or UPDATE statement

➤ SET CURSOR variable statement (on the right side)

In all these statements, Microsoft SQL Server raises an error if a referenced cursor variable exists but does not have a cursor currently allocated to it. If a referenced cursor variable does not exist, SQL Server raises the same error raised for an undeclared variable of another type.

A cursor variable:

➤ Can be the target of either a cursor type or another cursor variable. For more information, see SET *@local_variable*.

➤ Can be referenced as a target in an EXECUTE statement if the cursor variable does not have a cursor currently assigned to it.

➤ Should be regarded as a pointer to the cursor.

DECLARE CURSOR

Defines the attributes of a Transact-SQL server cursor, such as its scrolling behavior and the query used to build the result set on which the cursor operates. DECLARE CURSOR accepts both a syntax based on the SQL-92 standard and a syntax using a set of Transact-SQL extensions.

SQL-92 Syntax

```
DECLARE cursor_name [INSENSITIVE] [SCROLL] CURSOR
FOR select_statement
 [FOR {READ ONLY | UPDATE [OF column_list]}]
```

Transact-SQL Extended Syntax

```
DECLARE cursor_name CURSOR
 [LOCAL | GLOBAL]
 [FORWARD_ONLY | SCROLL]
 [STATIC | KEYSET | DYNAMIC]
 [READ_ONLY | SCROLL_LOCKS | OPTIMISTIC]
FOR select_statement
 [FOR {READ ONLY | UPDATE [OF column_list]}]
```

SQL-92 Arguments

cursor_name

> The name of the Transact-SQL server cursor being defined. The *cursor_name* must conform to the rules for identifiers.

INSENSITIVE

> Defines a cursor that makes a temporary copy of the data to be used by the cursor. All requests to the cursor are answered from this temporary table in tempdb; therefore, modifications made to base tables will not be reflected in the data returned by fetches made to this cursor, and this cursor does not allow modifications. When using SQL-92 syntax, if INSENSITIVE is omitted, committed deletes and updates made to the underlying tables (by any users) are reflected in subsequent fetches.

SCROLL

> Specifies that all fetch options (FIRST, LAST, PRIOR, NEXT, RELATIVE, ABSOLUTE) are available. If SCROLL is not specified in a SQL-92 DECLARE CURSOR, NEXT is the only fetch option supported.

select_statement

> A standard SELECT statement that defines the result set of the cursor. The keywords COMPUTE, COMPUTE BY, FOR BROWSE, and INTO are not allowed within the *select_statement* of a cursor declaration.
>
> If DISTINCT, UNION, GROUP BY, and/or HAVING are used, or an aggregate expression is included in the *select_list*, the cursor will be created as INSENSITIVE.
>
> If none of the underlying tables have a unique index and a SQL-92 SCROLL cursor is requested, it will automatically be an INSENSITIVE cursor.
>
> If the *select_statement* contains an ORDER BY where the columns are not unique row identifiers, a SQL-92 cursor will be INSENSITIVE even if the INSENSITIVE keyword is not specified.

READ ONLY

> Prevents updates from being made through this cursor. The cursor cannot be referenced in a WHERE CURRENT OF clause in an UPDATE or DELETE statement. This option overrides the default capability of a cursor to be updated.

UPDATE [OF *column_list*]

> Defines updatable columns within the cursor. If OF *column_list* is specified, only the columns listed will allow modifications. If UPDATE is specified with no column list, all columns can be updated.

Transact-SQL Extended Arguments

cursor_name

> The name of the Transact-SQL server cursor being defined. The *cursor_name* must conform to the rules for identifiers.

LOCAL

> Specifies that the scope of the cursor is local to the batch, stored procedure, or trigger in which the cursor was created. The cursor name is only valid within this scope. The cursor can be referenced by local cursor variables in the batch, stored procedure, or trigger, or a stored procedure OUTPUT parameter. An OUTPUT parameter in a stored procedure is used to pass the local cursor back to the calling batch, stored procedure, or trigger, which can assign the parameter to a cursor variable in order to reference the cursor after the stored procedure terminates. The cursor is implicitly deallocated when the batch, stored procedure, or trigger terminates, unless it was passed back in an OUTPUT parameter. If it is passed back in an OUTPUT parameter, the cursor is deallocated when the last variable referencing it is deallocated or goes out of scope.

GLOBAL

> Specifies that the scope of the cursor is global to the connection. The cursor name can be referenced in any stored procedure or batch executed by the connection. The cursor is only implicitly deallocated at disconnect.

FORWARD_ONLY

> Specifies that the cursor can only be scrolled from the first to the last row. FETCH NEXT is the only supported fetch option. If FORWARD_ONLY is specified without the STATIC, KEYSET, or DYNAMIC keywords, the cursor operates as a DYNAMIC cursor. When neither FORWARD_ONLY or SCROLL are specified, FORWARD_ONLY is the default unless the keywords STATIC, KEYSET, or DYNAMIC are specified. STATIC, KEYSET, and DYNAMIC cursors default to SCROLL. Unlike the database APIs such as ODBC and ADO, FORWARD_ONLY is supported with STATIC, KEYSET, and DYNAMIC Transact-SQL cursors.

STATIC

> Defines a cursor that makes a temporary copy of the data to be used by the cursor. All requests to the cursor are answered from this temporary table in tempdb; therefore, modifications made to base tables are not reflected in the data returned by fetches made to this cursor, and this cursor does not allow modifications.

KEYSET

> Specifies that the membership and order of rows in the cursor are fixed when the cursor is opened. The set of keys that uniquely identify the rows is built into a table in tempdb known as the keyset. Changes to nonkey values in the base tables, either made by the cursor owner or committed by other users, are visible as the owner scrolls around the cursor. Inserts made by other users are not visible (inserts cannot be made through a Transact-SQL server cursor). If a row is deleted, an attempt to fetch the row returns an @@FETCH_STATUS of –2. Updates of key values from outside the cursor resemble a delete of the old row followed by an insert of the new row. The row with the new values is not visible, and attempts to fetch the row with the old values return an @@FETCH_STATUS of –2. The new values are visible if the update is done through the cursor by specifying the WHERE CURRENT OF clause.

DYNAMIC

> Defines a cursor that reflects all data changes made to the rows in its result set as you scroll around the cursor. The data values, order, and membership of the rows can change on each fetch. The absolute and relative fetch options are not supported with dynamic cursors.

READ_ONLY

> Prevents updates from being made through this cursor. The cursor cannot be referenced in a WHERE CURRENT OF clause in an UPDATE or DELETE statement. This option overrides the default capability of a cursor to be updated.

SCROLL_LOCKS

> Specifies that positioned updates or deletes made through the cursor are guaranteed to succeed. Microsoft SQL Server locks the rows as they are read into the cursor to ensure their availability for later modifications.

OPTIMISTIC

> Specifies that positioned updates or deletes made through the cursor do not succeed if the row has been updated since it was read into the cursor. SQL Server does not lock rows as they are read into the cursor. It instead uses comparisons of **timestamp** column values, or a checksum value if the table has no **timestamp** column, to determine if the row was modified after it was read into the cursor. If the row was modified, the attempted positioned update or delete fails.

select_statement

> A standard SELECT statement that defines the result set of the cursor. The keywords COMPUTE, COMPUTE BY, FOR BROWSE, and INTO are not allowed within the *select_statement* of a cursor declaration.
>
> If DISTINCT, UNION, GROUP BY, and/or HAVING are used, or an aggregate expression is included in the *select_list*, the cursor will be created as STATIC.

If each of the underlying tables does not have a unique index and a Transact-SQL KEYSET cursor is requested, it will automatically be a STATIC cursor.

If the *select_statement* contains an ORDER BY where the columns are not unique row identifiers, a DYNAMIC cursor is converted to a KEYSET cursor, or to a STATIC cursor if a KEYSET cursor cannot be opened.

READ ONLY

Prevents updates from being made through this cursor. The cursor cannot be referenced in a WHERE CURRENT OF clause in an UPDATE or DELETE statement. This option overrides the default capability of a cursor to be updated. This READ ONLY keyword is different from the READ_ONLY concurrency option keyword specified above only by having a space between READ and ONLY instead of an underscore. The effects of both keywords are the same.

UPDATE [OF *column_list*]

Defines updatable columns within the cursor. If OF *column_list* is supplied, only the columns listed will allow modifications. If UPDATE is specified without a column list all columns can be updated, unless the READ_ONLY concurrency option was specified.

DEGREES

Given an angle in radians, returns the corresponding angle in degrees.

Syntax

DEGREES(*numeric_expression*)

Arguments

numeric_expression

An expression of the exact numeric or approximate numeric data type category, except for the **bit** data type.

Return Values: Same as input

DELETE

Removes rows from a table.

Syntax

```
DELETE
 [ FROM {table_name | view_name}]
{FROM <table_sources>}
 [ WHERE
{ <search_conditions>
| { [ CURRENT OF
{
{ [ GLOBAL ] cursor_name }
| cursor_variable_name
```

```
    }
  ]
  }
  ]
   [OPTION (<query_hints> [, ...n])]
<table_sources> ::=
{ <table_or_view>
| (select_statement) [AS] table_alias [ (column_alias [, ...n]) ]
| <table_or_view> CROSS JOIN <table_or_view>
| <table_or_view>
{ { INNER
| { FULL
| LEFT
| RIGHT
} [ OUTER ] [ <join_hints> ] [ JOIN ]
} <table_or_view> ON <join_condition>
}
| <rowset_function>
}
 [, ...n]
<table_or_view> ::=
{ table_name [ [AS] table_alias ] [ WITH (<table_hints> [...m]) ]
| view_name [ [AS] table_alias ]
}
<table_hints> ::=
{ INDEX(index_name | index_id)
| HOLDLOCK
| PAGLOCK
| READCOMMITTED
| REPEATABLEREAD
| ROWLOCK
| SERIALIZABLE
| TABLOCK
| TABLOCKX
}
<join_hints> ::=
{ HASH | LOOP | MERGE }
<query_hints> ::=
{ { HASH | ORDER } GROUP
| { CONCAT | HASH | MERGE } UNION
| FAST number_rows
| FORCE ORDER
| ROBUST PLAN
}
<join_condition> ::=
{ table_name | table_alias | view_name }.column_name
<logical_operator>
{ table_name | table_alias | view_name }.column_name
<logical_operator> ::=
```

```
{ = | > | < | >= | <= | <> | != | !< | !> }
<rowset_function> ::=
{ OPENQUERY (linked_server, 'query')
| OPENROWSET
 ( 'provider_name',
{
'datasource';'user_id';'password'
| 'provider_string'
},
{
 [catalog.][schema.]object_name
| 'query'
}
)
```

Arguments

FROM

> An optional keyword that can be used between the DELETE keyword and the *table_name* | *view_name* argument that identifies the table or view from which the rows are removed.

table_name | *view_name*

> The table or view from which the rows are removed. If the table or view exists in another database or has an owner other than the current user, use a four-part qualified name in the format *server_name.database.[owner].object_name*. If a view that references multiple tables is named, the delete operation can only remove rows from one of the underlying tables.

FROM <table_sources>

> Specifies a Transact-SQL FROM clause to use in identifying the rows to be deleted. A <from_clause> specifying a join can be used instead of a subquery in the WHERE clause to identify rows to be removed. For more information, see FROM.

<table_or_view>

> The name of the table or view that is used to provide criteria for the delete operation.

table_name

> The name of the table to provide criteria values for the delete operation.

table_alias

> The name of an alias. Each *table_name* or *view_name* can be given an alias, either for convenience or to distinguish a table or view in a self-join or a subquery. For more information, see FROM.

<table_hints>

> Specifies a table scan, one or more indexes to be used by the optimizer, or a locking method to be used by the optimizer with this table and for this SELECT.

Although this is an option, the optimizer can usually pick the best optimization method without hints being specified. Commas between <table_hints> are optional, but supported for backward compatibility. For more information, see the discussion of <table_hints> in SELECT.

INDEX(*index_name* | *index_id*)

Specifies the name or ID of the index to be used by SQL Server when processing the statement. Only one index hint per table can be specified. The alternative INDEX = syntax (which specifies a single index hint) is supported only for backward compatibility. Any index hints specified for a view are ignored, and SQL Server returns an error message.

SQL Server does not allow more than one table hint from each of the following groups:

➤ Granularity hints: PAGLOCK, NOLOCK, ROWLOCK, TABLOCK, or TABLOCKX.

➤ Isolation level hints: HOLDLOCK, NOLOCK, READCOMMITTED, REPEATABLEREAD, SERIALIZABLE.

In addition, the NOLOCK and READPAST <table_hints> are only allowed in SELECT statements and not in DELETE, INSERT, or UPDATE statements.

m

A placeholder indicating that multiple <table_hints> can be specified.

view_name

The name of the view to provide criteria values for the delete operation.

column_alias

A user-defined, temporary heading to replace the default column heading (the column name). For more information about column aliases, see FROM.

n

A placeholder used to indicate that the preceding item can be specified multiple times.

CROSS JOIN

Specifies the cross-product of two tables. Returns the same rows as if no WHERE clause was specified in an old-style, non-SQL-92-style join.

INNER

Specifies all matching pairs of rows are returned. Discards unmatched rows from both tables. This is the default if no join type is specified.

<join_hints>

Specifies that the query optimizer in Microsoft SQL Server use one *join_hint*, or *execution algorithm*, per join specified in the query's FROM clause. For more information, see the discussion of <join_hints> in SELECT.

Note If a <join_hints> is also specified for any particular pair of joined tables in the FROM clause, then it takes precedence over any <join_hint> specified in the OPTION clause.

HASH | LOOP | MERGE

    Specifies that the joins in the query use looping, hashing, or merging. If more than one join strategy is specified with the optional OPTION clause, the optimizer will select the least expensive strategy from those specified for each join.

JOIN

    A keyword to indicate that a SQL-92-style join be used in the DELETE operation.

ON <join_condition>

    Specifies the conditions upon which the join is based. For more information, see FROM.

WHERE

    Specifies the conditions used to limit the number of rows that are deleted. There are two forms of delete based on what is specified in the WHERE clause:

➤ Searched deletes specify *search_conditions* to qualify the rows to delete.

➤ Positioned deletes use the CURRENT OF clause to specify a cursor; the delete operation occurs at the current position of the cursor.

<search_conditions>

    Specifies the restricting conditions for the rows to be deleted. There is no limit to the number of <search_conditions> that can be included in a SQL statement. For additional details on <search_conditions>, see WHERE.

CURRENT OF

    Specifies the DELETE is done at the current position of the specified cursor.

GLOBAL

    Specifies that *cursor_name* refers to a global cursor.

cursor_name

    The name of the open cursor from which the fetch is made. If both a global and a local cursor exist with *cursor_name* as their name, then *cursor_name* refers to the global cursor if GLOBAL is specified. If GLOBAL is not specified, *cursor_name* refers to the local cursor. The cursor must allow updates.

cursor_variable_name

    The name of a cursor variable. The cursor variable must reference a cursor that allows updates.

OPTION (<query_hints>, [, ...*n*])

Keywords indicating that optimizer hints be used to customize SQL Server's processing of the statement.

{HASH | ORDER} GROUP

Specifies that the aggregations specified in the GROUP BY or COMPUTE clause of the query should use hashing or ordering.

{CONCAT | HASH | MERGE} UNION

Specifies that all UNION operations should be performed by merging, hashing, or concatenating UNION sets. If more than one UNION hint is specified, the optimizer will select the least expensive strategy from those hints specified.

FAST *number_rows*

Specifies that the query is optimized for fast retrieval of the first *number_rows* (a non-negative integer). After the first *number_rows* are returned, the query continues execution and produces its full result set.

FORCE ORDER

Specifies that the join order indicated by the query syntax be preserved during query optimization.

ROBUST PLAN

Forces the query optimizer to attempt a plan that works for the maximum potential row size at the expense of performance. If no such plan is possible, the optimizer returns an error rather than deferring error detection to query execution. Rows may contain variable-length columns; SQL Server allows rows to be defined whose maximum potential size is beyond the ability of SQL Server to process. Usually, despite the maximum potential size, an application stores rows whose actual size is within the limits that SQL Server can process. If SQL Server encounters a row that is too long, an execution error is returned.

OPENQUERY

Executes the specified pass-through query. For more information, see OPENQUERY.

OPENROWSET

Includes all connection information necessary to access remote data from a data source. For more information, see OPENROWSET.

DENY

Creates an entry in the security system that denies a permission from a security account in the current database and prevents the security account from inheriting the permission through its group or role memberships.

Syntax

Statement permissions:

```
DENY{ALL | statement[, ...n]}
```

```
TO security_account[, ...n]
```

Object permissions:

```
DENY {ALL [PRIVILEGES] | permission[, ...n]}
{[(column[, ...n])] ON {table|view}
|ON {table | view}[(column[, ...n])]
| {stored_procedure | extended_procedure}}
TO security_account
  [CASCADE]
```

Arguments

ALL

> Specifies that all applicable permissions are being denied. For statement permissions, ALL can be used only by those who have the sysadmin role. For object permissions, ALL can be used by members of the sysadmin and db_owner roles, and database object owners.

statement

> The statement for which permission is being denied. The statement list can include:

➤ CREATE DATABASE

➤ CREATE DEFAULT

➤ CREATE PROCEDURE

➤ CREATE RULE

➤ CREATE TABLE

➤ CREATE VIEW

➤ BACKUP DATABASE

➤ BACKUP LOG

n

> A placeholder indicating that the item can be repeated in a comma-separated list.

TO

> Specifies the security account list.

security_account

> The name of the security account in the current database affected by the denied permission. The security account can be a:

➤ Microsoft SQL Server user.

➤ SQL Server role.

➤ Microsoft Windows NT user.

➤ Windows NT group.

> When a permission is denied from a SQL Server user or Windows NT user account, the specified *security_account* is the only account affected by the

permission. If a permission is denied from a SQL Server role or a Windows NT group, the permission affects all users in the current database who are members of the group or role, regardless of the permissions that have been granted to the members of the group or role. If there are permission conflicts between a group or role and its members, the most restrictive permission (DENY) takes precedence.

Two special security accounts can be used with DENY. Permissions denied from the **public** role are applied to all users in the database. Permissions denied from the **guest** user are used by all users who do not have a user account in the database.

When denying permissions to a Windows NT local or global group, specify the domain or computer name the group is defined on, followed by a backslash, then the group name. However, to deny permissions to a Windows NT built-in local group, specify BUILTIN instead of the domain or computer name.

PRIVILEGES

An optional keyword that can be included for SQL-92 compliance.

permission

An object permission that is being denied. When permissions are denied on a table or a view, the permission list can include one or more of these statements: SELECT, INSERT, DELETE, or UPDATE.

Object permissions denied on a table can also include REFERENCES, and object permissions denied on a stored procedure or extended stored procedure can include EXECUTE. When permissions are denied on columns, the permissions list can include SELECT and/or UPDATE.

column

The name of the column in the current database for which permissions are being denied.

table

The name of the table in the current database for which permissions are being denied.

view

The name of the view in the current database for which permissions are being denied.

stored_procedure

The name of the stored procedure in the current database for which permissions are being denied.

extended_procedure

The name of an extended stored procedure for which permissions are being denied.

CASCADE

> Specifies that permissions are being denied from *security_account* as well as any other security accounts granted permissions by *security_account*. Use CASCADE when denying a grantable permission. If CASCADE is not specified and the specified user is granted WITH GRANT OPTION permission, an error is returned.

DIFFERENCE

Returns the difference between the SOUNDEX values of two character expressions as an integer.

Syntax

```
DIFFERENCE(character_expression, character_expression)
```

Arguments

character_expression

> An expression of type **char** or **varchar**.

Return Type: int

DROP DATABASE

Removes one or more databases from Microsoft SQL Server.

Syntax

```
DROP DATABASE database_name [, ...n]
```

Arguments

database_name

> Specifies the database to be removed. Execute sp_helpdb from the master database to see a list of databases.

Remarks

Removing a database deletes the database and the disk files used by the database.

Unlike earlier versions, DROP DATABASE will remove a damaged database that has been marked suspect. DROP DATABASE will remove any database except those that have been marked OFFLINE.

A database that has been dropped can only be re-created by restoring a backup. You cannot drop a database currently in use (open for reading or writing by any user). The master database should be backed up whenever a database is dropped.

Permissions

DROP DATABASE permission defaults to the database owner (DBO) and the system administrator (SA), and cannot be transferred. The database owner must be in the master database to use DROP DATABASE.

DROP DEFAULT

Removes one or more user-defined defaults from the current database.

The DROP DEFAULT statement does not apply to default constraints. For information about dropping default constraints (created by using the DEFAULT option of either the CREATE TABLE or ALTER TABLE statements), see ALTER TABLE.

Syntax

```
DROP DEFAULT {default} [, ...n]
```

Arguments

default

> The name of an existing default. To find out what defaults exist, execute sp_help. Specifying the default owner name is optional. Defaults must conform to the rules for identifiers.

n

> A placeholder indicating that multiple defaults can be specified.

Remarks

When dropping defaults using DROP DEFAULT:

➤ Before dropping a default, unbind the default by executing sp_unbindefault (if the default is currently bound to a column or a user-defined data type).

➤ After a default is dropped from a column that allows null values, NULL is inserted in that position when rows are added and no value is explicitly supplied. After a default is dropped from a NOT NULL column, an error message is returned when rows are added and no value is explicitly supplied. These rows are added later as part of the normal INSERT statement behavior.

➤ For information about creating defaults, see CREATE DEFAULT.

➤ For more information about changing the current database, see USE.

Permissions

DROP DEFAULT permission defaults to the owner of the default and is not transferable. However, members of the db_owner fixed database role and members of the sysadmin fixed database role can drop any default object by specifying the owner in DROP DEFAULT.

DROP INDEX

Removes one or more indexes from the current database.

The DROP INDEX statement does not apply to indexes created by creating primary key or unique constraints (created by using the PRIMARY KEY or UNIQUE options of either the CREATE TABLE or ALTER TABLE statements, respectively). For more information about primary or unique key constraints, see CREATE TABLE or ALTER TABLE.

Syntax

```
DROP INDEX 'table.index' [, ...n]
```

Arguments

table

> The table where the indexed column is located. Table names must conform to the rules for identifiers. If DROP INDEX is specified by the members of the db_owner fixed database role or members of the sysadmin fixed database role, then the owner name can be included to drop an index not owned by a member of the db_owner fixed database role. Specifying the table owner name is optional.

index

> The name of the index to be dropped. Index names must conform to the rules for identifiers.

n

> A placeholder indicating that multiple indexes can be specified.

Remarks

When dropping indexes using DROP INDEX:

> ➤ Once DROP INDEX is executed, all the space previously occupied by the index is regained. This space can then be used for any database object.

> ➤ DROP INDEX cannot be specified on an index on a system table.

> ➤ To get information about what indexes exist on a table, use sp_helpindex and specify the table name. For example, use sp_helpindex authors to determine what indexes exist on the Authors table of the Pubs database.

> ➤ To drop the indexes created to implement primary key or unique constraints, the constraint must be dropped. For more information about dropping constraints, see ALTER TABLE.

> ➤ Dropping a clustered index reindexes all the nonclustered indexes on that table. Creating a clustered index also reindexes all nonclustered indexes. To most efficiently reindex a clustered index, use DBCC DBREINDEX instead of DROP INDEX followed by CREATE INDEX. You can also use CREATE INDEX and the WITH DROP_EXISTING option on the clustered index to avoid dropping and re-creating the nonclustered indexes.

> ➤ Nonclustered indexes have different pointers to data rows depending on whether or not a clustered index is defined for the table. If there is a clustered index, the leaf rows of the nonclustered indexes use the clustered index keys to point to the data rows. If the table is a heap, the leaf rows of nonclustered indexes use row pointers. If you drop a clustered index on a table with nonclustered indexes, all the nonclustered indexes are rebuilt to replace the clustered index keys with row pointers.

Permissions

DROP INDEX permissions default to the table owner and are not transferable. However, members of the db_owner and sysadmin fixed database roles can drop any object by specifying the owner in DROP INDEX.

Examples

This example removes the index named au_id_ind in the Authors table.

```
USE pubs
IF EXISTS (SELECT name FROM sysindexes
WHERE name = 'au_id_ind')
DROP INDEX authors.au_id_ind
GO
```

DROP PROCEDURE

Removes one or more stored procedures or procedure groups from the current database.

Syntax

```
DROP PROCEDURE {procedure} [, ...n]
```

Arguments

procedure

> The name of the stored procedure(s) to be removed. Procedure names must conform to the rules for identifiers. Specifying the procedure owner name is optional, and a server name or database name cannot be specified.

n

> A placeholder indicating that multiple procedures can be specified.

Remarks

When dropping procedures using DROP PROCEDURE:

➤ When a stored procedure is dropped, information about the procedure is removed from the sysobjects and syscomments system tables.

➤ To see a list of procedure names, use sp_help. To display the procedure definition (which is stored in the syscomments system table), use sp_helptext.

➤ The *procedure* parameter can reference the name of an entire procedure group. A procedure group is a collection of procedures with the same name but different ;*number* suffixes:

```
CREATE PROCEDURE sampleproc;1 AS SELECT * FROM authors
CREATE PROCEDURE sampleproc;2 AS SELECT * FROM titles
```

When using DROP PROCEDURE and specifying a procedure group, the entire procedure group is dropped.

```
DROP PROCEDURE sampleproc
```

Individual procedures in the group cannot be dropped. For example, the following is not legal:

```
DROP PROCEDURE sampleproc;1
```

➤ User-defined system procedures (prefixed with sp_) are dropped from the master database whether or not it is the current database. If the system procedure is not found in the current database, Microsoft SQL Server tries to drop it from the master database.

➤ For information about creating or modifying existing procedures, see CREATE PROCEDURE and ALTER PROCEDURE, respectively.

➤ For more information about changing the current database, see USE.

Permissions

DROP PROCEDURE permission defaults to the procedure owner and is not transferable. However, members of the db_owner and sysadmin fixed database roles can drop any object by specifying the owner in DROP PROCEDURE.

DROP RULE

Removes one or more user-defined rules from the current database.

Syntax

```
DROP RULE {rule} [, ...n]
```

Arguments

rule

The rule to be removed. Rule names must conform to the rules for identifiers. Specifying the rule owner name is optional.

n

A placeholder indicating that multiple rules can be specified.

Remarks

When dropping rules using DROP RULE:

➤ To drop a rule, first unbind it if the rule is currently bound to a column or to a user-defined data type. Use sp_unbindrule to unbind the rule. If the rule is bound when attempting to drop it, an error message is displayed and the DROP RULE statement is canceled.

➤ After dropping a rule, new data entered into the columns previously governed by the rule is entered without these constraints. Existing data is not affected in any way.

➤ The DROP RULE statement does not apply to CHECK constraints. For more information about dropping check constraints, see ALTER TABLE.

➤ For information about creating rules, see CREATE RULE.

➤ To bind a rule, use sp_bindrule; to unbind a rule, use sp_unbindrule.

➤ For more information about changing the current database, see USE.

Permissions

DROP RULE permission defaults to the rule owner and is not transferable. However, members of the db_owner and sysadmin fixed database roles can drop any object by specifying the owner in DROP RULE.

DROP STATISTICS

Drops statistics for one or more columns within a given table (in the current database).

Syntax

```
DROP STATISTICS {table.column} [, ...n]
```

Arguments

table

> The name of the target table for which statistics should be dropped. Table names must conform to the rules for identifiers. Specifying the table owner name is optional.

column

> The name of the column for which statistics should be dropped. Column names must conform to the rules for identifiers.

n

> A placeholder indicating that more than one column name can be specified.

Remarks

For information about updating statistics, see UPDATE STATISTICS.

For more information about changing the current database, see USE.

Permissions

DROP STATISTICS permission defaults to the table owner and is not transferable. However, members of the db_owner and sysadmin fixed database roles can drop any object by specifying the owner in DROP STATISTICS.

DROP TABLE

Removes a table definition and all data, indexes, triggers, constraints, and permission specifications for that table. Any view on the dropped table must be explicitly dropped by using the DROP VIEW statement.

Syntax

```
DROP TABLE table_name
```

Arguments

table_name

> Specifies the table to be removed.

Remarks

The DROP TABLE statement cannot be used to drop a table being referenced by a FOREIGN KEY constraint. You must first drop the referencing FOREIGN KEY constraint or the referencing table.

If you are the table owner, you can drop a table in any database. When you drop a table, rules or defaults on it lose their binding, and any constraints or triggers associated with it are automatically dropped. If you re-create a table, you must rebind the appropriate rules and defaults, re-create any triggers, and add all necessary constraints.

You cannot use the DROP TABLE statement on system tables.

If you delete all rows in a table (DELETE *tablename*) or use the TRUNCATE TABLE statement, the table still exists until you drop it.

Permissions

DROP TABLE permission defaults to the table owner and is not transferable. However, the database owner (DBO), system administrator (SA), and DDL administrators can drop any object by specifying the owner in the DROP TABLE statement.

DROP TRIGGER

Removes one or more triggers from the current database.

Syntax

```
DROP TRIGGER {trigger} [, ...n]
```

Arguments

trigger

> The name of the trigger(s) to remove. Trigger names must conform to the rules for identifiers. Specifying the trigger owner name is optional.

n

> A placeholder indicating that multiple triggers can be specified.

Remarks

When dropping triggers using DROP TRIGGER:

➤ Remove a trigger by dropping it or by dropping the trigger table. When a table is dropped, all triggers associated with it are also dropped.

➤ If a new trigger is to replace the previous trigger, use the CREATE TRIGGER statement instead of DROP TRIGGER. For more information about creating a new trigger, see CREATE TRIGGER.

➤ For more information about modifying an existing trigger, see ALTER TRIGGER.

➤ When a trigger is dropped, information about the trigger is removed from the sysobjects and syscomments system tables.

Tip If entries are removed in syscomments rather than encrypted, Microsoft SQL Server cannot compile the stored procedure.

➤ For more information about changing the current database, see USE.

DROP VIEW

Removes one or more views from the current database. Any view on the dropped table (dropped by using the DROP TABLE statement) must be explicitly dropped by using DROP VIEW.

Syntax

```
DROP VIEW {view} [, ...n]
```

Arguments

view

The name of the view(s) to be removed. View names must conform to the rules for identifiers. Specifying the view owner name is optional.

n

A placeholder indicating that multiple views can be specified.

Remarks

When dropping views using DROP VIEW:

➤ When executing DROP VIEW, the definition of the view and other information about the view is deleted from the sysobjects, syscolumns, syscomments, sysdepends, and sysprotects system tables. All permissions for the view are also deleted.

➤ Microsoft SQL Server dynamically binds the view to the current object names of the objects referenced in the view definition at the time the view is executed. This behavior of using the object's current name in the view at view execution time is called *deferred name resolution*. For example, if view V1 references table T1 and table T1 is dropped and later re-created, view V1 then refers to the new table named T1. As long as the view definition matches the table schema, the view result is the same as if the table were never dropped and re-created.

However, even if the column names in both the base table and in the view definition match, the data stored in the columns of the new base table may be different from the originally stored data. The view may produce a different result set with the new table compared to the result set of the previously defined table. If a new view, view V2, refers to table T3, which is later renamed table T2, then view V2 becomes invalid because no table at query execution time named T2 exists. In addition, if a new table T3 is later created, then view V2 attempts to use the new table T3.

➤ For more information about creating views, see CREATE VIEW.

➤ For more information about modifying existing views, see ALTER VIEW.

➤ For more information about changing the current database, see USE.

DUMP

Makes a backup copy of a database (DUMP DATABASE) or makes a copy of the transaction log (DUMP TRANSACTION) in a form that can be read into Microsoft SQL Server using the BACKUP or LOAD statements.

ELSE (IF...ELSE)

Imposes conditions on the execution of a Transact-SQL statement. The Transact-SQL statement (*sql_statement*) following *Boolean_expression* is executed if *Boolean_expression* evaluates to TRUE. The optional ELSE keyword specifies the statement that is executed when *Boolean_expression* evaluates to FALSE or NULL.

Syntax

```
IF Boolean_expression
{
sql_statement
| statement_block
}
 [
ELSE
{
sql_statement
| statement_block
}
]
```

Arguments

Boolean_expression

An expression that returns TRUE or FALSE. If the Boolean expression contains a SELECT statement, the SELECT statement must be enclosed in parentheses.

{sql_statement | statement_block}

Any valid Transact-SQL statement or statement grouping as defined with a statement block. To define a statement block, use the control-of-flow language keywords BEGIN and END. Although all Transact-SQL statements are valid within a BEGIN...END block, certain Transact-SQL statements should not be grouped together within the same batch (statement block).

Result Type: Boolean

EXECUTE

Executes a system procedure, a user-defined stored procedure, or an extended stored procedure. Also supports the execution of a character string within a Transact-SQL batch.

Syntax

Execute a stored procedure:

```
[[EXEC[UTE]]
{
[@return_status =]
{procedure_name [;number] | @procedure_name_var
}
[[@parameter =] {value | @variable [OUTPUT] | [DEFAULT]]
[, ...n]
[WITH RECOMPILE]
```

Execute a character string:

```
EXEC[UTE] ({@string_variable | [N]'tsql_string'} [+ ...n])
```

Arguments

@return_status

An optional integer variable that stores the return status of a stored procedure. This variable must be declared in the batch or stored procedure before it is used in an EXECUTE statement.

procedure_name

The fully qualified or non-fully qualified name of the stored procedure to call. Procedure names must conform to the rules for identifiers. A procedure that has been created in another database can be executed if the user executing the procedure is the procedure owner or the user has the appropriate permission to execute it in that database. A procedure can be executed on another server running Microsoft SQL Server if the user executing the procedure has the appropriate permission to use that server (remote access) and to execute the procedure in that database. If a server name is specified but no database name is specified, Microsoft SQL Server looks for the procedure in the user's default database.

;number

An optional integer used to group procedures of the same name so that they can be dropped together with a single DROP PROCEDURE statement. Procedures used in the same application are often grouped this way. For example, the procedures used with the application *orders* might be named orderproc;1, orderproc;2, and so on. The statement DROP PROCEDURE orderproc drops the entire group. Once procedures have been grouped, individual procedures within the group cannot be dropped. For example, the statement DROP PROCEDURE orderproc;2 is not allowed. This parameter is not used for extended stored procedures. For more information about procedure groups, see CREATE PROCEDURE.

@procedure_name_var

The name of a locally defined variable that represents a stored procedure name.

@parameter

The parameter for a procedure, as defined in the CREATE PROCEDURE statement. Parameter names must be preceded by the at sign (@). When used with the *@parameter_name = value* form, parameter names and constants need not be supplied in the order defined in the CREATE PROCEDURE statement. However, if the *@parameter_name = value* form is used for any parameter, it must be used for all subsequent parameters.

Parameters are nullable, by default. If a NULL parameter value is passed and that parameter is used (in a CREATE or ALTER TABLE statement) where the column referenced does not allow NULLs (inserting into a non-NULL column), SQL Server generates an error. To prevent passing a NULL parameter value to a non-NULL column, either add programming logic to the procedure or use a default value (with the DEFAULT keyword of CREATE or ALTER TABLE) for the column.

value

The value of the parameter to the procedure. If parameter names are not specified, then parameter values must be supplied in the order defined in the CREATE PROCEDURE statement.

If the value of a parameter is an object name, character string, or qualified by a database name or owner name, the entire name must be enclosed in single quotation marks. If the value of a parameter is a keyword, the keyword must be enclosed in double quotation marks.

If a default is defined in the CREATE PROCEDURE statement, a user can execute the procedure without specifying a parameter. The default must be a constant and can include the wildcard characters %, _, [ ], and [^] if the procedure uses the parameter name with the LIKE keyword.

The default can also be NULL. Usually, the procedure definition specifies what action should be taken if a parameter value is NULL.

@variable

The variable that stores a parameter or a return parameter.

OUTPUT

Specifies that the stored procedure returns a parameter. The matching parameter in the stored procedure must also have been created with the keyword OUTPUT. Use this keyword when using cursor variables as parameters.

DEFAULT

Supplies the default value of the parameter as defined in the procedure. When the procedure expects a value for a parameter that does not have a defined default and either a parameter is missing or the DEFAULT keyword is specified, an error occurs.

n

> A placeholder indicating that the preceding item(s) can be repeated multiple times. For example, EXECUTE can specify one or more *@parameter*, *value*, or *@variable* items.

WITH RECOMPILE

> Forces a new plan to be compiled. Use this option if the parameter you are supplying is atypical or if the data has significantly changed. The changed plan is used in subsequent executions. This option is not used for extended stored procedures. It is recommended that you use this option sparingly because it is expensive.

@string_variable

> The name of a local variable. *@string_variable* can be of **char**, **varchar**, **nchar**, or **nvarchar** data type.

[N]'*tsql_string*'

> A constant string. *tsql_string* can be of **nvarchar** or **varchar** data type. If the N is included, the string is interpreted as **nvarchar** data type.

EXISTS

Specifies a subquery to test for the existence of rows.

Syntax

EXISTS {(*subquery*)}

Arguments

subquery

> A restricted SELECT statement (the COMPUTE clause and the INTO keyword are not allowed). For more information, see the discussion of subqueries in SELECT.

Result Type: Boolean

Result Value

Returns TRUE if a subquery contains any rows.

EXP

Returns the exponential value of the given **float** expression.

Syntax

EXP(*float_expression*)

Arguments

float_expression

> An expression of type **float**.

Return Type: float

FETCH

Retrieves a specific row from a Transact-SQL server cursor.

Syntax

```
FETCH
 [ [ NEXT | PRIOR | FIRST | LAST
 | ABSOLUTE {n | @nvar}
 | RELATIVE {n | @nvar}
 ]
 FROM
 ]
 { { [GLOBAL] cursor_name } | cursor_variable_name}
 [INTO @variable_name[, ...n] ]
```

Arguments

NEXT

> Returns the result row immediately following the current row, and increments the current row to the row returned. If FETCH NEXT is the first fetch against a cursor, it returns the first row in the result set. NEXT is the default cursor fetch option.

PRIOR

> Returns the result row immediately preceding the current row, and decrements the current row to the row returned. If FETCH PRIOR is the first fetch against a cursor, no row is returned and the cursor is left positioned before the first row.

FIRST

> Makes the first row in the cursor the current row and returns it.

LAST

> Makes the last row in the cursor the current row and returns it.

ABSOLUTE {n | @$nvar$}

> If n or @$nvar$ is positive, makes the row n rows from the front of the cursor the current row and returns it. If n or @$nvar$ is negative, makes the row n rows before the end of the cursor the current row and returns it. If n or @$nvar$ is 0, no rows are returned. n and @$nvar$ must be **smallint**, **tinyint**, or **int**.

RELATIVE {n | @$nvar$}

> If n or @$nvar$ is positive, returns the row n rows beyond the current row and makes the returned row the new current row. If n or @$nvar$ is negative, returns the row n rows prior to the current row and makes the returned row the new current row. If n or @$nvar$ is 0, returns the current row. If FETCH RELATIVE with n or @$nvar$ set to negative numbers or 0 is the first fetch done against a cursor, it returns no rows. n and @$nvar$ must be **smallint**, **tinyint**, or **int**.

GLOBAL

> Specifies that *cursor_name* refers to a global cursor.

cursor_name

> The name of the open cursor from which the fetch should be made. If both a global and a local cursor exist with *cursor_name* as their name, then *cursor_name* refers to the global cursor if GLOBAL is specified. If GLOBAL is not specified, *cursor_name* refers to the local cursor.

cursor_variable_name

> The name of a cursor variable referencing the open cursor from which the fetch should be made.

INTO @*variable_name* [, ...*n*]

> Allows data from the columns of a fetch to be placed into local variables. Each variable in the list, from left to right, is associated with the corresponding column in the cursor result set. The data type of each variable must either match or be a supported implicit conversion of the data type of the corresponding result set column. The number of variables must match the number of columns in the cursor select list.

FILE_ID

Returns the file identification number (file ID) for the given logical filename in the current database.

Syntax

```
FILE_ID('file_name')
```

Arguments

'file_name'

> The name of the file for which to return the file ID. *file_name* is **nchar(128)**.

Return Type: smallint

FILE_NAME

Returns the logical filename for the given file identification number (ID).

Syntax

```
FILE_NAME(file_id)
```

Arguments

file_id

> The file identification number for which to return the filename. *file_id* is **smallint**.

Return Type: nvarchar(128)

FILEGROUP_ID

Returns the filegroup identification number (ID) for the given filegroup name.

Syntax

```
FILEGROUP_ID('filegroup_name')
```

Arguments

'filegroup_name'

> The filegroup name for which to return the filegroup ID. *filegroup_name* is **nvarchar(128)**.

Return Type: smallint

FILEGROUP_NAME

Returns the filegroup name for the given filegroup identification number (ID).

Syntax

```
FILEGROUP_NAME(filegroup_id)
```

Arguments

filegroup_id

> The filegroup identification number (ID) for which to return the filegroup name. *filegroup_id* is **smallint**.

Return Type: nvarchar(128)

Remarks

filegroup_id corresponds to the groupid column in sysfilegroups.

FILEGROUPPROPERTY

Returns the specified filegroup property value when given a filegroup and property name.

Syntax

```
FILEGROUPPROPERTY('filegroup_name', 'property')
```

Arguments

'filegroup_name'

> The name of the filegroup for which to return the named property information. *filegroup_name* is **nvarchar(128)**.

'property'

> The name of the filegroup property to return. *property* is **varchar(128)**. *property* can be one of the following values:

property Value	Description	Value Returned
IsReadOnly	Filegroup name is read-only.	I = True 0 = False NULL = Value not found
IsDboOnly	Filegroup name is accessible only by the database owner (DBO).	I = True 0 = False NULL = Value not found

property Value	Description	Value Returned
IsUserDefinedFG	Filegroup name is a user-defined filegroup.	I = True 0 = False NULL = Value not found
IsDefault	Filegroup name is the default filegroup	I = True 0 = False NULL = Value not found

Return Type: integer

FILEPROPERTY

Returns the specified filename property value when given a filename and property name.

Syntax

```
FILEPROPERTY('file_name', 'property')
```

Arguments

'file_name'

The name of the file associated with the current database for which to return property information. *file_name* is **nchar(128)**.

'property'

The name of the file property to return. *property* is **varchar(128)**. *property* can be one of the following values:

property Value	Description	Value Returned
IsReadOnly	File is read-only.	I = True 0 = False NULL = Value not found
IsPrimaryFile	File is the primary file.	I = True 0 = False NULL = Value not found
IsLogFile	File is a log file.	I = True 0 = False NULL = Value not found
SpaceUsed	Amount of space used by the specified file.	Number of pages allocated in the file.

Return Type: integer

FLOOR

Returns the largest integer less than or equal to the given **numeric** expression.

Syntax

```
FLOOR(numeric_expression)
```

Arguments

numeric_expression

> An expression of the exact numeric or approximate numeric data type category, except for the **bit** data type.

FORMATMESSAGE

Constructs a message from an existing message in sysmessages. The functionality of FORMATMESSAGE resembles that of the RAISERROR statement; however, RAISERROR prints the message immediately, while FORMATMESSAGE returns the edited message for further processing.

Syntax

```
FORMATMESSAGE(msg_number, param_value[, ...n])
```

Arguments

msg_number

> The ID of the message that is stored in sysmessages. If the message does not exist in sysmessages, an error is returned.

param_value

> One or more parameter values for use in the message. The values must be specified in the order in which placeholder variables appear in the message. The maximum number of values is 20.

Return Type: nvarchar

FREETEXT

Searches columns containing character-based data types for values that match the meaning but not the exact wording of the words in the predicate.

Syntax

```
FREETEXT
 (
{column | * }, 'freetext_string'
)
```

Arguments

column

> The name of a specific column that has been registered for full-text searching. Columns of the character string data types are valid full-text searching columns.

*

> Specifies that all columns in the table that have been registered for full-text searching should be used to search for the given *freetext_string*(s).

freetext_string

> Text to search for in the specified *column*.

Remarks

With FREETEXT, any text, including words, phrases, or sentences, can be entered as the *freetext_string*. Syntax is not important within the *freetext_string*. The Microsoft SQL Server search engine identifies important words and phrases. No special meaning is given to any of the reserved keywords or wildcard characters that typically have meaning when specified in the <contains_search_condition> parameter of the CONTAINS predicate.

FREETEXTTABLE

> Returns a table of zero, one, or more rows for those columns containing character-based data types that return relevance ranking for each row. Searches columns containing character-based data types for values that match the meaning but not the exact wording of the words in the specified *freetext_string*.

Syntax

```
FREETEXTTABLE (table, {column | *}, 'freetext_string')
```

Arguments

table

> The name of the table which has been marked for full-text querying. *table* can be a one-part database object name or a multi-part database object name.

column

> The name of the column to search which resides within the specified *table*, which must be marked for full-text querying. Columns of the character string data types are valid full-text searching columns.

*

> Specifies that all columns in the table that have been registered for full-text searching should be used to search for the given <contains_search_condition>(s).

freetext_string

> Some text to search for in the specified *column*.

Remarks

Like the FREETEXT predicate, FREETEXTTABLE is used when searching against text-based columns for values that match the meaning but not the exact wording of the words in the predicate.

Permissions

FREETEXTTABLE can be invoked only by users with appropriate SELECT privileges for the specified *table* and/or the referenced columns of *table*.

FROM

Specifies the tables, views, derived tables, and joined tables used in DELETE, INSERT, SELECT, and UPDATE statements.

Syntax

```
FROM
{ <table_or_view>
| (select_statement) [AS] table_alias [ (column_alias [, ...n]) ]
| <table_or_view> CROSS JOIN <table_or_view>
{ { INNER
| { FULL
| LEFT
| RIGHT
} [OUTER] [<join_hints>] JOIN
} <table_or_view> ON <join_condition>
}
| <rowset_function>
}[, ...n]
<table_or_view> ::=
{ table_name [ [AS] table_alias ] [ <table_hints> [, ...m] ]
| view_name [ [AS] table_alias ]
}
<table_hints> ::=
{ INDEX(index_name | index_id)
| FASTFIRSTROW
| HOLDLOCK
| NOLOCK
| PAGLOCK
| READCOMMITTED
| READPAST
| READUNCOMMITTED
| REPEATABLEREAD
| ROWLOCK
| SERIALIZABLE
| TABLOCK
| TABLOCKX
| UPDLOCK
}
<join_hint> ::=
{ HASH | LOOP | MERGE }
<join_condition> ::=
{ table_name | table_alias | view_name }.column_name
<logical_operator>
{ table_name | table_alias | view_name }.column_name
<logical_operator>::=
{ = | > | < | >= | <= | <> | != | !< | !> }
<rowset_function> ::=
{ CONTAINSTABLE [ [ AS] table_alias]
```

```
( table, { column | * }, '<contains_search_condition>'
)
| FREETEXTTABLE [ [ AS] table_alias]
( table, { column | * }, 'freetext_string'
)
| OPENQUERY (linked_server, 'query')
| OPENROWSET
( 'provider_name',
{
'datasource';'user_id';'password'
| 'provider_string'
},
{
[catalog.][schema.]object_name
| 'query'
}
)
}
```

Arguments

<table_or_view>

> Specifies the table or view, both with or without an alias, to use in the statement.

table_name

> The name(s) of the table(s) or joined table used in the SELECT statement. Up to 256 tables can be used in a DELETE, INSERT, UPDATE, or SELECT statement. If the tables exist in other databases on the same computer running Microsoft SQL Server, use a fully qualified table or view name, such as *database.owner.object_name*. If the table or view exists outside the local server in a linked server, use the four-part name of *linked_server.catalog.schema.object*. A joined table is the result set that is the product of two or more tables being combined. The order of the tables and views after the FROM keyword does not affect the result set returned. Errors are reported when redundant table names appear in the FROM clause.

table_alias

> The name of an alias. Each *table_name* or *view_name* can be given an alias, either for convenience or to distinguish a table or view in a self-join or subquery. Derived tables require an alias. An alias, when used in a join, is a shortened table name. Aliases are usually used to refer to specific columns from one of the tables involved in a join. If the same column name exists for more than one table involved in the join, SQL Server requires that the table name be specified. Therefore, defined aliases must be used for any ambiguous column references and must always match the alias reference (the full table name cannot be used if an alias has been defined).

Note Non-SQL-92-style joins (*= and =*) used in earlier versions of SQL Server did not allow nested outer joins or inner joins nested within an outer join. However, when using the SQL-92-style syntax for joined tables, nested outer joins or inner joins nested within an outer join are now supported.

\<table_hints\>

Specifies a table scan, one or more indexes to be used by the optimizer, or a locking method to be used by the optimizer with this table and for this SELECT. Although this is an option, the optimizer can usually pick the best optimization method without hints being specified. Commas between \<table_hints\> are optional but supported for backward compatibility. For more information, see the discussion of \<table_hints\> in SELECT.

INDEX(*index_name* | *index_id*)

Specifies the name or ID of the index to be used by SQL Server when processing the statement. Only one index hint per table can be specified. The alternative INDEX = syntax (which specifies a single index hint) is supported only for backward compatibility. Any index hints specified for a view are ignored, and SQL Server returns an error message.

Note If an index hint referring to multiple indexes is used on the fact table in a star join, SQL Server ignores the index hint and returns an error message. Also, index ORing is disallowed for a table with a specified index hint specified.

SQL Server does not allow more than one table hint from each of the following groups:

➤ Granularity hints: PAGLOCK, NOLOCK, ROWLOCK, TABLOCK, or TABLOCKX.

➤ Isolation level hints: HOLDLOCK, NOLOCK, READCOMMITTED, REPEATABLEREAD, SERIALIZABLE.

In addition, the NOLOCK and READPAST \<table_hints\> are only allowed in SELECT statements and not in DELETE, INSERT, or UPDATE statements.

m

A placeholder indicating that multiple \<table_hints\> can be specified.

view_name

The name(s) of the view(s) used in the DELETE, INSERT, UPDATE, or SELECT statement. If the views exist in other databases, use a fully qualified table or view name, such as *database.owner.object_name* or the four-part name of *linked_server.catalog.schema.object*.

select_statement

> The statement, also called a derived table, that retrieves rows from the database. A derived table is a subquery as specified in *select_statement* and uses the result set of the subquery as the input to the query being executed.

column_alias

> A user-defined, temporary heading to replace the default column heading (the column name). There are three methods for specifying a column heading different from the column name:

> ➤ Use *column_name* AS *column_alias*. This is the SQL-92-standard syntax.
> ➤ Use *column_alias* = *column_name*.
> ➤ Use *column_name column_alias*.

n

> A placeholder indicating that any of the preceding items can be repeated multiple times.

CROSS JOIN

> Specifies the cross-product of two tables. Returns the same rows as if no WHERE clause was specified in an old-style, non-SQL-92-style join.

> **Note** Old-style, non-SQL-92-style joins specify join conditions in the WHERE clause while SQL-92-style joins specify join conditions in the FROM clause of a SELECT statement.

INNER

> Specifies all matching pairs of rows are returned. Discards unmatched rows from both tables. This is the default if no join type is specified.

FULL [OUTER]

> If a row from either the left or right table does not match the selection criteria, specifies the row be included in the result set and output columns that correspond to the other table be set to NULL. This is in addition to all rows normally returned by INNER JOIN.

> **Note** Earlier versions of SQL Server joins (using the *= and =* syntax in the WHERE clause) cannot be used within the same statement as SQL-92-style joins.

LEFT [OUTER]

> Specifies all rows from the left table not meeting the condition specified are included in the result set, and output columns from the other table are set to NULL in addition to all rows returned by the INNER JOIN.

RIGHT [OUTER]

> Specifies all rows from the right table not meeting the condition specified are included in the result set, and output columns corresponding to the other table are set to NULL in addition to all rows returned by the INNER JOIN.

<join_hints>

> Specifies that SQL Server's query optimizer use one *join_hint*, or *execution algorithm*, per join specified in the query's FROM clause. For more information, see the discussion of <join_hints> in SELECT.

JOIN

> Indicates that the specified join operation should take place between the given tables or views.

ON <join_condition>

> Specifies the criteria that must match for the specified JOIN to be performed. As part of the <join_condition>, specify a common *column_name* from each table in the join. A <join_condition> also specifies a <logical_operator>.

<logical_operator>

> Specifies the condition that rows to be returned must meet.

<rowset_function>

> Specifies that one of the rowset functions is to be used.

CONTAINSTABLE

> When used with a SELECT statement only, returns a table of zero, one, or more rows for those columns containing character-based data types for precise or "fuzzy" (less precise) matches to single words and phrases, the proximity of words within a certain distance of one another, and weighted matches. For more information, see CONTAINSTABLE.

FREETEXTTABLE

> When used with a SELECT statement only, returns a table of zero, one, or more rows for those columns containing character-based data types for values that match the meaning but not the exact wording of the words in the predicate. For more information, see FREETEXTTABLE.

OPENQUERY

> Executes the specified pass-through query. For more information, see OPENQUERY.

OPENROWSET

> Includes all connection information necessary to access remote data from a data source. For more information, see OPENROWSET.

Remarks

The FROM clause supports the SQL-92-style syntax for joined tables and derived tables. SQL-92 syntax provides the INNER, LEFT OUTER, RIGHT OUTER, and FULL OUTER join operators.

Although the outer join operators from earlier versions of SQL Server are supported, you cannot use both outer join operators and SQL-92-style joined tables in the same FROM clause.

UNION and JOIN within a FROM clause are supported within views as well as in derived tables and subqueries.

A self-join is a table that joins upon itself. Inserts or updates that are based on a self-join follow the order in the FROM clause.

Permissions

FROM permissions default the permissions for the DELETE, INSERT, SELECT, or UPDATE statement.

FULLTEXTCATALOGPROPERTY

Returns information about full-text catalog properties

Syntaxt

```
FULLTEXTCATALOGPROPERTY( 'catalog_name', 'property')
```

Arguments

'*catalog_name*'

> The name of the full-text catalog.

'*property*'

> The name of the full-text catalog property to return. *property* can be one of the following values:

property	Value
PopulateStatus	0 = Idle 1 = Population in progress 2 = Paused 3 = Throttled 4 = Recovering 5 = Shutdown 6 = Incremental population in progress 7 = Updating index
ItemCount	Number of full-text indexed items currently in the full-text catalog.
IndexSize	Size of the full-text index in megabytes.
UniqueKeyCount	Number of unique words (keys) that make up the full-text index in this catalog. This is an approximation of the number of non-noise words stored in the full-text catalog.
LogSize	Size of the last full-text index population in megabytes.
PopulateCompletionAge	The difference in seconds between the completion of the last full-text index population and 01/01/1990 00:00:00.

Return Type: integer

FULLTEXTSERVICEPROPERTY

Returns full-text service-level properties.

Syntaxt

```
FULLTEXTSERVICEPROPERTY('property')
```

Arguments

'*property*'

The name of the property. *property* can be one of these values:

property	Value
ResourceUsage	A value from 1 (background) through 5 (dedicated).
ConnectTimeout	This number, when multiplied by 4, is the time in seconds that is given to Microsoft Search Service to set up and initialize for full-text index population.
IsFulltextInstalled	1 = Microsoft Search (Full-text) Service is installed on the computer. 0 = Otherwise

Return Type: integer

GETANSINULL

Returns the default nullability for the database for this session.

Syntax

```
GETANSINULL(['database'])
```

Arguments

'*database*'

The name of the database for which to return nullability information. *database* is either **char** or **nchar**. If **char**, *database* is implicitly converted to **nchar**.

Return Type: int

GETDATE

Returns the current system date and time in the Microsoft SQL Server standard internal format for **datetime** values.

Syntax

```
GETDATE()
```

Return Type: datetime

Remarks

Date functions can be used in the SELECT statement select list or in the WHERE clause of a query.

In designing a report, GETDATE can be used to print the current date and time every time the report is produced. GETDATE is also useful for tracking activity, such as logging the time a transaction occurred on an account.

GO

Signals the end of a batch of Transact-SQL statements to the Microsoft SQL Server utilities.

Syntax

```
GO
```

Remarks

GO is a command and is used with either **osql** or the SQL Server Query Analyzer.

SQL Server utilities interpret GO as a signal that they should send the current batch of Transact-SQL statements to SQL Server. The current batch of statements is composed of all statements entered since the last GO, or since the start of the ad hoc session or script if this is the first GO. SQL Server Query Analyzer and the **osql** and **isql** command-prompt utilities implement GO differently.

A Transact-SQL statement cannot occupy the same line as a GO command. However, the line can contain comments.

Users must follow the rules for batches. For example, any execution of a stored procedure after the first statement in a batch must include the EXECUTE keyword. The scope of local (user-defined) variables is limited to a batch, and cannot be referenced after a GO command.

```
USE pubs
GO
DECLARE @MyMsg VARCHAR(50)
SELECT @MyMsg = 'Hello, World.'
GO -- @MyMsg is not valid after this GO ends the batch.
-- Yields an error because @MyMsg not declared in this batch.
PRINT @MyMsg
GO
SELECT @@version;
-- Yields an error: Must be EXEC sp_who if not first statement in
-- batch.
sp_who
GO
```

SQL Server applications can send multiple Transact-SQL statements to SQL Server for execution as a batch. The statements in the batch are then compiled into a single execution plan. Programmers executing ad hoc statements in the SQL Server utilities or building scripts of Transact-SQL statements to run through the SQL Server utilities use GO to signal the end of a batch.

Applications based on the DB-Library, ODBC, or OLE DB APIs receive a syntax error if they attempt to execute a GO command. The SQL Server utilities never send a GO command to the server.

GOTO

Alters the flow of execution to a label. The Transact-SQL statements following GOTO are skipped and processing continues at the label. GOTO statements and labels can be used anywhere within a procedure, batch, or statement block. GOTO statements can be nested.

Syntax
Define the label:

```
label:
```

Alter the execution:

```
GOTO label
```

Arguments

label

> The point after which processing begins if a GOTO is targeted to that label. Labels must follow the rules for identifiers. A label can be used as a commenting method whether or not GOTO is used.

Remarks

GOTO can exist within conditional control-of-flow statements, statement blocks, or procedures, but it cannot go to a label outside of the batch. GOTO branching can go to a label defined before or after GOTO.

Permissions

GOTO permissions default to any valid user.

GRANT

Creates an entry in the security system that allows a user in the current database to work with data in the current database or execute specific Transact-SQL statements.

Syntax
Statement permissions:

```
GRANT {ALL | statement [, ...n]}
TO security_account[, ...n]
```

Object permissions:

```
GRANT
{
```

```
{ALL | permission[, ...n]} [(column[, ...n])] ON {table | view}
| ON {stored_procedure | extended_procedure}
}
TO security_account [, ...n]
 [WITH GRANT OPTION]
 [AS {group | role}]
```

Arguments

ALL

Specifies that all applicable permissions are being granted. For statement permissions, ALL can be used only by members of the sysadmin role. For object permissions, ALL can be used by members of the sysadmin and db_owner roles and database object owners.

statement

The statement for which permission is being granted. The statement list can include:

➤ CREATE DATABASE

➤ CREATE DEFAULT

➤ CREATE PROCEDURE

➤ CREATE RULE

➤ CREATE TABLE

➤ CREATE VIEW

➤ BACKUP DATABASE

➤ BACKUP LOG

n

A placeholder indicating that the item can be repeated in a comma-separated list.

TO

Specifies the security account list.

security_account

The security account to which the permissions are applied. The security account can be a:

➤ Microsoft SQL Server user.

➤ SQL Server role.

➤ Microsoft Windows NT user.

➤ Windows NT group.

When a permission is granted to a SQL Server user or Windows NT user account, the specified *security_account* is the only account affected by the permission. If a permission is granted to a SQL Server role or a Windows NT group, the permission affects all users in the current database who are members of the group or role. If there are permission conflicts between a group or role and its

members, the most restrictive permission (DENY) takes precedence.
security_account must exist in the current database; permissions cannot be granted to a user, role, or group in another database, unless the user has already been created or given access to the current database.

Two special security accounts can be used with GRANT. Permissions granted to the **public** role are applied to all users in the database. Permissions granted to the **guest** user are used by all users who do not have a user account in the database.

When granting permissions to a Windows NT local or global group, specify the domain or computer name the group is defined on, followed by a backslash, then the group name. However, to grant permissions to a Windows NT built-in local group, specify BUILTIN instead of the domain or computer name.

permission

An object permission that is being granted. When permissions are granted on a table or a view, the permission list can include one or more of these statements: SELECT, INSERT, DELETE, or UPDATE.

Object permissions granted on a table can also include REFERENCES, and object permissions granted on a procedure can include EXECUTE. When permissions are granted on columns, the permissions list can include SELECT and/or UPDATE. When permissions are granted on stored procedures, the permissions list can include only EXECUTE.

When a user adds a row to a table with a FOREIGN KEY constraint, or changes data in a column with a FOREIGN KEY constraint, SQL Server must validate the data in the column with the data referenced in the FOREIGN KEY constraint. If the user does not have SELECT permissions on the referenced column or table, the REFERENCES permission for the column must be granted to the user. The REFERENCES permission cannot be granted for a system table.

column

The name of a column in the current database for which permissions are being granted.

table

The name of the table in the current database for which permissions are being granted.

view

The name of the view in the current database for which permissions are being granted.

stored_procedure

The name of the stored procedure in the current database for which permissions are being granted.

extended_procedure

The name of the extended stored procedure for which permissions are being granted.

WITH GRANT OPTION

Specifies that *security_account* is given the ability to grant the specified permission object to the other security accounts. The WITH GRANT OPTION clause is only valid with object permissions.

AS {*group | role*}

Specifies the name of the security account that has the permissions necessary to execute the GRANT statement. The AS option is required when the user executing the GRANT statement belongs to multiple groups or roles. If there are conflicts between the permissions applied to the users through their group and role membership, the AS option must be used to indicate the group with the permissions necessary to allow them to use the GRANT statement. The group and role must exist in the current database.

GROUP BY

Divides a table into groups. Groups can consist of column names or results or computed columns.

HAVING

Specifies the restricting conditions for the groups returned in the result set.

HOST_ID

Returns the workstation identification number.

Syntax

```
HOST_ID( )
```

Return Type: int

Remarks

When the parameter to a system function is optional, the current database, host computer, server user, or database user is assumed. Built-in functions must always be followed by parentheses.

System functions can be used in the select list, in the WHERE clause, and anywhere an expression is allowed.

HOST_NAME

Returns the workstation name.

Syntax

```
HOST_NAME( )
```

Return Type: nchar

Remarks

When the parameter to a system function is optional, the current database, host computer, server user, or database user is assumed. Built-in functions must always be followed by parentheses.

System functions can be used in the select list, in the WHERE clause, and anywhere an expression is allowed.

IDENT_INCR

Returns the increment value (returned as **numeric(@@maxprecision**,0)) specified during the creation of an identity column in a table or view that has an identity column.

Syntax

```
IDENT_INCR('table_or_view')
```

Arguments

'table_or_view'

> An expression specifying the table or view to check for a valid identity increment value. *table_or_view* can be a character string constant enclosed in quotation marks, a variable, a function, or a column name. *table_or_view* is **char**, **nchar**, **varchar**, or **nvarchar**.

Return Type: numeric

IDENT_SEED

Returns the seed value (returned as **numeric(@@maxprecision**,0)) specified during the creation of an identity column in a table or a view that has an identity column.

Syntax

```
IDENT_SEED('table_or_view')
```

Arguments

'table_or_view'

> An expression specifying the table or view to check for a valid identity seed value. *table_or_view* can be a character string constant enclosed in quotation marks, a variable, a function, or a column name. *table_or_view* is **char**, **nchar**, **varchar**, or **nvarchar**.

Return Type: numeric

IDENTITY

Creates an identity column in a table.

Remarks

An identity column is often used for primary keys for identification numbers or any other value that should be an automatically incrementing value. By using IDENTITY for primary keys, each row in the table has a unique value within a database, the primary key number is automatically generated, and the index is short, so it is relatively quick to find the necessary record or records. When inserting data, no value is needed for an identity column.

If an identity column exists for a table with frequent deletions, gaps can occur between identity values. If this is a concern, do not use the IDENTITY property. However, to ensure that no gaps have been created or to fill an existing gap, evaluate the existing identity values before explicitly entering one with SET IDENTITY_INSERT ON.

IF...ELSE

Imposes conditions on the execution of a Transact-SQL statement. The Transact-SQL statement following an IF keyword and its condition is executed if the condition is satisfied (when the Boolean expression returns TRUE). The optional ELSE keyword introduces an alternate Transact-SQL statement that is executed when the IF condition is not satisfied (when the Boolean expression returns FALSE).

Syntax

```
IF Boolean_expression
{sql_statement | statement_block}
 [ELSE
{sql_statement | statement_block}]
```

Arguments

Boolean_expression

An expression that returns TRUE or FALSE. If the Boolean expression contains a SELECT statement, the SELECT statement must be enclosed in parentheses.

{sql_statement | statement_block}

Any Transact-SQL statement or statement grouping as defined with a statement block. The IF or ELSE condition can affect the performance of only one Transact-SQL statement, unless a statement block is used. To define a statement block, use the control-of-flow keywords BEGIN and END. CREATE TABLE or SELECT INTO statements must refer to the same table name if the CREATE TABLE or SELECT INTO statements are used in both the IF and ELSE areas of the IF...ELSE block.

IN

Determines if a given value matches any value in a list.

Syntax

```
test_expression IN
 (
subquery
| expression [, ...n]
)
```

Arguments

test_expression

Any valid Microsoft SQL Server expression.

subquery

A subquery whose result set has one column. This column must have the same data type as *test_expression*.

Result Type: Boolean

INDEXPROPERTY

Returns the named index property value given a table identification number, index name, and property name.

Syntax

```
INDEXPROPERTY(table_ID, 'index', 'property')
```

Arguments

table_ID

The identification number of the table for which to provide index property information. *table_ID* is **int**.

'index'

The name of the index for which to return property information. *index* is **nvarchar(128)**.

'property'

The name of the database property to return. *property* is **varchar(128)**. *property* can be one of these values:

property Value	Description	Value Returned
IsClustered	Index is clustered.	1 = True 0 = False NULL = Value not found
IsUnique	Index is unique.	1 = True 0 = False NULL = Value not found
IndexFillFactor	Index specifies its own fill factor.	A number that is the fill factor used when the index was created or last rebuilt.
IsPadIndex	Index specifies space to leave open on each interior node.	1 = True 0 = False NULL = Value not found

property Value	Description	Value Returned
IsFulltextKey	Index is the Full-Text key for a table	I = True 0 = False NULL = invalid table or invalid index name.

Return Type: integer

INDEX_COL

Returns the indexed column name.

Syntax

```
INDEX_COL('table', index_id, key_id)
```

Arguments

'table'

> The name of the table to be used.

index_id

> The ID of the index to be used.

key_id

> The ID of the key to be used.

Return Type: nchar

INSERT

Adds a new row to a table or a view.

Syntax

```
INSERT [INTO] {<table_sources>}
{
{
 [(column_list)] VALUES
 (
{
DEFAULT
| constant_expression
}[, ...n]
)
| select_statement
| execute_statement
}
| DEFAULT VALUES
}
<table_sources> ::=
{ <table_or_view>
| (select_statement) [AS] table_alias [ (column_alias [, ...n]) ]
| <table_or_view> CROSS JOIN <table_or_view>
{ { INNER
```

```
|  { FULL
|  LEFT
|  RIGHT
}  [OUTER] [<join_hints>] JOIN
}  <table_or_view> ON <join_condition>
}
|  <rowset_function>
}[, ...n]
<table_or_view> ::=
{ table_name [ [AS] table_alias ] [ WITH (<table_hints> [, ...m]) ]
| view_name [ [AS] table_alias ]
}
<table_hints> ::=
{ INDEX(index_name | index_id)
| HOLDLOCK
| PAGLOCK
| READCOMMITTED
| REPEATABLEREAD
| ROWLOCK
| SERIALIZABLE
| TABLOCK
| TABLOCKX
}
<join_hints> ::=
{
HASH
| LOOP
| MERGE
}
<rowset_function> ::=
{ OPENQUERY (linked_server, 'query')
| OPENROWSET
 ( 'provider_name',
{
'datasource';'user_id';'password'
| 'provider_string'
},
{
 [catalog.][schema.]object_name
| 'query'
}
)
}
```

Arguments

INTO

   Specifies that the given data should be inserted into the specified table or view.

column_list

A list of one or more columns in which to insert data. *column_list* must be enclosed in parentheses and delimited by commas. If the values in the VALUES clause are not in the same order as the columns in the table or do not have a value for each column in the table, the *column_list* option must be used to explicitly specify the column that stores each incoming value.

VALUES

Introduces the list of data values to be inserted. There must be one data value for each column in *column_list* (if specified) or in the table.

DEFAULT

Forces Microsoft SQL Server to load the default value defined for a column. If a default does not exist for the column and the column allows nulls, NULL will be inserted. For a column defined with the **timestamp** data type, the next timestamp value will be inserted. DEFAULT is not valid for an identity column.

constant_expression

A literal value, a variable, or an expression that returns a single value. The expression cannot contain a SELECT or EXECUTE statement.

n

A placeholder indicating that multiple values separated by commas can be specified in the parenthetical VALUES list.

select_statement

Any valid SELECT statement that returns rows of data to be loaded into the table.

execute_statement

A valid EXECUTE statement that returns data with SELECT or READTEXT statements.

If the EXECUTE option is used with INSERT, each result set returned must be compatible with the columns in the table or in the *column_list*. The EXECUTE option can be used to execute stored procedures on the same server or another remote server. The procedure in the remote server will be executed, and the result sets will be returned to the local server and loaded into the table in the local server. If the EXECUTE option returns data with the READTEXT statement, each individual READTEXT statement can return a maximum of one megabyte (1,024 K) of data. The EXECUTE option can also be used with extended procedures, and will insert the data returned by the main thread of the extended procedure. Output from threads other than the main thread will not be inserted.

DEFAULT VALUES

Forces the new row to contain the default values defined for each column.

The name of the table or view that will be used to provide criteria for the INSERT operation.

table_name

The name of a table in which the data is loaded. If the table is not in the current database or is owned by a different user, use a fully qualified name in the format [*database.*][*owner.*]*tablename.*

table_alias

The name of an alias. Each table or view can be given an alias, either for convenience or to distinguish a table or view in a self-join or a subquery.

column_alias

A user-defined, temporary heading to replace the default column heading (the column name). For more information about column aliases, see FROM.

CROSS JOIN

Specifies the cross-product of two tables. Returns the same rows as if no WHERE clause was specified in an old-style, non-SQL-92-style join.

INNER

Specifies all matching pairs of rows are returned. Discards unmatched rows from both tables. This is the default if no join type is specified.

<join_hints>

Specifies that SQL Server's query optimizer use one *join_hint*, or *execution algorithm*, per join specified in the query's FROM clause. For more information, see the discussion of <join_hints> in SELECT.

HASH | LOOP | MERGE

Specifies that the joins in the query use looping, hashing, or merging. If more than one join strategy is specified with the optional OPTION clause, the optimizer will select the least expensive strategy from those specified for each join.

JOIN

A keyword to indicate that an SQL-92-style join be used in the INSERT operation.

<table_hints>

Specifies a table scan, one or more indexes to be used by the optimizer, or a locking method to be used by the optimizer with this table and for this SELECT. Although this is an option, the optimizer can usually pick the best optimization method without hints being specified. Commas between <table_hints> are optional but supported for backward compatibility. For more information, see the discussion of <table_hints> in SELECT.

m

A placeholder indicating that multiple <table_hints> can be specified.

view_name

The name of a view. The rows are inserted into the table in the view definition. INSERT cannot be used with multitable views or views containing aggregates (AVG, COUNT, MIN, MAX, SUM) or expressions in the view's column definition.

INDEX(*index_name* | *index_id*)

Specifies the name or ID of the index to be used by SQL Server when processing the statement. Only one index hint per table can be specified. The alternative INDEX = syntax (which specifies a single index hint) is supported only for backward compatibility. Any index hints specified for a view are ignored, and SQL Server returns an error message.

Note If an index hint referring to multiple indexes is used on the fact table in a star join, SQL Server ignores the index hint and returns an error message. Also, index ORing is disallowed for a table with a specified index hint specified.

SQL Server does not allow more than one table hint from each of the following groups:

➤ Granularity hints: PAGLOCK, NOLOCK, ROWLOCK, TABLOCK, or TABLOCKX.

➤ Isolation level hints: HOLDLOCK, NOLOCK, READCOMMITTED, REPEATABLEREAD, SERIALIZABLE.

In addition, the NOLOCK and READPAST <table_hints> are only allowed in SELECT statements and not in DELETE, INSERT, or UPDATE statements.

OPENQUERY

Executes the specified pass-through query. For more information, see OPENQUERY.

OPENROWSET

Includes all connection information necessary to access remote data from a data source. For more information, see OPENROWSET.

Remarks

INSERT appends new rows to a table. To replace data in a table, the DELETE or TRUNCATE TABLE statements must be used to clear existing data before loading new data with INSERT. To modify column values in existing rows, use UPDATE. To create a new table and load it with data in one step, use the INTO option of the SELECT statement.

If the values to be loaded as a new row are not in the same order or do not have a value for each column, the *column_list* option must be used to explicitly specify the column for each value. If a column is not in *column_list*, SQL Server must be able to provide a value based on the definition of the column; otherwise the row cannot be loaded. SQL Server automatically provides a value for the column if:

➤ It has an IDENTITY property. The next incremental identity value will be used.

➤ It has a default. The default value for the column will be used.

➤ It has a **timestamp** data type. The current timestamp value will be used.

➤ It is nullable. A NULL value will be used.

The *column_list* and *values_list* must be used when inserting explicit values into an identity column, and the IDENTITY_INSERT setting must be TRUE for the table.

Columns created with the **uniqueidentifier** data type store specially formatted 16-byte binary values. Unlike identity columns, SQL Server does not automatically generate values for columns with the **uniqueidentifier** data type. Variables with a data type of **uniqueidentifier** and string constants in the form:

xxxxxxxx-xxxx-xxxx-xxxx-xxxxxxxxxxxx

(36 characters including hyphens, where x is a hexadecimal digit in the range 0-9 or a-f) can be used for **uniqueidentifier** columns during INSERT. For example, 6F9619FF-8B86-D011-B42D-00C04FC964FF is a valid value for a **uniqueidentifier** variable or column. The NEWID function should be used to provide a GUID (globally unique ID).

When inserting rows, these rules apply:

➤ If a value is being loaded into columns with a **char**, **varchar**, or **varbinary** data type, the padding or truncation of trailing blanks (spaces for char and **varchar**, zeroes for **varbinary**) is determined by the SET ANSI_PADDING setting defined for the column when the table was created.

This table shows the default operation for SET ANSI_PADDING to OFF.

Data Type	Default Operation
char	Pad value with spaces to defined width of column.
varchar	Remove trailing spaces to the last non-space character or to a single space character for strings consisting of only spaces.
varbinary	Remove trailing zeroes.

➤ If an empty string (' ') is loaded into a column with a **varchar** or **text** data type, the default operation is to load a zero-length string. If the compatibility level for the database is less than 70, the value is converted to a single space.

➤ If an INSERT statement violates a constraint or rule, or if it has a value incompatible with the data type of the column, the statement fails and SQL Server displays an error message.

➤ Inserting a null value into a **text** or **image** column does not create a valid text pointer, nor does it preallocate an 8 K text page.

➤ If INSERT is loading multiple rows with SELECT or EXECUTE, any violation of a rule or constraint that occurs from the values being loaded will cause the entire statement to be terminated, and no rows will be loaded.

When an INSERT statement encounters an arithmetic error (overflow, divide by zero, or a domain error) occurring during expression evaluation, SQL Server handles these errors as if SET ARITHABORT is ON so the remainder of the batch is aborted. An error message is returned.

Permissions

INSERT permissions default to members of the sysadmin fixed database role, the database owner, and table owner, who can transfer them to other users.

IS_MEMBER

Indicates whether the current user is a member of the specified Microsoft Windows NT group or Microsoft SQL Server™ role.

Syntax

IS_MEMBER ({'group' | 'role'})

Arguments

'group'

The name of the Windows NT group being checked; must be in the domain\group format. *group* is sysname.

'role'

The name of the SQL Server role being checked. *role* is sysname. Can include the database fixed roles or user-defined roles, but not server roles.

Remarks

IS_MEMBER returns.

Return Value	Description
0	Current user is not a member of *group* or *role*.
I	Current user is a member of *group* or *role*.
NULL	Either *group* or *role* is not valid.

This function can be useful to programmatically detect whether the current user can perform an activity that depends on the permissions applied to a group or role.

IS_SRVROLEMEMBER

Indicates whether the current user login is a member of the specified server role.

Syntax

IS_SRVROLEMEMBER ('role' [,'login'])

Arguments

'role'

> The name of the server role being checked. *role* is sysname.

'login'

> The optional name of the login to check. *login* is sysname, with a default of NULL. If not specified, the login account for the current user will be used.

Remarks

IS_SRVROLEMEMBER returns.

Return Value	Description
0	Login is not a member of *role*.
I	Login is a member of *role*.
NULL	*Role* and/or *login* is not valid.

This function can be useful to programmatically detect whether the current user can perform an activity requiring the server role's permissions.

The valid values for *role* are: sysadmin, dbcreator, diskadmin, processadmin, serveradmin, setupadmin, and securityadmin.

ISDATE

Checks a variable or column with **varchar** data type for valid date format. The function returns 1 when the variable or column contains a valid date; otherwise, it returns 0.

Syntax

```
ISDATE(expression)
```

Arguments

expression

> A variable or column of **varchar** data type.

IS [NOT] NULL

Determines whether or not a given expression is NULL.

Syntax

```
expression IS [NOT] NULL
```

Arguments

expression

> Any valid Microsoft SQL Server expression.

NOT

> Specifies that the Boolean expression specified by the predicate is negated.

Result Type: Boolean

ISNULL

Replaces NULL value with the specified replacement value.

Syntax

ISNULL(*check_expression, replacement_value*)

Arguments

check_expression

The expression to be checked for NULL value. *check_expression* can be of any type.

replacement_value

The expression to be returned if the value of *check_expression* is NULL. *replacement_value* must have the same type as *check_expresssion*.

Return Type: Same as *check_expression*

ISNUMERIC

Returns 1 when the input expression evaluates to a valid integer, floating-point number, money, or decimal type. Returns 0 otherwise. A return of 1 guarantees that the input string expression can be converted to one of these numeric types.

Syntax

ISNUMERIC(*expression*)

Arguments

expression

An expression to be evaluated.

Return Type: integer

KILL

Terminates a user process based on the system process ID (SPID). If the specified SPID has a lot of work to undo, the KILL may take some time to complete.

Syntax

KILL {*spid*} [WITH {ABORT | COMMIT}]

Arguments

spid

The SPID of the process to terminate. The SPID value is a unique integer (**smallint**) assigned to each user connection when the connection is made; no user is permanently assigned a SPID.

WITH ABORT

When used with a distributed transaction only, specifies that the specified SPID is aborted. SQL Server returns an error message if this option is specified for a SPID that is not involved in a distributed transaction.

WITH COMMIT

When used with a distributed transaction only, specifies that the specified SPID is committed. If there are network disconnects with a client or if previous KILL statements have been issued, WITH COMMIT may not commit the distributed transaction-related SPID. Consult the SQL Server error log to determine the status of distributed transaction-related SPIDs and related KILL statements. SQL Server returns an error message if this option is specified for a SPID that is not involved in a distributed transaction.

Remarks

When using KILL to terminate a user process:

➤ KILL is commonly used to terminate a process that is blocking other important processes with locks, or to terminate a process that is executing a query that is using necessary system resources. System processes and processes running an extended stored procedure cannot be terminated.

➤ Use KILL very carefully, especially when critical processes are running. Remember that you cannot kill your own process. Processes not to kill are:

  ➤ AWAITING COMMAND
  ➤ CHECKPOINT SLEEP
  ➤ LAZY WRITER
  ➤ LOCK MONITOR
  ➤ SELECT
  ➤ SIGNAL HANDLER

Execute sp_who to get a report on valid SPID values. Use @@spid to display the SPID value for the current session.

Permissions

KILL permissions default to the members of the sysadmin fixed database role. Permissions are not transferable.

LEFT

Returns the number of characters from the left of the specified character string.

Syntax

```
LEFT(character_expression, integer_expression)
```

Arguments

character_expression

> An expression of character or binary data. *character_expression* can be a constant, variable, or column. *character_expression* must be of a data type that can be implicitly convertible to **varchar**. Otherwise, use the CAST function to explicitly convert *character_expression*.

integer_expression

> A positive whole number. If *integer_expression* is negative, a null string is returned.

Return Type: varchar

LEN

Returns the number of characters, rather than the number of bytes, of the given string expression, excluding trailing blanks.

Syntax

```
LEN(string_expression)
```

Arguments

string_expression

> The string expression to be evaluated.

Return Type: int

LIKE

Determines whether or not a given character string matches a specified *pattern*, which can include regular characters and wildcard characters. During pattern matching, regular characters must exactly match the characters specified in the character string; wildcard characters, however, may be matched with arbitrary fragments of the character string. Using wildcard characters makes the LIKE operator more flexible than regular string comparison which uses the = and != operators. If any of the arguments are not of character string data type, Microsoft SQL Server converts them to character string data type, if possible.

Syntax

```
match_expression [NOT] LIKE pattern [ESCAPE escape_character]
```

Arguments

match_expression

> Any valid SQL Server expression of character string data type.

pattern

> The pattern to search for in *match_expression*. Can be one of these valid SQL Server wildcard characters:

Wildcard Character	Description	Example
%	Any string of zero or more characters.	WHERE title LIKE '%computer%' finds all book titles with the word 'computer' anywhere in the book title.
_ (underscore)	Any single character.	WHERE au_fname LIKE '_ean' finds all four-letter first names that end with 'ean' (Dean, Sean, and so on).
[ ]	Any single character within the specified range ([a-f]) or set ([abcdef])	WHERE au_lname LIKE '[C-P]arsen' finds author last names ending with 'arsen' and beginning with any single character between C and P, for example Carsen, Larsen, Karsen, and so on.
[^]	Any single character not within the specified range ([^a-f]) or set ([^abcdef])	WHERE au_lname LIKE 'de[^l]%' finds all author last names beginning with 'de' and where the following letter is not 'l'.

escape_character

Any valid SQL Server expression of character string data type. Must consist of only one character. There is no default *escape_character*.

Result Type: Boolean

LOAD

Loads a backup copy of one of the following:

➤ User database (LOAD DATABASE)

➤ Transaction log (LOAD TRANSACTION)

➤ Header information about the dump (LOAD HEADERONLY)

LOG

Returns the natural logarithm of the given **float** expression.

Syntax

LOG(*float_expression*)

Arguments

float_expression

An expression of the **float** data type.

Return Type: float

LOG10

Returns the base-10 logarithm of the given **float** expression.

Syntax

LOG10(*float_expression*)

Arguments

float_expression

> An expression of the **float** data type.

Return Type: float

LOWER

Returns a character expression after converting uppercase character data to lowercase.

Syntax

LOWER(*character_expression*)

Arguments

character_expression

> An expression of character or binary data. *character_expression* can be a constant, variable, or column.

Return Type: varchar

LTRIM

Returns a character expression after removing leading blanks.

Syntax

LTRIM(*character_expression*)

Arguments

character_expression

> An expression of character or binary data. *character_expression* can be a constant, variable, or column.

Return Type: varchar

MAX

Returns the maximum value in the expression.

Syntax

MAX([ALL | DISTINCT] *expression*)

Arguments

ALL

> Applies the aggregate function to all values. ALL is the default.

DISTINCT

> Specifies that each unique value is considered. DISTINCT is not meaningful with MAX and is available for ANSI compatibility only.

expression

A constant, column name, or function, and any combination of arithmetic, bitwise, and string operators. MAX can be used with numeric, character, and **datetime** columns, but not with **bit** columns. Aggregate functions and subqueries are not permitted.

Return Type: Same as *expression*.

MIN

Returns the minimum value in the expression.

Syntax

MIN([ALL | DISTINCT] *expression*)

Arguments

ALL

Applies the aggregate function to all values. ALL is the default.

DISTINCT

Specifies that each unique value is considered. DISTINCT is not meaningful with MIN and is available for ANSI compatibility only.

expression

A constant, column name, or function, and any combination of arithmetic, bitwise, and string operators. MIN can be used with numeric, **char**, **varchar**, or **datetime** columns, but not with **bit** columns. Aggregate functions and subqueries are not permitted.

Return Type: Same as *expression*.

MONTH

Returns an integer that represents the month part of a specified date.

Syntax

MONTH(*date*)

Arguments

date

An expression returning a **datetime** or **smalldatetime** value, or a character string in a date format. Use the **datetime** data type only for dates after January 1, 1753.

Return Type: int

NCHAR

Returns the Unicode character with the given integer code, as defined by the Unicode standard.

Syntax

NCHAR(*integer_expression*)

Arguments

integer_expression

> A positive whole number from 0 through 65,535. If a value outside this range is specified, NULL is returned.

Return Type: nchar(1)

NEWID

Creates a unique value of type **uniqueidentifier**.

Syntax

NEWID()

Return Type: uniqueidentifier

NOT

Negates a Boolean input.

Syntax

[NOT] *boolean_expression*

Arguments

boolean_expression

> Any valid Microsoft SQL Server Boolean expression.

Remarks

The use of NOT negates an expression.

This table shows the results of comparing TRUE and FALSE values using the NOT operator.

NOT	
TRUE	TRUE
FALSE	FALSE
UNKNOWN	UNKNOWN

NULLIF

Returns a null value if the two specified expressions are equivalent.

Syntax

NULLIF(*expression, expression*)

Arguments

expression

> A constant, column name, function, subquery, or any combination of arithmetic, bitwise, and string operators.

Return Type: A null value when both expressions are equivalent.

OBJECT_ID

> Returns the database object identification number.

Syntax

```
OBJECT_ID('object')
```

Arguments

'object'

> The object to be used. *object* is either **char** or **nchar**. If *object* is specified as **char**, then it is implicitly converted to **nchar**.

Return Type: int

OBJECT_NAME

> Returns the database object name.

Syntax

```
OBJECT_NAME(object_id)
```

Arguments

object_id

> The ID of the object to be used.

Return Type: nchar

OBJECTPROPERTY

> Returns information about objects in the current database.

Syntax

```
OBJECTPROPERTY(id, 'property')
```

Arguments

id

> The ID of the object in the current database.

'property'

The information to be returned for the object specified by *id*. *property* can be one of these values:

property Value	Object Type	Object Definition
'CnstIsClustKey'	Constraint	Primary key with a clustered index
'CnstIsColumn'	Constraint	COLUMN constraint
'CnstIsDisabled'	Constraint	Disabled constraint
'CnstIsNonclustKey'	Constraint	Primary key with a nonclustered index
'CnstIsNotRepl'	Constraint	Constraint defined with the NOT FOR REPLICATION keywords
'ExecIsAnsiNullsOn'	Procedure, Trigger, View	Setting of ANSI_NULLS at creation time
'ExecIsDeleteTrigger'	Trigger	A delete trigger
'ExecIsInsertTrigger'	Trigger	An insert trigger
'ExecIsQuotedIdentOn'	Procedure, Trigger, View	Setting of QUOTED_IDENTIFIER at creation time
'ExecIsStartup'	Procedure	Startup procedure
'ExecIsTriggerDisabled'	Trigger	Disabled trigger
'ExecIsUpdateTrigger'	Trigger	Update trigger
'IsCheckCnst'	Any	CHECK constraint
'IsConstraint'	Any	Constraint

OPEN

Opens a Transact-SQL server cursor and fills the cursor by executing the Transact-SQL statement specified on the DECLARE CURSOR or SET *cursor_variable* statement.

Syntax

```
OPEN { { [GLOBAL] cursor_name } | cursor_variable_name}
```

Arguments

GLOBAL

Specifies that *cursor_name* refers to a global cursor.

cursor_name

The name of a declared cursor. If both a global and a local cursor exist with *cursor_name* as their name, then *cursor_name* refers to the global cursor if GLOBAL is specified. If GLOBAL is not specified, *cursor_name* refers to the local cursor.

cursor_variable_name

The name of a cursor variable referencing a cursor.

Remarks

If the cursor is declared with the INSENSITIVE or STATIC option, OPEN creates a temporary table to hold the result set. The size of the rows in the result set cannot exceed the maximum row size for Microsoft SQL Server tables; if so, OPEN fails. If the cursor is declared with the KEYSET option, OPEN creates a temporary table to hold the keyset.

OPENQUERY

Executes the specified pass-through query on the given *linked_server* which is an OLE DB data source. The OPENQUERY function can be referenced in the FROM clause of a query as though it is a table name. The OPENQUERY function can also be referenced as the target table of an INSERT, UPDATE, or DELETE statement, subject to the capabilities of the OLE DB provider.

Syntax

```
OPENQUERY(linked_server, 'query')
```

Arguments

linked_server

    An identifier representing the name of the linked server.

'query'

    The query string executed in the linked server.

OPENROWSET

Includes all connection information necessary to access remote data from an OLE DB data source. This method is an alternative to accessing tables in a linked server and is a one-time, ad hoc method of connecting and accessing remote data using OLE DB. The OPENROWSET function can be referenced in the FROM clause of a query as though it is a table name. The OPENROWSET function can also be referenced as the target table of an INSERT, UPDATE, or DELETE statement, subject to the capabilities of the OLE DB provider.

Syntax

```
OPENROWSET('provider_name'
{
'datasource';'user_id';'password'
| 'provider_string'
},
{
 [catalog.][schema.]object
| 'query'
})
```

Arguments

'provider_name'

A character string that represents the friendly name of the OLE DB provider as specified in the registry. *provider_name* has no default value.

'datasource'

A string literal that corresponds to a particular OLE DB data source. *datasource* is the DBPROP_INIT_DATASOURCE property to be passed to the provider's IDBProperties interface to initialize the provider. Typically, this string includes the name of the database file, the name of a database server, or a name that the provider understands to locate the database(s).

'user_id'

A string literal that is the user name that will be passed to the specified OLE DB provider. *user_id* specifies the security context for the connection and is passed in as the DBPROP_INIT_USERID property to initialize the provider.

'password'

A string literal that is the user password to be passed to the OLE DB provider. *password* is passed in as the DBPROP_INIT_PASSWORD property when initializing the provider.

'provider_string'

A provider-specific connection string that is passed in as the DBPROP_INIT_PROVIDERSTRING property to initialize the OLE DB provider. *provider_string* typically encapsulates all the connection information needed to initialize the provider.

catalog

The name of the catalog or database in which the specified object resides.

schema

The name of the schema or object owner for the specified object.

object

The object name that uniquely identifies the object to manipulate.

'query'

A string literal to be sent to and executed by the provider. Microsoft SQL Server does not process this query, but processes query results returned by the provider. This is called a *pass-through query*. Pass-through queries are useful when used on providers that do not expose their tabular data through table names, but only through a command language. *query* can also perform a pass-through query on the remote server, as long as the query provider supports the OLE DB Command object and its mandatory interfaces.

PARSENAME

Returns the specified part of an object name. Parts of an object that can be retrieved are the object name, owner name, database name, and server name.

Note The PARSENAME function does not indicate whether or not an object by the specified name exists. It just returns the specified piece of the given object name.

Syntax

PARSENAME('*object_name* ', *object_piece*)

Arguments

'*object_name*'

The name of the object for which to retrieve the specified object part. *object_name* is sysname. This parameter is an optionally qualified object name. If all parts of the object name are qualified, this name can consist of four parts: the server name, the database name, the owner name, and the object name.

object_piece

The object part to return. *object_piece* is **int**, and can have these values:

Value	Description
1	Object name
2	Owner name
3	Database name
4	Server name

Return Type: nchar

PATINDEX

Returns the starting position of the first occurrence of a pattern in a specified expression, or zeroes if the pattern is not found, on all valid text and character data types.

PERMISSIONS

Returns a value containing a bitmap that indicates the statement, object, or column permissions for the current user.

Syntax

PERMISSIONS([*objectid* [, '*column*']])

Arguments

objectid

The ID of an object. If *objectid* is not specified, the bitmap value contains statement permissions for the current user; otherwise, the bitmap contains object permissions on the object ID for the current user. The object specified must be in the current database. Use the OBJECT_ID function with an object name to determine the *objectid* value.

'column'

The optional name of a column for which permission information is being returned. The column must be a valid column name in the table specified by *objectid*.

Return Type: int

Remarks

PERMISSIONS can be used to determine whether the current user has the necessary permissions to execute a statement or to grant a permission on an object to another user.

The permissions information returned is a 32-bit bitmap.

The lower 16 bits reflect permissions granted to the security account for the current user, as well as permissions applied to Microsoft Windows NT groups or Microsoft SQL Server roles of which the current user is a member. For example, a returned value of 66 (hex value 0x42), when no *objectid* is specified, indicates the current user has permissions to execute the CREATE TABLE (decimal value 2) and BACKUP DATABASE (decimal value 64) statement permissions.

The upper 16 bits reflect the permissions that the current user can grant to other users. The upper 16 bits are interpreted exactly as those for the lower 16 bits described in the following tables, except they are shifted to the left by 16 bits (multiplied by 65,536). For example, 0x8 (decimal value 8) is the bit indicating INSERT permissions when an *objectid* is specified, whereas 0x80000 (decimal value 524,288) indicates the ability to grant INSERT permissions, because 524,288 = 8 x 65,536. Due to membership in roles, it is possible to not have a permission to execute a statement, but still be able to grant that permission to someone else.

The table below shows the bits used for statement permissions (*objectid* is not specified):

Bit (dec)	Bit (hex)	Statement Permission
1	0x1	CREATE DATABASE (master database only)
2	0x2	CREATE TABLE
4	0x4	CREATE PROCEDURE
8	0x8	CREATE VIEW
16	0x10	CREATE RULE
32	0x20	CREATE DEFAULT

Bit (dec)	Bit (hex)	Statement Permission
64	0x40	BACKUP DATABASE
128	0x80	BACKUP LOG
256	0x100	BACKUP TABLE

The following table shows the bits used for object permissions, returned when only *objectid* is specified.

Bit (dec)	Bit (hex)	Statement Permission
1	0x1	SELECT ALL
2	0x2	UPDATE ALL
4	0x4	REFERENCES ALL
8	0x8	INSERT
16	0x10	DELETE
32	0x20	EXECUTE (procedures only)
4096	0x1000	SELECT ANY (at least one column)
8192	0x2000	UPDATE ANY
16384	0x4000	REFERENCES ANY

The following table shows the bits used for column-level object permissions, returned when both *objectid* and *column* are specified.

Bit (dec)	Bit (hex)	Statement Permission
1	0x1	SELECT
2	0x2	UPDATE
4	0x4	REFERENCES

A NULL is returned if a specified parameter is NULL or invalid (for example, an *objectid* or *column* that does not exist). The bit values for permissions that do not apply (for example, EXECUTE permissions, bit 0x20, for a table) are undefined.

Use the bitwise AND (&) operator to determine each bit set in the bitmap returned by the PERMISSIONS function.

The sp_helprotect system stored procedure can also be used to return a list of object permissions for a user in the current database.

PI

Returns the constant value of pi.

Syntax

```
PI()
```

Return Type: float

POWER

Returns the value of the given expression to the specified power.

Syntax

```
POWER(numeric_expression, y)
```

Arguments

numeric_expression

An expression of the exact numeric or approximate numeric data type category, except for the **bit** data type.

y

The power to which to raise *numeric_expression*. *y* can be an expression of the exact numeric or approximate numeric data type category, except for the **bit** data type.

Return Type: Same as *numeric_expression*.

PRINT

Returns a user-defined message to the client's message handler.

Syntax

```
PRINT 'any ASCII text' | @local_variable | @@function | string_expr
```

Arguments

'any ASCII text'

A string of text.

@local_variable

A variable of any valid character data type. *@local_variable* must be **char** or **varchar**, or be able to be implicitly converted to those data types.

@@function

A function that returns string results. *@@function* must be **char** or **varchar**, or be able to be implicitly converted to those data types.

string_expr

An expression that returns a string. Can include concatenated literal values and variables.

QUOTENAME

Returns a Unicode string with the delimiters added to make the input string a valid Microsoft SQL Server delimited identifier.

Syntax

```
QUOTENAME('character_string'[, 'quote_character'])
```

Arguments

'*character_string*'

> A string of Unicode character data. *character_string* is sysname.

'*quote_character*'

> A one-character string to use as the delimiter. Can be a single quotation mark ('),
> a left or right bracket ([]), or a double quotation mark (").

Return Type: nvarchar(129)

RADIANS

Returns radians given a numeric expression in degrees. The result of the RADIANS
function is the same data type as the given *numeric_expression*.

Syntax

```
RADIANS(numeric_expression)
```

Arguments

numeric_expression

> An expression of the exact numeric or approximate numeric data type category,
> except for the **bit** data type.

Return Type: float

RAISERROR

Returns a user-defined error message and sets a system flag to record that an error
has occurred. Using RAISERROR, the client can either retrieve an entry from the sysmessages table or build a message dynamically with user-specified severity and state
information. After the message is defined it is sent back to the client as a server error
message.

Syntax

```
RAISERROR ({msg_id | msg_str}{, severity, state}
  [, argument
  [, ...n]] )
  [WITH option]
```

Arguments

msg_id

> A user-defined error message stored in the sysmessages table. Error numbers for
> user-defined error messages should be greater than 50,000. Ad hoc messages
> will raise an error of 50,000. The maximum value for *msg_id* is 2,147,483,647
> ($2^{31} - 1$).

msg_str

> An ad hoc message with formatting similar to the C PRINTF format style. The error message can have as many as 8,000 characters. All ad hoc messages have a standard message ID of 14,000.
>
> This format is supported for *msg_str*:
>
> % [[*flag*] [*width*] [*precision*] [{h | l}]] *type*
>
> The parameters that can be used in *msg_str* are:

flag

> A code that determines the spacing and justification of the user-defined error message, as described below:

flag Code	Prefix or Justification	Description
– (minus)	Left-justified	Left-justify the result within the given field width.
+ (plus)	+ (plus) or – (minus) prefix	Preface the output value with a sign (+ or –) if the output value is of signed type.
0 (zero)	Zero padding	If width is prefaced with 0, zeroes are added until the minimum width is reached. When 0 and – appear, 0 is ignored. When 0 is specified with an integer format (i, u, x, X, o, d), 0 is ignored.
# (number)	0x prefix for hexadecimal type of x or X	When used with the o, x, or X format, the # flag prefaces any nonzero value with 0, 0x, or 0X, respectively. When d, i, or u are prefaced by the # flag, the flag is ignored.
' ' (blank)	Space padding	Preface the output value with blank spaces if the value is signed and positive. This is ignored when included with the + flag.

width

> An integer defining the minimum width. An asterisk (*) allows the *precision* argument to determine the width.

precision

> The maximum number of characters printed for the output field or the minimum number of digits printed for integer values. An asterisk (*) allows the argument to determine the precision.

{h | l} *type*

> Used with types d, i, o, x, X, or u, and creates **short int** (h) or **long int** (l) values.

Character Type	Represents
d or i	Signed integer
o	Unsigned octal
p	Pointer
s	String

Character Type	Represents
u	Unsigned integer
x or X	Unsigned hexadecimal

Note The **float**, double-, and single-character types are not supported.

severity

The user-defined severity level associated with this message. Severity levels from 0 through 18 can be used by any user. Severity levels 19 through 25 are used only by members of the sysadmin fixed database role. For severity levels 19 through 25, the WITH LOG option is required.

Caution Severity levels 20 through 25 are considered fatal. If a fatal severity level is encountered, the client connection is terminated after receiving the message, and the error is logged in the error log and the event log.

state

An arbitrary integer from 1 through 127 that represents information about the invocation state of the error. A negative value for *state* defaults to 1.

argument

The parameters used in the substitution for variables defined in the *msg_str* or the message corresponding to the *msg_id*. There can be zero or more substitution parameters; however, the total number of substitution parameters cannot exceed 20. Each substitution parameter can be a local variable or any of these data types: **int1**, **int2**, **int4**, **char**, **varchar**, **binary**, or **varbinary**. No other data types are supported.

option

The custom options for the error. *option* can be one of these values:

option Value	Description
LOG	Logs the error in the server error log and the event log. This option is required for messages with a severity level of 19 through 25, and it can be issued only by members of the sysadmin fixed database role.
NOWAIT	Sends messages immediately to the client server.
SETERROR	Sets @@error value to *msg_id* or 50,000, regardless of the severity level.

Remarks

If a sysmessages error is used and the message was created using the format shown for *msg_str*, then supplied arguments (*argument1*, *argument2*, and so on) are passed to the message of the supplied *msg_id*.

When using RAISERROR to create and return user-defined error messages, use sp_addmessage to add user-defined error messages and sp_dropmessage to delete user-defined error messages.

When an error is raised, the error number is placed in the @@ERROR function, which stores the most recently generated error number. @@ERROR is set to 0 by default for messages with a severity of 1 through 10.

RAND

Returns a random **float** value between 0 and 1 given some *seed* value of **int**, **smallint**, or **tinyint** data type.

Syntax

```
RAND([seed])
```

Arguments

seed

> An integer expression (**tinyint**, **smallint**, or **int**) giving the seed or starting value.

Return Type: float

READTEXT

Reads **text**, **ntext**, or **image** values from a **text** or **image** column, starting from a specified offset and reading the specified number of bytes.

Syntax

```
READTEXT {table.column text_ptr offset size} [HOLDLOCK]
```

Arguments

table.column

> The name of a table and column from which to read. Table and column names must conform to the rules for identifiers. Specifying the table and column names is required; however, specifying the database name and owner name is optional.

text_ptr

> A valid text pointer. *text_ptr* must be **binary(16)**.

offset

> The number of bytes (when using the **text** or **image** data types) or characters (when using the **ntext** data type) to skip before starting to read the **text**, **image**, or **ntext** data. When using **ntext** data type, *offset* is the number of

characters to skip before starting to read the data. When using **text** or **image** data types, *offset* is the number of bytes to skip before starting to read the data.

size

The number of bytes (when using the **text** or **image** data types) or characters (when using the **ntext** data type) of data to read. If *size* is 0, 4 K bytes of data are read.

HOLDLOCK

Causes the text value to be locked for reads until the end of the transaction. Other users can read the value, but they cannot modify it.

RECONFIGURE

Updates the currently configured value (the config_value column in the sp_configure result set) of a configuration option changed with the sp_configure system stored procedure. Since some configuration options require a server stop and restart to update the currently running value, RECONFIGURE does not always update the currently running value (the run_value column in the sp_configure result set) for a changed configuration value.

Syntax

```
RECONFIGURE [WITH OVERRIDE]
```

Arguments

RECONFIGURE

Specifies that, if the configuration setting does not require a server stop and restart, the currently running value should be updated. RECONFIGURE also checks the new configuration value for either invalid values (for example, a sort order value that does not exist in syscharsets) or non-recommended values (for example, setting Allow Updates to 1). With those configuration options not requiring a server stop and restart, the currently running value and the currently configured values for the configuration option should be the same value after specifying RECONFIGURE.

WITH OVERRIDE

Disables the configuration value checking (for invalid values or for non-recommended values) for the Allow Updates, Recovery Interval, or Time Slice advanced configuration options. In addition, RECONFIGURE WITH OVERRIDE forces the reconfiguration with the specified value. For example, the Min Server Memory configuration option could be configured with a value greater than the value specified in the Max Server Memory configuration option. However, this is considered a fatal error. Therefore, specifying RECONFIGURE WITH OVERRIDE would not disable configuration value checking. Any configuration option can be reconfigured using the WITH OVERRIDE option.

REPLACE

Replaces all occurrences of the second given string expression in the first string expression with a third expression.

Syntax

REPLACE('*string_expression1*', '*string_expression2*', '*string_expression3*')

Arguments

'*string_expression1*'

The string expression to search for *string_expression2*. *string_expression1* can be of character or binary data type.

'*string_expression2*'

The string expression for which to search in *string_expression1* and to replace with *string_expression3*. *string_expression2* can be of character or binary data type.

'*string_expression3*'

The new string expression that replaces *string_expression2* in *string_expression1*. *string_expression3* can be of character or binary data type.

Return Type: Returns character data if the *string_expression* (1, 2, or 3) is one of the supported character data types. Returns binary data if *string_expression* (1, 2, or 3) is one of the supported binary data types.

REPLICATE

Repeats a character expression a specified number of times.

Syntax

REPLICATE(*character_expression, integer_expression*)

Arguments

character_expression

An alphanumeric expression of character data. *character_expression* can be a constant, variable, or column of either character or binary data.

integer_expression

A positive whole number. If *integer_expression* is negative, a null string is returned.

Return Type: varchar

character_expression must be of a data type that is implicitly convertible to **varchar**. Otherwise, use the CAST function to convert explicitly *character_expression*.

Remarks

Compatibility levels can affect return values.

RESTORE

Restores an entire database and log, database file(s), or a log. For more information about database back up and restore operations, see Chapter 18.

Caution Backups created with the evaluation version of Microsoft SQL Server found on the companion CD cannot be restored to an earlier version of SQL Server.

Syntax

Restore an entire database:

```
RESTORE DATABASE {database_name | @database_name_var}
 [FROM <backup_device> [, ...n]]
 [WITH
 [DBO_ONLY]
 [[,] FILE = file_number]
 [[,] MEDIANAME = {media_name | @media_name_variable}]
 [[,] MOVE 'logical_file_name' TO 'operating_system_file_name']
 [, ...p]
 [[,] {NORECOVERY | RECOVERY | STANDBY = undo_file_name}]
 [[,] {NOUNLOAD | UNLOAD}]
 [[,] REPLACE]
 [[,] RESTART]
 [[,] STATS [= percentage]]
]
```

Restore specific files or filegroups:

```
RESTORE DATABASE {database_name | @database_name_var}
<file_or_filegroup> [, ...m]
 [FROM <backup_device> [, ...n]]
 [WITH
 [DBO_ONLY]
 [[,] FILE = file_number]
 [[,] MEDIANAME = {media_name | @media_name_variable}]
 [[,] NORECOVERY]
 [[,] {NOUNLOAD | UNLOAD}]
 [[,] REPLACE]
 [[,] RESTART]
 [[,] STATS [= percentage]]
]
```

Restore a transaction log:

```
RESTORE LOG {database_name | @database_name_var}
 [FROM <backup_device> [, ...n]]
 [WITH
 [DBO_ONLY]
```

```
[[,] FILE = file_number]
[[,] MEDIANAME = {media_name | @media_name_variable}]
[[,] {NORECOVERY | RECOVERY | STANDBY = undo_file_name}]
[[,] {NOUNLOAD | UNLOAD}]
[[,] RESTART]
[[,] STATS [= percentage]]
[[,] STOPAT = {date_time | @date_time_var}]
]
<backup_device> ::=
{
{'backup_device_name' | @backup_device_name_var}
| {DISK | TAPE | PIPE} =
{'temp_backup_device' | @temp_backup_device_var}
}
<file_or_filegroup> ::=
{
FILE = {logical_file_name | @logical_file_name_var}
|
FILEGROUP = {logical_filegroup_name | @logical_filegroup_name_var}
}
```

Arguments

DATABASE

>Specifies the complete restore of the database from a backup. If a list of files and filegroups is specified, then only those files and filegroups are restored.

{*database_name* | *@database_name_var*}

>The database that the log or complete database will be restored into. If supplied as a variable (*@database_name_var*), this name can be specified either as a string constant (*@database_name_var* = *database name*) or as a variable of character string data type, except for the **ntext** or **text** data types.

FROM

>Specifies the backup devices from which to restore the backup. If the FROM clause is not specified, the restore of a backup does not take place. Instead, the database is recovered. Omitting the FROM clause can be used to attempt recovery of a non-suspect database that has been restored with the NORECOVERY option, or to switch over to a standby server. If the FROM clause is omitted, either NORECOVERY, RECOVERY, or STANDBY must be specified.

<backup_device>

>Specifies the permanent or temporary backup devices to use for the restore operation. Can be one or more of the following:

{'*backup_device_name*' | *@backup_device_name_var*}

>The logical name, which must follow the rules for identifiers, of the backup device(s) created by sp_addumpdevice from which the database is restored. The maximum number of backup devices in a single RESTORE statement is 32. If supplied as a variable (*@backup_device_name_var*), the backup device name can

be specified either as a string constant (*@backup_device_name_var =
backup_device_name*) or as a variable of character string data type, except for the
ntext or **text** data types.

{DISK | TAPE | PIPE} = '*temp_backup_device*' | *@temp_backup_device_var*

Allows backups to be restored from the named disk, tape, or pipe device. The
device types of disk and tape should be specified with the actual name (for
example, complete path and file name) of the device. For example, DISK =
'c:\mssql7\backup\mybackup.dat' or TAPE = \\.\TAPE0. A device type of pipe
should specify the name of the named pipe that will be used by the client
application. If specified as a variable (*@temp_backup_device_var*), the device
name can be specified either as a string constant (*@temp_backup_device_var =
'temp_backup_device*') or as a variable of character string data type, except for
the **ntext** or **text** data types. Pipe devices have been added to allow third-party
vendors a flexible and powerful way to connect their own software. For typical
Transact-SQL use, the pipe device is not used.

If you are using either a network server with a UNC name or a redirected drive
letter, specify a device type of DISK.

n

A placeholder indicating that multiple backup devices and temporary backup
devices may be specified. The maximum number of backup devices or temporary
backup devices is 32.

DBO_ONLY

Restricts access for the newly restored database to only the DBO. Causes the
DBO Use Only option of sp_dboption to be set to TRUE. This database option
restricts access to the database owner after the restore operation until the option
is set to FALSE by executing sp_dboption. If this option is not specified, then the
setting of the DBO Use Only database option may or may not change. Use with
the RECOVERY option.

FILE = *file_number*

Identifies the backup set to be restored. For example, a *file_number* of 1 indicates
the first backup set on the backup medium and a *file_number* of 2 indicates the
second backup set.

MEDIANAME = {*media_name* | *@media_name_variable*}

Specifies the media name for the entire backup set. If provided, the media name
must match the media name on the backup volume(s); otherwise, the restore
operation terminates. If no media name is given in the RESTORE statement, then
the check for a matching media name on the backup volume(s) is not
performed.

Tip Consistently using media names in BACKUP and RESTORE operations provides an extra safety check for the media selected for the restore operation.

MOVE '*logical_file_name*' TO '*operating_system_file_name*'

Specifies that the given *logical_file_name* should be moved to *operating_system_file_name*. By default, the *logical_file_name* is restored to its original location. If either the BACKUP or RESTORE statements is used to copy a database to the same or different server, the MOVE option may be needed to relocate the database files and to avoid collisions with existing files. Each logical file in the database can be specified in different MOVE statements.

p

A placeholder indicating that more than one logical file can be moved by specifying multiple MOVE statements.

NORECOVERY

Instructs the restore operation to not rollback any uncommitted transactions. Either the NORECOVERY or STANDBY option <u>must</u> be specified if another transaction log needs to be applied. If neither NORECOVERY, RECOVERY, nor STANDBY is specified, RECOVERY is the default.

SQL Server requires that the WITH NORECOVERY option be used on all but the final RESTORE statement when restoring a database backup and multiple transaction logs or when multiple RESTORE stateme1ts are needed (for example, a full database backup followed by a differential database backup).

Note When specifying the NORECOVERY option, the database is not usable in this intermediate, nonrecovered state.

When used with a file or filegroup restore operation, this forces the database to remain in load state after the restore operation. This is useful when either:

➤ A restore script is being run and the log is always wanted to be applied.

Or

➤ A sequence of file restores is used and the database is not wanted to be usable between two of the restore operations.

RECOVERY

Instructs the restore operation to rollback any uncommitted transactions. After the recovery process, the database is ready for use. However, RECOVERY should not be specified when another transaction log must be applied to the database. If neither NORECOVERY, RECOVERY, nor STANDBY is specified, RECOVERY is the default. The database version is updated for databases and transaction logs if RECOVERY is specified.

STANDBY = *undo_file_name*

Specifies the undo filename so the recovery effects may be undone. This file is of unlimited size. If neither NORECOVERY, RECOVERY, nor STANDBY is specified, RECOVERY is the default.

STANDBY allows a database to be brought up for read-only access between transaction log restores and can be used with either warm backup server situations or special recovery situations where it is useful to check the database between log restores.

If the specified *undo_file_name* does not exist, SQL Server creates it. If the file does exist, SQL Server overwrites it unless the file contains current undo information for a database.

The same undo file may be used for consecutive restores of the same database.

Tip If free disk space is exhausted on the drive containing the specified *undo_file_name*, the restore operation aborts.

NOUNLOAD

Specifies that the tape will not be unloaded automatically from the tape drive after a restore. NOUNLOAD remains set until UNLOAD is specified. This option is used only for tape devices. If a nontape device is being used for the restore, this option is ignored.

UNLOAD

Specifies that the tape is automatically rewound and unloaded when the restore is finished. UNLOAD is set by default when a new user session is started. It remains set until that user specifies NOUNLOAD. This option is used only for tape devices. If a nontape device is being used for the restore, this option is ignored.

REPLACE

Specifies that SQL Server should create the specified database and its related files regardless if another database already exists with the same name. In such a case, the existing database is first destroyed. When the REPLACE option is not specified, a safety check occurs (which prevents overwriting a different database by accident). The safety check ensures that the RESTORE DATABASE statement will not restore the database to the current server if:

The database named in the RESTORE statement already exists on the current server, and

➤ Either the database name is different from the database name recorded in the backup set.

Or

➤ The set of files in the database is different from the set of database files contained in the backup set. Differences in file size are ignored.

When used with a file or filegroup restore operation, allows overwriting of an existing file, which is useful only when attempting to restore a file on a disk that is replacing a failed disk.

RESTART

Specifies that SQL Server should restart the restore operation that was interrupted. The RESTART option saves time since it will restart the restore operation at the point it was interrupted. To restart a specific restore operation that was interrupted, repeat the entire RESTORE statement and add the RESTART option. Using the RESTART option is not required but can save time.

Tip This option can only be used for restores directed from tape media and for restores that span multiple tape volumes.

STATS [= *percentage*]

Displays a message every time another percentage completes and is used to gauge progress. If *percentage* is omitted, SQL Server displays a message after every 10% is completed.

<file_or_filegroup>

Specifies the names of the logical files or filegroups to include in the database restore. Multiple files or filegroups may be specified.

FILE = {*logical_file_name* | *@logical_file_name_var*}

Names one or more files to include in the database restore.

FILEGROUP = {*logical_filegroup_name* | *@logical_filegroup_name_var*}

Names one or more filegroups to include in the database restore.

When using this option, you must apply the log to the database files immediately after the last file or filegroup restore operation to roll the files forward to be consistent with the rest of the database. If all files being restored have not been modified since they were last backed up, then no log needs to be applied. The RESTORE statement informs the user of this situation.

The RESTORE statement requires that one or more filegroups be restored in a single operation if indexes were created on these filegroups since the last time these files were backed up. This requirement of restoring the entire set of filegroup(s) is necessary whether the restore is from a filegroup backup or a full database backup. The RESTORE statement detects this filegroup situation and communicates to the restore user the minimum filegroups that must be restored.

m

A placeholder indicating that multiple files and filegroups may be specified. There is no maximum number of files or filegroups.

LOG

Specifies that a transaction log backup is to be applied to this database. Logs must be applied in sequential order. SQL Server checks the backed-up log to make sure that the transactions are being loaded into the correct database and in the correct sequence. In order to apply multiple transaction logs, use the NORECOVERY option on all restore operations except the last.

STOPAT = *date_time* | *@date_time_var*

Specifies that the database be restored to the state it was in as of the specified date and time. If a variable is used for STOPAT, the variable must be either **varchar**, **char**, **smalldatetime**, or **datetime** data type. Only log records written before the specified date and time are applied to the database.

RESTORE FILELISTONLY

Returns a result set with a list of the database and log files contained in the backup set.

Syntax

```
RESTORE FILELISTONLY
FROM <backup_device>
 [WITH
 [FILE = file_number]
 [[, ] {NOUNLOAD | UNLOAD}]
]
<backup_device> :: =
{
{'backup_device_name' | @backup_device_namevar}
| {DISK | TAPE | PIPE} =
{'temp_backup_device' | @temp_backup_device_var}
}
```

Arguments

<backup_device>

Specifies the permanent or temporary backup device(s) to use for the restore. Can be one or more of the following:

{'*backup_device_name*' | *@backup_device_namevar*}

The logical name, which must follow the rules for identifiers, of the backup device created by sp_addumpdevice from which the database is restored. If supplied as a variable (*@backup_device_name_var*), the backup device name can be specified either as a string constant (*@backup_device_name_var* = '*backup_device_name*') or as a variable of character string data type, except for the **ntext** or **text** data types.

{DISK | TAPE | PIPE} = '*temp_backup_device*' | *@temp_backup_device_var*

Allows backups to be restored from the named disk, tape, or pipe device. The device types of disk and tape should be specified with the actual name (for example, complete path and file name) of the device. For example, DISK = 'c:\mssql7\backup\mybackup.dat' or TAPE = \\.\TAPE0. A device type of pipe should specify the name of the named pipe that is used by the client application. If specified as a variable (*@temp_backup_device_var*), the device name can be specified either as a string constant (*@temp_backup_device_var* = '*temp_backup_device*') or as a variable of character string data type, except for the **ntext** or **text** data types.

Pipe devices have been added to allow third-party vendors a flexible and powerful way to connect their own software. For typical Transact-SQL use, the pipe device is not used.

If you are using either a network server with a UNC name or a redirected drive letter, specify a device type of DISK.

FILE = *file_number*

Identifies the backup set to be processed. For example, a *file_number* of 1 indicates the first backup set and a *file_number* of 2 indicates the second backup set. If no *file_number* is supplied, the first backup set on the specified <backup_device> is assumed.

NOUNLOAD

Specifies that the tape will not be unloaded automatically from the tape drive after a backup. NOUNLOAD remains set until UNLOAD is specified. This option is used only for tape devices.

UNLOAD

Specifies that the tape is automatically rewound and unloaded when the backup is finished. UNLOAD is set by default when a new user session is started. It remains set until that user specifies NOUNLOAD. This option is used only for tape devices.

Permissions

RESTORE permissions default to the server DBLOAD operator and are not transferable.

RESTORE HEADERONLY

Retrieves all the backup header information for all backup sets on a particular backup device. The result from executing RESTORE HEADERONLY is a result set.

Syntax

```
RESTORE HEADERONLY
FROM <backup_device>
 [WITH {NOUNLOAD | UNLOAD}]
<backup_device> :: =
```

```
{
{'backup_device_name' | @backup_device_name_var}
| {DISK | TAPE | PIPE} =
{'temp_backup_device' | @temp_backup_device_var}
}
```

Arguments

\<backup_device\>

Specifies the permanent or temporary backup device(s) to use for the restore. Can be one of the following:

{*'backup_device_name'* | *@backup_device_name_var*}

The logical name, which must follow the rules for identifiers, of the backup device created by sp_addumpdevice from which the database will be restored. If supplied as a variable (*@backup_device_name_var*), the backup device name can be specified either as a string constant (*@backup_device_name_var* = *'backup_device_name'*) or as a variable of character string data type, except for the **ntext** or **text** data types.

{DISK | TAPE | PIPE} = *'temp_backup_device'* | *@backup_device_var*

Allows backups to be restored from the named disk, tape, or pipe device. The device types of disk and tape should be specified with the actual name (for example, complete path and file name) of the device. For example, DISK = 'c:\mssql7\backup\mybackup.dat' or TAPE = \\.\TAPE0. A device type of pipe should specify the name of the named pipe that is used by the client application. If specified as a variable (*@temp_backup_device_var*), the device name can be specified either as a string constant (*@temp_backup_device_var* = *'temp_backup_device'*) or as a variable of character string data type, except for the **ntext** or **text** data types.

Pipe devices have been added to allow third-party vendors a flexible and powerful way to connect their own software. For typical Transact-SQL use, the pipe device is not used.

If you are using either a network server with a UNC name or a redirected drive letter, specify a device type of DISK.

NOUNLOAD

Specifies that the tape is not unloaded automatically from the tape drive after a backup. NOUNLOAD remains set until UNLOAD is specified. This option is used only for tape devices.

UNLOAD

Specifies that the tape is automatically rewound and unloaded when the backup is finished. UNLOAD is set by default when a new user session is started. It remains set until that user specifies NOUNLOAD. This option is used only for tape devices.

RESTORE LABELONLY

Returns a result set containing information about the backup media identified by the given <backup_device>.

Syntax

```
RESTORE LABELONLY
FROM <backup_device>
<backup_device> ::=
{
{'backup_device_name' | @backup_device_name_var}
| {DISK | TAPE | PIPE} =
{'temp_backup_device' | @temp_backup_device_var}
}
```

Arguments

<backup_device>

Specifies the permanent or temporary backup device to use for the restore. Can be one of the following:

{'*backup_device__name*' | *@backup_device_name_var*}

The logical name, which must follow the rules for identifiers, of the backup device created by sp_addumpdevice from which the database is restored.

{DISK | TAPE | PIPE} = '*temp_backup_device*' | *@temp_backup_device_var*

Allows backups to be restored from the named disk, tape, or pipe device. The device types of disk and tape should be specified with the actual name (for example, complete path and file name) of the device. For example, DISK = 'c:\mssql7\backup\mybackup.dat' or TAPE = \\.\TAPE0. A device type of pipe should specify the name of the named pipe that is used by the client application. If specified as a variable (*@temp_backup_device_var*), the device name can be specified either as a string constant (*@temp_backup_device_var* = '*temp_backup_device*') or as a variable of character string data type, except for the **ntext** or **text** data types.

Pipe devices have been added to allow third-party vendors a flexible and powerful way to connect their own software. For Transact-SQL use, the pipe device is not used.

If you are using either a network server with a UNC name or a redirected drive letter, specify a device type of DISK.

Permissions

RESTORE permissions default to the server DBLOAD operator and are not transferable.

RESTORE VERIFYONLY

Verifies the backup but does not restore the backup. Checks to see that the backup set is complete and that all volumes are readable. However, RESTORE VERIFYONLY does not attempt to verify the structure of the data contained in the backup volumes. If the backup is valid, Microsoft SQL Server returns a message, "The backup set is valid."

Syntax

```
RESTORE VERIFYONLY
FROM <backup_device> [, ...n]
 [WITH
 [FILE = file_number]
 [[,] {UNLOAD | NOUNLOAD}]
 [[,] LOADHISTORY]
]
<backup_device> ::=
{
{'backup_device_name' | @backup_device_name_var}
| {DISK | TAPE | PIPE} =
{'temp_backup_device' | @temp_backup_device_var}
}
```

Arguments

<backup_device>

Specifies the permanent or temporary backup device(s) to use for the restore. Can be one or more of the following:

{'*backup_device_name*' | @*backup_device_name_var*}

The logical name, which must follow the rules for identifiers, of the backup device(s) created by sp_addumpdevice from which the database is restored. The maximum number of backup devices in a single RESTORE statement is 32. If supplied as a variable (@*backup_device_name_var*), the backup device name can be specified either as a string constant (@*backup_device_name_var* = '*backup_device_name*') or as a variable of character string data type, except for the **ntext** or **text** data types.

{DISK | TAPE | PIPE} = '*temp_backup_device*' | @*temp_backup_device_var*

Allows backups to be restored from the named disk, tape, or pipe device. The device types of disk and tape should be specified with the actual name (for example, complete path and file name) of the device. For example, DISK = 'c:\mssql7\backup\mybackup.dat' or TAPE = \\.\TAPE0. A device type of pipe should specify the name of the named pipe that is used by the client application. If specified as a variable (@*temp_backup_device_var*), the device name can be specified either as a string constant (@*temp_backup_device_var* = '*temp_backup_device*') or as a variable of character string data type, except for the **ntext** or **text** data types.

Pipe devices have been added to allow third-party vendors a flexible and powerful way to connect their own software. For Transact-SQL use, the pipe device is not used.

If you are using either a network server with a UNC name or a redirected drive letter, specify a device type of DISK.

n

A placeholder indicating that multiple backup devices and temporary backup devices may be specified. The maximum number of backup devices or temporary backup devices in a single RESTORE VERIFYONLY statement is 32.

Note In order to specify multiple backup devices for <backup_device>, all backup devices specified must be part of the same media set.

FILE = *file_number*

Identifies the backup set to be restored or processed. For example, a *file_number* of 1 indicates the first backup set and a *file_number* of 2 indicates the second backup set. If no *file_number* is supplied, the first backup set on the specified <backup_device> is assumed.

UNLOAD

Specifies that the tape is automatically rewound and unloaded when the restore is finished. UNLOAD is set by default when a new user session is started. It remains set until that user specifies NOUNLOAD. This option is used only for tape devices. If a nontape device is being used for the restore, this option is ignored.

NOUNLOAD

Specifies that the tape is not unloaded automatically from the tape drive after a restore. NOUNLOAD remains set until UNLOAD is specified. This option is used only for tape devices. If a nontape device is being used for the restore, this option is ignored.

LOADHISTORY

Specifies that the RESTORE operation load the information into the msdb history tables. The LOADHISTORY option loads information, for the single backup set being verified, about SQL Server backups stored on the media set to the backup and restore history tables in the msdb database. No information for non-SQL Server backups is loaded into these history tables.

RETURN

Exits unconditionally from a query or procedure. RETURN is immediate and complete and can be used at any point to exit from a procedure, batch, or statement block. Statements following RETURN are not executed.

Syntax

```
RETURN [(integer_expression)]
```

Arguments

integer_expression

> The integer value returned. Stored procedures can return an integer value to a calling procedure or an application.

Return Type: Optionally returns **int**.

SQL Server reserves 0 to indicate a successful return and negative values from –1 through –99 to indicate different reasons for failure. If more than one error occurs during execution, the status with the highest absolute value is returned.

User-defined return values always take precedence over those supplied by SQL Server. User-defined return status values should not conflict with those reserved by SQL Server. If no user-defined return value is provided, the SQL Server value is used. The values 0 through –14 are currently used.

Reserved Return Status Value	Description
0	Procedure was executed successfully.
-1	Object is missing.
-2	Data type error occurred.
-3	Process was chosen as deadlock victim.
-4	Permission error occurred.
-5	Syntax error occurred.
-6	Miscellaneous user error occurred.
-7	Resource error, such as out of space, occurred.
-8	Nonfatal internal problem was encountered.
-9	System limit was reached.
-10	Fatal internal inconsistency occurred.
-11	Fatal internal inconsistency occurred.
-12	Table or index is corrupt.
-13	Database is corrupt.
-14	Hardware error occurred.

REVERSE

Returns the reverse of a character expression.

Syntax

REVERSE(*character_expression*)

Arguments

character_expression

> An expression of character data. *character_expression* can be a constant, variable, or column of either character or binary data.

Return Type: varchar

REVOKE

Removes a previously granted or denied permission from a user in the current database.

Syntax

Statement permissions:

```
REVOKE {ALL | statement[, ...n]}
FROM security_account[, ...n]
```

Object permissions:

```
REVOKE [GRANT OPTION FOR]
{ALL [PRIVILEGES] | permission[, ...n]}
{
{[(column[, ...n])] ON {table | view}
| {stored_procedure | extended_procedure}
}
FROM security_account[, ...n] [CASCADE]
 [AS {group | role}]
```

Arguments

ALL

> Specifies that all applicable permissions are being removed. For statement permissions, ALL can be used only by members of the sysadmin role. For object permissions, ALL can be used by members of the sysadmin and db_owner roles, and database object owners.

statement

> A granted statement for which permission is being removed. The statement list can include: CREATE DATABASE, CREATE DEFAULT, CREATE PROCEDURE, CREATE RULE, CREATE TABLE, CREATE VIEW, BACKUP DATABASE, BACKUP LOG.

n

> A placeholder indicating the item can be repeated in a comma-separated list.

FROM

> Specifies that a security account or list of security accounts is being specified.

security_account

> The security account in the current database from which the permissions are being removed. The security account can be a:

> ➤ Microsoft SQL Server user.
> ➤ SQL Server role.
> ➤ Microsoft Windows NT user.
> ➤ Windows NT group.

Permissions cannot be revoked from the system roles, such as sysadmin. When permissions are revoked from a SQL Server or Windows NT user account, the specified *security_account* is the only account affected by the permissions. If permissions are revoked from a SQL Server role or a Windows NT group, the permissions affect all users in the current database who are members of the group or role, unless the user has already been explicitly granted or denied a permission.

There are two special security accounts that can be used with REVOKE. Permissions revoked from the **public** role are applied to all users in the database. Permissions revoked from the **guest** user are used by all users who do not have a user account in the database.

When revoking permissions to a Windows NT local or global group, specify the domain or computer name the group is defined on, followed by a backslash, then the group name, for example, London\JoeB. However, to revoke permissions to a Windows NT built-in local group, specify BUILTIN instead of the domain or computer name, for example, BUILTIN\Users.

GRANT OPTION FOR

Specifies that WITH GRANT OPTION permissions are being removed. Use the GRANT OPTION FOR keywords with REVOKE to remove the effects of the WITH GRANT OPTION setting specified in the GRANT statement. The user still has the permissions but cannot grant the permissions to other users.

PRIVILEGES

An optional keyword that can be included for SQL-92 compliance.

permission

An object permission that is being revoked. When permissions are revoked on a table or a view, the permission list can include one or more of these statements: SELECT, INSERT, DELETE, or UPDATE.

Object permissions revoked on a table can also include REFERENCES, and object permissions revoked on a stored procedure or extended stored procedure can be EXECUTE. When permissions are revoked on columns, the permissions list can include SELECT and/or UPDATE.

column

The name of the column in the current database for which permissions are being removed.

table

The name of the table in the current database for which permissions are being removed.

view

The name of the view in the current database for which permissions are being removed.

stored_procedure

> The name of the stored procedure in the current database for which permissions are being removed.

extended_procedure

> The name of an extended stored procedure for which permissions are being removed.

CASCADE

> Specifies that permissions are being removed from *security_account* as well as any other security accounts that were granted permissions by *security_account*. Use when revoking a grantable permission. By using CASCADE, not only are the specified user's permissions revoked, but also permissions are revoked for all those to whom the specified user granted permissions. If CASCADE is not specified and the specified user is granted WITH GRANT OPTION permission, an error is returned.

AS {*group* | *role*}

> Specifies the optional name of the security account in the current database that has the permissions necessary to execute REVOKE. AS is required when the user executing REVOKE belongs to multiple groups or roles, which may apply conflicting permissions. AS must be used to indicate the group with the permissions necessary to allow REVOKE to be used.

Remarks

Only use REVOKE with permissions in the current database.

A revoked permission removes the granted or denied permission only at the level revoked (user, group, or role). For example, permission to view the Authors table is explicitly granted to the Andrew user account, which is a member of the employees role only. If the employees role is revoked access to view the Authors table, Andrew can still view the table because permission has been explicitly granted. Andrew is unable to view the Authors table only if Andrew is revoked permission as well. If Andrew is never explicitly granted permissions to view Authors, then revoking permission from the employees role prevents Andrew from viewing the table.

RIGHT

Returns the part of a character string starting *integer_expression* characters from the right.

Syntax

```
RIGHT(character_expression, integer_expression)
```

Arguments

character_expression

> An expression of character data. *character_expression* can be a constant, variable, or column of either character or binary data.

integer_expression

> A positive whole number. If *integer_expression* is negative, a null string is returned.

Return Type: varchar

ROLLBACK TRANSACTION

> Rolls back an explicit or implicit transaction to the beginning of the transaction, or to a savepoint inside a transaction.

Syntax

```
ROLLBACK [TRAN[SACTION] [transaction_name |
@tran_name_variable |
savepoint_name |
@savepoint_variable] ]
```

Arguments

transaction_name

> The name assigned to the transaction in BEGIN TRANSACTION. The *transaction_name* must conform to the rules for identifiers. When nesting transactions, *transaction_name* must be the name from the outermost BEGIN TRANSACTION statement.

@tran_name_variable

> The name of a user-defined variable containing a valid transaction name. The variable must be declared with a **char**, **varchar**, **nchar**, or **nvarchar** data type.

savepoint_name

> The *savepoint_name* from a SAVE TRANSACTION statement. The *savepoint_name* must conform to the rules for identifiers. Use *savepoint_name* when a conditional rollback should affect only part of the transaction.

@savepoint_variable

> The name of a user-defined variable containing a valid savepoint name. The variable must be declared with a **char**, **varchar**, **nchar**, or **nvarchar** data type.

Remarks

ROLLBACK TRANSACTION erases all data modifications made since the start of the transaction or to a savepoint. It also frees resources held by the transaction.

ROLLBACK TRANSACTION without a *savepoint_name* or *transaction_name* rolls back to the beginning of the transaction. When nesting transactions, this same statement rolls back all inner transactions to the outermost BEGIN TRANSACTION statement. In both cases, ROLLBACK TRANSACTION decrements the global variable @@TRANCOUNT to 0. ROLLBACK TRANSACTION *savepoint_name* does not decrement @@TRANCOUNT.

A ROLLBACK TRANSACTION statement specifying a *savepoint_name* does not free any locks.

A transaction cannot be rolled back after a COMMIT TRANSACTION statement is executed.

Within a transaction, duplicate *savepoint_names* are allowed, but a ROLLBACK TRANSACTION using the duplicate *savepoint_name* rolls back only to the most recent SAVE TRANSACTION using that *savepoint_name*.

In stored procedures, ROLLBACK TRANSACTION statements without a *save-point_name* or *transaction_name* roll back all statements to the outermost BEGIN TRANSACTION. A ROLLBACK TRANSACTION statement in a stored procedure that causes @@TRANCOUNT to have a different value when the trigger completes than the @@TRANCOUNT value when the stored procedure was called produces an informational message. This message does not affect subsequent processing.

If a ROLLBACK TRANSACTION is issued in a trigger:

➤ All data modifications made to that point in the current transaction are rolled back, including any that were made by the trigger.

➤ The trigger continues executing any remaining statements after the ROLLBACK statement. If any of these statements modify data, the modifications are not rolled back. No nested triggers are fired by the execution of these remaining statements.

➤ None of the statements in the batch after the statement that fired the trigger are executed.

@@TRANCOUNT is incremented by one when entering a trigger, even when in auto-commit mode. (The system treats a trigger as an implied nested transaction.)

ROLLBACK TRANSACTION statements in stored procedures do not affect subsequent statements in the batch that called the procedure; subsequent statements in the batch are executed. ROLLBACK TRANSACTION statements in triggers terminate the batch containing the statement that fired the trigger; subsequent statements in the batch are not executed.

ROLLBACK WORK

Rolls back a user-specified transaction to the beginning of a transaction.

Syntax

```
ROLLBACK [WORK]
```

Remarks

This statement functions identically to ROLLBACK TRANSACTION except that ROLLBACK TRANSACTION accepts a user-defined transaction name. With or without specifying the optional WORK keyword, this ROLLBACK syntax is SQL-92-compatible.

When nesting transactions, ROLLBACK WORK always rolls back to the outermost BEGIN TRANSACTION statement and decrements the global variable @@trancount to 0.

ROUND

Returns a numeric expression, rounded to the specified length or precision.

Syntax

```
ROUND(numeric_expression, length[, function])
```

Arguments

numeric_expression

An expression of the exact numeric or approximate numeric data type category, except for the **bit** data type.

length

The precision to which *numeric_expression* is to be rounded. Must be **tinyint**, **smallint**, or **int**.

> ➤ When *length* is a positive number, *numeric_expression* is rounded to the number of decimal places specified by *length*.

> ➤ When *length* is a negative number, *numeric_expression* is rounded on the left side of the decimal point, as specified by *length*.

function

The type of operation to perform. Must be **tinyint**, **smallint**, or **int**. When *function* is omitted or has a value of 0 (default), *numeric_expression* is rounded. When a value other than 0 is specified, *numeric_expression* is truncated.

Return Type: Same as *numeric_expression*

RTRIM

Returns a character string after removing all trailing blanks.

Syntax

```
RTRIM(character_expression)
```

Arguments

character_expression

An expression of character data. *character_expression* can be a constant, variable, or column of either character or binary data.

Return Type: varchar

Remarks

character_expression must be of a data type that is implicitly convertible to **varchar**. Otherwise, use the CAST function to explicitly convert *character_expression*.

Note Compatibility levels can affect return values.

SAVE TRANSACTION

Sets a savepoint within a transaction.

Syntax

SAVE TRAN[SACTION] {*savepoint_name* | @*savepoint_variable*}

Arguments

savepoint_name

The name assigned to the savepoint. Savepoint names must conform to the rules for identifiers.

@savepoint_variable

The name of a user-defined variable containing a valid savepoint name. The variable must be declared with a **char**, **varchar**, **nchar**, or **nvarchar** data type.

Remarks

A user can set a savepoint, or marker, within a transaction. It defines a location to which a transaction can return if part of the transaction might be conditionally canceled. If a transaction is rolled back to a savepoint, it must proceed to completion (with more Transact-SQL statements if needed and a COMMIT TRANSACTION statement), or it must be canceled altogether (by rolling it back to its beginning). To cancel an entire transaction, use the form ROLLBACK TRANSACTION *transaction_name*. All the statements or procedures of the transaction are undone.

SELECT

Retrieves rows from the database. Allows selection of one or many rows or columns from one or many tables. The SELECT statement has several optional clauses including GROUP BY, FROM, and WHERE.

The FROM clause:

➤ Specifies the table where the columns are located.

➤ Is required except when the <select_list> contains only constants, variables, and arithmetic expressions (no column names).

The WHERE clause specifies which rows in the table to retrieve.

The UNION operator can be used (between SELECT statements) to combine the results of two or more queries into a single result set consisting of all the rows belonging to all queries in the union. For information about the UNION operator, see UNION.

Syntax

```
SELECT [ ALL | DISTINCT ]
  [ TOP n [PERCENT] [ WITH TIES] ] <select_list>
  [ INTO new_table_name ]
  [ FROM <table_sources> ]
  [ WHERE <search_conditions> ]
  [ [ GROUP BY [ALL] group_by_expression [, ...n]]
  [HAVING <search_conditions> ]
  [ WITH { CUBE | ROLLUP } ]
]
  [ ORDER BY { column_name [ ASC | DESC ] } [, ...n] ]
  [ COMPUTE
{ { AVG | COUNT | MAX | MIN | SUM } (expression) } [, ...n]
  [ BY expression [, ...n]
]
  [ FOR BROWSE ]
  [ OPTION (<query_hints>) ]
<select_list> ::=
{ [ { <table_or_view> | table_alias }.]*
| { column_name | expression | IDENTITYCOL | ROWGUIDCOL }
  [ [AS] column_alias ]
| new_column_name = IDENTITY(data_type, seed, increment)
| GROUPING (column_name)
| { table_name | table_alias}.RANK
| column_alias = expression
| expression column_name
} [, ...n]
<table_sources> ::=
{ <table_or_view>
| (select_statement) [AS] table_alias [ (column_alias [, ...m]) ]
| <table_or_view> CROSS JOIN <table_or_view>
| <table_or_view>
{ { INNER
| { FULL | LEFT | RIGHT }
  [ OUTER ] [ <join_hints> ] [ JOIN ]
} <table_or_view> ON <join_condition>
}
| <rowset_function>
}
  [, ...n]
<table_or_view> ::=
{ table_name [ [AS] table_alias ] [ WITH (<table_hints> [, ...m]) ]
| view_name [ [AS] table_alias ]
}
<table_hints> ::=
{ INDEX(index_name | index_id)
| FASTFIRSTROW
| HOLDLOCK
```

```
      | NOLOCK
      | PAGLOCK
      | READCOMMITTED
      | READPAST
      | READUNCOMMITTED
      | REPEATABLEREAD
      | ROWLOCK
      | SERIALIZABLE
      | TABLOCK
      | TABLOCKX
      | UPDLOCK
      }
      <join_hints> ::=
      { HASH | LOOP | MERGE }
      <query_hints> ::=
      { { HASH | ORDER } GROUP
      | { CONCAT | HASH | MERGE } UNION
      | FAST number_rows
      | FORCE ORDER
      | MAXDOP number
      | ROBUST PLAN
      }
      <join_condition> ::=
      { table_name | table_alias | view_name }.column_name
      <logical_operator>
      { table_name | table_alias | view_name }.column_name
      <logical_operator>::=
      { = | > | < | >= | <= | <> | != | !< | !> }
      <rowset_function> ::=
      { CONTAINSTABLE [ [ AS] table_alias]
       ( table, { column | *}, '<contains_search_condition>'
      )
      | FREETEXTTABLE [ [ AS] table_alias]
       ( table, {column | * }, 'freetext_string'
      )
      | OPENQUERY (linked_server, 'query')
      | OPENROWSET
       ( 'provider_name',
      {
      'datasource';'user_id';'password'
      | 'provider_string'
      },
      {
       [catalog.][schema.]object_name
      | 'query'
      }
      )
      <search_conditions> ::=
      { [ NOT ] <predicate> [ { AND | OR } [ NOT ] <predicate> ]
```

```
| CONTAINS
 ( {column | * }, '<contains_search_condition>'
)
| FREETEXT
 (
{column | * }, 'freetext_string'
)
| fulltext_table.fulltext_key_column = fulltext_table.[KEY]
} [, ...n]
<predicate> ::=
{
expression { = | <> | != | > | >= | !> | < | <= | !< } expression
| string_expression [NOT] LIKE string_expression
 [ESCAPE 'escape_character']
| expression [NOT] BETWEEN expression AND expression
| expression IS [NOT] NULL
| expression [NOT] IN (subquery | expression [, ...n])
| expression { = | <> | != | > | >= | !> | < | <= | !< }
{ALL | SOME | ANY} (subquery)
| EXISTS (subquery)     .
}
```

Arguments

ALL

> Specifies that duplicate rows can appear in the result set. Duplicate rows appear only if the ALL keyword is specified immediately following the SELECT keyword.

DISTINCT

> Specifies that only unique rows can appear in the result set. Null values are considered equal for the purposes of the DISTINCT keyword.

> **Tip** Distinct aggregates, for example, AVG(DISTINCT *column_name*), COUNT(DISTINCT *column_name*), MAX(DISTINCT *column_name*), MIN(DISTINCT *column_name*), and SUM(DISTINCT *column_name*), are not supported when using CUBE or ROLLUP. If used, Microsoft SQL Server returns an error message and aborts the query.

TOP *n*

> Specifies that only the first *n* rows are to be output from the query result set. When the query includes an ORDER BY clause, this causes the first *n* rows ordered by the ORDER BY clause to be output. When the query has no ORDER BY clause, then the *n* number of rows is arbitrary.

PERCENT

> Specifies that only the first *n*% of the rows (rounded to the next integer value if the percentage yields a fractional row) be output from the query result set.

When the query includes an ORDER BY clause, this causes the first *n*% rows ordered by the ORDER BY clause to be output. When the query has no ORDER BY clause, then the *n*% of rows is arbitrary.

WITH TIES

When used with TOP *n* or PERCENT, specifies that additional rows be returned from the base result set with the same value in the ORDER BY columns appearing as the last of the TOP *n* (PERCENT) rows. TOP WITH TIES can only be specified when an ORDER BY clause exists.

<select_list>

Specifies the list of columns, expressions, and/or keywords to select.

<table_or_view>

Specifies the name of the table or view.

table_name

The name of the table or joined table used in the SELECT statement. Up to 256 tables can be used in a DELETE, INSERT, UPDATE, or SELECT statement. For more information, see FROM.

Tip When creating a derived table, the SELECT statement does not support the use of the INTO, ORDER BY, COMPUTE, or COMPUTE BY clauses.

table_alias

The name of the table (specified as an alias) used in the SELECT statement. For more information, see FROM.

<table_hints>

Specifies a table scan, one or more indexes to be used by the optimizer, or a locking method to be used by the optimizer with this table and for this SELECT. Although this is an option, the optimizer can usually pick the best optimization method without hints being specified. Commas between <table_hints> are optional but supported for backward compatibility.

If a table (including system tables) contains computed columns and the computed columns are computed by expressions or functions accessing columns in other tables, then the table hints are not used on those tables (the table hints are not propagated). For example, a NOLOCK table hint is specified on a table in the query. This table has computed columns that are computed by a combination of expressions and functions (accessing columns in another table). The tables referenced by the expressions and functions will not use the NOLOCK table hint when accessed.

INDEX(*index_name* | *index_id*)

Specifies the name or ID of the index to be used by SQL Server when processing the statement. Only one index hint per table can only be specified. The alternative INDEX = syntax (which specifies a single index hint) is supported only for backward compatibility. If a clustered index exists, INDEX = 0 forces a clustered index scan and INDEX = 1 forces a clustered index scan or seek. If no clustered index exists, INDEX = 0 forces a table scan and INDEX = 1 is interpreted as an error. Any index hints specified for a view are ignored, and SQL Server returns an error message.

Note If an index hint referring to multiple indexes is used on the fact table in a star join, SQL Server ignores the index hint and returns an error message. Also, index ORing is disallowed for a table with a specified index hint specified.

SQL Server does not allow more than one table hint from each of the following groups:

➤ Granularity hints: PAGLOCK, NOLOCK, ROWLOCK, TABLOCK, or TABLOCKX.

➤ Isolation level hints: HOLDLOCK, NOLOCK, READCOMMITTED, REPEATABLEREAD, SERIALIZABLE.

In addition, the NOLOCK and READPAST <table_hints> are only allowed in SELECT statements and not in DELETE, INSERT, or UPDATE statements.

FASTFIRSTROW

Equivalent to OPTION (FAST 1).

Tip You can use the <table_hints> in any combination, but some of them do not make sense to use together, for example, TABLOCK and PAGLOCK. When multiple options are specified, separate them with a space; the more restrictive option takes precedence.

HOLDLOCK

Equivalent to SERIALIZABLE. The HOLDLOCK option applies only to the table or view for which it is specified and only for the duration of the transaction defined by the statement in which it is used. The HOLDLOCK option cannot be used in a SELECT statement including the FOR BROWSE option.

NOLOCK

Allows dirty reads, which means that no shared locks are issued and no exclusive locks are honored. This can result in higher concurrency, but at the cost of lower consistency. If this option is specified, it is possible to read an uncommitted transaction or to read a set of pages rolled back in the middle of the read, so error messages might result. If you receive error messages 605, 606, 624, or 625 when NOLOCK is specified, resolve them as you would a deadlock error (1205) and retry your statement.

PAGLOCK

Takes shared page locks where a single shared table lock is normally taken.

READCOMMITTED

Performs a scan with the same locking semantics as a transaction running at READ COMMITTED isolation level.

READPAST

Reads past locked rows and basically skips them. For example, assume table T1 contains a single integer column with the values of 1, 2, 3, 4, 5. If transaction A changes the value of 3 to 8 but has not yet committed, a SELECT * FROM T1 (READPAST) yields values 1, 2, 4, 5. READPAST only applies to transactions operating at READ COMMITTED isolation and only reads past row-level locks. This lock hint is primarily used to implement a work queue on a SQL Server table.

READUNCOMMITTED

Equivalent to NOLOCK.

REPEATABLEREAD

Performs a scan with the same locking semantics as a transaction running at REPEATABLE READ isolation level.

ROWLOCK

Takes a shared row lock where a single shared page or table lock is normally taken.

SERIALIZABLE

Equivalent to HOLDLOCK. Makes shared locks more restrictive by holding them until the completion of a transaction (instead of releasing the shared lock as soon as the required table or data page is no longer needed, whether or not the transaction has been completed). The scan is performed with the same semantics as a transaction running at the SERIALIZABLE isolation level.

TABLOCK

Takes a shared table lock on the table held until the end-of-statement. If HOLDLOCK is also specified, the shared table lock is held until the end of the transaction.

TABLOCKX

Takes an exclusive table lock on the table held until the end-of-statement or end-of-transaction.

UPDLOCK

Takes update locks instead of shared locks while reading the table and holds them until the end-of-statement or end-of-transaction.

n

> A placeholder indicating that any of the preceding item(s) can be repeated multiple times. The maximum number of indexes in the <table_hints> is 250 non-clustered indexes.

view_name

> The names of the views used in the SELECT statement. For more information, see FROM.

*

> Specifies that all columns, in the order in which they were specified in the CREATE TABLE statement, should be retrieved. Using * in the <select_list> affects all tables in the SELECT statement's FROM clause. Although unusual, * can be specified more than once in the same query. For example, to retrieve all columns from two or more tables in a join operation. Returns all columns enabled for full-text querying, if applicable. For more information about full-text querying, see CONTAINS, CONTAINSTABLE, FREETEXT, and FREETEXTTABLE.

column_name

> The name of the column to retrieve. To select multiple column names, separate the names with commas. When used with the optional COMPUTE clause, *column_name* is the column used by the row aggregate function.

expression

> A column name, constant, or function, any combination of column names, constants, and functions connected by an operator(s), or a subquery.

> Only expressions of the numeric data type category can be used with SUM and AVG.

> When used with SELECT INTO, the expression can be used to set up an identity column by using the IDENTITY() function with SELECT INTO. For example, ID = IDENTITY(int,1,1).

> When using an expression with a COMPUTE clause, remember the following:

> ➤ When used as a row aggregate function, an expression is usually the name of a column.

> ➤ One COMPUTE clause can apply the same function to several columns or several functions to one column.

IDENTITYCOL

> Produces the actual column name of the identity column. For more information, see IDENTITY, ALTER TABLE, and CREATE TABLE.

ROWGUIDCOL

> A keyword indicating that the new column is a row global unique identifier column (ROWGUIDCOL). Columns of ROWGUIDCOL may be used for merge replication. Only one **uniqueidentifier** column per table can be designated as

the ROWGUIDCOL column. The ROWGUIDCOL property can be assigned only to a **uniqueidentifier** column.

column_alias

A user-defined, temporary heading to replace the default column heading (the column name). For more information about column aliases, see FROM.

new_column_name

A new column name (of the integer data type category except for the **bit** data type, or **decimal** data type) that does not allow null values.

IDENTITY

Specifies that the specified column in the new table should use the IDENTITY property. For more information, see IDENTITY, ALTER TABLE, and CREATE TABLE.

Note When used in a SELECT statement, IDENTITY must be used with an INTO clause.

data_type

The data type of the identity column. Valid data types for an identity column are any data types of the integer data type category (except for the **bit** data type), or **decimal** data type.

seed

The value to be assigned to the first row in the table. Each subsequent row is assigned the next identity value, which is equal to the last IDENTITY value plus the *increment* value. If neither *seed* nor *increment* is specified, both default to 1.

increment

The increment to add to the *seed* value for successive rows in the table.

GROUPING

Causes an additional column to be output with a value of 1, when the row is added by either the CUBE or ROLLUP operator, or 0, which distinguishes those null values appearing in summary rows from the null values appearing in a GROUP BY column. The GROUPING function is applied to a *column_name* in <select_list>. The *column_name* must be one of the columns appearing in the GROUP BY clause. A value of 1 is returned when NULL is returned in the result set for *column_name* when it appears in a summary row. A value of 0 is returned when NULL is returned in the result set for *column_name*. This function is allowed only with a GROUP BY clause and either the CUBE or ROLLUP operator.

RANK

Specifies that the ranking value for each row returned by a full-text query is to be displayed. Use with a table that has been registered and enabled for full-text querying. For more information about full-text querying and ranking, see CONTAINSTABLE.

INTO *new_table_name*

The name of a new table to be created based on the columns specified in the <select_list> and the rows chosen in the WHERE clause. To select into a permanent table, execute sp_dboption to turn on the Select Into/Bulkcopy option. By default, the Select Into/Bulkcopy option is off in newly created databases. *new_table_name* must follow the same rules as *table* with these exceptions:

➤ If Select Into/Bulkcopy is on in the database where the table is to be created, a permanent table is created. The table name must be unique in the database and conform to the rules for identifiers.

➤ If Select Into/Bulkcopy is not on in the database where the table is to be created, permanent tables cannot be created using SELECT INTO; only local or global temporary tables can be created. To create a temporary table, the table name must begin with a number sign (#). For details on temporary tables, see CREATE TABLE.

SELECT INTO is a two-step operation. The first step creates the table. The user executing the statement must have CREATE TABLE permission in the destination database. The second step inserts the specified rows into the new table.

You can use SELECT INTO to create an identical table definition (different table name) with no data by having a false condition in the WHERE clause.

You cannot use SELECT INTO with the COMPUTE clause or inside a user-defined transaction.

When selecting an existing identity column into a new table, the new column inherits the IDENTITY property unless one of the following conditions is true:

➤ The SELECT statement contains a join, GROUP BY clause, or aggregate function.

➤ Multiple SELECT statements are joined with UNION.

➤ The identity column is listed more than once in the <select_list>.

➤ The identity column is part of an expression.

➤ If any of these conditions is true, the column is created NOT NULL instead of inheriting the IDENTITY property. If none of the conditions is true, the new table will inherit the identity column. All rules and restrictions for the identity columns apply to the new table.

FROM <table_sources>

Specifies the table(s) from which to retrieve information. For more information about FROM, see FROM.

select_statement

A nested SELECT statement, retrieving rows from the specified database and table(s). When used with the AS keyword and a *table_alias*, refers to a derived table.

CROSS JOIN

Specifies the cross-product of two tables. Returns the same rows as if no WHERE clause was specified in an old-style, non-SQL-92-style join.

INNER

Specifies all matching pairs of rows are returned. Discards unmatched rows from both tables. This is the default if no join type is specified.

LEFT [OUTER]

Specifies all rows from the left table not meeting the condition specified are included in the result set, and output columns from the other table are set to NULL in addition to all rows returned by the INNER JOIN.

RIGHT [OUTER]

Specifies all rows from the right table not meeting the condition specified are included in the result set, and output columns corresponding to the other table are set to NULL in addition to all rows returned by the INNER JOIN.

FULL [OUTER]

If a row from either the left or right table does not match the selection criteria, specifies the row be included in the result set and output columns that correspond to the other table be set to NULL. This is in addition to all rows normally returned by INNER JOIN.

Note Earlier versions of SQL Server joins (using the *= and =* syntax in the WHERE clause) cannot be used within the same statement as SQL-92-style joins. For more information, see Non-SQL-92 Joins later in this topic.

<join_hints>

Specifies one <join hint>, or *execution algorithm*, per join is specified in the query's FROM clause. If a <join_hint> is specified for any two tables, the query optimizer automatically enforces the join order for all joined tables in the query, based on the position of the ON keywords. In the case of FULL OUTER JOINS, when the ON clauses are not used, parentheses can be used to indicate the desired join order.

{LOOP | HASH | MERGE}

Specifies that the join in the query should use looping, hashing, or merging. Using LOOP | HASH | MERGE JOIN in the FROM clause, with SQL-92-style join syntax, enforces a particular join between two tables.

JOIN

Indicates that the specified join operation should take place between the given tables or views.

ON <join_condition>

Specifies the criteria that must match for the specified JOIN to be performed. As part of the <join_condition>, specify a common *column_name* from each table in the join. A <join_condition> also specifies a <logical_operator>.

<logical_operator>

Specifies the condition that rows to be returned must meet.

<rowset_function>

Specifies that one of the rowset functions is to be used.

CONTAINSTABLE

Returns a table of zero, one, or more rows for those columns containing character-based data types for precise or "fuzzy" (less precise) matches to single words and phrases, the proximity of words within a certain distance of one another, and weighted matches. For more information, see CONTAINSTABLE.

FREETEXTTABLE

Returns a table of zero, one, or more rows for those columns containing character-based data types for values that match the meaning but not the exact wording of the words in the predicate. For more information, see FREETEXTTABLE.

OPENQUERY

Executes the specified pass-through query. For more information, see OPENQUERY.

OPENROWSET

Includes all connection information necessary to access remote data from a data source. For more information, see OPENROWSET.

n

A placeholder indicating that any of the preceding items can be repeated multiple times.

WHERE

Specifies that a WHERE clause is used to restrict the rows returned.

Note Earlier versions of SQL Server joins (using the *= and =* syntax in the WHERE clause) cannot be used within the same statement as SQL-92-style joins. For more information, see Non-SQL-92 Joins later in this topic.

<search_conditions>

Specifies the restricting condition(s) for the rows returned in the result set. There is no limit to the number of <search_conditions> that can be included in a SQL statement. When a WHERE clause is used, the <search_conditions> restrict the rows included in the calculation of the aggregate function but do not restrict the rows returned by the query. For more information about valid <search_conditions> or predicates, see WHERE.

GROUP BY

Specifies the groups into which the table is partitioned and, if aggregate functions are included in the <select_list>, finds a summary value for each group. The groups are formed by collecting rows having the same value for the expressions in the GROUP BY clause into a group. You can refer to the new summary columns in the HAVING clause. The **text**, **image**, and **bit** data types cannot be used in a GROUP BY clause.

When a GROUP BY clause is used, each item in <select_list> must produce a single value for each group. A table can be grouped by any combination of columns; however, you cannot group by a column heading. You must use a column name or an expression. In Transact-SQL, any valid expression is allowed in the GROUP BY clause as long as it does not involve aggregate functions (although not with column headings).

Any column referenced in <select_list> must also be referenced in the GROUP BY clause unless the column is being used in an aggregate function. Null values in the GROUP BY column are put into a single group when the GROUP BY column is also contained in <select_list>.

You cannot group by an alias. You can list more than one column in the GROUP BY clause to nest groups; that is, you can group a table by any combination of columns.

You can use a WHERE clause in a query containing a GROUP BY clause. Rows that do not satisfy the conditions in the WHERE clause are eliminated before any grouping is done.

Note If the ORDER BY clause is not specified, groups returned using the GROUP BY clause are not in any particular order. It is recommended that you always use the ORDER BY clause to specify a particular ordering of the data.

A maximum of 10 grouping expressions are permitted in a GROUP BY clause when CUBE or ROLLUP is specified. Otherwise, the number of grouping expressions is limited based on the GROUP BY column sizes, the aggregated columns, and the aggregate values involved in the query. This limit originates from the limit of 8,060 bytes on the intermediate work table needed for holding intermediate query results.

The aggregate functions, which calculate summary values from the non-null values in a column, can be divided into two groups:

Aggregate Function Groups	Description
Scalar	Aggregate functions are applied to all the rows in a table (producing a single value per function) with the GROUP BY clause and, optionally, the HAVING clause. An aggregate function in <select_list> with no GROUP BY clause applies to the whole table and is one example of a scalar.
Vector	Aggregate functions are applied to all rows that have the same value in a specified column or expression with the GROUP BY clause and, optionally, the HAVING clause (producing a value for each group per function).

You cannot specify the GROUP BY ALL clause when you use the CUBE or ROLLUP operators.

ALL

Includes all groups and result sets, even those that do not have any rows that meet the <search_conditions> specified in the WHERE clause. If ALL is specified, null values are returned for summary columns for groups that do not meet the <search_conditions>.

group_by_expresssion

The expression upon which to perform the GROUP BY operation.

Note This definition applies only to the ALL keyword specified immediately following the GROUP BY clause.

HAVING <search_conditions>

Specifies the conditions for aggregate functions in <select_list>; the <search_conditions> restrict the rows returned by the query but do not affect the calculations of the aggregate function(s). The HAVING clause sets conditions for the GROUP BY clause similar to the way that WHERE sets conditions for the SELECT statement. Because the HAVING clause is used to restrict groups, it is recommended that HAVING always be specified with a GROUP BY clause. However, if HAVING is specified without a GROUP BY clause, then a single group is produced and HAVING limits the data returned. When multiple conditions are included in the HAVING clause, they are combined with AND, OR, or NOT. For more information about <search_conditions>, see WHERE.

There is no limit on the number of conditions that can be included in <search_conditions>. When the HAVING clause is used with GROUP BY ALL, all predicates containing aggregates in the HAVING clause are applied on the results of the aggregation. This is the same behavior as if HAVING is used with GROUP BY.

The **text**, **image**, and **ntext** data types cannot be used in a HAVING clause.

Note Using the HAVING clause in the SELECT statement does not affect the way the CUBE operator groups the result set and returns summary aggregate rows.

CUBE

Specifies that, in addition to the usual aggregate rows provided by GROUP BY, *super-aggregate* rows are introduced into the result set. A super-aggregate row is a summary row generated by grouping on a subset of the *expressions* in the GROUP BY clause. Result sets with the super-aggregate rows are typically used for reports.

Tip Distinct aggregates, for example, AVG(DISTINCT *column_name*), COUNT(DISTINCT *column_name*), MAX(DISTINCT *column_name*), MIN(DISTINCT *column_name*), and SUM(DISTINCT *column_name*), are not supported when using CUBE or ROLLUP. If used, SQL Server returns an error message and aborts the query.

Columns included in the GROUP BY clause are cross-referenced to produce a superset of groups. The aggregate function specified in <select_list> is applied to these groups to produce summary values for the additional super-aggregate rows. The number of extra groups in the result set is determined by the number of columns included in the GROUP BY clause. Each operand (column) in the GROUP BY clause is bound under the null value and grouping is applied to all other operands (columns). The null value in this case represents all the values in a particular column.

The aggregate function used in the SELECT statement is applied to the cross-referenced columns for the super-aggregate calculation. The CUBE operator can be applied to all aggregate functions, including AVG, SUM, MAX, MIN, and COUNT.

You can use the CUBE operator to present cross-referenced information without having to write additional procedures. Consider a personnel department report that includes information such as job titles, home addresses, and modes of transportation to work. The SELECT statement reports on these records for each employee. By introducing the CUBE operator and the COUNT aggregate function, you can obtain statistics such as the number of people who drive to work and from what locations, and whether their jobs may be related to where they live or how they get to work.

For example, if your query was computing the average price of an automobile, grouped by manufacturer, a single super-aggregate row would be added that contained the average price of all cars. Suppose your query was grouped instead by manufacturer and color. The result set would then contain super-aggregates for each manufacturer, regardless of color, and separate super-aggregates for each color, regardless of manufacturer.

You might also apply the CUBE operator to a company sales management report that records sales personnel, customers, products, and quantities sold of each product. A SELECT statement used with the SUM aggregate function produces a report of how many of each product were sold, to which customers, and by which salespersons.

The CUBE operator expands the information returned by cross-referencing and reporting data such as the products that particular customers frequently buy, which sales personnel sell the most of a particular product, and which products are the most popular. By using application or programming tools, this information can then be fed into charts and graphs that convey results and relationships visually and effectively.

Here are guidelines for using the CUBE operator:

➤ The maximum size of a GROUP BY column list is 8,060 bytes.

➤ A maximum of 10 columns or expressions are permitted when WITH CUBE or WITH ROLLUP is specified.

➤ Columns or expressions must be specified in the GROUP BY clause; GROUP BY ALL is not permitted.

ROLLUP

Specifies a subset of super-aggregates is computed along with the usual aggregate rows for elements within a GROUP BY clause. This is useful when you have sets within sets.

Tip Distinct aggregates, for example, AVG(DISTINCT *column_name*), COUNT(DISTINCT *column_name*), MAX(DISTINCT *column_name*), MIN(DISTINCT *column_name*), and SUM(DISTINCT *column_name*), are not supported when using CUBE or ROLLUP. If used, SQL Server returns an error message and aborts the query.

The ROLLUP operator is applicable to cumulative aggregates such as running sums or running averages. It differs from the CUBE operator only in that it is sensitive to the position of the column in the GROUP BY clause. Aggregate groupings are made up of columns to the right of the current column value.

The ROLLUP operator can be used by report writers to extract statistics and summary information from result sets. The cumulative aggregates, such as running sums, can be used in reports, charts, and graphs.

The ROLLUP operator creates groupings by moving in only one direction, from right to left, along the list of columns in the GROUP BY clause. It then applies the aggregate function to these groupings. The CUBE operator creates all combinations of groupings from the list of columns in the GROUP BY clause.

Consider grouping by the expressions, column1, column2, and column3, and for an aggregate function, agg(column4). Applying the ROLLUP operator results in these rows:

```
column1 column2 column3 agg(column4)
column1 column2 NULL agg(column4)
column1 NULL NULL agg(column4)
NULL NULL NULL agg(column4)
```

ORDER BY

Specifies the sort order used on columns returned. Either specify a *column_name* (which can be qualified by the table or view name), or specify a non-negative integer representing the position of the column name, column heading, alias, or expression in <select_list>. If the result set is sorted by the column number, the columns to which the ORDER BY clause refers must be included in the <select_list>.

There is no limit on the number of items in the ORDER BY clause. However, there is a limit of 8,060 bytes for the row size of intermediate work tables needed for sort operations. This limits the total size of columns specified in an ORDER BY clause and the select list. In Transact-SQL, the ORDER BY clause can include items not appearing in <select_list>. You can sort by a column name, a column heading (or alias), an expression, or by the *select_list_number*. <select_list> can be a single asterisk (*). If you use COMPUTE BY, you must also specify an ORDER BY clause. If SELECT DISTINCT is specified, the ORDER BY items must appear in the <select_list>.

Null values are sorted before all others, and **ntext**, **text**, or **image** columns cannot be used in an ORDER BY clause. Subqueries and view definitions cannot include an ORDER BY clause, a COMPUTE clause, or the INTO keyword. However, through Transact-SQL extensions, you can sort by expressions and aggregates if you use their *select_list_number* in the ORDER BY clause.

ASC

Specifies that the sorted result set should be returned in ascending order, from the smallest value to the largest value.

DESC

Specifies that the sorted result set should be returned in descending order, from the largest value to the smallest value.

COMPUTE

Generates summary values that appear as additional rows in the query results for row aggregate functions (unlike the aggregate function results, which appear as new columns in a SELECT statement). Use the COMPUTE clause to calculate summary values for subgroups, or to calculate more than one aggregate function for the same group. COMPUTE and the row aggregate functions are

Transact-SQL enhancements to standard SQL specifying that control-break summary changes are generated for row aggregate functions (SUM, AVG, MIN, MAX, and COUNT).

The summary values appear as additional rows in the query results, allowing you to see detail rows and summary rows within one result set. You can calculate summary values for subgroups, and you can calculate more than one aggregate function for the same group.

The COMPUTE clause cannot be used with INTO and cannot contain aliases for column names, although aliases can be used in <select_list>.

The columns in the COMPUTE clause must appear in the select list.

You cannot use COMPUTE in a SELECT INTO statement because statements including COMPUTE generate tables and their summary results are not stored in the database. Therefore, any calculations produced by COMPUTE do not appear in the new table created with the SELECT INTO statement.

If you use COMPUTE BY, you must also use an ORDER BY clause. The columns listed after COMPUTE BY must be identical to or a subset of those listed after ORDER BY, and they must be in the same left-to-right order, start with the same expression, and not skip any expressions.

The COMPUTE keyword can be used without BY to generate grand totals, grand counts, and so on. ORDER BY is optional if you use the COMPUTE keyword without BY.

When you add or average integer data, SQL Server treats the result as an **int** value, even if the data type of the column is **smallint** or **tinyint**.

Note To reduce the possibility of overflow errors in ODBC and DB-Library programs, make all variable declarations for the results of averages or sums data type **int**.

In a SELECT statement with a COMPUTE clause, the order of columns in the select list overrides the order of the aggregate functions in the COMPUTE clause. ODBC and DB-Library programmers must be aware of this order requirement to put the aggregate function results in the correct place.

Note **ntext**, **text**, or **image** data types cannot be specified in a COMPUTE or COMPUTE BY clause.

BY

Specifies that the values for row aggregate functions be calculated for subgroups.

When the value of BY items changes, row aggregate function values are generated. If you use BY, you must also use an ORDER BY clause. Listing more than one item after BY breaks a group into subgroups and applies the aggregate function at each level of grouping. The columns listed after a COMPUTE clause must be identical to or a subset of those listed after an ORDER BY clause, and must be in the same left-to-right order, start with the same expression, and not skip any expression.

For example, if the ORDER BY clause is:

```
ORDER BY a, b, c
```

The COMPUTE clause can be any (or all) of these:

```
COMPUTE BY a, b, c
COMPUTE BY a, b
COMPUTE BY a
```

FOR BROWSE

Specifies updates be allowed while viewing data in client applications using DB-Library.

A table can be browsed in an application under these conditions:

➤ The table includes a time-stamped column (defined with the **timestamp** data type).

➤ The table has a unique index.

➤ The FOR BROWSE option is at the end of the SELECT statement(s) sent to SQL Server.

Note It is not possible to use the <lock_hint> HOLDLOCK in a SELECT statement that includes the FOR BROWSE option.

The FOR BROWSE option cannot appear in SELECT statements joined by the UNION operator.

<query_hints>

Specifies that the indicated <query_hint> should be used throughout the entire query. Each query hint can be specified only once even though multiple <query_hints> can be specified. The OPTION clause must be specified with the outermost SELECT of the statement. <query_hints> affects all operators in the statement. If a UNION is involved in the main query, then only the last SELECT statements involving a UNION operator can have the OPTION clause. If one or more <query_hints> causes the optimizer to not generate a valid plan, then SQL Server recompiles the query without the specified query hints and issues a SQL Server Profiler event.

Caution Because the query optimizer of SQL Server usually selects the best execution plan for a query, it is recommended that <join_hints> and <query_hints> only be used as a last resort by experienced database administrators.

{HASH | ORDER} GROUP

Specifies aggregations described in the GROUP BY or COMPUTE clause of the query should use hashing or ordering.

{MERGE | HASH | CONCAT} UNION

Specifies all UNION operations are performed by merging, hashing, or concatenating UNION sets. If more than one UNION hint is specified, the optimizer selects the least expensive strategy from those hints specified.

FAST *number_rows*

Specifies that the query is optimized for fast retrieval of the first *number_rows* (a non-negative integer). After the first *number_rows* are returned, the query continues execution and produces its full result set.

FORCE ORDER

Specifies the join order indicated by the query syntax is preserved during query optimization.

MAXDOP *number*

Changes the Max Degree of Parallelism configuration option (of sp_configure) only for the query specifying this option. All semantic rules used with the Max Degree of Parallelism configuration option are applicable when using MAXDOP <query_hint>.

ROBUST PLAN

Forces the query optimizer to attempt a plan that works for the maximum potential row size at the expense of performance. If no such plan is possible, the optimizer returns an error rather than deferring error detection to query execution. Rows can contain variable-length columns; SQL Server allows rows to be defined whose maximum potential size is beyond the ability of SQL Server to process them. Typically, despite the maximum potential size, an application stores rows whose actual size is within the limits that SQL Server can process. If SQL Server encounters a row that is too long, an execution error is returned.

Remarks

The order of the clauses in the SELECT statement is significant. Any of the optional clauses can be omitted, but when used, they must appear in the appropriate order.

The length returned for **text** or **ntext** columns included in the <select_list> defaults to the smallest of the actual size of the **text**, the default TEXTSIZE session setting, or the hardcoded application limit. To change the length of returned text for the session, use the SET statement. By default, the limit on the length of text data returned with a SELECT statement is 4,000 bytes.

SQL Server raises exception 511 and rolls back the current executing statement if either:

➤ The SELECT statement produces a result row or an intermediate work table row exceeding 8,060 bytes.

Or

➤ The DELETE, INSERT, or UPDATE statement attempts action on a row exceeding 8,060 bytes.

Note In SQL Server, an error occurs if no column name is given to a column created by a SELECT INTO or CREATE VIEW statement.

Non-SQL-92 Joins

Old-style, non-SQL-92-style joins specify join conditions in the WHERE clause and use the *= and =* syntax; SQL-92-style joins specify join conditions in the FROM clause and do not use the *= and =* syntax. Earlier versions of SQL Server joins cannot be used within the same statement as SQL-92-style joins.

It is recommended that queries be rewritten to use the SQL-92 join syntax.

Using the GROUP BY clause and the HAVING clause

This list shows the requirements for processing a SELECT with the GROUP BY clause and the HAVING clause, and it shows how the rows returned in the result set are derived:

➤ The WHERE clause excludes rows not meeting its <search_conditions>.

➤ The GROUP BY clause collects the selected rows into one group for each unique value in the GROUP BY clause. Omitting the GROUP BY clause creates a single group for the whole table.

➤ The HAVING clause excludes rows not meeting its <search_conditions>. Typically, HAVING is used with a GROUP BY clause. The GROUP BY clause creates the applicable groups from the rows. Then, HAVING further filters those grouped rows. It is possible to specify HAVING without a GROUP BY clause. Then, HAVING behaves as a WHERE clause.

➤ Aggregate functions specified in the <select_list> calculate summary values for each surviving group.

For the GROUP BY clause, the HAVING clause, and aggregate functions to accomplish the goal of one row and one summary value per group, SQL-92-standard SQL requires:

➤ Columns in <select_list> must also be in the GROUP BY clause or be parameters of aggregate functions.

➤ Columns in a HAVING clause must have only one value per group. For example, they must be either GROUP BY columns or aggregate functions of non-GROUP BY columns.

➤ A query with a HAVING clause should have a GROUP BY clause. But if it does not, all the rows not excluded by the WHERE clause are considered to be a single group.

Transact-SQL extensions to standard SQL make displaying data more flexible by allowing references to columns and expressions that are not used for creating groups or summary calculations. For example:

➤ The GROUP BY clause can include expressions.

➤ When the HAVING clause is used with GROUP BY ALL, all predicates containing aggregates in the HAVING clause are applied on the results of the aggregation. This is the same behavior as if HAVING is used with GROUP BY.

Rules for COMPUTE Clauses

➤ The DISTINCT keyword is not allowed with row aggregate functions.

➤ The columns in a COMPUTE clause must appear in the statement's select list.

➤ SELECT INTO cannot be used in the same statement as a COMPUTE clause because statements that include COMPUTE do not generate normal rows.

➤ If using COMPUTE BY, an ORDER BY clause must also be specified. The columns listed after COMPUTE BY must be identical to or a subset of those listed after ORDER BY. They must be in the same left-to-right order, start with the same expression, and not skip any expressions.

For example, if the ORDER BY clause is:

```
ORDER BY a, b, c
```

The COMPUTE BY clause can be any of these:

```
COMPUTE row_aggregate (column_name) BY a, b, c
COMPUTE row_aggregate (column_name) BY a, b
COMPUTE row_aggregate (column_name) BY a
```

The COMPUTE BY clause cannot be any of these:

```
COMPUTE row_aggregate (column_name) BY b, c
COMPUTE row_aggregate (column_name) BY a, c
COMPUTE row_aggregate (column_name) BY c
```

➤ Use a column name or an expression in the ORDER BY clause; sorting cannot be performed by specifying a column heading.

➤ The COMPUTE keyword can be used without BY to generate grand totals, grand counts, and so on. ORDER BY is optional if the COMPUTE keyword is used without BY.

Row Aggregate Functions and the COMPUTE Clause

These row aggregate functions are used with COMPUTE:

Row Aggregate Function	Result
SUM	Total of the values in the numeric expression
AVG	Average of the values in the numeric expression
MAX	Highest value in the expression
MIN	Lowest value in the expression
COUNT	Number of selected rows

SUM, AVG, MAX, MIN, and COUNT ignore null values.

These row aggregate functions are the same aggregate functions that can be used with GROUP BY, except that there is no equivalent to COUNT(*). To find the summary information produced by GROUP BY and COUNT(*), use a COMPUTE clause without BY.

Permissions

SELECT permission defaults to the owner of the table or view, who can grant it to other users using the GRANT statement. If the INTO clause is used to create a permanent table, then the user must have CREATE TABLE permission in the destination database.

SELECT @local_variable

Specifies the given local variable (created using DECLARE @local_variable) should be given the specified expression (variable assignment). It is recommended that SET @local_variable be used for variable assignment rather than SELECT @local_variable. For more information, see SET @local_variable.

Syntax

```
@local_variable = expression
```

Arguments

@local_variable

> The previously declared variable for which a value is to be assigned. The SELECT statement that assigns a value to the variable usually returns a single value. If the SELECT variable assignment statement returns more than one value, the variable is assigned the last value returned. If the SELECT variable assignment statement returns no rows, the variable retains its present value unless the variable assignment is made with a subquery. Only if the subquery returns no rows is the variable set to NULL. The SELECT statement that assigns a value to variables cannot retrieve data in the same statement. One SELECT statement can initialize several local variables at one time.

expression

Any valid Microsoft SQL Server expression.

SESSION_USER

A niladic function that allows a system-supplied value for the current session's user name to be inserted into a table when no default value is specified. Also allows the user name to be used in queries, error messages, and so on.

Syntax

SESSION_USER

Return Type: nchar

Remarks

Use SESSION_USER with DEFAULT constraints in either the CREATE TABLE or ALTER TABLE statements, or use as any standard function.

SET

The Transact-SQL programming language provides several SET statements that alter the current session handling of specific information. These SET statements range from SQL-92 settings to locking statements.

The SET statements are grouped into these categories.

Category	Explanation
Date and Time Statements	Alter the current session settings for handling date and time data.
Locking Statements	Alter the current session settings for handling SQL Server locking.
Miscellaneous Statements	Alter the current session settings for miscellaneous SQL Server functionality.
Query Execution Statements	Alter the current session settings for query execution and processing.
SQL-92 Settings Statements	Alter the current session settings to use the SQL-92 default settings.
Statistics Statements	Alter the current session settings for displaying statistics information.
Transactions Statements	Alter the current session settings for handling SQL Server transactions.

Date and Time Statements

SET DATEFIRST   SET DATEFORMAT

Locking Statements

SET DEADLOCK_PRIORITY   SET LOCK_TIMEOUT

Miscellaneous Statements

SET CONCAT_NULL_YIELDS_NULL

SET CURSOR_CLOSE_ON_COMMIT

SET DISABLE_DEF_CNST_CHK

SET FIPS_FLAGGER

SET IDENTITY_INSERT

SET LANGUAGE

SET OFFSETS

SET PROCID

SET QUOTED_IDENTIFIER

Query Execution Statements

SET ARITHABORT

SET ARITHIGNORE

SET FMTONLY

SET NOCOUNT

SET NOEXEC

SET NUMERIC_ROUNDABORT

SET PARSEONLY

SET QUERY_GOVERNOR_COST_LIMIT

SET ROWCOUNT

SET TEXTSIZE

SQL-92 Settings Statements

SET ANSI_DEFAULTS

SET ANSI_NULL_DFLT_OFF

SET ANSI_NULL_DFLT_ON

SET ANSI_NULLS

SET ANSI_PADDING

SET ANSI_WARNINGS

Statistics Statements

SET FORCEPLAN

SET SHOWPLAN_ALL

SET SHOWPLAN_TEXT

SET STATISTICS IO

SET STATISTICS TIME

Transactions Statements

SET IMPLICIT_TRANSACTIONS

SET REMOTE_PROC_TRANSACTIONS

SET TRANSACTION ISOLATION LEVEL

SET XACT_ABORT

SET @local_variable

Sets the specified local variable, previously created with the DECLARE *@local_variable* statement, to the given value.

Syntax

```
SET
{
{@local_variable = expression}
| { @cursor_variable =
{ @cursor_variable
| cursor_name
| { CURSOR
[FORWARD_ONLY | SCROLL]
[STATIC | KEYSET | DYNAMIC]
```

```
[READ_ONLY | SCROLL_LOCKS | OPTIMISTIC]
FOR select_statement
[FOR {READ ONLY | UPDATE [OF column_list] } ]
}
}
}
}
```

Arguments

@local_variable

> The name of a variable of any type except cursor. Variable names must begin with only one at sign (@). Variable names must conform to the rules for identifiers. The variable must have been previously declared with a DECLARE *@local_variable* statement.

expression

> Any valid Microsoft SQL Server expression.

cursor_variable

> The name of a cursor variable. If the target cursor variable previously referenced a different cursor, that previous reference is removed.

cursor_name

> The name of the cursor declared using the DECLARE CURSOR statement.

CURSOR

> Specifies that the SET statement contains a declaration of a cursor.

SCROLL

> Specifies that the cursor supports all fetch options (FIRST, LAST, NEXT, PRIOR, RELATIVE, and ABSOLUTE).

FORWARD_ONLY

> Specifies that the cursor only supports the FETCH NEXT option. The cursor can only be retrieved in one direction, from the first to the last row. If FORWARD_ONLY is specified without the STATIC, KEYSET, or DYNAMIC keywords, the cursor is implemented as DYNAMIC. When neither FORWARD_ONLY or SCROLL are specified, FORWARD_ONLY is the default unless the keywords STATIC, KEYSET, or DYNAMIC are specified. STATIC, KEYSET, and DYNAMIC cursors default to SCROLL.

STATIC

> Defines a cursor that makes a temporary copy of the data to be used by the cursor. All requests to the cursor are answered from this temporary table in tempdb; therefore, modifications made to base tables are not reflected in the data returned by fetches made to this cursor, and this cursor does not allow modifications.

KEYSET

Specifies that the membership and order of rows in the cursor are fixed when the cursor is opened. The set of keys that uniquely identify the rows is built into a table in tempdb known as the keyset. Changes to nonkey values in the base tables, either made by the cursor owner or committed by other users, are visible as the owner scrolls around the cursor. Inserts made by other users are not visible (inserts cannot be made through a Transact-SQL server cursor). If a row is deleted, an attempt to fetch the row returns an @@FETCH_STATUS of –2. Updates of key values from outside the cursor resemble a delete of the old row followed by an insert of the new row. The row with the new values is not visible, and attempts to fetch the row with the old values return an @@FETCH_STATUS of –2. The new values are visible if the update is done through the cursor by specifying the WHERE CURRENT OF clause.

DYNAMIC

Defines a cursor that reflects all data changes made to the rows in its result set as you scroll around the cursor. The data values, order, and membership of the rows can change on each fetch. The absolute and relative fetch options are not supported with dynamic cursors.

READ_ONLY

Prevents updates from being made through this cursor. The cursor cannot be referenced in a WHERE CURRENT OF clause in an UPDATE or DELETE statement. This option overrides the default capability of a cursor to be updated.

SCROLL LOCKS

Specifies that positioned updates or deletes made through the cursor are guaranteed to succeed. SQL Server locks the rows as they are read into the cursor to ensure their availability for later modifications.

OPTIMISTIC

Specifies that positioned updates or deletes made through the cursor do not succeed if the row has been updated since it was read into the cursor. SQL Server does not lock rows as they are read into the cursor. It instead uses comparisons of **timestamp** column values, or a checksum value if the table has no **timestamp** column, to determine if the row was modified after it was read into the cursor. If the row was modified, the attempted positioned update or delete fails.

FOR *select_statement*

A standard SELECT statement that defines the result set of the cursor. The keywords COMPUTE, COMPUTE BY, FOR BROWSE, and INTO are not allowed within the *select_statement* of a cursor declaration.

If DISTINCT, UNION, GROUP BY, and/or HAVING are used, or an aggregate expression is included in the *select_list*, the cursor will be created as STATIC.

If each of the underlying tables does not have a unique index and a SQL-92 SCROLL cursor or a Transact-SQL KEYSET cursor is requested, it will automatically be a STATIC cursor.

If the *select_statement* contains an ORDER BY where the columns are not unique row identifiers, a DYNAMIC cursor is converted to a KEYSET cursor, or to a STATIC cursor if a KEYSET cursor cannot be opened. This also happens for a cursor defined using SQL-92 syntax but without the STATIC keyword.

READ ONLY

Prevents updates from being made through this cursor. The cursor cannot be referenced in a WHERE CURRENT OF clause in an UPDATE or DELETE statement. This option overrides the default capability of a cursor to be updated. This keyword varies from the previous READ_ONLY by having a space instead of an underscore between READ and ONLY.

UPDATE [OF *column_list*]

Defines updatable columns within the cursor. If OF *column_list* is supplied, only the columns listed will allow modifications. If no list is supplied, all columns can be updated unless the cursor has been defined as READ_ONLY.

SETUSER

Allows a member of the sysadmin or db_owner roles to impersonate another user.

Tip SETUSER is only included in Microsoft SQL Server version 7.0 for backward compatibility, and is not recommended to be used. This statement may not be supported in future releases of SQL Server.

Syntax

```
SETUSER ['username' [WITH NORESET]]
```

Arguments

'*username*'

The name of a SQL Server or Microsoft Windows NT user in the current database who is impersonated. When *username* is not specified, the original identity of the system administrator or database owner impersonating the user is reestablished.

WITH NORESET

Specifies that subsequent SETUSER statements (with no specified *username*) do not reset to the system administrator or database owner.

SHUTDOWN

Immediately stops Microsoft SQL Server.

Syntax

SHUTDOWN [WITH NOWAIT]

Arguments

WITH NOWAIT

> Shuts down SQL Server immediately, without performing checkpoints in every database. SQL Server exits after attempting to terminate all user processes, and a rollback operation occurs for each active transaction.

SIGN

Returns the positive (+), zero (0), or negative (–) sign of the given expression.

Syntax

SIGN(*numeric_expression*)

Arguments

numeric_expression

> An expression of the exact numeric or approximate numeric data type category, except for the **bit** data type.

Return Type: float

SIN

Returns the trigonometric sine of the given angle (in radians) in an approximate numeric (**float**) expression.

Syntax

SIN(*float_expression*)

Arguments

float_expression

> An expression of type **float**.

Return Type: float

SOUNDEX

Returns a four-character (SOUNDEX) code to evaluate the similarity of two strings.

Syntax

SOUNDEX(*character_expression*)

Arguments

character_expression

> An alphanumeric expression of character data. *character_expression* can be a constant, variable, or column.

Return Type: char

SPACE

Returns a string of repeated spaces.

Syntax

SPACE(*integer_expression*)

Arguments

integer_expression

A positive integer that indicates the number of spaces. If *integer_expression* is negative, a null string is returned.

Return Type: char

SQRT

Returns the square root of the given expression.

Syntax

SQRT(*float_expression*)

Arguments

float_expression

An expression of type **float**.

Return Type: float

SQUARE

Returns the square of the given expression.

Syntax

SQUARE(*float_expression*)

Arguments

float_expression

An expression of type **float**.

Return Type: float

STATS_DATE

Returns the date that the statistics for the specified index were last updated.

Syntax

STATS_DATE(*table_id*, *index_id*)

Arguments

table_id

The ID of the table used.

index_id

> The ID of the index used.

Return Type: datetime

STDEV

An aggregate function that returns the statistical standard deviation of all values in the given expression. If STDEV is used on all items in a SELECT statement, each value in the result set is included in the calculation. STDEV can be used with numeric columns only. Null values are ignored.

Syntax

STDEV(*expression*)

Arguments

expression

> A constant, column, or function, and any combination of arithmetic, bitwise, and string operators. Aggregate functions and subqueries are not permitted. *expression* is an expression of the exact numeric or approximate numeric data type category, except for the **bit** data type.

Return Type: float

STDEVP

An aggregate function that returns the statistical standard deviation for the population for all values in the given expression. If STDEVP is used on all items in a SELECT statement, each value in the result set is included in the calculation. STDEVP can be used with numeric columns only. Null values are ignored.

Syntax

STDEVP(*expression*)

Arguments

expression

> A constant, column, or function, and any combination of arithmetic, bitwise, and string operators. Aggregate functions and subqueries are not permitted. *expression* is an expression of the exact numeric or approximate numeric data type category, except for the **bit** data type.

Return Type: float

STR

Returns character data converted from numeric data.

Syntax

STR(*float_expression*[, *length*[, *decimal*]])

Arguments

float_expression

> An approximate numeric (**float**) data type with a decimal point.

length

> The total length, including decimal point, sign, digits, and spaces. The default for *length* is 10.

decimal

> The number of spaces to the right of the decimal point.

Return Type: char

STUFF

Deletes *length* characters from the first *character_expression* at *start* and inserts the second *character_expression* into the first *character_expression* at *start*.

Syntax

```
STUFF(character_expression, start, length, character_expression)
```

Arguments

character_expression

> An expression of character data. *character_expression* can be a constant, variable, or column of either character or binary data.

start

> An integer value specifying the starting location to begin deletion and insertion. If the *start* position or the *length* is negative, a null string is returned. If the *start* position is longer than the first *character_expression*, a null string is returned.

length

> An integer value specifying the number of characters to delete. If the *length* to delete is longer than the first *character_expression*, deletion occurs up to the first character in the first *character_expression*.

Return Type: Returns character data if *character_expression* is one of the supported character data types. Returns binary data if *character_expression* is one of the supported binary data types.

SUBSTRING

Returns part of a character, binary, text, or image expression.

Syntax

```
SUBSTRING(expression, start, length)
```

Arguments

expression

> A character string, binary string, text, image, column, or expression that includes a column. (Do not use expressions that include aggregate functions.)

start

> An integer value that specifies where the substring begins.

length

> An integer value that specifies the length of the substring (the number of characters or bytes to return).

> **Note** Because *start* and *length* specify the number of bytes when SUBSTRING is used on **text** data, DBCS data, such as Kanji, may result in split characters at the beginning or end of the result. This behavior is consistent with the way in which READTEXT handles DBCS; however, because of the occasional strange result, it is advisable to use **ntext** instead of **text** for DBCS characters.

Return Type: Returns character data if *character_expression* is one of the supported character data types. Returns binary data if *character_expression* is one of the supported binary data types.

SUM

Returns the sum of all the values, or only the DISTINCT values, in the expression. SUM can be used with numeric columns only. Null values are ignored.

Syntax

```
SUM([ALL | DISTINCT] expression)
```

Arguments

ALL

> Applies the aggregate function to all values. ALL is the default.

DISTINCT

> Specifies that SUM return the sum of unique values.

expression

> A constant, column, or function, and any combination of arithmetic, bitwise, and string operators. *expression* is an expression of the exact numeric or approximate numeric data type category, except for the **bit** data type. Aggregate functions and subqueries are not permitted.

Return Type: Returns the summation of all *expression* values in most precise *expression* data type.

SUSER_ID

Returns the user's login identification number. The SUSER_ID system function is included in Microsoft SQL Server version 7.0 for backward compatibility. Use SUSER_SID instead.

Syntax

```
SUSER_ID(['login'])
```

Arguments

'login'

> The user's login identification name. *login*, which is optional, is **nchar**; if *login* is specified as **char**, it is implicitly converted to **nchar**. *login* can be any SQL Server login or Microsoft Windows NT user or group that has permission to connect to SQL Server. If *login* is not specified, the login identification number for the current user is returned.

Return Type: int

SUSER_NAME

Returns the user's login identification name. The SUSER_NAME system function is included in Microsoft SQL Server version 7.0 for backward compatibility only. Use SUSER_SNAME instead.

Syntax

```
SUSER_NAME([server_user_id])
```

Arguments

server_user_id

> The user's login identification number. *server_user_id*, which is optional, is **int**. *server_user_id* can be the login identification number of any SQL Server login or Microsoft Windows NT user or group that has permission to connect to SQL Server. If *server_user_id* is not specified, the login identification name for the current user is returned.

Return Type: nchar

SUSER_SID

Returns the security identification number (SID) for the user's login name.

Syntax

```
SUSER_SID(['login'])
```

Arguments

'login'

> The user's login name. *login* is **sysname**. *login*, which is optional, can be any Microsoft SQL Server login or Microsoft Windows NT user or group that has

permission to connect to SQL Server. The login name must already exist. If login is not specified, information about the current user is returned.

Return Type: int

SUSER_SNAME

Returns the login identification name from a user's security identification number (SID).

Syntax

SUSER_SNAME([*server_user_sid*])

Arguments

server_user_sid

The user security identification number. *server_user_sid*, which is optional, is **varbinary(85)**. *server_user_sid* can be the security identification number of any Microsoft SQL Server login or Microsoft Windows NT user or group that has permission to connect to SQL Server. The security identification number must already exist. If *server_user_sid* is not specified, information about the current user is returned.

Return Type: nchar

SYSTEM_USER

Allows a system-supplied value for the current system username to be inserted into a table when no default value is specified.

Syntax

SYSTEM_USER

Remarks

Use the SYSTEM_USER niladic function with DEFAULT constraints in either the CREATE TABLE or ALTER TABLE statements, or use as any standard function.

If the current user is logged in to Microsoft SQL Server using Microsoft Windows NT Authentication, SYSTEM_USER returns the Windows NT login identification name, for example, DOMAIN\user_login_name. However, if the current user is logged in to SQL Server using SQL Server Authentication, SYSTEM_USER returns the SQL Server login identification name, for example, sa for a user logged in as **sa**.

TAN

Returns the tangent of the input expression.

Syntax

TAN(*float_expression*)

Arguments

float_expression

> An expression of type **float** or **real**, interpreted as number of radians.

Return Type: float

TEXTPTR

Returns the text-pointer value in **varbinary** format. The text pointer is checked to ensure that it points to the first text page.

Syntax

TEXTPTR(*column*)

Arguments

column

> The **text**, **ntext**, or **image** column to be used.

Remarks

If a **text**, **ntext**, or **image** column has not been initialized by an INSERT or UPDATE statement, TEXTPTR returns a null pointer. Use TEXTVALID to check whether a text pointer exists. You cannot use UPDATETEXT, WRITETEXT, or READTEXT without a valid text pointer.

These functions and statements are also useful with **text**, **ntext**, and **image** data.

Function or Statement	Description
PATINDEX('%*pattern*%', *expression*)	The character position of a given character string in **text** or **ntext** columns.
DATALENGTH(*expression*)	The length of data in **text**, **ntext**, and **image** columns.
SET TEXTSIZE	The limit, in bytes, of the **text**, **ntext**, or **image** data to be returned with a SELECT statement.
SUBSTRING(*text_column*, *start*, *length*)	Returns a **varchar** string specified by the given *start* offset and *length*. The length should be less than 8 K.

TEXTVALID

A **text**, **ntext**, or **image** function that checks whether a given text pointer is valid.

Syntax

TEXTVALID('*table.column*', *text_ptr*)

Arguments

table

> The name of the table to be used.

column

> The name of the column to be used.

text_ptr

The text pointer to be checked.

Remarks

Returns 1 if the pointer is valid and 0 if the pointer is invalid. Note that the identifier for the **text** column must include the table name. If a **text**, **ntext**, or **image** column has not been initialized by an INSERT or UPDATE statement, TEXTPTR returns a null pointer. Use TEXTVALID to check whether a text pointer exists. You cannot use UPDATETEXT, WRITETEXT, or READTEXT without a valid text pointer.

These functions and statements are also useful with **text**, **ntext**, and **image** data.

Function or Statement	Description
PATINDEX('%*pattern*%', *expression*)	The character position of a given character string in **text** and **ntext** columns.
DATALENGTH(*expression*)	The length of data in **text**, **ntext**, and **image** columns.
SET TEXTSIZE	The limit, in bytes, of the **text**, **ntext**, or **image** data to be returned with a SELECT statement.

TRIGGER_NESTLEVEL

Returns the number of triggers executed for the UPDATE, INSERT, or DELETE statement that fired the trigger.

Syntax

```
TRIGGER_NESTLEVEL( [ object_id ] )
```

Arguments

object_id

The object ID of a trigger. If *object_id* is specified, TRIGGER_NESTLEVEL reports how many times the specified trigger has been executed for the statement. If *object_id* is not specified, TRIGGER_NESTLEVEL reports how many times all triggers have been executed for the statement.

TRUNCATE TABLE

Removes all rows from a table without logging the individual row deletes.

Syntax

```
TRUNCATE TABLE name
```

Arguments

name

The name of the table to truncate or remove all rows from.

Remarks

TRUNCATE TABLE is functionally identical to the DELETE statement with no WHERE clause: Both remove all rows in the table. But TRUNCATE TABLE is faster and uses fewer system and transaction log resources than DELETE.

The DELETE statement removes rows one at a time and records an entry in the transaction log for each deleted row. TRUNCATE TABLE removes the data by deallocating the data pages used to store the table's data, and only the page deallocations are recorded in the transaction log. This means that DELETE statements can be rolled back, but TRUNCATE TABLE cannot.

TRUNCATE TABLE removes all rows from a table, but the table structure and its columns, constraints, indexes and so on remain. The counter used by an identity for new rows is reset to the seed for the column. If you want to retain the identity counter, use DELETE instead. If you want to remove table definition and its data, use the DROP TABLE statement.

You cannot use TRUNCATE TABLE on a table referenced by a FOREIGN KEY constraint; instead, use DELETE without a WHERE clause. Because TRUNCATE TABLE is not logged, it cannot activate a trigger.

TYPEPROPERTY

Returns information about a data type.

Syntax

TYPEPROPERTY (*type, property*)

Arguments

type

> The name of the data type.

property

> The type of information to be returned for the data type. Can be one of these values:

property	Description	Value Returned
Precision	The precision for the data type.	The number of digits or characters NULL= Data type not found
Scale	The scale for the data type.	The number of decimal places for the data type NULL= Data type not **numeric** or not found
AllowsNull	The data type allows null values.	1=True 0=False NULL= Data type not found
UsesAnsiTrim	The ANSI padding setting was ON when the data type was created.	1=True 0=False NULL= Data type not found, or it is not a binary or string data type

Return Type: Returns the values as shown in the above table.

UNICODE

Returns the integer value, as defined by the Unicode standard, for the first character of the input expression.

Syntax

UNICODE('*ncharacter_expression*')

Arguments

'*ncharacter_expression*'

An **nchar** or **nvarchar** expression.

Return Type: int

UNION

Combines the results of two or more queries into a single result set consisting of all the rows belonging to all queries in the union.

Syntax

```
select_statement
UNION [ALL]
select_statement
 [UNION [ALL] select_statement][, ...n]
```

Arguments

select_statement

A SELECT statement that returns data to be combined with the data from another SELECT statement.

UNION

A keyword to indicate that multiple result sets are to be combined and returned as a single result set.

ALL

Incorporates all rows into the results, including duplicates. If not specified, duplicate rows will be removed.

n

A placeholder indicating that multiple SELECT statements can be added with multiple UNION keywords.

Remarks

The benefit of UNION is that it allows you to combine rows from two queries and return them as one result set. This is different from using joins that combine columns from two tables.

The basic rule about combining the result sets of two queries with UNION is that the number and the order of the columns must be identical in all queries, and the data types must be compatible. For example, the following statement is invalid because the first select list is longer than the second:

```
SELECT au_id, title_id, au_ord
FROM titleauthor
UNION
SELECT stor_id, date
FROM sales
```

The definitions of the columns that are part of a UNION operation do not have to be identical, but they have to be compatible through implicit conversion. The following table shows the rules for comparing the data types and options of corresponding (*ith*) columns.

Data Type of *ith* Column	Data Type of *ith* Column of Results Table
Not data type-compatible (data conversion not handled implicitly by SQL Server).	Error returned by SQL Server.
Both fixed-length **char** with lengths L1 and L2.	Fixed-length **char** with length equal to the greater of L1 and L2.
Both fixed-length **binary** with lengths L1 and L2.	Fixed-length **binary** with length equal to the greater of L1 and L2.
Either or both variable-length **char**.	Variable-length **char** with length equal to the maximum of the lengths specified for the *ith* columns.
Either or both variable-length **binary**.	Variable-length **binary** with length equal to the maximum of the lengths specified for the *ith* columns.
Both numeric data types (for example, **smallint**, **int**, **float**, **money**).	Data type equal to the maximum precision of the two columns. For example, if the *ith* column of table A is of type **int** and the *ith* column of table B is of type **float**, then the data type of the *ith* column of the results table is **float**, because **float** is more precise than **int**.
Both columns' descriptions specify NOT NULL.	Specifies NOT NULL.

The columns in the SELECT statements can include:

➤ An asterisk (*), representing all columns listed in the order in which they were specified in CREATE TABLE for all tables in the FROM clause, in the order they appear.

➤ A list of column names, specified in the order in which you want to see them.

➤ A column name and column heading that replaces the column name in the heading.

➤ An expression (a column name, variable, constant, function, or any combination of column names, variables, constants, and functions connected by an operator(s), a CASE function, or a subquery).

➤ The IDENTITYCOL keyword instead of the name of a column that has the IDENTITY property.

Other rules and options for using UNION are:

➤ If you need to combine UNION operators with different use of ALL for more than two tables, you can use parentheses to control when duplicates are removed.

➤ If you need to create a new table and load it with data using UNION, you must use the INTO keyword in the first query; INTO cannot be used in the later queries.

➤ The UNION operator can appear within an INSERT-SELECT statement to load the results into a table.

➤ GROUP BY and HAVING clauses can be used only within individual queries and cannot be used to affect the final result set.

➤ ORDER BY and COMPUTE clauses are allowed only at the end of the UNION operator to define the order of the final results or to compute summary values.

➤ You cannot specify the FOR BROWSE option in queries with the UNION operator.

UPDATE

Changes existing data in a table.

Syntax

```
UPDATE {<table_or_view>}
SET
{column_name = {expression | DEFAULT}
| @variable = expression} [, ...n]
 [FROM
{
<table_or_view>
| (select_statement) [AS] table_alias [ (column_alias [, ...m]) ]
| <table_or_view> CROSS JOIN <table_or_view>
| INNER [<join_hints>] JOIN
<table_or_view> ON <join_condition>
| <rowset_function>
}[, ...n]
]
 [WHERE
<search_conditions>
| CURRENT OF
{ { [GLOBAL] cursor_name } | cursor_variable_name} }
]
 [OPTION (<query_hints>, [, ...n] )]
<table_or_view> ::=
{ table_name [ [AS] table_alias ] [ WITH (<table_hints> [...m]) ]
| view_name [ [AS] table_alias ]
}
<table_hints> ::=
{ INDEX(index_name | index_id)
| FASTFIRSTROW
| HOLDLOCK
```

```
  | PAGLOCK
  | READCOMMITTED
  | REPEATABLEREAD
  | ROWLOCK
  | SERIALIZABLE
  | TABLOCK
  | TABLOCKX
  }
<join_hints> ::=
{ HASH | LOOP | MERGE }
<query_hints> ::=
{ { HASH | ORDER } GROUP
| { CONCAT | HASH | MERGE } UNION
| FAST number_rows
| FORCE ORDER
| ROBUST PLAN
}
<join_condition> ::=
{ table_name | table_alias | view_name }.column_name
<logical_operator>
{ table_name | table_alias | view_name }.column_name
<logical_operator> ::=
{ = | > | < | >= | <= | <> | != | !< | !> }
<rowset_function> ::=
{ OPENQUERY (linked_server, 'query')
| OPENROWSET
 ( 'provider_name',
{
'datasource';'user_id';'password'
| 'provider_string'
},
{
 [catalog.][schema.]object_name
| 'query'
}
)
}
<search_conditions> ::=
{ [ NOT ] <predicate> [ { AND | OR } [ NOT ] <predicate> ]
} [, ...n]
<predicate> ::=
{
expression { = | <> | != | > | >= | !> | < | <= | !< } expression
| string_expression [NOT] LIKE string_expression
 [ESCAPE 'escape_character']
| expression [NOT] BETWEEN expression AND expression
| expression IS [NOT] NULL
| expression [NOT] IN (subquery | expression [, ...n])
| expression { = | <> | != | > | >= | !> | < | <= | !< }
```

```
{ALL | SOME | ANY} (subquery)
| EXISTS (subquery)
}
```

Arguments

<table_or_view>

> The name of the table or view that is used to provide criteria for the UPDATE operation.

table_name | view_name

> Name of the table or view in which data is updated. The name can be qualified with the linked server, database, and/or owner name if the object is not in the current server or database, or is not owned by the current user. If *view_name* refers to multiple tables, only one of the tables can be updated.

table_alias

> The name of an alias. Each table or view can be given an alias, either for convenience or to distinguish a table or view in a self-join or a subquery.

column_alias

> A user-defined, temporary heading to replace the default column heading (the column name). For more information about column aliases, see FROM.

<table_hints>

> Specifies a table scan, one or more indexes to be used by the optimizer, or a locking method to be used by the optimizer with this table and for this SELECT. Although this is an option, the optimizer can usually pick the best optimization method without hints being specified. Commas between <table_hints> are optional but supported for backward compatibility. For more information, see the discussion of <table_hints> in SELECT.

INDEX(*index_name | index_id*)

> Specifies the name or ID of the index to be used by Microsoft SQL Server when processing the statement. Only one index hint per table can be specified. The alternative INDEX = syntax (which specifies a single index hint) is supported only for backward compatibility. Any index hints specified for a view are ignored, and SQL Server returns an error message.

Note If an index hint referring to multiple indexes is used on the fact table in a star join, SQL Server ignores the index hint and returns an error message. Also, index ORing is disallowed for a table with a specified index hint.

> SQL Server does not allow more than one table hint from each of the following groups:

> ➤ Granularity hints: PAGLOCK, NOLOCK, ROWLOCK, TABLOCK, or TABLOCKX.

➤ Isolation level hints: HOLDLOCK, NOLOCK, READCOMMITTED, REPEATABLEREAD, SERIALIZABLE.

In addition, the NOLOCK and READPAST <table_hints> are only allowed in SELECT statements and not in DELETE, INSERT, or UPDATE statements.

m

A placeholder indicating that multiple <table_hints> can be specified.

m

A placeholder indicating that more than one *column_alias* can be specified.

<rowset_function>

Specifies that one of the rowset functions is to be used.

OPENQUERY

Executes the specified pass-through query. For more information, see OPENQUERY.

OPENROWSET

Includes all connection information necessary to access remote data from a data source. For more information, see OPENROWSET.

SET

Introduces the list of column or variable names to be updated.

column_name

A column in the updated table that will be changed. When multiple columns are to be updated in *table_name*, each should be separated by commas.

Tip Any column prefix specified in the SET clause must match the table or view name specified after the UPDATE keyword. For example, the following is valid:

```
UPDATE authors
SET authors.au_fname = 'Annie'
WHERE au_fname = 'Anne'
```

expression

A variable, literal value, expression, or a parenthetical subSELECT statement that returns a single value. The value returned by *expression* replaces the existing value(s) in *column* or *@variable*.

DEFAULT

Indicates that the default defined for the column will replace the existing values in the column. This can also be used to change the column to NULL if the column has no default and is defined to allow NULL values.

@variable

A declared variable that is set to the value returned by *expression*.

n

> A placeholder to indicate that the preceding item can be specified multiple times.

FROM

> Specifies that another table is used to provide criteria values for the UPDATE operation. For more detailed information about the FROM clause, see FROM.

table_name

> The name of the table to provide criteria values for the UPDATE operation.

view_name

> The name of the view to provide criteria values for the UPDATE operation.

CROSS JOIN

> Specifies the cross-product of two tables. Returns the same rows as if no WHERE clause was specified in an old-style, non-SQL-92-style join.

INNER

> Specifies all matching pairs of rows are returned. Discards unmatched rows from both tables. This is the default if no join type is specified.

<join_hints>

> Specifies that SQL Server's query optimizer use one <join_hints>, or *execution algorithm*, per join specified in the query's FROM clause. For more information about <join_hints>, see SELECT.

ON <join_condition>

> Specifies the conditions upon which the join is based. For more information about <join_condition>, see FROM.

WHERE

> Specifies the conditions used to limit the number of rows that are updated. There are two forms of update based on what is specified in the WHERE clause:
>
> ➤ Searched updates specify <search_conditions> to qualify the rows to delete.
>
> ➤ Positioned updates use the CURRENT OF clause to specify a cursor; the delete operation occurs at the current position of the cursor.

<search_conditions>

> Specifies the restricting conditions upon which the join is based or for the rows to be updated. There is no limit to the number of <search_conditions> that can be included in a SQL statement. For additional details on <search_conditions>, see WHERE.

CURRENT OF

> Specifies that the update is performed at the current position of the specified cursor.

GLOBAL

> Specifies that *cursor_name* refers to a global cursor.

cursor_name

> The name of the open cursor from which the fetch should be made. If both a global and a local cursor exist with *cursor_name* as their name, then *cursor_name* refers to the global cursor if GLOBAL is specified. If GLOBAL is not specified, *cursor_name* refers to the local cursor. The cursor must allow updates.

cursor_variable_name

> The name of a cursor variable. The cursor variable must reference a cursor that allows updates.

OPTION (<query_hints>, [, ...*n*])

> Keywords to indicate that optimizer hints are used to customize SQL Server's processing of the statement.

{HASH | ORDER} GROUP

> Specifies that the aggregations specified in the GROUP BY or COMPUTE clause of the query should use hashing or ordering.

{MERGE | HASH | CONCAT} UNION

> Specifies that all UNION operations should be performed by merging, hashing, or concatenating UNION sets. If more than one UNION hint is specified, the optimizer will select the least expensive strategy from those hints specified.

Note If a <joint_hint> is also specified for any particular pair of joined tables in the FROM clause, then it takes precedence over any <join_hint> specified in the OPTION clause.

FAST *number_rows*

> Specifies that the query is optimized for fast retrieval of the first *number_rows* (a non-negative integer). After the first *number_rows* are returned, the query continues execution and produces its full result set.

FORCE ORDER

> Specifies that the join order indicated by the query syntax should be preserved during query optimization.

ROBUST PLAN

> Forces the query optimizer to attempt a plan that works for the maximum potential row size at the expense of performance. If no such plan is possible, the optimizer returns an error rather than deferring error detection to query execution. Rows may contain variable-length columns; SQL Server allows rows to be defined whose maximum potential size is beyond the ability of SQL Server to process them. Normally, despite the maximum potential size, an application

stores rows whose actual size is within the limits that SQL Server can process. If SQL Server encounters a row that is too long, an execution error is returned.

Remarks

UPDATE can be used to change existing rows in one or more tables and does not return any rows of data. To load new rows into a table, see the INSERT and INTO options of the SELECT statement. To return rows of data, use SELECT. To delete rows, use DELETE or TRUNCATE TABLE.

A positioned UPDATE using a WHERE CURRENT OF clause updates the single row at the current position of the cursor. This can be more accurate than a searched UPDATE that uses a WHERE *search_conditions* clause to qualify the rows to be updated. A searched UPDATE updates multiple rows if the *search_conditions* do not uniquely identify a single row.

When updating rows, these rules apply:

➤ Identity columns cannot be updated.

➤ All **char** and **nchar** columns are right-padded to the defined length.

➤ If ANSI_PADDING is set OFF, all trailing spaces are removed from data inserted into **varchar** and **nvarchar** columns, except in strings containing only spaces. These strings are truncated to an empty string. If ANSI_PADDING is set ON, trailing spaces are inserted. The Microsoft SQL Server ODBC driver and SQL Server OLE DB provider automatically set ANSI_PADDING ON for each connection. This can be configured in ODBC data sources or by setting connection attributes or properties.

➤ If an update to a record violates a constraint or rule, if it violates the NULL setting for the column, or if the new value is an incompatible data type, the statement is canceled, an error is returned, and no records will be updated.

➤ Modifying a **text**, **ntext**, or **image** column with UPDATE initializes it, assigns a valid text pointer to it, and allocates at least one data page unless updating the column with NULL.

➤ If an update query may alter more than one row while updating both the clustering key and one or more **text**, **image**, or Unicode columns, then the update operation fails and SQL Server returns an error message.

➤ If an update to a column or columns participating in a clustered index causes the size of the clustered index and the row to exceed 8,092 bytes, the update will fail and an error message is returned.

➤ When an UPDATE statement encounters an arithmetic error (overflow, divide by zero, or a domain error) during expression evaluation, the update is not performed. The remainder of the batch is not executed, and an error message is returned.

Note The UPDATE statement is logged; if you are replacing or modifying large blocks of **text**, **ntext**, or **image** data, use the WRITETEXT or UPDATETEXT statement instead of the UPDATE statement. The WRITETEXT and UPDATETEXT statements (by default) are not logged.

Setting Variables and Columns

Variable names can be used in UPDATE statements to show the old and new values affected. This should only be used when the UPDATE statement affects a single record; if the UPDATE statement affects multiple records, the variables will only contain the values for one of the updated rows.

Permissions

UPDATE permissions default to the table owner, who can transfer them to other users. SELECT permissions are also required for the table being updated if the UPDATE statement contains a WHERE clause, or if *expression* in the SET clause uses a column in the table.

UPDATE STATISTICS

Updates information about the distribution of key values for one or more indexes in the specified table. UPDATE STATISTICS is run automatically when an index is created on a table that already contains data.

Syntax

```
UPDATE STATISTICS {table}
 [
index
| (index_or_column
 [, ...n])
]
 [WITH
 [
 [FULLSCAN]
| SAMPLE number {PERCENT | ROWS}]
]
 [[,] [ALL | COLUMNS | INDEX]
 [[,] NORECOMPUTE]
]
```

Arguments

table

> The table for which statistics are being updated. Table names must conform to the rules for identifiers. *table* is the table with which the index is associated. Because index names are not unique within each database, *table* must be specified. Specifying the database or table owner is optional.

index

> The index for which statistics are being updated. Index names must conform to the rules for identifiers. If *index* is not specified, the distribution statistics for all indexes in the specified table are updated. To see a list of index names and descriptions, execute sp_helpindex with the table name.

index_or_column

> The name of the column(s) or index(es) for which statistics are being updated. Index and column names must conform to the rules for identifiers. *index_or_column* is required only when the INDEX or COLUMN options are specified.

Note Columns consisting of **ntext**, **text**, **image**, or **bit** data types, and computed columns cannot be specified as statistics columns.

n

> A placeholder indicating that multiple index or column names can be specified.

FULLSCAN

> Causes Microsoft SQL Server to perform a full scan of the index or table when gathering statistics.

SAMPLE *number* {PERCENT | ROWS}

> Specifies the percentage of the table or the number of rows that are being sampled when collecting statistics for larger tables. To use the default sampling behavior for larger tables, use SAMPLE *number* with PERCENT or ROWS. SQL Server ensures a minimum number of values are sampled to ensure useful statistics. If the PERCENT, ROWS, or *number* option results in too few rows being sampled, SQL Server automatically corrects the sampling based on the number of existing rows in the table.

Note The default behavior is to perform a sample scan on the target table. SQL Server automatically computes the required sample size.

ALL | COLUMNS | INDEX

> Specifies whether the UPDATE STATISTICS statement affects column statistics, index statistics, or all existing statistics. If no option is specified, the UPDATE STATISTICS statement affects existing indexes only. When COLUMN is specified, statistics are created or updated (if they already exist) for columns that do not have preexisting statistics.

NORECOMPUTE

> Specifies that statistics that become out of date are not automatically recomputed. Statistics become out of date depending on the number of INSERT,

UPDATE, and DELETE operations performed on indexed columns. When specified, this option causes SQL Server to never automatically rebuild statistics and disables automatic statistics rebuilding. To restore automatic statistics recomputation, reissue UPDATE STATISTICS without the NORECOMPUTE option or execute sp_autostats.

UPDATETEXT

Updates an existing **text**, **ntext**, or **image** field. Use UPDATETEXT to change only a portion of a **text**, **ntext**, or **image** column in place. Use WRITETEXT to update and replace an entire **text**, **ntext**, or **image** field.

Syntax

```
UPDATETEXT {table_name.dest_column_name dest_text_ptr}
{
NULL
| insert_offset
}
{
NULL
| delete_length
}
 [WITH LOG]
[
inserted_data
| [{table_name.src_column_name src_text_ptr}
]
```

Arguments

table_name.dest_column_name

The name of the table and **text**, **ntext**, or **image** column to be updated. Table names and column names must conform to the rules for identifiers. Specifying the database name and owner name is optional.

dest_text_ptr

A text pointer value (returned by the TEXTPTR function) that points to the **text**, **ntext**, or **image** data to be updated. *dest_text_ptr* must be **binary(16)**.

insert_offset

The zero-based starting position for the update. For **text** or **image** columns, *insert_offset* is the number of bytes to skip from the start of the existing column before inserting new data. For **ntext** columns, *insert_offset* is the number of characters (each **ntext** character uses 2 bytes). The existing **text**, **ntext**, or **image** data beginning at this zero-based starting position is shifted to the right to make room for the new data. A value of 0 inserts the new data at the beginning of the existing data. A value of NULL appends the new data to the existing data value.

delete_length

> The length of data to delete from the existing **text**, **ntext**, or **image** column, starting at the *insert_offset* position. The *delete_length* value is specified in bytes for **text** and **image** columns and in characters for **ntext** columns. Each **ntext** character uses 2 bytes. A value of 0 deletes no data. A value of NULL deletes all data from the *insert_offset* position to the end of the existing **text** or **image** column.

WITH LOG

> Specifies that the inserted **text**, **ntext**, or **image** data is logged. This option allows recovery, but it can quickly increase the size of the transaction log.

inserted_data

> The data to be inserted into the existing **text**, **ntext**, or **image** column at the *insert_offset* location. This is a single **char**, **nchar**, **varchar**, **nvarchar**, **binary**, **varbinary**, **text**, **ntext**, or **image** constant.

table_name.src_column_name

> The name of the table and **text**, **ntext**, or **image** column used as the source of the inserted data. Table names and column names must conform to the rules for identifers.

src_text_ptr

> A text pointer value (returned by the TEXTPTR function) that points to a **text**, **ntext**, or **image** column used as the source of the inserted data.

UPPER

Returns a character expression with lowercase character data converted to uppercase.

Syntax

UPPER(*character_expression*)

Arguments

character_expression

> An expression of character data. *character_expression* can be a constant, variable, or column of either character or binary data.

Return Type: varchar

Remarks

character_expression must be of a data type that is implicitly convertible to **varchar**. Otherwise, use the CAST function to explicitly convert *character_expression*.

USE

Changes the database context to the specified database.

Syntax

```
USE {database}
```

Arguments

database

> The name of the database to which the user context is switched. Database names must conform to the rules for identifiers.

Remarks

The USE statement executes at both compile and execution time and takes effect immediately. Therefore, statements that appear in a batch after the USE statement are executed in the specified database.

When logging in to Microsoft SQL Server, it is likely that users will be automatically connected to the master database. Unless a default database has been set up for each user's login ID, each user must execute the USE statement to change from master to another database.

To change context to a different database, it is necessary to have a security account for that database. The owner of the database must provide users access by adding a security account for those selected users in the database.

Permissions

USE permissions default to those users who are assigned permissions by members of the db_owner fixed database role executing sp_adduser. Users without a security account in the destination database can still be allowed access if a guest user exists in that database.

USER

A niladic function that allows a system-supplied value for the current user's database username to be inserted into a table when no default value is specified.

Syntax

```
USER
```

Return Type: char

Remarks

This statement provides the same functionality as the USER_NAME system function.

Use USER with DEFAULT constraints in either the CREATE TABLE or ALTER TABLE statements, or use as any standard function.

USER_ID

Returns the user's database identification number.

Syntax

```
USER_ID(['user'])
```

Arguments

'user'

> The user name to be used. The *user* parameter is of **nchar** data type. If a **char** value is specified, it will be implicitly converted to **nchar**.

Return Type: int

Remarks

When the parameter to a system function is optional, the current database, host computer, server user, or database user is assumed. Built-in functions must always be followed by parentheses.

System functions can be used in the select list, in the WHERE clause, and anywhere an expression is allowed.

USER_NAME

A niladic function that returns the user's database username given an identification number.

Syntax

```
USER_NAME([id])
```

Arguments

id

> The identification number of the user to return a user's name. The *id* parameter is of **int** data type.

Return Type: nchar

Remarks

When the parameter to a system function is optional, the current database, host computer, server user, or database user is assumed. Built-in functions must always be followed by parentheses.

VAR

An aggregate function that returns the statistical variance of all values in the given expression. If VAR is used on all items in a SELECT statement, then each value in the result set is included in the calculation. VAR can be used with numeric columns only. Null values are ignored.

Syntax

```
VAR(expression)
```

Arguments

expression

> A constant, column, or function, and any combination of arithmetic, bitwise, and string operators. *expression* is an expression of the exact numeric or approximate

numeric data type category, except for the **bit** data type. Aggregate functions and subqueries are not permitted.

Return Type: float

VARP

An aggregate function that returns the statistical variance for the population for all values in the given expression. If VARP is used on all items in a SELECT statement, each value in the result set is included in the calculation. VARP can be used with numeric columns only. Null values are ignored.

Syntax

VARP(*expression*)

Arguments

expression

A constant, column name, or function, and any combination of arithmetic, bitwise, and string operators. *expression* is an expression of the exact numeric or approximate numeric data type category, except for the **bit** data type. Aggregate functions and subqueries are not permitted.

Return Type: float

WAITFOR

Specifies a time, time interval, or event that triggers execution of a statement block, stored procedure, or transaction.

Syntax

WAITFOR {DELAY '*time*' | TIME '*time*'}

Arguments

DELAY

Instructs Microsoft SQL Server to wait until the specified amount of time has passed, up to a maximum of 24 hours.

'*time*'

Specifies a time in one of the acceptable formats for **datetime** data. The time you specify can include hours, minutes, and seconds. Use the format *hh:mm:ss*. You cannot specify dates; the date portion of the **datetime** value is not allowed. You can also specify a local variable in place of the *time* string.

TIME

Instructs SQL Server to wait until the specified time.

Remarks

After executing the WAITFOR statement, you cannot use your connection to SQL Server until the time or event that you specified occurs.

WHERE

Specifies the criteria for which rows to retrieve. HAVING is used only with GROUP BY in a SELECT statement.

Syntax

```
WHERE <search_conditions>
```

Or:

```
HAVING <search_conditions>
<search_conditions> ::=
{ [ NOT ] <predicate> [ { AND | OR } [ NOT ] <predicate> ]
| CONTAINS
 ( {column | * }, '<contains_search_condition>'
)
| FREETEXT
 (
{column | * }, 'freetext_string'
)
| fulltext_table.fulltext_key_column = fulltext_table.[KEY]
} [, ...n]
<predicate> ::=
{
expression { = | <> | != | > | >= | !> | < | <= | !< } expression
| string_expression [NOT] LIKE string_expression
 [ESCAPE 'escape_character']
| expression [NOT] BETWEEN expression AND expression
| expression IS [NOT] NULL
| expression [NOT] IN (subquery | expression [, ...n])
| expression { = | <> | != | > | >= | !> | < | <= | !< }
{ALL | SOME | ANY} (subquery)
| EXISTS (subquery)
}
```

Arguments

WHERE

Specifies the restricting conditions for the rows returned in the result set. There is no limit to the number of <search_conditions> that can be included in a Transact-SQL statement.

HAVING

Specifies the restricting conditions for the groups returned in the result set. When used with a GROUP BY CLAUSE, HAVING functions similarly to the WHERE clause when WHERE is used in a SELECT statement.

<search_conditions>

Specifies the conditions for the rows returned in the result set. There is no limit to the number of <search_conditions> that can be included in a Transact-SQL statement. If <search_conditions> contains Unicode data, precede the <search_conditions> with 'N'.

NOT

Negates the Boolean expression specified by the predicate.

<predicate>

An expression that returns TRUE or FALSE.

AND

Combines two conditions and evaluates to TRUE when both of the conditions are true.

OR

Combines two conditions and evaluates to TRUE when both of the conditions are true.

n

A placeholder indicating that multiple predicates may exist in one SELECT statement.

expression

A column name, constant, function, variable, subquery, or any combination of column names, constants, and functions connected by an operator(s) or a subquery. The expression may also contain the CASE function.

=

A symbol used to test the equality between two expressions.

<>

A symbol used to test the condition of two expressions not being equal to each other.

!=

A symbol used to test the condition of two expressions not being equal to each other.

>

A symbol used to test the condition of one expression being greater than the other.

>=

A symbol used to test the condition of one expression being greater than or equal to the other expression.

!>

A symbol used to test the condition of one expression not being greater than the other expression.

<

A symbol used to test the condition of one expression being less than the other.

< =

A symbol used to test the condition of one expression being less than or equal to the other expression.

!<

A symbol used to test the condition of one expression not being less than the other expression.

string_expression

A string of characters and wildcard characters enclosed in quotation marks.

LIKE

Indicates the following character string (enclosed by quotation marks) is to be used with pattern matching.

ESCAPE

Specifies the given wildcard character should be searched for in a character string(s) instead of functioning as a wildcard character.

'escape_character'

The character before a wildcard character indicating the wildcard character will be treated and searched for as a regular character rather than as a wildcard character.

BETWEEN

Specifies an inclusive range of values. Use AND for the range-end value. A range of expression BETWEEN x AND y, unlike a range of expression $> x$ and expression $< y$, is inclusive.

IS [NOT] NULL

Specifies that the expression should evaluate and search for either NULL or NOT NULL values, depending on which keywords are used. An expression with a bitwise or arithmetic operator evaluates to NULL if any of the operands is NULL.

IN

Allows values to be selected that match any one of a list of values. The expression can be a constant or a column name, and the list can be a set of constants or, more commonly, a subquery. Enclose the list of values in parentheses.

subquery

A restricted SELECT statement (the ORDER BY clause, the COMPUTE clause, and the INTO keyword are not allowed). For more information, see the discussion of subqueries in SELECT.

ALL

Used with a comparison operator and a subquery. Returns TRUE in the <predicate> when all values retrieved in the subquery match the expression, or FALSE when not all values match or when the subquery returns no rows to the outer statement.

{SOME | ANY}

Used with a comparison operator and a subquery. Returns TRUE in the <predicate> when any value retrieved in a subquery satisfies the comparison predicate in the expression or FALSE when the comparison returns false for all rows in a subquery or when a subquery returns no rows to the outer statement. Otherwise, the expression is unknown.

EXISTS

Used with a subquery to test for the existence of rows returned by the subquery.

fulltext_table

The name of the table (or alias) which has been marked for full-text querying. For more information about full-text querying using the RANK keyword, see CONTAINSTABLE, FROM, and FREETEXTTABLE.

CONTAINS

When used with a SELECT statement only, searches columns containing character-based data types for precise or "fuzzy" (less precise) matches to single words and phrases, the proximity of words within a certain distance of one another, and weighted matches. Can only be used with SELECT statements. For more information, see CONTAINS.

FREETEXT

When used with a SELECT statement only, searches columns containing character-based data types for values that match the meaning but not the exact wording of the words in the predicate. Can only be used with SELECT statements. For more information, see FREETEXT.

fulltext_table

The name of the table (or alias) which has been marked for full-text querying. Can only be used with SELECT statements. For more information, see CONTAINSTABLE or FREETEXTTABLE.

fulltext_key_column

The name of the full-text key column which resides in the *fulltext_table* that has been registered for full-text querying. Can only be used with SELECT statements.

[KEY]

Specifies that the rows matching the <contains_search_condition> are to be selected. Can only be used with SELECT statements. For more information, see CONTAINSTABLE and FREETEXTTABLE.

WHILE

Sets a condition for the repeated execution of a *sql_statement* or statement block. The statements are executed repeatedly as long as the specified condition is true. The execution of statements in the WHILE loop can be controlled from inside the loop with the BREAK and CONTINUE keywords.

Syntax

```
WHILE Boolean_expression
{sql_statement | statement_block}
  [BREAK]
{sql_statement | statement_block}
  [CONTINUE]
```

Arguments

Boolean_expression

> An expression that returns TRUE or FALSE. If the Boolean expression contains a SELECT statement, the SELECT statement must be enclosed in parentheses.

{sql_statement | statement_block}

> Any Transact-SQL statement or statement grouping as defined with a statement block. To define a statement block, use the control-of-flow keywords BEGIN and END.

BREAK

> Causes an exit from the innermost WHILE loop. Any statements appearing after the END keyword, marking the end of the loop, are executed.

CONTINUE

> Causes the WHILE loop to restart, ignoring any statements after the CONTINUE keyword.

Remarks

If two or more WHILE loops are nested, the inner BREAK exits to the next outermost loop. First, all the statements after the end of the inner loop run, and then the next outermost loop restarts.

WRITETEXT

Permits nonlogged, interactive updating of an existing **text**, **ntext**, or **image** column. This statement completely overwrites any existing data in the column it affects. WRITETEXT cannot be used on **text**, **ntext**, and **image** columns in views. By default, WRITETEXT statements are not logged; therefore, the transaction log does not fill up with the large amounts of data that often make up these data types.

Syntax

```
WRITETEXT {table.column text_ptr}
  [WITH LOG] {data}
```

Arguments

table.column

> The name of the table and **text**, **ntext**, or **image** column to update. Table and column names must conform to the rules for identifiers. Specifying the database name and owner names is optional.

text_ptr

> A value that stores the pointer to the **text**, **ntext** or **image** data. *text_ptr* must be **binary(16)**. To create a text pointer, execute an INSERT or UPDATE statement with data that is not NULL for the **text**, **ntext**, or **image** column. For more information about creating a text pointer, see either INSERT or UPDATE.

WITH LOG

> Logs the inserted **text**, **ntext**, or **image** data, which aids media recovery. Because **text** data quickly increases the size of the transaction log, ensure the transaction log has enough space to grow.

data

> The actual **text**, **ntext** or **image** data to store. The maximum length of text that can be inserted interactively with WRITETEXT is approximately 120 K for **text**, **ntext**, and **image** data.

Remarks

Use WRITETEXT to replace **text**, **ntext**, and **image** data and UPDATETEXT to modify **text**, **ntext**, and **image** data. UPDATETEXT is more flexible because it changes only a portion of a **text**, **ntext**, or **image** column rather than the entire column.

By default, WRITETEXT is a nonlogged operation. This means **text**, **ntext**, or **image** data is not logged when it is written to the database. To use WRITETEXT in its default, nonlogged state, members of the sysadmin fixed database role must use sp_dboption to set Select Into/Bulkcopy, which allows nonlogged data to be inserted.

For WRITETEXT to work properly, the column must already contain a valid text pointer.

Microsoft SQL Server saves space by not initializing **text** columns when explicit or implicit null values are placed in **text** columns with INSERT.

The DB-Library dbwritetext and dbmoretext functions and the ODBC SQLPutData function are faster and use less dynamic memory than WRITETEXT. These functions can insert up to 2 gigabytes of **text**, **ntext**, or **image** data.

Caution After using the WRITETEXT statement, execute BACKUP DATABASE. After nonlogged operations occur within a database, the BACKUP LOG statement cannot be performed. For more information, see BACKUP.

To initialize **text** columns to NULL, use UPDATETEXT when the compatibility setting of sp_dbcmptlevel is equal to 65. If the compatibility setting of sp_dbcmptlevel is equal to 70, use WRITETEXT to initialize **text** columns to NULL; otherwise, UPDATETEXT initializes **text** columns to an empty string.

Permissions

WRITETEXT permissions default to those users with SELECT permissions on the specified table. Permissions are transferable when SELECT permissions are transferred.

YEAR

Returns an integer that represents the year part of a specified date.

Syntax

YEAR(*date*)

Arguments

date

An expression of type **datetime** or **smalldatetime**.

Return Type: int

Appendix *B*

Installing the Software

Installing SQL Server 7 Evaluation Software

Before you install the companion CD-ROM, be sure your system has the following requirements to install the Evaluation Edition of Microsoft SQL Server 7.0:

➤ PC with a Pentium (166 MHz or higher) or Alpha processor
➤ Windows NT Server 4.0 with Service Pack 4
➤ Internet Explorer 4.01 (included on the CD-ROM)
➤ 32 MB of RAM
➤ CD-ROM drive

Hard drive space required:

➤ 65-180 MB for Server
➤ 25-50 MB for OLAP Services
➤ 24-36 MB for English Query

To install the desktop version you must have the same server configuration requirements with the following exceptions:

➤ Windows 95 or Windows 98, Windows NT 4.0 Server with Service Pack 4.

Simply insert the CD into your CD-ROM drive. If it is configured as auto run, the program will load itself. If this does not happen, select the CD-ROM drive letter using My Computer and click on the Install/Setup icon.

You must check the SQL Server 7 requirements in order to assure your machine is ready for SQL Server 7. Click on Install SQL Server 7.0 Components. The program will copy the installation program.

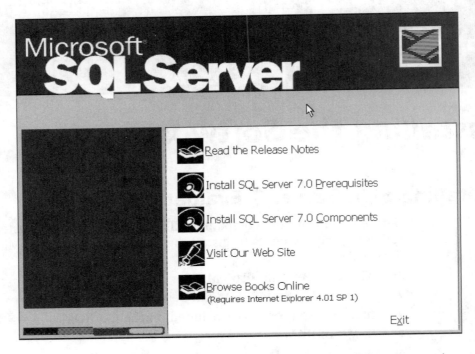

In the screen that appears, as shown below, click on Next to continue.

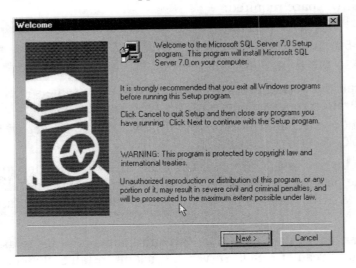

The license agreement screen will come up, as shown on the next page. Press Yes if you agree with the license agreement. You must accept the license agreement presented during the setup program in order to use the Evaluation Edition of Microsoft SQL Server 7.0 included on the companion CD-ROM. If you do not accept the terms of this license agreement, you are not authorized to use this software.

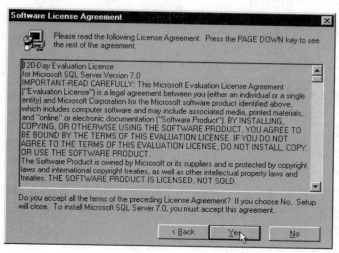

The next step requires you to confirm or change the user name and organization. Press Next.

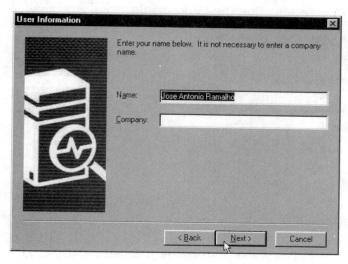

The Setup Type dialog that appears shows the disk space requirements and your available space.

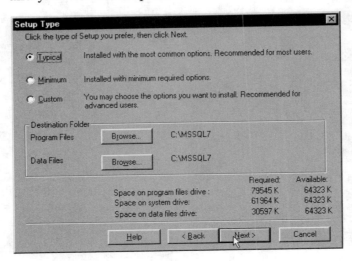

My machine did not have the amount required on drive C. If you do have the required space, press Next. Otherwise, you will have to change the default directories using the Choose Folder dialog.

After you press the Next button, the files will be copied. It takes about 20 to 30 minutes, depending on your machine processor and memory.

When all files are installed, you will receive a dialog box asking you to restart the machine.

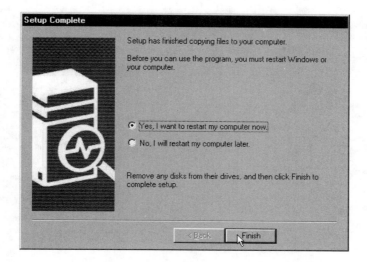

Select Yes or No, according to your preference, and click Finish.

If you want to install other SQL Server 7 components, such as the Microsoft English Query or DSS, repeat the steps above.

Installing the FoodMart Database

Open the CD-ROM drive using My Computer. Select the FoodMart directory.

Copy the Foodmart.exe file to a hard drive folder and click on the FoodMart icon in order to uncompress installation files. Follow the instructions to install files. You must run the program twice if you want to install the files used in Chapters 15 and 17.

Index

On the CD

The CD-ROM that accompanies this book contains the Evaluation Edition of Microsoft SQL Server 7.0, along with the FoodMart database used in the chapter exercises.

See Appendix B for information on installing the programs from the CD.

 Caution Opening the CD package makes this book nonreturnable.